Empire Builders Series: Masterclasses in Business and Law

Legal Ink

ALSO BY AUTHORSDOOR GROUP

Empire Builders Series: Masterclasses in Business and Law

Legal Ink

Navigating the Legalese of Publishing

L. A. MOESZINGER

AuthorsDoor Group
an imprint of The Ridge Publishing Group

Library of Congress Control Number: 2024920985

Legal Ink: Navigating the Legalese of Publishing / by L. A. Moeszinger

ISBN 978-1-956905-36-6 (e-book)
ISBN 978-1-956905-35-9 (softcover)

1. Law / Intellectual Property / Copyright. 2. Law / Contracts. 3. Business & Economics / Negotiating. 4. Reference / Writing Skills. 5. Language Arts & Disciplines / Publishing.
I. Title. II. Series

Printed in the United States of America

To all the writers whose creativity fuels their craft, may this book light your path through the legal labyrinth of publishing.

AuthorsDoor Group
Coeur d'Alene, Idaho

INTRODUCTION TO THE
AUTHORSDOOR LEADERSHIP PROGRAM

The AuthorsDoor Leadership Program, separate from the Builders Empire Series, is a new initiative designed to empower authors and publishers with the skills to effectively sell books. It features three tailored series: (1) AuthorsDoor Series: *Publisher & Her World*, (2) AuthorsDoor Advanced Series: *Publisher & Her World*, and (3) AuthorsDoor Masterclass Series: *Publisher & Her World*; each series is meticulously structured to guide participants from foundational concepts to advanced strategies in selling books, book by book, in a chronological format. The courses, offered for free on our YouTube channels—Publisher & Her World at Ridge Publishing Group, AuthorsDoor Group: Publisher & Her World, and Authors Red Door #Shorts—complement the books and workbooks, each providing unique and valuable teachings.

Explore additional resources to enhance your journey:

- Follow our blog at AuthorsRedDoor.com.
- Subscribe to our Newsletters at AuthorsDoor.com.
- Join our AuthorsDoor Strategy Forum Facebook Group.
- Connect with our Facebook Page at AuthorsDoor Group.
- Become a fan on our social media channels @AuthorsDoor1.

For feedback or questions, contact us at info@authorsdoor.com. We are here to support your journey from writing to successfully selling your books.

Warm regards,

L. A. Moeszinger #PubHerWorld

Contents

PART 4: MANAGING FINANCES

PART 5: CONCLUDING THE RELATIONSHIP

Introduction

Unlocking the Secrets to Legal and Business Mastery for Entrepreneurs and Creators

So, you've written a book—a beautiful, soul-stirring, possibly life-changing work of art. You've nurtured every chapter like it's your literary baby, coaxing it from messy scribbles to polished prose. And now, you're ready to launch it into the world. But before you pop the champagne, there's one small, yet incredibly important thing standing between you and your dream of bestselling glory: legalese.

Yes, my fellow authors, this book isn't just about writing; it's about navigating the treacherous waters of the publishing world—contracts, rights, royalties, and all the delightful, jargon-filled clauses you didn't know could exist. Welcome to "Legal Ink: Navigating the Legalese of Publishing"—your guide to mastering the business side of creativity.

Think of this as your very own publishing survival kit, packed with everything you need to protect your intellectual property, negotiate like a pro, and ensure that your masterpiece doesn't get lost in the labyrinth of legal mumbo jumbo. We're not just here to talk contracts—we're here to show you how to turn your book into a bulletproof business that rewards your hard work. It's about keeping those creative fires burning while also making sure you keep control of your rights, your royalties, and your future.

You're not just a writer—you're a creator, an entrepreneur, and now, a savvy negotiator ready to decode those complex contracts and make them work for you. This book will help you unlock the hidden secrets of the publishing industry's legal framework, covering topics like:

- **Publishing Rights**: What are they? Why should you care? And how can you use them to turn your midnight scribbles into royalties that last a lifetime?

- **Negotiation Tactics**: Ever felt like you were signing your life away without truly understanding the fine print? We'll give you the tools to negotiate fair deals that put more money in your pocket without selling your soul—or your sequel.

- **Subsidiary Rights**: Film adaptations, audiobooks, foreign translations, and merchandise—your book isn't just words on a page, it's a potential franchise. Learn how to keep the rights to your story, even when Hollywood comes knocking.

- **Copyright and Intellectual Property Protection**: It's your story, your characters, your world. We'll teach you how to keep it that way, even when someone tries to "borrow" your work without asking.

But don't worry—we're not here to bore you with dry legal mumbo-jumbo. This book has witty insights, practical tips, and a dash of humor to make sure the journey through contracts, clauses, and copyright doesn't leave you feeling like you've just been swallowed by a legal black hole. We're turning complex legal frameworks into approachable, bite-sized chunks, with just the right amount of sass to keep you entertained along the way.

You'll also get a crash course in when to call in the big guns: agents and lawyers. These unsung heroes of the publishing world can help you secure the best deals and ensure you never sign anything you'll regret. We'll walk you through the art of knowing when to hire them, how to choose the right professionals, and what they can do to protect your rights and earnings.

By the end of this book, you'll be equipped with the knowledge and confidence to navigate the wild world of publishing with the poise of a seasoned pro. You'll understand the true power of a well-negotiated contract, the value of your intellectual property, and how to keep your creative empire flourishing long after your book hits the shelves.

So, grab your favorite coffee mug, settle in, and let's demystify the legal labyrinth of publishing. After all, writing the book was the hard part—navigating the business side should be a breeze with "Legal Ink" by your side.

Empowering Authors to Take Control of Their Careers

It's time to grab the reins, fellow wordsmiths. Welcome to the part of your writing journey where creativity meets business, and you, the author, become the one in control. No more blindly signing contracts or relying on someone else to explain the fine print—"Legal Ink" is here to empower you to take full ownership of your career, both creatively and financially.

Think of this section as a power-up in your author toolkit. You've mastered the art of storytelling; now it's time to master the art of protecting your work and negotiating deals that not only reward you for your efforts but also set the stage for long-term success. Gone are the days when the legal side of publishing was something you avoided or handed off without fully understanding. With the knowledge you'll gain from this book, you'll be prepared to sit at the negotiation table with confidence, fully aware of your rights and ready to fight for the terms you deserve.

The Old Way: Feeling Powerless at the Negotiation Table

Let's face it—legal contracts are designed to be intimidating. When you first glance at a publishing agreement, it can feel like you're stepping into a foreign land where people speak a language only they understand. And for many authors, the default approach has been to trust someone else—whether it's an agent or a lawyer—or, worse, to just sign and hope for the best.

But here's the thing: you are your own best advocate. No one cares as much about your work, your rights, or your future as you do. Agents and lawyers are invaluable resources (we'll get into that later), but at the end of the day, you need to understand what's at stake and make informed decisions about your career. You wouldn't sign a blank check, so why would you sign a contract you don't fully understand?

The traditional publishing landscape has often put authors in a reactive position, waiting for someone else to explain what's going on. But in today's world, with self-publishing and hybrid models rising, the game has changed. Authors now have more control over their work than ever before. However, with great power comes great responsibility. Understanding the legal aspects of your career is the key to using that control effectively.

The New Way: The Empowered Author

This book is about making sure that the balance of power shifts back into your hands. Understanding your contracts, protecting your rights, and negotiating better deals aren't just business tasks—they're essential parts of being a modern author. Here's how empowering yourself with legal knowledge will change the game for you:

1. **You'll Protect Your Intellectual Property**: Your stories, characters, and ideas are the core of your career. By understanding how copyright works, how to secure it, and how to enforce it, you'll ensure that your creations remain yours—no matter what.

2. **You'll Negotiate Better Deals**: When you know what you're worth and how the publishing world operates, you can negotiate deals that reflect your value. Whether it's securing higher advances, better royalties, or retaining subsidiary rights (like film or audiobook rights), you'll be able to stand your ground and walk away with the best possible terms.

3. **You'll Retain Control Over Your Work**: One of the biggest mistakes new authors make is signing away too much control—whether it's the ability to publish future works in the same genre or giving up creative control over adaptations. With this book, you'll learn how to keep as

much control as possible, so your work continues to serve your interests long after publication.

4. **You'll Build a Sustainable Career**: Understanding the business side of writing helps you make decisions that are good for the long haul. You'll be able to plan for future works, negotiate contracts that support sequels or spin-offs, and build a career that isn't reliant on one-time success but grows with each new project.

5. **You'll Have the Confidence to Make Informed Choices**: Knowledge is power. The more you know about your legal rights and the business of publishing, the more confident you'll be in making decisions that align with your goals. Whether you're choosing between publishers, deciding to self-publish, or negotiating subsidiary rights, you'll do so from a position of strength.

Take the Lead in Your Publishing Journey

Empowerment is about ownership—ownership of your career, your rights, and your future. You're not just a passive participant in the publishing process. You're a key player, and every decision you make can have long-lasting effects on your success.

This book is your roadmap to navigating the complex, and sometimes confusing, world of publishing law. Each chapter will give you the tools you need to take control—whether it's understanding your publishing rights, negotiating contracts, protecting your intellectual property, or hiring the right professionals to help you along the way. By the end of this journey, you'll be a more empowered, informed, and savvy author.

So, let's flip the script. Instead of feeling overwhelmed by the legal side of things, embrace it as another part of your creative process. After all, building a successful writing career isn't just about writing great stories—it's about owning them, and ensuring you reap the rewards of your hard work.

In the next chapter, we'll dive into the nuts and bolts of publishing rights, the foundation of every author's career. But for now, remember this: You are the author of your destiny—both in words and in business. And it's time to start writing your own rules.

Common Pitfalls to Avoid

Ah, the glamorous life of an author. You've finished your masterpiece, the words flow like fine wine, and you're ready to unleash it upon the world. But wait—before you sign that publishing contract and pop the champagne, let's talk about the landmines scattered along the path to literary stardom. These are the common pitfalls that countless authors—brilliant, talented authors—have fallen into, often without even realizing it until it's too late. The goal here? To ensure you don't become a cautionary tale.

Contracts and legal agreements can seem like a minor detail, an afterthought even, compared to the creative process of writing. But if you don't pay attention, they can quickly turn into the villain of your publishing journey. By recognizing these pitfalls ahead of time, you can steer clear of them and emerge not only as a successful author but as one who's in control of their creative and financial future.

1. Signing Away All Your Rights

One of the most common and damaging mistakes authors make is unknowingly signing away all their rights to a publisher. When you see the words "exclusive" or "all rights" in your contract, alarm bells should be ringing. These clauses could mean that you're giving up control over your book not just for the initial print run, but indefinitely. Even worse, it could cover rights you didn't even think to consider—like film adaptations, audiobook versions, or even merchandise based on your characters.

- **What to Look Out For**: Watch out for overly broad or vague language in the rights section of your contract. You want to retain as much control as possible, especially over subsidiary rights like film, TV, and audiobook rights, which could be worth a fortune down the line.

- **Avoid This Pitfall**: Make sure the contract clearly defines what rights the publisher is acquiring and for how long. If possible, negotiate to keep subsidiary rights or limit the contract to specific formats (like print and eBook), leaving the rest for you to explore later.

2. Accepting Low Royalties or Unfavorable Terms

You've poured your heart and soul into writing your book, so it's important to make sure you're fairly compensated for your work. However, many authors get swept up in the excitement of a publishing deal and overlook unfavorable royalty rates or contract terms. This can lead to long-term financial losses, especially if your book becomes a hit.

- **What to Look Out For**: Low royalty percentages (especially for eBooks and foreign sales) and long payment periods. Some contracts might also include clauses that allow publishers to withhold royalties for "returns" or give them the ability to delay payments indefinitely due to vague conditions.

- **Avoid This Pitfall**: Negotiate royalty rates that reflect the industry standard (or higher, if you can). Don't be afraid to push back on clauses that allow for unnecessary withholding of payments. Always make sure the contract specifies clear timelines for royalty payments, so you know when to expect your earnings.

3. Falling Into the Non-Compete Trap

Many publishing contracts include a non-compete clause, which restricts you from publishing any other works within a certain timeframe, or in the same genre, or even under a different pen name. This might seem harmless at first, but it can become a creativity killer if it prevents you from exploring other writing opportunities—or locks you into a deal where you're stuck waiting while your publisher decides when (or if) to release your book.

- **What to Look Out For**: Vague or overly broad non-compete clauses that prohibit you from publishing anything that might be seen as competition with your contracted work. This can restrict your ability to write other books in the same genre, even if they're completely unrelated to the book under contract.

- **Avoid This Pitfall**: Push for a narrower non-compete clause that limits restrictions to just the specific work you're contracting for. Make sure the terms are clear about what you can and can't do, and consider negotiating a shorter timeframe for the non-compete clause.

4. Underestimating the Importance of Reversion Clauses

Many authors are so excited to get their book published that they don't think about what happens if the book stops selling or the publisher decides to let it sit on a virtual shelf. This is where the reversion of rights clause comes in—an often-overlooked section of the contract that can determine whether you regain control over your work after a certain period or if the publisher keeps it forever, regardless of how well it's performing.

- **What to Look Out For**: Contracts without a clear reversion of rights clause or ones that set unreasonably high sales thresholds before rights revert to you. If your book isn't actively being marketed or sold, you should be able to take it back and explore other opportunities.

- **Avoid This Pitfall**: Ensure there's a clear reversion clause that specifies when and how the rights to your book will revert to you—especially if sales fall below a certain threshold or the book goes out of print. This allows you to republish or pursue other opportunities if the publisher is no longer actively supporting your book.

5. Overlooking Subsidiary and Foreign Rights

Remember when we talked about film rights, audiobook rights, and foreign sales? These can be some of the most lucrative parts of your book deal, but they're often buried in the fine print of your contract. Many authors unknowingly sign these rights over to the publisher, only to miss out on the financial windfall they could have earned by keeping control of them.

- **What to Look Out For**: Contracts that grant the publisher control over all subsidiary rights without additional compensation or the ability to sell those rights on your behalf. If you sign these away, you may miss out on a potential film adaptation or a series of lucrative foreign translations.

- **Avoid This Pitfall**: Retain control over subsidiary and foreign rights whenever possible, or at least ensure that the publisher splits the revenue from these deals fairly. If the publisher wants to sell these rights, make sure you're entitled to a significant percentage of any income they generate.

6. Misunderstanding the Advance Structure

Many authors hear the word "advance" and immediately think it's a giant check headed their way. But advances are usually paid out in installments—sometimes over years—and can be recoupable against your royalties, meaning you won't see any additional money until your book earns out its advance. This can lead to disappointment if you expect a quick financial windfall.

- **What to Look Out For**: Advances that are paid out over long periods or that are contingent on certain milestones (like manuscript delivery, publication, or paperback release). It's also important to understand that once the advance is paid, royalties don't start flowing until the publisher recoups their initial investment.

- **Avoid This Pitfall**: Ask for a clear breakdown of when and how the advance will be paid. Negotiate for quicker payment schedules if possible, and understand that you might not receive additional royalties until after the advance has been fully recouped by the publisher.

7. Failing to Seek Professional Help

Let's be real—publishing contracts are dense and filled with legal jargon. Many authors try to navigate them alone, either out of excitement or in an attempt to avoid legal fees. But going in without an experienced eye can lead to costly mistakes. Agents and lawyers exist for a reason: to protect your interests.

- **What to Look Out For**: The temptation to go it alone, especially when a contract seems straightforward or you're eager to sign quickly. Even well-meaning publishers may include clauses that work in their favor rather than yours.

- **Avoid This Pitfall**: Invest in professional help. A literary agent or an entertainment lawyer can help you understand what you're signing, negotiate better terms, and ensure your rights are protected. It's a small price to pay for long-term peace of mind and protection.

Avoiding the Pitfalls: Your Key to a Stronger Career

These common pitfalls have tripped up even the most seasoned authors, but they don't have to trip you. By being aware of the red flags in publishing contracts and understanding the implications of every clause, you'll position yourself to make better decisions for your career.

Remember, the publishing process is as much about business as it is about creativity. A little extra vigilance and some strategic negotiations can make all the difference between a contract that works for you and one that works against you. Throughout this book, we'll equip you with the tools and knowledge you need to avoid these pitfalls and emerge from every negotiation stronger, smarter, and in control of your writing destiny.

Now that we've covered the potential landmines, it's time to dive into the first chapter: Understanding Publishing Rights: The Foundation of Your Book's Journey.

The Evolving Publishing Landscape

Welcome to the wild west of the publishing world—where the rules are constantly changing, the opportunities are endless, and the traditional gatekeepers no longer hold all the keys. The publishing landscape has evolved dramatically over the past decade, opening up new avenues for authors to get their work out there and create long-lasting careers. But with these changes come new challenges, and if you don't keep up, you might find yourself lost in the shuffle.

Gone are the days when publishing success was defined by signing with a major publisher and hoping for a big print run. Today, authors have more options than ever, from self-publishing on digital platforms to pursuing hybrid models where they retain more control over their work. But navigating this new terrain requires understanding not only the creative side of writing but also the business and legal aspects of the evolving industry.

In this section, we'll explore how the publishing landscape has transformed, what it means for you as an author, and how you can take advantage of these shifts to build a sustainable, profitable career.

1. The Rise of Self-Publishing: Author as Publisher

Not so long ago, the phrase "self-publishing" might have carried a bit of stigma. It was often seen as a last resort for authors who couldn't land a traditional book deal. But today, self-publishing is not only legitimate; it's thriving. Authors have found tremendous success by taking control of their careers, publishing on platforms like Amazon's Kindle Direct Publishing (KDP), IngramSpark, or even creating audiobooks through services like ACX.

With self-publishing, the power is in your hands—but so is the responsibility. When you choose to self-publish, you become not only the author but also the publisher, marketer, and legal manager of your own work. That means you need to understand how to protect your rights, set competitive prices, handle distribution, and ensure you're getting the best financial return for your efforts.

Here's why self-publishing is a game-changer:

- **Creative Control**: You call the shots. Want to release a series in rapid succession? Go for it. Want to design your own cover or set your own pricing strategy? You have complete creative control.

- **Higher Royalties**: Self-published authors often keep 70% of their royalties or more, compared to the standard 10-15% royalty from traditional publishers. The trade-off? You're doing more of the heavy lifting.

- **Faster Time to Market**: You don't have to wait months or even years for a publisher's release schedule. Once your manuscript is ready, you can get it to market quickly, capitalizing on trends or the momentum of your fan base.

The Legal Angle: As a self-publisher, you need to be vigilant about copyright protection, trademarking, and managing your distribution rights. Platforms like Amazon give you global reach, but you need to be sure that your rights are protected in every territory where your book is sold. This is where understanding your territorial rights becomes crucial.

2. The Hybrid Publishing Model: Best of Both Worlds?

For some authors, neither traditional publishing nor self-publishing is the perfect fit. Enter hybrid publishing—a model that offers the creative freedom of self-publishing but with some of the support of a traditional publishing house. Hybrid publishers often provide services like editing, cover design, and distribution, but you retain more control over your rights and royalties.

Hybrid publishing allows you to:

- **Maintain Ownership of Your Rights**: Unlike many traditional contracts where the publisher controls your rights for years, hybrid models often allow authors to keep ownership of their intellectual property.

- **Keep a Bigger Share of Royalties**: While hybrid publishers take a fee or percentage for their services, you'll typically earn a higher royalty rate than you would with a traditional deal.

- **Get Professional Services**: You get the benefit of professional editing, design, and marketing assistance, which can help you produce a polished product while still having a say in how your book is marketed and distributed.

The Legal Angle: Hybrid publishing contracts can vary widely, so it's critical to carefully review the terms. Make sure the publisher isn't demanding exclusive rights unless you're comfortable with that arrangement. Hybrid deals can sometimes blur the lines, so work with a lawyer to ensure you're not signing away more control than intended.

3. Audiobooks, Podcasts, and Beyond: The Multimedia Explosion

In the evolving landscape, audiobooks and podcasts are two of the fastest-growing segments in publishing. Readers are increasingly turning to audio content—whether it's during their commute, their workout, or while they're doing chores. This opens up a whole new frontier for authors.

You no longer have to think of your book as just a physical or digital product—it can become an audiobook, a podcast series, or even an interactive experience. But to make the most of these opportunities, you need to understand the legal nuances of adapting your work into different formats.

Here's why exploring these formats is crucial:

- **New Revenue Streams**: Audiobooks can bring in a whole new set of royalties, especially as platforms like Audible and Spotify continue to grow. The more formats your book exists in, the more potential revenue you can generate.

- **Expanded Audience**: Some readers prefer audiobooks or podcasts to sitting down with a physical book. By offering your work in these formats, you're reaching a larger audience.

- **Cross-Promotion**: Imagine launching your audiobook alongside your print book or hosting a podcast that delves into the themes of your novel. These multimedia formats can cross-promote each other, expanding your reach and visibility.

The Legal Angle: When it comes to audio content, make sure your contract includes clear language about who holds the rights to audiobooks and any other audio formats. If you're self-publishing, platforms like ACX make it easier to create your own audiobook, but you still need to ensure that your intellectual property is protected across all formats and territories.

4. The Importance of Building Your Brand

In today's publishing world, you are the brand. It's not just about the book anymore—it's about you as an author, your social media presence, your email list, and your ability to connect with readers. Building an author platform is now more important than ever, whether you're self-publishing or working with a traditional publisher.

But here's the kicker: when you're a brand, you're also a business, and that comes with its own set of legal considerations.

Why branding matters:

- **Reader Loyalty**: A strong brand creates a community around your work, turning casual readers into loyal fans who are eager to buy everything you publish.

- **Better Deals**: The more visible and established your brand, the more leverage you'll have in negotiations—whether that's for higher advances, better royalties, or retaining more control over your intellectual property.

- **More Opportunities**: A strong brand can lead to opportunities beyond books—such as speaking engagements, collaborations, or even film and TV deals.

The Legal Angle: As you build your brand, make sure to protect it legally. This includes trademarking your author name, book series, or any unique branding elements. If your brand extends into merchandise, you'll need to ensure you own the rights to your characters and any other intellectual property that might be used in your branding.

5. Traditional Publishing: Still a Viable Path?

With all the new opportunities in self-publishing, hybrid publishing, and digital formats, you might wonder if traditional publishing is still worth pursuing. The answer is: absolutely—if you know how to navigate it. Traditional publishers still offer significant advantages, such as:

- **Access to Established Distribution Channels**: Big publishers have relationships with major retailers, libraries, and international markets, helping your book reach a wide audience.

- **Professional Editing and Marketing**: Working with experienced editors, marketers, and publicists can elevate the quality of your book and its visibility.

- **Prestige and Recognition**: For some authors, the backing of a traditional publisher still carries a certain prestige and credibility that can open doors to media coverage, awards, and other opportunities.

The Legal Angle: When entering the traditional publishing world, it's essential to understand the contract terms, especially when it comes to rights, royalties, and advances. Be sure to negotiate for fair royalty rates and retain as many subsidiary rights as possible. We'll dive deep into how to negotiate those deals later in the book.

In this ever-evolving publishing landscape, authors are no longer limited by one-size-fits-all models. Whether you're going the self-publishing route, exploring hybrid models, or sticking with traditional publishers, the power to shape your career is now in your hands. The key to thriving in this environment? Understanding your rights and making informed, strategic decisions about how you publish, distribute, and protect your work.

With more opportunities come more legal complexities—but don't worry, we're here to help you navigate them all. In the next section, we'll take a deep dive into publishing rights—the foundation of your book's journey and one of the most important legal aspects to understand.

A Roadmap for a Long, Sustainable Career

It's every author's dream to not only publish a book but to build a long, sustainable career in writing. Sure, the thrill of seeing your name on the spine of a book is incredible, but what about the bigger picture? How do you ensure that you're not just a flash in the pan, but a seasoned author with a body of work that generates steady income and continues to find new readers for years to come?

In today's rapidly evolving publishing world, the path to success isn't as clear-cut as it used to be. But that's not a bad thing. It means you have more opportunities to shape your career on your own terms. Whether you're dreaming of writing a best-selling series, creating an entire world of interconnected novels, or mastering multiple formats like audiobooks and eBooks, having a long-term strategy is key.

In this section, we'll walk you through a roadmap to creating a sustainable writing career—one that's built to last, with multiple revenue streams and the flexibility to grow as the industry changes. It's not just about your next book, it's about your next ten books, and how to maximize your success over the long haul.

1. Think Like a Business: Protect and Leverage Your Rights

As an author, your creative work is more than just a passion—it's a business asset. Each book you write is intellectual property that can generate income not just today but for years to come. To build a sustainable career, you need to think like a business owner and treat your books like valuable assets that need protection and management.

Here's how to start thinking long-term about your career:

- **Retain Ownership of Your Rights**: The most valuable asset you have as an author is the ownership of your rights. This includes not just the publishing rights to your book but also subsidiary rights like film, TV, audio, and foreign rights. Always negotiate to keep as many of these rights as possible, so you have the freedom to exploit them in different ways later.

- **Plan for Future Works**: Don't just think about the book you're working on now—consider how it fits into a broader strategy. Are you writing a standalone novel, or could this turn into a series? Are you building a world that could expand into multiple books, or even spin-offs? Mapping out your future works allows you to make smart decisions about contracts, rights, and marketing that benefit you in the long term.

- **Monetize Across Platforms**: Your book can be more than just a paperback on a bookstore shelf. Explore opportunities in eBooks, audiobooks, and foreign markets to ensure that your work reaches as many readers (and markets) as possible. The more formats and platforms your book exists in, the more potential it has to generate revenue.

Example: You publish your first novel and retain the audiobook rights. A year later, you decide to produce the audiobook yourself, using a platform like ACX, and it becomes a hit with a whole new audience. The audiobook success also boosts sales of your print and eBook versions, creating a virtuous cycle of revenue across formats.

2. Build a Body of Work: The Power of the Backlist

The key to a sustainable writing career is not just writing one great book but creating a body of work—a collection of books that continue to sell and bring in revenue long after they've been published. This is often referred to as your backlist, and it's one of the most powerful tools you have as an author.

Here's why the backlist matters:

- **Steady Income Stream**: Once you've built a catalog of books, your backlist can generate passive income as new readers discover your older works. Many successful authors make a significant portion of their income from their backlist, which continues to sell as they release new titles.

- **Cross-Promotion**: Your new books can drive readers to your older titles and vice versa. If a reader loves your latest book, they're likely to seek out everything else you've written. By creating a consistent brand and writing style, you turn casual readers into lifelong fans.

- **Series and Spin-Off Potential**: If your books are connected—either as part of a series or through shared characters or worlds—you can encourage readers to move seamlessly from one book to the next. This creates a long-term relationship with your audience and ensures that your career is built on more than just standalone success.

Example: You write a successful fantasy novel, and over the next few years, you release two sequels. Fans of the first book eagerly buy the next two, and each time a new reader discovers the series, they purchase all three books. Your backlist becomes a self-sustaining revenue stream, continually driving sales as new readers discover your work.

3. Diversify Your Income Streams: Multiple Ways to Monetize Your Work

To build a sustainable career, you need to think beyond just book sales. Successful authors often have multiple income streams, from royalties to speaking engagements, workshops, merchandising, and even TV or film adaptations. The more ways you can monetize your work, the more stable your income will be.

Here are some ways to diversify your income:

- **Foreign Rights Sales**: Your book may have a strong market in other countries. Selling the foreign translation rights to publishers in different regions can open up new revenue streams and significantly boost your overall earnings.

- **Audiobooks**: As the popularity of audiobooks continues to grow, producing an audiobook version of your work is a must. Audiobooks have become a major revenue source for authors, and some readers even prefer to consume books in this format.

- **Merchandising**: If your book has a dedicated fanbase, consider creating merchandise based on your characters, world, or quotes from your story. From t-shirts to mugs to exclusive signed editions, merchandising is a great way to engage fans and generate extra income.

- **Workshops, Courses, and Speaking Engagements**: If you've established yourself as an expert in a particular genre or topic, you could offer workshops or courses on writing. This not only brings in extra income but also helps build your author brand and connects you with your audience on a deeper level.

Example: After your fantasy novel becomes a bestseller, you start receiving requests from schools and libraries to speak about your writing process. You turn this into a side business, offering workshops and talks that generate additional income while also helping you build a stronger connection with your readers.

4. Future-Proof Your Career: Stay Adaptable in a Changing Industry

The publishing world is constantly evolving, and what works today might not be the best strategy five years from now. The most successful authors are those who can adapt to industry changes, whether it's the rise of digital platforms, the growing demand for audiobooks, or the increasing influence of social media marketing.

To future-proof your career, you need to:

- **Stay Educated**: The more you know about the changes in the industry, the better equipped you'll be to navigate them. Keep an eye on publishing trends, new platforms, and emerging technologies that could impact your career.

- **Be Open to New Formats**: Don't limit yourself to one format or platform. Whether it's exploring audiobooks, foreign translations, or new digital distribution models, staying flexible will help you tap into new opportunities.

- **Leverage Technology**: From email marketing to social media to automated tools for tracking royalties and sales, technology can help you manage your career more efficiently. The more you embrace these tools, the more time you'll have to focus on your writing and the long-term strategy of your career.

Example: After noticing the rise in popularity of podcasts, you decide to launch your own podcast where you discuss your world-building process and interview other authors. Not only does this provide an additional revenue stream, but it also introduces your work to a new audience who may not have discovered your books otherwise.

5. Plan for the Future: Contracts That Set You Up for Success

Building a sustainable career also means planning for the legal side of your future. The contracts you sign today can have long-lasting impacts on your ability to continue building your career tomorrow. Whether it's negotiating sequel rights, ensuring a fair reversion of rights clause, or retaining control of subsidiary rights, the decisions you make now will affect your ability to capitalize on your work later.

- **Negotiate Sequel and Spin-Off Rights**: If you're writing a series, ensure that your contract allows for future books or spin-offs. Retaining control of your characters, world, and overarching story will give you more flexibility in expanding your body of work.

- **Reversion Clauses**: Make sure your contract includes a reversion of rights clause, which allows you to regain control of your work after a certain period or if sales drop below a certain threshold. This gives you the option to self-publish your backlist or find a new publisher later in your career.

- **Consider Long-Term Licensing**: When licensing your work for film, TV, or merchandise, make sure the terms are favorable to you not just now, but years down the line. A savvy lawyer can help you ensure that your rights and earnings are protected as your career evolves.

Example: When signing a contract for your fantasy series, you negotiate a clause that allows you to retain the film adaptation rights. Years later, when your series takes off, you're able to license the film rights to a major studio, creating a whole new revenue stream that could have been lost if you had signed away those rights earlier.

The key to a long, sustainable writing career is strategic thinking and planning for the future. By protecting your rights, diversifying your income streams, and building a strong backlist, you'll set yourself up for success—not just with your next book, but with the next ten. Remember, a successful career in writing isn't about a single breakthrough; it's about consistency, adaptability, and business savvy. Let "Legal Ink" be your guide as you chart your path to long-term success in the ever-changing world of publishing.

Turning Knowledge Into Action

Alright, you've soaked up the insights, decoded the legal jargon, and hopefully had a few lightbulb moments. But here's the thing—knowledge without action is like a book without pages: all concept, no content. Now that you're equipped with the understanding of how the publishing world works and how to navigate its legal minefields, it's time to put that knowledge to work. This section is all about taking action, turning what you've learned into concrete steps that will advance your career, protect your rights, and ensure that your literary empire flourishes.

Knowing your rights and understanding publishing contracts is half the battle; the other half is applying this knowledge with precision and confidence. The goal here is to take proactive steps to not only avoid mistakes but to maximize your opportunities. Let's turn all those aha moments into real-world decisions that will elevate your career and protect your creative interests.

1. Create Your Own Publishing Playbook

Every author's journey is different, and no single strategy fits everyone. So, the first step is to create your own publishing playbook—a personalized strategy that reflects your career goals, whether that's becoming a bestselling author, mastering self-publishing, or building a brand that extends beyond books.

Here's how to start:

- **Define Your Goals**: Are you aiming to publish traditionally or self-publish? Is your focus on creating a long-term series or writing a variety of standalone novels? Do you want to expand into audiobooks, film, or TV adaptations? Get clear on what success looks like for you.

- **Map Out Your Rights Strategy**: Now that you understand publishing rights, decide which rights you want to keep and which ones you're willing to license. For instance, you might want to retain audiobook rights while allowing a traditional publisher to handle print and eBook formats. Having a clear vision of your rights strategy will help you negotiate better deals.

- **Prioritize Your Contracts**: What's negotiable, and what's non-negotiable? If maintaining control over subsidiary rights is a priority, make sure that's at the top of your list in every contract negotiation. Your playbook should include a list of key contract elements you'll focus on, such as royalty rates, reversion clauses, and the scope of rights.

Example: You've decided to self-publish your first novel but want to retain the rights for audiobook production. You create a step-by-step plan in your playbook for securing an audiobook narrator, deciding on distribution platforms like ACX, and releasing the audiobook six months after the print version to keep the momentum going.

2. Take a Proactive Approach to Negotiation

Contracts don't have to be intimidating if you approach them with a clear strategy. Whether you're working with a traditional publisher, self-publishing, or exploring hybrid options, negotiation is key to protecting your interests and maximizing your earnings. But negotiation isn't just about getting what you want—it's about knowing what to ask for and how to ask for it.

Here's how to take action during negotiations:

- **Know Your Worth**: Before sitting down to negotiate, research industry standards for advances, royalties, and subsidiary rights. This will help you confidently ask for terms that reflect the value of your work. If you don't know what's possible, you can't negotiate effectively.

- **Have Clear Priorities**: Don't enter negotiations trying to win every point. Instead, know which terms are non-negotiable for you (such as retaining film rights or securing a higher royalty rate on eBooks) and be flexible on the rest. Your willingness to compromise on smaller points can help you win on the big ones.

- **Use Your Rights as Leverage**: If you're keeping certain rights (like foreign or audiobook rights), use that as leverage to negotiate a better deal. Publishers may offer you a higher advance or royalty rate if you're open to letting them handle more aspects of your book's distribution.

Example: During negotiations with a traditional publisher, you focus on securing a reversion of rights clause that allows you to regain control of your book if sales fall below a certain threshold. This ensures that if the publisher no longer actively markets your book, you can take back the rights and explore self-publishing or other opportunities.

3. Build a Sustainable Marketing and Distribution Plan

Understanding the legal side of publishing is one thing, but it's also crucial to think about how you're going to get your book into readers' hands—and keep it there. A solid marketing and distribution plan is an essential part of turning your book into a long-term success, and it needs to be crafted with your legal rights in mind.

Here's how to build a smart marketing and distribution plan:

- **Leverage Multiple Formats**: Don't limit your book to just one format. By releasing your work in print, eBook, and audiobook formats, you increase its chances of reaching different types of readers and generating multiple revenue streams. Make sure your contracts reflect your ability to distribute across different formats.

- **Plan for Long-Term Marketing**: Your book launch is just the beginning. Plan out a 12-month marketing calendar that includes ongoing promotions, new release announcements, and ways to engage your audience over time. By keeping your book in the public eye, you extend its shelf life and improve your chances of long-term sales.

- **Keep Control of Your Brand**: Whether you're self-publishing or working with a traditional publisher, make sure you retain control over your author brand. This includes managing your website, email list, and social media accounts, which will help you build a direct relationship with your readers. Your brand is an asset that can grow with each new release, so make sure it's not tied up in your publishing contracts.

Example: You release your book in both eBook and print formats and negotiate to retain audiobook rights. Six months later, you release the audiobook version, using your email list and social media presence to promote it to readers who've already bought the print edition. The result is a steady sales boost as fans explore new ways to enjoy your book.

4. Protect Your Rights, Every Step of the Way

Now that you understand the importance of protecting your rights, it's time to put that knowledge into action. This doesn't mean just signing good contracts—it means actively monitoring your rights and making sure they're enforced. Keep track of where your work is being used, how much revenue it's generating, and whether your contractual agreements are being honored.

Here's how to stay proactive about protecting your rights:

- **Track Your Royalties**: Don't just assume you're being paid what you're owed. Regularly review your royalty statements and compare them against your sales data. If you spot discrepancies, address them immediately by contacting your publisher or distributor. If necessary, exercise your audit rights.

- **Monitor for Infringement**: Protecting your intellectual property doesn't stop once your book is published. Regularly monitor platforms where your work is sold or shared to ensure there's no unauthorized use. If you discover infringement, act quickly by sending a cease-and-desist letter or working with a lawyer to resolve the issue.

- **Plan for Rights Reversion**: Don't wait until your book's sales start to decline. Keep an eye on your reversion clauses and make a plan for what you'll do when the rights revert to you. This might mean re-releasing the book in a new format, offering a limited edition, or even exploring new publishing options.

Example: A year after publishing your novel, you notice that your royalty payments don't seem to match your sales numbers. You contact the publisher and discover a miscalculation in the royalties owed to you. By staying on top of your rights, you ensure that you receive the correct payment and avoid a potential loss of income.

5. Stay Flexible, Stay Informed

The publishing world is constantly changing, and the most successful authors are those who stay informed and adaptable. You've learned a lot from this book, but the journey doesn't end here. The best way to stay ahead is to keep learning, keep networking, and stay open to new opportunities as they arise.

Here's how to keep your knowledge fresh and stay on the cutting edge of publishing:

- **Continue Your Education**: Publishing laws and trends evolve, and so should your knowledge. Keep reading industry blogs, attending writer conferences, and staying updated on changes in the legal and business side of publishing.

- **Build a Network**: Surround yourself with other authors, agents, and legal professionals who can offer support and advice as you navigate your career. Your network can alert you to new opportunities, share valuable insights, and help you avoid common pitfalls.

- **Stay Adaptable**: Don't get too comfortable with one way of doing things. The best authors are those who can pivot as new platforms and formats emerge. Whether it's self-publishing, audiobooks, or new distribution models, stay open to what's coming next and be ready to evolve.

Example: After successfully self-publishing your first novel, you decide to explore the possibility of turning it into a limited podcast series to attract a new audience. You research podcasting rights, work with a lawyer to create a contract with the production company, and launch the series as a way to cross-promote your book and expand your brand.

Turning knowledge into action is what will set you apart as an author who's not only creative but also savvy and strategic. By building a publishing playbook, negotiating smartly, protecting your rights, and staying adaptable, you'll be able to turn your understanding of the publishing industry into tangible success. Each step you take will bring you closer to a long, fulfilling, and profitable career as an empowered author.

In the next section, we'll dive deeper into publishing rights, the core of every author's business strategy. Stay tuned, because understanding these rights will be key to taking full control of your career.

Bringing Legal Jargon Down to Earth

Ah, legal jargon—the great intimidator. Those contracts filled with words like "subsidiary rights," "territorial exclusivity," and "royalty escalation clauses" can make even the most seasoned authors feel like they're wading through quicksand. But here's the good news: you don't need a law degree to understand what's going on in your publishing agreements. You just need a little translation help, and that's where "Legal Ink" comes in.

Let's face it, legalese is designed to confuse and intimidate. It's why so many authors sign contracts without fully understanding what they're agreeing to. But we're here to cut through the confusion, bring those fancy terms down to earth, and empower you to walk into any negotiation with your head held high. By the end of this book, you'll not only be able to read a contract, but you'll also be able to own it—because you'll know exactly what it says, and more importantly, what it means for your career.

So let's demystify the legal language of publishing and turn it into something approachable, actionable, and yes—even a little bit fun.

1. Decoding the Jargon: What Those Big Words Really Mean

Legal contracts love their big words. But what's important isn't the complexity of the language—it's the meaning behind it. Let's take a look at some of the most common terms you'll encounter in publishing agreements, and break them down in plain English:

- **Grant of Rights**: This is the section of the contract where you (the author) grant certain rights to the publisher. Essentially, it outlines what you're giving them permission to do with your work. For example, if you grant "exclusive worldwide rights," you're giving the publisher the sole right to publish your book anywhere in the world. Simple, right?

- **Territorial Rights**: This refers to the geographic areas where the publisher has the right to sell your book. If you've granted "worldwide rights," the publisher can distribute your book globally. If you've only granted "North American rights," they can sell the book only in the U.S. and Canada. This section is crucial if you're hoping to sell foreign rights separately.

- **Royalties**: Royalties are the percentage of sales that you, the author, earn for each book sold. The contract will specify what percentage you'll earn on different formats (eBooks, paperbacks, hardcovers) and in different territories. Royalties are paid after you've earned out your advance, meaning once the publisher has recouped the money they gave you upfront.

- **Advance**: An advance is the money the publisher pays you before the book is published. It's essentially an advance against future royalties, so you won't see any royalty checks until your book sales surpass the amount of the advance. But hey, getting paid upfront is always nice, right?

- **Subsidiary Rights**: This is where things get juicy. Subsidiary rights refer to the rights to adapt your book into other formats—like film, TV, audiobooks, or foreign translations. These rights can be incredibly lucrative, so it's important to negotiate who controls them. Do you keep the rights, or does the publisher? If they sell the rights to a film studio, do you get a percentage of the deal?

- **Reversion of Rights**: This clause outlines when and how the rights to your book will revert back to you. This usually happens when a book goes out of print or when sales drop below a certain threshold. Having a strong reversion clause is key if you want to regain control of your book and possibly re-publish it later.

- **Exclusivity**: This term refers to whether the publisher has exclusive rights to publish your book, meaning no one else can publish it in the agreed-upon territory or format. Non-exclusive rights, on the other hand, would allow you to publish your book in multiple places or formats simultaneously.

Example: You've just signed a contract with a traditional publisher, but you've held onto audiobook rights and plan to create an audiobook on your own. Because you've only granted exclusive print and eBook rights, you're free to create an audiobook, distribute it on Audible, and earn royalties on it—while still benefiting from your publisher's work on the print and digital versions.

2. Why the Fine Print Matters: Read Before You Sign

It's tempting to skim through a contract, especially when you're eager to start working with a publisher or distributor. But here's the thing: the devil is in the details. Those tiny clauses buried deep in the contract can have a big impact on your future earnings, your rights to your work, and your overall career.

Here's why the fine print matters:

- **Royalties and Advances**: It's easy to focus on the advance payment (because who doesn't love upfront cash?), but what about the royalty percentages? Will you still be earning from your book five years down the line, or will the terms of your contract mean you're missing out on long-term earnings? The fine print here can make a huge difference in how much you ultimately take home.

- **Subsidiary Rights**: Are you unknowingly signing away the rights to a potential film adaptation or a foreign translation deal? Make sure the contract clearly states who controls subsidiary rights—and if it's the publisher, be sure you're getting a fair cut of any deals they make on your behalf.

- **Reversion Clauses**: Your book may not sell forever, and eventually, you'll want the rights back to republish, adapt, or even explore self-publishing. The reversion clause should spell out exactly when and how you can get those rights back. If the language is vague or restrictive, you might be waiting a lot longer than you'd like.

- **Non-Compete Clauses**: Some contracts include non-compete clauses, which prevent you from publishing other works that could compete with your current book. Make sure these clauses are reasonable and don't limit your ability to write or publish future works. If the terms are too broad, they could stifle your creativity or slow down your publishing schedule.

Example: Imagine you sign a contract that includes a vague reversion clause, stating that rights revert back to you if the book is "no longer in print." Sounds reasonable, right? But what happens if the publisher keeps the book available as an eBook indefinitely? Without a clearer definition of "no longer in print," you might never get your rights back—even if sales have completely dried up.

3. Keep Your Eyes on the Money: Understanding Royalty Calculations

Let's talk about royalties, because this is where the financial rubber meets the road. Royalties are often not as straightforward as they seem. Depending on your contract, there could be all kinds of deductions—distribution fees, marketing costs, printing costs—that get taken out before you ever see a check.

Here's what you need to know:

- **Net vs. Gross Royalties**: Some contracts pay royalties on the net sales, meaning you're paid a percentage after costs like printing, shipping, and marketing are deducted. Other contracts pay on gross sales, meaning you're paid a percentage based on the total sales price of each book. Gross royalties are almost always better for the author.

- **Royalty Escalation Clauses**: Some contracts include clauses that increase your royalty rate after certain sales milestones are hit. For example, you might earn 10% royalties on the first 10,000 copies sold, and 12% on any sales beyond that. This can be a great incentive if your book takes off, so make sure you know if and when your royalties increase.

- **Advances and Earning Out**: If you receive an advance, it's important to know that you won't see additional royalties until your book earns out that advance. That means if you receive a $10,000 advance, you won't receive royalty payments until the book has generated enough sales to cover that amount. Keep an eye on the fine print to ensure that the math works in your favor.

Example: You sign a contract with a publisher that offers 15% royalties on net sales. After the book is released, you notice that your royalty checks are lower than expected. You review your royalty statement and see that distribution and marketing fees were deducted before calculating your percentage. By understanding the difference between gross and net royalties, you can negotiate a better deal for future projects.

4. Asking the Right Questions: What to Clarify Before You Sign

When you're handed a contract, don't be afraid to ask questions—even if you're working with an agent or lawyer. It's your work, your career, and your future on the line, so make sure you fully understand the terms before signing.

Here are a few questions to always ask:

- **What specific rights am I granting?** Make sure the contract is clear about which rights you're giving to the publisher and which you're keeping for yourself.

- **What happens if sales are low?** Ensure that there's a reversion of rights clause that allows you to take back control of your book if it's no longer selling or being actively marketed.

- **How are royalties calculated?** Clarify whether your royalties are based on gross or net sales, and ask about any deductions that will be taken before royalties are paid out.

- **Who controls subsidiary rights?** If you're granting subsidiary rights (like film or TV rights), make sure the contract specifies how much of any deal you'll receive—and whether you have a say in the final decision.

- **How long will this contract last?** Make sure you know the duration of the contract and what triggers the reversion of rights. If possible, negotiate for shorter terms or options to renew.

Example: You're about to sign a contract with a small press, but you notice that the royalty rates seem low. You ask for clarification and discover that the royalties are calculated based on net sales after significant distribution costs. You negotiate for a higher percentage or a royalty structure based on gross sales, ensuring that you get a bigger slice of the pie.

Bringing legal jargon down to earth is all about making sure you, as the author, feel empowered to understand every part of your publishing journey. Contracts may be filled with big words and complicated clauses, but when you break them down, they're really just tools for protecting your rights and maximizing your success.

In the next section, we'll dive into negotiation strategies that will help you get the best possible deal and protect your work for years to come. Stay tuned—because when it comes to contracts, knowledge truly is power!

The Importance of Agents and Lawyers

Let's be honest: the publishing world is a bit like a high-stakes poker game. You've got your cards (your manuscript), the pot (your potential earnings), and a table full of seasoned players (publishers, editors, and distributors) all looking for the best deal. While you've learned a lot about how to play the game, sometimes you need a trusted partner to help you make the right moves and ensure that you're not just holding a good hand, but winning the game. That's where agents and lawyers come in.

Agents and lawyers are the unsung heroes behind many literary success stories. They are your allies, advocates, and advisors. They're there to help you negotiate contracts, protect your rights, and ensure that you're getting the best possible deal. But they do more than just read the fine print—they're experts in the business of publishing, and they can open doors that you might not even know exist.

In this section, we'll explore why agents and lawyers are so important, what they bring to the table, and how to know when it's time to bring one (or both) onto your team. Whether you're negotiating your first book deal or managing a complex portfolio of contracts, having the right professional support can make all the difference.

1. Literary Agents: Your Career's GPS

Think of a literary agent as your publishing GPS. They know the terrain, the best routes to take, and how to avoid roadblocks. An agent's job is to guide you through the labyrinth of the publishing world, helping you land the best deals, protecting your interests, and helping you navigate everything from editorial feedback to movie deals.

Here's why having an agent is a game-changer:

- **Access to Bigger Publishers**: Many large publishing houses won't even consider unsolicited manuscripts. But if you're represented by a well-connected agent, doors that were previously closed can suddenly swing open. Agents have relationships with editors and publishers that can give you a leg up in landing that coveted book deal.

- **Expert Negotiators**: An agent's bread and butter is negotiating contracts. They know what a fair advance looks like, how to get you the best royalty rates, and how to ensure you retain as many rights as possible. They're skilled at identifying red flags in contracts and negotiating favorable terms.

- **Long-Term Career Management**: Agents don't just work on a single book deal; they're invested in your long-term success. They help you strategize your career, plan future works, and explore new opportunities. Whether it's negotiating a sequel, licensing foreign rights, or securing a film adaptation, a good agent is always thinking several steps ahead.

- **Protecting Your Rights**: Agents understand the importance of subsidiary rights, such as film, TV, audiobook, and foreign translations. They'll fight to retain as many of these rights as possible so that you can explore future revenue streams.

Example: You've written a science fiction novel that has the potential to become a blockbuster series. With an agent on your side, not only do you secure a great deal with a major publisher, but your agent also negotiates a separate deal for audiobook rights and foreign rights in Europe. A year later, your book is optioned for a TV series, and your agent ensures you're compensated fairly for that deal as well.

2. Lawyers: Your Legal Bodyguards

While agents focus on getting you the best deal, entertainment lawyers are the ones who ensure that every contract is legally sound and bulletproof. If your agent is your GPS, then your lawyer is your bodyguard, standing between you and any potential legal issues. Lawyers have one job: to protect your legal and financial interests. They read every line of your contract with the precision of a hawk, ensuring that your rights are safeguarded and that you won't run into any nasty surprises down the road.

Here's why you need a lawyer in your corner:

- **Contract Expertise**: Lawyers are trained to analyze contracts in a way that even the most experienced agent can't. They'll catch clauses that might seem harmless but could end up costing you down the line—like vague reversion terms, excessive non-compete clauses, or royalties calculated in ways that benefit the publisher, not you.

- **Resolving Disputes**: If a dispute arises—whether it's over royalty payments, rights reversion, or breach of contract—your lawyer is the one who steps in to resolve it. They'll help you navigate mediation, arbitration, or litigation, ensuring that your rights are protected and that you're fairly compensated.

- **Rights Management**: Lawyers are experts at managing subsidiary rights (like film, TV, and foreign rights) and can help you structure deals that allow you to retain as much control as possible while maximizing your earnings. They'll ensure that you're not signing away future revenue streams unknowingly.

- **Navigating Complex Deals**: If your book is picked up for a film adaptation or licensed for international markets, your lawyer will ensure that every contract is airtight. They'll handle the nitty-gritty details that can make or break a deal—like how long the studio has to make the film, what happens if they don't, and how much you'll earn from box office or streaming revenue.

Example: You've secured a book deal, and everything seems straightforward—until your lawyer reviews the contract and discovers a non-compete clause that would prevent you from writing another book in the same genre for five years. Thanks to your lawyer's sharp eye, you renegotiate the clause to a more reasonable one-year window, ensuring that your future projects aren't held up.

3. Agents and Lawyers Working Together: The Dream Team

When it comes to building a long-term, sustainable career, the combination of an agent and a lawyer is often the ideal scenario. Together, they form a dream team that covers all your bases: your agent works to secure the best deals and long-term opportunities, while your lawyer ensures that the legal side of things is watertight.

Here's how they complement each other:

- **Agents focus on the big picture**: They're your career strategist, helping you navigate the publishing world, land the best deals, and plan your future moves. Agents are in it for the long haul, helping you manage your career over multiple books and projects.

- **Lawyers focus on the legal details**: They ensure that every contract you sign is in your best interest. Whether it's reviewing publishing agreements, managing intellectual property rights, or handling disputes, they've got your back on the legal side.

- **Collaboration for Complex Deals**: When big deals arise—like film or TV adaptations, merchandising agreements, or international sales—having both an agent and a lawyer ensures that you're not only getting a great deal but that the legal side is fully protected. Your agent will negotiate the terms, while your lawyer will make sure that those terms are legally sound.

Example: You've written a successful trilogy, and a Hollywood studio is interested in adapting it into a movie. Your agent negotiates the terms of the deal, securing a hefty upfront payment and a percentage of box office revenue. Meanwhile, your lawyer ensures that the contract includes provisions for creative control, reversion of rights if the film isn't made within a certain timeframe, and a clear royalty structure for future streaming earnings. Together, they secure both a great deal and strong legal protection.

4. When to Bring Them On Board: Timing Is Everything

Now that you understand the importance of agents and lawyers, the next question is: When do you need them? The answer depends on where you are in your career and the complexity of the deals you're navigating.

Here are a few guidelines:

- **When You're Submitting to Traditional Publishers**: If you're pursuing a traditional publishing deal with a large or mid-sized publisher, having an agent is almost always a good idea. They can help you land a better deal, retain more rights, and navigate the editorial process.

- **When You're Negotiating Major Contracts**: Whether it's your first publishing contract, a movie adaptation deal, or a foreign rights agreement, you'll want a lawyer to review the contract before you sign. Even if you're working with an agent, a lawyer will ensure that every detail is in your favor.

- **When Disputes Arise**: If you run into issues with royalty payments, rights reversion, or breach of contract, it's time to bring in a lawyer. They'll help you resolve the issue, whether through mediation, arbitration, or legal action.

- **When Your Career Is Taking Off**: As your career grows and you're managing multiple projects, contracts, and revenue streams, having both an agent and a lawyer on your team will ensure that you're making the most of every opportunity while staying legally protected.

Example: You're a self-published author who's had great success on Amazon, and now a traditional publisher is offering you a multi-book deal. You decide it's time to bring an agent on board to help negotiate the terms of the deal and explore future opportunities, like foreign translations and audiobook rights. You also hire a lawyer to review the contract, ensuring that your intellectual property rights are protected.

Agents and lawyers aren't just for blockbuster authors or big-time Hollywood deals—they're invaluable resources for any author looking to protect their rights, maximize their earnings, and navigate the complex world of publishing. Whether you're negotiating your first book contract or managing a multi-book empire, having the right professional support can be the difference between a good deal and a great career.

In the next section, we'll talk about how to find the right agent or lawyer and what to look for when bringing one onto your team. Stay tuned, because the next steps could be game-changing for your career!

Encouraging a Mindset Shift

Success in the publishing world isn't just about mastering the craft of writing or understanding legal jargon—it's about cultivating the right mindset. To thrive in an industry as unpredictable and evolving as publishing, you need to think not only as an artist but also as an entrepreneur, advocate, and lifelong learner. This section is all about making the mindset shift that will help you navigate your career with confidence and purpose.

Often, authors focus so much on their creative work that they overlook the business aspects that can make or break their careers. But embracing a business mindset doesn't mean compromising your artistic integrity—it means empowering yourself to make informed decisions, protect your work, and ultimately, reach more readers.

Here's why shifting your mindset is crucial for long-term success:

1. From Writer to Authorpreneur: Embrace the Business Side

If you want to build a sustainable career in publishing, you have to start thinking like an authorpreneur—a writer who also understands the business and marketing side of being an author. This mindset shift requires seeing yourself not just as a creative but as a business owner, with your books as the products you sell and your intellectual property as the assets you manage.

Here's what this shift looks like:

- **Taking Ownership**: Don't leave the business side to agents or publishers—understand the financials, the contracts, and your rights. When you take ownership of the business side of your writing, you're in control of your career trajectory.

- **Building Your Brand**: Every successful entrepreneur understands the importance of branding, and the same goes for authors. Developing your author brand and using it to connect with readers can set you apart and build a loyal audience that follows your career.

- **Thinking Long-Term**: As an authorpreneur, your focus isn't just on your current project but on the long-term vision for your career. That means planning multiple books, expanding into new formats (like audiobooks or merchandise), and diversifying your revenue streams.

Example: You've written your first novel, but instead of simply handing it off to a publisher, you think about how you can turn it into a multi-book series, a merchandise line, or an audiobook. You research the best ways to retain rights, negotiate contracts, and build your brand on social media, ensuring that your work continues to generate income long after its initial release.

2. Negotiating with Confidence: You Have More Power Than You Think

Many authors approach contract negotiations with a sense of powerlessness, feeling lucky just to have a deal on the table. But here's the truth: you have more power than you think. The key is recognizing the value of your work and walking into every negotiation with the confidence that comes from being well-prepared and well-informed.

Shifting your mindset around negotiation means:

- **Valuing Your Work**: The more you understand the market and the value of your intellectual property, the more confident you'll be when negotiating with agents, publishers, or distributors. Recognize that your work has value and that you're not just taking what's offered—you're **creating opportunities**.

- **Being Willing to Walk Away**: True negotiation power comes when you're willing to walk away from a bad deal. If the terms don't align with your long-term goals, or if you feel like you're signing away too many rights, don't be afraid to walk. There will be other opportunities, and protecting your work is paramount.

- **Seeing Negotiation as a Partnership**: Negotiation isn't about getting everything your way; it's about building a mutually beneficial partnership. Shifting your mindset to view publishers, agents, and distributors as collaborators (rather than adversaries) can create more fruitful, long-lasting relationships.

Example: You're offered a publishing deal with a low royalty rate and limited control over subsidiary rights. Instead of feeling pressured to sign, you confidently ask for better terms based on your research. You emphasize the potential for future projects and negotiate a more favorable royalty structure, keeping the audiobook and foreign rights for yourself.

3. Adaptability: Embrace Change and Stay Open to New Opportunities

The publishing industry is constantly evolving. From the rise of self-publishing to the growing dominance of digital and audio formats, authors today have more opportunities than ever before—but only if they're willing to adapt. The key to long-term success is staying open to change, learning new skills, and embracing new platforms and strategies as they emerge.

Here's how to shift to a mindset of adaptability:

- **Be Open to New Formats**: Don't limit yourself to traditional publishing. Explore the possibilities of eBooks, audiobooks, podcasts, and digital marketing. The more flexible you are with how your work is delivered to readers, the more opportunities you have to generate revenue.

- **Keep Learning**: Stay on top of industry trends, changes in publishing laws, and emerging platforms. Whether it's attending writer conferences, joining online forums, or reading industry blogs, continuous learning ensures you're always at the forefront of the industry.

- **Diversify Your Approach**: Adaptability means not relying on one book, one platform, or one type of deal. Create multiple revenue streams— write across genres, expand into non-fiction, or explore foreign markets. By diversifying your approach, you protect yourself from the ups and downs of the market.

Example: You've published a successful fantasy novel, but instead of resting on your laurels, you explore how to adapt the world you've created into an audiobook and a tabletop game. By keeping an open mind and learning how to branch into new formats, you expand your brand and reach new audiences who wouldn't have discovered your book otherwise.

4. Self-Advocacy: You Are Your Own Best Champion

No one will advocate for your work more passionately than you. Agents, lawyers, and publishers are valuable allies, but ultimately, you are your own best champion. Shifting to a mindset of self-advocacy means taking an active role in every aspect of your career, from marketing to contracts to reader engagement.

Here's what self-advocacy looks like:

- **Own Your Career**: Don't wait for others to make decisions for you. Take ownership of every part of your career—from how your book is marketed to the deals you pursue. This doesn't mean you have to do everything alone, but it does mean being an active participant in your success.

- **Ask Questions**: Never be afraid to ask questions about contracts, royalties, or anything that feels unclear. The more you understand the business, the more empowered you'll be to make decisions that benefit you in the long run.

- **Build Your Network**: Surround yourself with other authors, industry professionals, and legal advisors who can offer support, advice, and opportunities. Your network can be one of your most valuable assets as you grow your career.

Example: After signing with a publisher, you notice that the marketing plan seems underwhelming. Instead of leaving it to chance, you work with your agent to advocate for more promotional resources and take it upon yourself to run a targeted social media campaign, boosting your book's visibility and sales.

Shifting your mindset from just "a writer" to a business-savvy authorpreneur is the first step in building a successful, long-term career. When you approach your writing as both a creative endeavor and a business venture, you empower yourself to make smart decisions, protect your work, and maximize your success.

In the next section, we'll dive into practical strategies for turning your newly empowered mindset into real-world action—because knowing is only half the battle!

An Invitation to Keep Learning

Congratulations—you've taken the first big step by diving into the world of "Legal Ink: Navigating the Legalese of Publishing." But here's the thing: mastering the legal and business side of publishing isn't a one-time achievement. It's a continuous journey, and we're just getting started. The publishing industry is always evolving, new challenges arise, and opportunities pop up in unexpected places. The key to thriving in this dynamic world is to keep learning, growing, and adapting as your career progresses.

This book is your foundation—a guide that demystifies the complexities of contracts, rights, and royalties, empowering you to take control of your career. But there's so much more to explore! With each new book, each contract, and each opportunity, you'll encounter new questions and challenges. Whether you're negotiating a subsidiary rights deal, launching a self-publishing empire, or exploring the world of foreign translations, there's always something new to learn.

Here's your invitation: stay curious, stay proactive, and keep building on what you've learned.

- **Stay Informed**: The publishing world is constantly changing, from new digital platforms to shifts in copyright law. Stay informed by keeping up with industry news, attending writing conferences, and joining author communities. The more you know, the more equipped you'll be to seize opportunities and avoid pitfalls.

- **Keep Asking Questions**: No matter how much experience you gain, there will always be new challenges and unfamiliar terms. Never stop asking questions—whether it's about contracts, royalty statements, or marketing strategies. The more you dig, the more confident you'll become in navigating your career.

- **Learn from Others**: Connect with other authors, agents, and legal professionals. Share your experiences, ask for advice, and offer support. The best part about being in the publishing world is that there's a wealth of knowledge in the community, and learning from others is one of the best ways to grow.

- **Embrace New Opportunities**: As the industry evolves, so do the opportunities available to you. Whether it's experimenting with audiobooks, launching a podcast based on your book, or branching into film and TV rights, don't be afraid to embrace new formats and strategies.

By reading this book, you've already shown that you're dedicated to more than just writing—you're committed to building a successful, long-term career in publishing. The knowledge you've gained here is the foundation, but the journey doesn't end with the last page. Keep pushing forward, stay curious, and most importantly, continue to empower yourself through knowledge.

Welcome to the next chapter of your career!

Now that you've started on this path, I invite you to continue your learning journey with confidence. With every new skill and every new piece of knowledge, you're building a stronger, more resilient foundation for your future as an author. Whether you're navigating contracts, strategizing marketing, or exploring new publishing platforms, the best part is that you're never alone on this journey. So, keep writing, keep learning, and most importantly—keep thriving.

Let's get started, shall we?

PART ONE

Starting the Journey

Part I of "Legal Ink: Navigating the Legalese of Publishing" lays the essential groundwork for authors entering the complex world of publishing contracts. From understanding the significance of publishing rights to negotiating terms that secure both fair value and creative control, this section guides authors through the foundational elements of contract agreements. You'll learn how to identify and leverage the "Grant of Rights" clause, unlock new income streams with subsidiary rights, and develop strategies to protect your work's long-term value. With practical insights into the intricacies of publishing law, Part I equips you with the knowledge to start your publishing journey on solid legal footing.

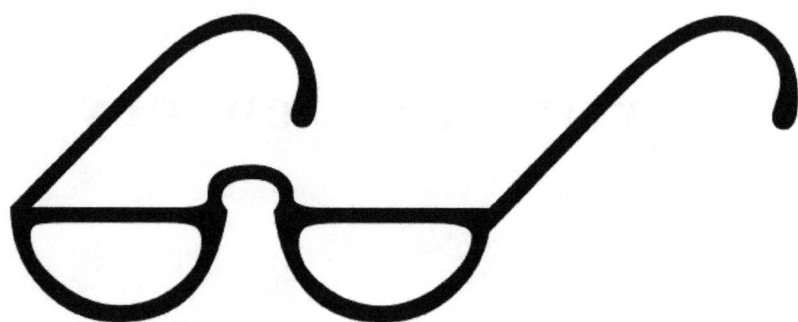

Understanding Publishing Rights: The Foundation of Your Book's Journey

"Mastering your publishing rights isn't just about understanding the fine print—it's about crafting the passport for your book's global journey." — J. K. ROWLING, AUTHOR

W elcome to Chapter One, "Understanding Publishing Rights: The Foundation of Your Book's Journey," where we're diving headfirst into the alphabet soup of rights, licenses, and permissions. Strap on your intellectual property helmets because this is where your journey from a writer with a dream to a published author with a legally sound contract begins.

Think of publishing rights as the golden tickets of the literary world; they're what turn your midnight scribbles into books that travel across continents and perhaps, if you play your cards right, into film adaptations where Hollywood stars butcher your beloved characters. We'll navigate the treacherous waters of copyright, translation rights, and those pesky electronic rights that have more layers than your favorite lasagna.

By the end of this chapter, not only will you understand the ins and outs of what it means to own, sell, or buy publishing rights, but you'll also be equipped to shout "Aha!" instead of "Huh?" when your publisher starts throwing around terms like "first serial rights" and "subsidiary rights." Get ready to grip the reins of your book's destiny with the confidence of a seasoned literary conqueror.

What Are Publishing Rights?

Publishing rights are the legal foundation upon which the entire publishing industry is built. Simply put, these are the permissions and licenses that determine who has the authority to print, distribute, and otherwise reproduce a book. When you, as the author, write your manuscript, you automatically hold the copyright to your work. However, when it comes time to publish, you often grant certain rights to publishers, allowing them to print and sell your book in exchange for an advance or royalties.

Think of publishing rights like a set of keys that unlock various doors in your literary career. Some doors lead to domestic book deals, others to translations in foreign languages, audiobooks, or even movie adaptations. The rights you grant— or choose to keep—directly affect the reach and success of your book. They dictate how your work will be distributed, who can access it, and in what formats.

Publishing rights are usually divided into primary rights (such as print and digital publishing) and secondary or subsidiary rights (like film, television, or merchandise). Understanding the differences between these rights and how they function in a contract is essential. If you don't fully grasp what you're signing over, you might find yourself locked out of valuable opportunities for your book.

As you embark on your publishing journey, it's crucial to remember that retaining certain rights can open doors to future negotiations, while granting others may provide short-term gains but long-term limitations. A clear understanding of publishing rights gives you the power to make informed decisions and control the fate of your work in the literary marketplace.

The Different Types of Publishing Rights

When you enter the world of publishing, you'll quickly find that publishing rights come in many forms, each offering unique opportunities to expand the reach of your book. Understanding these rights is essential to making informed decisions that not only protect your work but also maximize its potential across different formats, markets, and even genres. In this section, we'll explore the primary and subsidiary rights that can be part of your publishing contract, and how they can impact your book's future.

1. Primary Rights

Primary rights are the core rights that govern how your book is first published and distributed. They are typically the first to be negotiated and set the foundation for your book's journey into the world.

- **Print Rights**: The most straightforward of all, print rights give the publisher permission to print and distribute physical copies of your book. This includes hardcover, paperback, and any special or limited editions they may choose to release. The size of the print run and distribution methods should be clearly outlined in your contract. Print rights can vary between traditional and independent publishing routes, and it's vital to know whether you are granting global print rights or just for specific regions.

- **Digital Rights**: In today's digital era, eBooks are a significant part of the market. Digital rights cover the publication of your book in electronic formats, which can include ePub, PDF, Kindle, and other digital formats. Retaining or selling these rights is a critical decision since eBooks can reach global markets instantly, allowing for a broader audience. Some authors may negotiate to hold onto their digital rights to self-publish the eBook version while selling the print rights to a traditional publisher.

- **Audio Rights**: Audiobooks have become an essential part of the publishing landscape, offering readers another way to consume books, especially with the rise of platforms like Audible. Audio rights give a publisher or audio production company the permission to record and distribute your book in audio format. These rights are often sold separately from print and digital rights, so authors need to pay close attention to whether they are part of the overall deal or being negotiated individually.

2. Subsidiary Rights

While primary rights focus on getting your book into the hands of readers for the first time, subsidiary rights unlock additional revenue streams and audience opportunities. These rights can be incredibly valuable, so it's crucial to negotiate them carefully.

- **Translation Rights**: One of the most exciting subsidiary rights is translation rights, which allow your book to be translated into other languages and sold in international markets. Some publishers may want to acquire global rights and handle translation themselves, but many authors prefer to retain these rights to negotiate individual deals with foreign publishers. Keeping these rights can lead to multiple streams of income as your book reaches readers in different countries and cultures.

- **Serial Rights**: Serial rights refer to the permission to publish parts of your book in magazines, journals, or other media, often before or after the book's official release. There are two main types:

  - **First Serial Rights**: These allow for the publication of an excerpt or chapter of your book before its official release. First serial rights are often used for promotional purposes, giving readers a taste of what's to come and building excitement before the book hits shelves.

  - **Second Serial Rights**: These rights allow for parts of your book to be published after the full book is already on the market. This might happen when a chapter or excerpt from your book fits into a themed magazine issue or is included in a special feature.

- **Film and TV Rights**: The Holy Grail of subsidiary rights, film and TV rights give a production company permission to adapt your book for the screen. This can range from a feature-length movie to a multi-season television series. The terms of a film or TV rights deal often include options for creative input or approval, but in many cases, authors may lose significant creative control once these rights are sold. It's vital to work with an experienced agent or lawyer when negotiating film and TV rights, as the potential payoff can be substantial, but so are the stakes.

- **Merchandising Rights**: These rights allow your book's title, characters, or themes to be used for merchandise like T-shirts, posters, action figures, or even video games. If your book has the potential to create a lasting brand, retaining these rights can open up lucrative opportunities down the line. Publishers often look to include these rights in their contracts, but you may want to keep control over how your book's intellectual property is commercialized.

- **Dramatic Rights**: Beyond film and TV, dramatic rights pertain to stage adaptations of your book, such as plays, musicals, or even operas. While not every book lends itself to a dramatic adaptation, some stories translate beautifully to the stage, and holding onto these rights can provide another path for your work to find new audiences.

3. Electronic and Digital Media Rights

With technology continually evolving, electronic and digital media rights are becoming more complex. These rights cover any use of your work in electronic formats beyond just eBooks, potentially including apps, interactive experiences, and even augmented reality adaptations. If your work lends itself to creative multimedia interpretations, these rights could be immensely valuable.

- **Interactive Rights**: This category is becoming increasingly relevant as books are being adapted into interactive experiences, whether through apps or virtual reality. For example, children's books often have interactive versions where the reader can engage with the characters and story through games or multimedia content. If your book has the potential for these types of adaptations, retaining these rights might be worth considering.

- **App Rights**: In some cases, books are adapted into standalone apps, offering readers a digital experience that goes beyond reading. This is especially common in educational or children's literature, where apps can provide interactive learning tools. App rights can be bundled with other digital media rights or sold separately, depending on the publisher's business model.

4. Reprint and Anthology Rights

Reprint and anthology rights allow for parts of your book, or sometimes the entire book, to be republished or included in a collection after its initial release. These rights can be particularly valuable for keeping your work in circulation long after the first print run has sold out.

- **Reprint Rights**: These rights allow for your book to be reprinted in different formats or by different publishers. For example, you may sell reprint rights to a publisher that wants to produce a mass-market paperback edition after the hardcover has been out for a while. Reprint rights are often time-sensitive, meaning they become negotiable after a certain period once the original edition has been published.

- **Anthology Rights**: This refers to the right to include a portion of your book, such as a chapter or excerpt, in a collection or anthology. Anthologies are often themed around a particular genre or topic, and including your work can expose it to new readers who may not have encountered it otherwise. Authors who retain anthology rights can often negotiate new deals as their work becomes part of curated collections.

Each of these rights opens up new doors for your book, allowing it to reach different markets, mediums, and formats. While it may be tempting to grant as many rights as possible in your first deal to secure a lucrative advance, remember that once those rights are sold, they may be gone for good. Balancing what you sell with what you retain is the key to ensuring that your book reaches its full potential while still keeping you in control of its future.

By understanding the different types of publishing rights, you'll be better equipped to protect your work, maximize your earnings, and make strategic decisions about how your book evolves across various platforms.

How Publishing Rights Impact Your Book's Reach

Publishing rights are more than just legal jargon on a contract—they play a critical role in determining how far your book can travel, both geographically and across different media. From print editions to digital formats and film adaptations, the rights you retain or sign away will directly impact how your book is distributed, marketed, and consumed. Let's explore the various ways publishing rights can affect your book's reach, ensuring you make the most of every opportunity.

1. Geographic Reach: Local, National, and International Markets

One of the most immediate impacts of your publishing rights is where your book will be sold. When negotiating your contract, it's essential to understand the scope of distribution.

- **Territorial Rights**: These define where your publisher has the right to distribute your book. You can sell worldwide rights to a single publisher, giving them the ability to distribute your book globally. However, many authors choose to break up territorial rights, selling domestic rights to one publisher and foreign rights to others. This allows for greater control and often results in multiple revenue streams, as foreign publishers may offer advances and royalties separate from your domestic deal.

- **Translation Rights**: If your book has international appeal, retaining or selling translation rights can significantly extend your book's reach. Translation rights allow foreign publishers to publish your book in different languages, opening up entirely new markets. For example, a book that resonates in English-speaking markets may find an even larger audience when translated into Spanish, Chinese, or other languages. By carefully negotiating translation rights, you can tap into global markets and build a worldwide readership.

2. Format Reach: Print, Digital, and Audiobook Markets

The format in which your book is published also has a profound effect on how many readers you can reach. Different formats cater to different audiences, and each offers unique advantages.

- **Print**: Traditional print books, whether in hardcover or paperback, are still the foundation of the publishing industry. Selling print rights allows your book to be sold in physical stores and online retailers, reaching readers who prefer the tactile experience of holding a book. However, print books have limitations when it comes to global distribution— shipping costs, import regulations, and the availability of your book in different markets can all limit its reach.

- **Digital**: Digital rights, including eBooks, open up your book to a global audience with no physical barriers. With eBooks, your work can be instantly available worldwide through platforms like Kindle, Apple Books, and Kobo. Digital formats allow readers to access your book at the click of a button, providing you with the potential for a much larger reach than print alone. Digital rights are particularly important for independent authors, who often rely on the flexibility and global accessibility of eBooks to build their audience.

- **Audiobooks**: The audiobook market has exploded in recent years, with more readers than ever choosing to listen to books while commuting, exercising, or multitasking. If you sell your audio rights, your book can reach an entirely new segment of readers who prefer listening to reading. Platforms like Audible, iTunes, and Google Play have made audiobooks widely accessible, giving your story a voice—literally—and the potential to engage listeners worldwide.

3. Media Reach: Expanding Beyond the Book

One of the most exciting possibilities for authors is the potential to expand their story beyond the written word. Selling film, TV, and other media rights can take your book to new heights, introducing it to entirely different audiences who may never have encountered it otherwise.

- **Film and Television**: If your book is optioned for a movie or TV series, it can reach millions of viewers who may not typically read books. However, selling these rights requires careful consideration, as you may lose creative control over how your story is adapted. The reach of your book can be dramatically amplified through these mediums, often bringing renewed interest to the original book and driving up sales.

- **Merchandising and Brand Extensions**: Merchandising rights can extend your book's impact even further, allowing for products like apparel, toys, posters, and more. Books with strong fan bases, especially in genres like fantasy and science fiction, often benefit from brand extensions, building a dedicated audience that interacts with the story across multiple formats.

4. Control vs. Opportunity: Finding the Right Balance

As you navigate your publishing contract, one of the biggest decisions you'll face is how much control you want to retain versus how much you're willing to grant to your publisher. The more rights you retain, the more opportunities you have to negotiate separate deals for foreign editions, audiobooks, and other formats. However, selling certain rights can open doors to opportunities that might otherwise be out of reach, such as wide distribution, robust marketing campaigns, or major media deals.

Finding the right balance between control and opportunity is key. For example, you may decide to grant worldwide print rights to a major publisher for the promise of strong global distribution but hold onto your audiobook rights to self-publish on platforms like Audible. Or, you may negotiate a higher advance in exchange for your film and TV rights, knowing that the possibility of a big-screen adaptation could bring your story to millions of new fans.

5. Long-Term Reach: The Power of Reversion Rights

One critical aspect of publishing rights that authors sometimes overlook is what happens when the contract ends. Many publishing agreements include a clause for rights reversion, which allows the author to regain certain rights after a specified period or if the book goes out of print. Rights reversion can be incredibly valuable because it gives you the opportunity to republish your work in new formats, markets, or even with a new publisher.

For instance, if your book goes out of print, and you regain the rights, you can self-publish it as an eBook or offer it to foreign publishers. By planning ahead and negotiating a strong reversion clause, you can ensure that your book remains available to readers even after the initial contract has expired.

Ultimately, publishing rights dictate how far and wide your book will travel. They shape the life of your book not just at the moment of release, but long into the future, influencing its potential across global markets, different formats, and media adaptations. By understanding how these rights impact your book's reach, you can make informed decisions that will set your book up for success in the marketplace and beyond.

Protecting and Managing Your Rights

As an author, your publishing rights are one of your most valuable assets, and it's crucial to take active steps to protect and manage them throughout your career. Navigating the complex world of publishing contracts can be daunting, but by understanding your rights and staying vigilant, you can safeguard your work and ensure that you maintain control over its future. In this section, we'll discuss key strategies for protecting your rights and offer tips on how to manage them effectively over the long term.

1. Understand Every Clause in Your Contract

The first step in protecting your rights is having a thorough understanding of your publishing contract. Every clause matters, and vague language or seemingly minor details can have significant consequences. Before signing any agreement, make sure you understand what rights you're granting, what rights you're retaining, and how those rights will be exercised.

- **Grant of Rights Clause**: This is one of the most important sections of your contract. It details exactly which rights you are granting to the publisher and for how long. Are you giving away print rights only, or are digital and audiobook rights included? Is the contract limited to specific territories, or does it grant worldwide rights? Understanding this clause is critical because it outlines the scope of what the publisher is entitled to do with your book.

- **Reversion of Rights**: As mentioned earlier, reversion rights allow you to regain control of your work after a certain period of time or if certain conditions are met (such as the book going out of print). Ensure that your contract includes a reversion clause that works in your favor, giving you the flexibility to republish or renegotiate the terms once the original contract ends. Pay attention to the triggers for reversion—whether it's a sales threshold, a time frame, or a specific event—so you know when and how you can reclaim your rights.

- **Subsidiary Rights Clauses**: If your contract includes subsidiary rights, make sure the terms for each are clearly defined. For example, if your publisher has the rights to negotiate foreign translations or film adaptations, understand what kind of cut you'll receive and how much control you retain over those decisions. Many authors negotiate to keep certain subsidiary rights, such as film or merchandise, to explore those opportunities independently.

- **Non-Compete Clauses**: Be wary of non-compete clauses, which may limit your ability to publish other works during or after the contract's term. These clauses can sometimes be overly broad, restricting your ability to write or publish similar works even if they are unrelated to your current project. If a non-compete clause is included, negotiate to make sure it is narrow and reasonable, allowing you the freedom to pursue other writing opportunities without unnecessary restrictions.

2. Work with Professionals: Agents and Lawyers

Protecting your rights doesn't have to be a solo endeavor. Publishing contracts are complex legal documents, and having an experienced literary agent or lawyer by your side can make all the difference. A good agent will not only negotiate better deals on your behalf but will also ensure that you fully understand the implications of the rights you're granting and the ones you're retaining.

- **Literary Agents**: A reputable literary agent has the experience and industry connections to negotiate the best possible terms for your book.

Agents know the ins and outs of publishing contracts and will advocate for you to retain as many rights as possible while still securing a favorable deal. They'll also help you manage your rights over the long term, seeking out opportunities for subsidiary rights like foreign translations, audiobooks, and film adaptations.

- **Publishing Lawyers**: Even if you have an agent, hiring a lawyer with expertise in intellectual property and publishing law is a smart move, especially when dealing with complex contracts. A lawyer can help you understand the fine print, flag potential red flags, and negotiate terms that might otherwise go unnoticed. Having legal counsel ensures that you are fully protected and that your rights are not compromised.

3. Monitor the Use of Your Rights

Once your book is published, your work isn't done. Protecting your rights means staying vigilant and monitoring how your publisher is using them. Keep track of where and how your book is being distributed, both domestically and internationally, as well as in what formats. Make sure your publisher is adhering to the terms of your contract and that you are receiving the royalties and advances to which you're entitled.

- **Royalty Statements**: Regularly review your royalty statements to ensure you're being paid accurately. If you notice discrepancies or feel that your book's sales don't match the reported earnings, you may want to exercise your audit rights (if included in your contract) to verify the publisher's accounting. Many authors find that keeping a close eye on their financials helps prevent issues down the line.

- **Subsidiary Rights Management**: If you've granted subsidiary rights to your publisher, stay informed about their efforts to sell those rights. Are they actively pursuing translation deals or audiobook opportunities? If not, you may be able to negotiate a reversion of those rights to explore the opportunities on your own. Make sure your contract includes a clause that allows for rights to revert if they're not being exploited within a certain time frame.

4. Keep Good Records

Managing your rights effectively requires organization. Keep detailed records of all contracts, amendments, royalty statements, and correspondence with your publisher. If you negotiate additional deals for subsidiary rights or reversion clauses, make sure everything is documented in writing. Good record-keeping ensures that you have the evidence and information you need if any disputes arise or if you need to revisit the terms of your contract in the future.

- **Contract Files**: Create a dedicated file (digital or physical) for each of your publishing contracts, keeping track of important details like contract expiration dates, royalty rates, and reversion terms. If you're working with an agent or lawyer, they will likely keep copies of all your contracts, but having your own organized system is crucial for staying on top of your rights management.

- **Communication Logs**: Whenever you communicate with your publisher—whether about royalty payments, subsidiary rights, or contractual obligations—document the conversation. This ensures you have a clear record of what was agreed upon and can help prevent misunderstandings later on. Email is often the best medium for these communications, as it provides a written record that can be easily referenced.

5. Plan for the Future: Managing Rights Long-Term

Your publishing rights are not just about the present; they are about the future of your career. It's essential to have a long-term strategy for managing your rights, particularly if you plan to build a body of work over time.

- **Reversion and Renewal**: As the term of your contract comes to an end, start planning for what happens next. Will you seek to renew the contract with the same publisher? Will you look for a new publishing partner, or will you take advantage of self-publishing opportunities with reverted rights? Keeping an eye on contract deadlines and preparing for the next stage will help you stay in control of your book's future.

- **Future Works and Series**: If your contract includes options for future works (such as a series), consider how granting those rights will affect your flexibility. Series options can lock you into working with the same publisher for multiple books, which may be beneficial in some cases but restrictive in others. If you have long-term plans for your book series, make sure your contract allows you the freedom to pursue those plans without unnecessary limitations.

- **Protecting Your Intellectual Property**: Beyond your current book, it's important to protect your intellectual property as a whole. This includes not only your written work but also any branding, merchandising, or media opportunities related to your book. Make sure you have a strategy in place to defend your intellectual property rights and ensure that your work is not used without your permission.

In the world of publishing, your rights are your most valuable asset. By understanding your contract, working with professionals, monitoring the use of your rights, and planning for the future, you can protect and manage your rights effectively. With the right strategy, you'll not only safeguard your current book but also ensure that you're in control of your career for years to come.

Quick Tips and Recap

- **Understand Your Rights**: Know what rights you're granting, retaining, or selling in your publishing contract, including print, digital, audio, and subsidiary rights.

- **Negotiate Smart**: Pay close attention to key clauses like Grant of Rights, Subsidiary Rights, and Reversion of Rights to maintain control over your work.

- **Watch Out for Non-Compete Clauses**: Ensure non-compete clauses are reasonable and don't overly restrict your ability to publish other works.

- **Work with Professionals**: Hire a literary agent or lawyer to help negotiate your contract and protect your rights long-term.

- **Monitor Your Rights**: Keep track of how your book is being distributed and ensure royalties and advances align with your contract terms.

- **Exercise Reversion Rights**: Be aware of your contract's reversion terms, and act when you can regain control of your work for future opportunities.

- **Keep Detailed Records**: Document contracts, royalty statements, and all communications with your publisher to avoid disputes.

- **Plan for the Long-Term**: Think about how your current contract affects your future works and intellectual property, especially if writing a series or planning for media adaptations.

- **Stay in Control**: Protect your rights and plan strategically to maintain flexibility and maximize your book's reach and profitability over time.

Negotiating Your Rights: Strategies for a Fair Deal

"Negotiation is the subtle art of getting the best deal without compromising the worth of your creation." — RICHARD BRANSON, FOUNDER OF VIRGIN GROUP

Welcome to Chapter Two, "Negotiating Your Rights: Strategies for a Fair Deal," where we treat the art of negotiation like a high-stakes poker game—but instead of bluffing with cards, you're armed with chapters and characters. This is where you learn to hold your ground like a tree with deep roots when publishers wave contracts in your face.

Think of this as your guide to not just surviving the negotiation table but walking away with a grin that says, "I knew what I was doing." We'll unpack the mysteries of advance payments, royalty rates, and why you should care about things like the reversion of rights—because, let's face it, your great-grandchildren might one day thank you for it.

By the end of this chapter, you'll not only be able to spot a bad deal from a mile away but also have the savvy to turn it around in your favor. Prepare to sharpen your negotiation skills to a fine point, ensuring that your signature at the bottom of a contract is a cause for celebration, not regret. Let's dial up your deal-making prowess and ensure your work earns what it's truly worth.

Understanding the Basics: Key Terms in Publishing Contracts

Before you can negotiate a fair deal, you need to understand the playing field—and that starts with mastering the essential terms in publishing contracts. These terms might seem like a foreign language at first, but they hold the key to ensuring you don't sign away more than you intend or accept less than you deserve. In this section, we'll break down the critical concepts and clauses that will shape your negotiations, giving you the confidence to know exactly what you're agreeing to when you sign on the dotted line.

1. Advances

An advance is the upfront payment you receive from the publisher, typically split into installments, such as upon signing the contract, delivering the manuscript, and publication. This is essentially a loan against your future royalties—meaning you won't receive royalty payments until your book earns enough to cover the advance amount. The larger the advance, the more confident the publisher is in the book's potential success. However, an advance is not just free money—it's a financial gauge of the publisher's expectations, and you should consider it carefully when negotiating.

- **Key Tip**: Don't be afraid to negotiate a higher advance if you believe your book has strong commercial potential, but be realistic. A higher advance can signal strong publisher support, but it also means you'll need to sell more copies to see additional royalties.

2. Royalties

Royalties are the ongoing payments you receive for each sale of your book once the advance has been earned back. Royalties are usually calculated as a percentage of the book's sale price or net sales, and they can vary depending on the format of the book (print, eBook, audiobook). For example, print royalties might range from 7-15%, while digital royalties are often higher, around 25% of net sales. Knowing the standard royalty rates for your genre and format gives you leverage in negotiations.

- **Key Tip**: Focus on securing higher royalties for formats where your book is likely to perform well. If you expect strong eBook sales, push for better terms on digital royalties.

3. Territorial Rights

Territorial rights determine where your book can be sold and distributed. There are three primary options:

- **Worldwide Rights**: The publisher has the rights to sell your book globally.

- **Territory-Specific Rights**: The publisher can only sell your book in specific regions, such as North America or the United Kingdom.

- **Translation Rights**: These are a subset of territorial rights, allowing the publisher to sell your book in translated editions in non-English-speaking markets.

Retaining the rights to sell your book in multiple territories, or selling them to different publishers in each region, can maximize your earnings. If a publisher wants worldwide rights, consider whether they have the global reach to distribute your book effectively.

- **Key Tip**: Negotiate to retain foreign or translation rights if the publisher doesn't have strong distribution in certain markets, so you can explore separate deals in those regions.

4. Subsidiary Rights

Subsidiary rights refer to additional ways your book can be sold or adapted, such as:

- **Film and TV Rights**: The right to adapt your book into a movie or television series.

- **Audiobook Rights**: The right to produce and distribute your book as an audiobook.

- **Merchandising Rights**: The right to create products based on your book, like T-shirts, posters, or action figures.

- **Translation Rights**: The right to publish your book in other languages (if not already included in the territorial rights).

If your book has strong media potential, these subsidiary rights can be incredibly valuable. Many authors choose to retain these rights or negotiate separate deals to maximize their earnings.

- **Key Tip**: Don't automatically sign away all subsidiary rights. Retaining control over film, TV, and merchandising rights can offer significant long-term benefits, especially if your book has franchise potential.

5. Reversion of Rights

Reversion of rights is a clause that outlines when and how the rights to your book will return to you, the author. Typically, this happens when the book goes out of print or sales drop below a certain threshold. Reversion clauses are critical because they allow you to reclaim your book and explore new publishing opportunities—whether by self-publishing or finding a new publisher.

- **Key Tip**: Negotiate a reversion clause that allows you to regain rights within a reasonable timeframe. For example, if your book sells fewer than 100 copies in a 12-month period, you should have the right to request the return of your rights.

6. Option Clauses

An option clause gives the publisher the right to publish your next book under similar terms to the current contract. While it can seem like a vote of confidence in your future work, an option clause can also limit your ability to negotiate with other publishers for your next project. If your current deal is less than favorable, being locked into another contract under similar terms might not be ideal.

- **Key Tip**: If you agree to an option clause, make sure it's limited to your next work, and negotiate favorable terms in advance. This ensures you maintain some freedom to shop your future projects around to other publishers.

Understanding these key terms gives you the foundation to negotiate from a position of strength. By familiarizing yourself with advances, royalties, rights, and contractual clauses, you can avoid signing deals that undermine your long-term success. In the next section, we'll dive into specific strategies for negotiating better advances and royalties to ensure that every contract you sign is a win for your career.

How to Negotiate Advances and Royalties

Negotiating advances and royalties is where the rubber meets the road in publishing contracts. These two elements directly impact how much money you make from your book, both upfront and in the long term. Knowing how to secure a good advance and favorable royalty rates can significantly boost your earnings and give you more control over your financial future. In this section, we'll explore the strategies you can use to maximize both your advance and your royalties, ensuring that your book deal works for you now and for years to come.

1. Negotiating the Advance: Balance Between Upfront Payment and Long-Term Royalties

An advance is the upfront payment you receive when you sign a book deal, and it's typically paid in installments. While it's tempting to focus on getting the biggest advance possible, it's essential to balance that with the long-term potential of your royalties. A large advance may seem like a win, but if your book doesn't sell enough to "earn out" (recoup the advance through royalties), you won't see any additional income from royalties.

- **Strategy 1: Understand Industry Standards**. Before negotiating your advance, do some research on what's typical for your genre and level of experience. Advances can vary widely depending on whether you're publishing fiction or non-fiction, genre, and whether you're a debut author or a seasoned writer. Literary agents often have insights into these industry norms, but if you're negotiating on your own, look for benchmarks in your niche to avoid underselling yourself.

- **Strategy 2: Leverage Multiple Offers**. If you have interest from multiple publishers, use this as a bargaining chip to negotiate a higher advance. Publishers may increase their offer if they know there's competition, as they don't want to lose out on a potentially profitable book. Even if you don't have competing offers, you can still hint at the possibility of exploring other options, showing the publisher that you have alternatives.

- **Strategy 3: Consider the Advance Payment Schedule**. Advances are often split into two or three payments, such as upon signing, manuscript delivery, and publication. Negotiate to have as much of the advance paid upfront as possible. This gives you more immediate financial security and reduces the risk of delays in receiving your full advance if publication is postponed.

- **Strategy 4: Know When to Push and When to Compromise**. While it's crucial to negotiate confidently, sometimes it's better to accept a moderate advance if the royalty terms are more favorable or if the publisher has a robust marketing and distribution plan. A modest advance with higher royalty rates can lead to more money in the long term if your book performs well.

2. Maximizing Your Royalties: Ensuring Ongoing Income

While an advance gets you money upfront, royalties are where the long-term earnings potential comes in. Royalties are the percentage of each book sale that you receive once the advance is earned out. The key to maximizing your royalties lies in understanding the various types of royalty structures and pushing for the best terms.

- **Strategy 1: Understand How Royalties Are Calculated**. Royalties can be based on two primary methods:

  o **List Price Royalties**: A percentage of the book's cover price. For example, if your royalty rate is 10% and your book sells for $20, you earn $2 per copy sold.

  o **Net Sales Royalties**: A percentage of the publisher's net revenue from the sale of the book, after discounts and expenses. This is often lower than the list price, meaning a royalty rate of 25% of net sales may not be as lucrative as it seems.

In general, royalties based on the list price are more transparent and easier to calculate, while net sales royalties can vary depending on how the publisher prices and sells the book. Always ask for list price royalties when possible, or negotiate a higher percentage of net sales if the publisher insists on using that model.

- **Strategy 2: Push for Higher Royalties on Different Formats**. Royalty rates often differ based on the format of the book. For example, hardcover royalties might be higher than paperback, while eBook royalties are often the most lucrative due to lower production costs. Here are typical royalty ranges:

  o **Hardcover**: 10-15% of the cover price.

  o **Paperback**: 5-8% of the cover price.

  o **eBooks**: 25-50% of net sales (depending on the publisher).

Since eBooks and audiobooks are growing markets with lower production costs, push for higher royalties on these formats. Publishers are often more flexible in this area because of the minimal overhead, and you stand to earn more in the long run.

- **Strategy 3: Consider Escalating Royalties**. Escalating royalties (or "royalty escalators") mean that the percentage you earn increases as more copies of the book are sold. For example, you might start with a

10% royalty for the first 5,000 copies sold, but after that, your royalty increases to 12%, and then to 15% after 10,000 copies are sold.

Escalating royalties are beneficial because they reward the book's success. If your book performs well, you'll earn a higher percentage per sale, boosting your long-term income. Don't be afraid to ask for an escalating royalty structure, especially if you're confident that your book has strong sales potential.

- **Strategy 4: Watch Out for "Deep Discount" Royalties**. Many contracts include clauses that allow publishers to reduce your royalties if they sell your book at a deep discount, such as to book clubs, wholesalers, or bulk buyers. These clauses can drastically reduce your earnings if a significant portion of sales comes from discounted outlets.

Negotiate to limit these deep discount clauses, or at least ensure that your royalty percentage doesn't drop below a certain threshold. For example, you can negotiate that deep discount royalties will only apply if the book is sold at a discount of more than 50%, or that your royalties can't fall below 50% of your standard rate.

3. Leveraging Negotiation Tactics: When to Push, When to Settle

Negotiating advances and royalties is an art. You need to know when to push for more favorable terms and when it's smarter to compromise for the sake of the overall deal. Here are a few tactics to keep in mind:

- **Start High but Stay Realistic**: Always aim high when entering negotiations. Publishers expect authors to negotiate, and they rarely offer their best deal upfront. However, don't push for unrealistic terms that might scare off the publisher, especially if you're a debut author. Find a balance between ambition and practicality.

- **Use Leverage Wisely**: If you have a literary agent or if there's interest from multiple publishers, use that as leverage. If a publisher knows they're competing for your book, they may be more willing to offer a higher advance or better royalty rates to secure the deal.

- **Think Long-Term**: Sometimes a smaller advance with better royalty rates or stronger marketing support is a smarter choice. If your publisher is committed to long-term marketing and promotion, your book may have a longer shelf life, leading to more royalties down the line. Always consider the long-term earning potential when evaluating the deal.

4. Negotiating Without an Agent: What to Know

If you don't have a literary agent, you'll need to handle the negotiations yourself. Here are a few tips for successfully negotiating your advance and royalties without an agent:

- **Do Your Research**: Knowledge is power. Research industry standards for advances and royalties in your genre, and be prepared to justify why you deserve a higher advance or better royalty terms.

- **Ask Questions**: If something in the contract is unclear, ask for clarification. Don't feel pressured to sign a contract if you don't fully understand the terms. Publishers expect authors to have questions, and a good publisher will take the time to explain the details.

- **Get Legal Advice**: If you're negotiating on your own, it's wise to hire a lawyer who specializes in publishing contracts. They can help you understand the fine print and ensure you're getting a fair deal.

Negotiating advances and royalties is a crucial step in securing a fair and rewarding book deal. By understanding the factors that affect your earnings and using strategic negotiation tactics, you can maximize both your upfront payment and long-term income. In the next section, we'll explore how to handle subsidiary rights, offering you even more ways to increase your book's value over time.

Navigating Subsidiary Rights: Maximizing Long-Term Value

Subsidiary rights offer authors a significant opportunity to increase the long-term value of their work. These rights allow your book to reach audiences beyond the traditional print and eBook formats, potentially leading to adaptations in film, television, audiobooks, translations, and more. While primary rights focus on publishing and selling the book itself, subsidiary rights refer to any additional ways your book can generate revenue and exposure. By carefully negotiating and managing these rights, you can unlock new streams of income and maximize your book's potential. In this section, we'll guide you through the different types of subsidiary rights and how to navigate them to your advantage.

1. Understanding the Key Types of Subsidiary Rights

Subsidiary rights encompass a wide range of opportunities for your book. Knowing what each right entails and how it can be used is the first step in making smart decisions about whether to retain or sell these rights to your publisher.

- **Film and Television Rights**: These rights allow your book to be adapted into a movie or television series. For many authors, selling film or TV rights is the ultimate dream, as these deals can result in significant financial rewards and bring your story to a much larger audience. However, selling these rights often means giving up creative control over how your book is adapted.

  o **Strategy**: If your book has cinematic potential, it may be worth retaining these rights or negotiating a separate deal for them, rather than bundling them into your initial publishing contract. Work with a literary agent or entertainment lawyer who specializes in film and TV adaptations to ensure you get the best possible terms.

- **Audiobook Rights**: The audiobook market has exploded in recent years, and selling the rights to produce and distribute an audiobook can be a lucrative opportunity. Audiobooks cater to a different segment of the reading population—those who prefer listening to books while commuting or multitasking.

  o **Strategy**: Consider whether you want to sell your audiobook rights to your publisher or retain them to produce and distribute the audiobook independently. If your publisher doesn't have a strong audiobook division, it might be better to hold onto these rights and work directly with an audiobook production company like Audible or Findaway Voices. Negotiate for higher royalty rates on audiobooks, as they tend to have lower production costs than print books.

- **Translation Rights**: If your book has international appeal, translation rights allow it to be translated into other languages and sold in foreign markets. These rights can open the door to global readership and additional streams of revenue.

  o **Strategy**: Rather than selling worldwide translation rights to a single publisher, consider retaining them and negotiating separate deals for different territories. This allows you to target publishers in specific regions who specialize in those markets. Alternatively, if you sell translation rights, negotiate for higher royalties on foreign editions, as these deals can be highly profitable.

- **First and Second Serial Rights**: Serial rights allow for parts of your book—such as chapters or excerpts—to be published in magazines, newspapers, or online platforms.

  o **First Serial Rights**: These give a publication the right to publish an excerpt of your book before it's officially released, often as a promotional tool.

  o **Second Serial Rights**: These allow excerpts to be published after your book has already been released, usually to generate continued interest.

  o **Strategy**: Retaining serial rights can be a smart move, as they can provide additional income and publicity for your book. You can negotiate separate deals with periodicals or online publications to publish excerpts, helping to build anticipation for your book or keep the buzz alive post-publication.

- **Merchandising Rights**: Merchandising rights allow the use of your book's characters, title, or themes to create products like T-shirts, posters, toys, or even video games. This is particularly valuable for books with strong fan bases, such as fantasy or young adult series.

  o **Strategy**: Unless your book is part of a major franchise with immediate merchandising potential, it's usually best to retain these rights until you see a clear opportunity. However, if your publisher has plans for marketing and merchandising, negotiate for a share of the profits or control over how your characters and themes are used.

2. Retaining vs. Selling Subsidiary Rights: What to Consider

Deciding whether to retain or sell subsidiary rights can be tricky, as it requires balancing short-term gains with long-term potential. In some cases, selling these rights as part of your initial publishing deal can provide an immediate boost to your advance, but in other cases, holding onto them might result in more control and higher earnings down the road.

- **Short-Term Gains**: Selling subsidiary rights up front can increase your advance or overall earnings from the deal. Publishers may offer more money if they know they'll control the film, TV, or translation rights. However, be cautious—once those rights are sold, they're often gone for good, and you may lose out on future opportunities.

- **Long-Term Potential**: Retaining subsidiary rights gives you the freedom to negotiate separate deals with companies that specialize in each area (audiobook producers, foreign publishers, film studios). This can lead to higher earnings, as you can command separate advances or royalties for each format and market. Retaining rights also allows you to retain more creative control over how your book is adapted and marketed.

- **Negotiating Split Rights**: Another option is to split rights between you and your publisher. For example, you might sell audiobook rights but retain film rights, or sell translation rights for specific languages while keeping control over others. This approach allows you to benefit from your publisher's marketing and distribution capabilities while still holding onto valuable opportunities.

- **Working with an Agent or Lawyer**: If you're unsure about how to handle subsidiary rights, consult with a literary agent or entertainment lawyer. These professionals can help you evaluate the value of your rights, negotiate the best possible deals, and ensure that you retain the flexibility and control you need to make the most of your work.

3. Maximizing Value Through Strategic Partnerships

Retaining subsidiary rights doesn't mean you have to handle everything yourself. Forming strategic partnerships with companies that specialize in specific formats—such as audiobook producers, foreign publishers, or film studios—can help you get the most value from these rights.

- **Audiobook Producers**: If you retain your audiobook rights, consider partnering with a professional audiobook producer to ensure your book is recorded and distributed effectively. Platforms like Audible, Findaway Voices, and Libro.fm offer services that connect authors with narrators, producers, and distributors, giving you control over the final product while tapping into a larger audience.

- **Foreign Publishers**: If you retain your translation rights, work with foreign literary agents or scouts to help you sell your book in international markets. These professionals know the local publishing landscape and can negotiate deals with foreign publishers to bring your book to readers around the world.

- **Film and TV Producers**: If you retain your film and TV rights, consider partnering with a literary agent who specializes in film adaptations. They can help you pitch your book to studios, production companies, or streaming services like Netflix or Amazon, ensuring that you find the right fit for your story. Keep in mind that even retaining some creative control over the adaptation process can make a significant difference in how your story is represented on screen.

4. Building a Long-Term Strategy for Subsidiary Rights

Maximizing the long-term value of your subsidiary rights requires strategic thinking and careful planning. Here's how to create a long-term strategy for managing these rights:

- **Identify the Most Valuable Rights**: Not every book will have equal potential across all subsidiary rights. For example, a memoir might not have strong merchandising prospects, but it could have significant audiobook and film potential. Identify which subsidiary rights are most valuable for your particular book and prioritize them in your negotiations.

- **Stagger Deals for Maximum Revenue**: If you retain multiple subsidiary rights, stagger your deals over time to maximize revenue. For instance, you might first sell audiobook rights, then wait until your book gains traction before negotiating film or translation deals. This approach ensures that you're not giving away too much too soon and allows you to capitalize on your book's success as it builds.

- **Monitor Your Rights**: Keep track of which subsidiary rights you've sold, which you've retained, and when they revert back to you. Stay proactive about exploring new opportunities—whether that's partnering with a foreign publisher or pitching your story to a streaming service—so you don't miss out on valuable deals down the line.

By understanding the different types of subsidiary rights and knowing when to retain or sell them, you can unlock additional streams of income and significantly extend the reach of your book. Whether through audiobooks, film adaptations, or international translations, these rights offer endless possibilities for your story to reach new audiences and markets. In the next section, we'll explore how to protect your future with reversion, renewal, and exit clauses, ensuring you remain in control of your book's destiny.

Reversion, Renewal, and Exit clauses: Protecting Your Future

When negotiating a publishing contract, it's easy to focus on the immediate benefits—advances, royalties, and subsidiary rights—but protecting your long-term interests is just as important. Reversion, renewal, and exit clauses are critical tools that ensure you retain control over your work as your career evolves. These clauses provide flexibility and protection, allowing you to reclaim your rights, renegotiate deals, or exit agreements when necessary. In this section, we'll explore how each of these clauses works and how to negotiate them to safeguard your future.

1. Reversion of Rights: Taking Back Control

A reversion of rights clause allows you to regain the rights to your book after a certain period or under specific conditions. This is one of the most important clauses in your contract because it gives you the power to reclaim your work if it's no longer being actively published or promoted. Without a strong reversion clause, your book could remain tied to a publisher indefinitely, even if it's no longer available to readers.

- **When Rights Revert**: Reversion clauses typically trigger when a book goes out of print or if sales fall below a certain threshold. For example, if your book sells fewer than 100 copies in a 12-month period, you might have the right to request a reversion of rights. In the case of eBooks, where books rarely go "out of print," the contract should specify a minimum sales threshold that would allow you to reclaim your rights.

- **Why Reversion Is Important**: Once your rights revert, you're free to republish your book, whether through self-publishing, a new traditional publisher, or even as part of an updated edition. Reverting rights gives you the opportunity to breathe new life into your book, especially if you believe it still has untapped potential or new markets to explore.

- **Strategy**: When negotiating your reversion clause, push for a clear and reasonable time frame or sales threshold that gives you the ability to regain control. For example, a clause that triggers after 12 months of low sales is more favorable than one that requires several years of inactivity. Additionally, ensure that the clause covers all formats—print, digital, and audiobook—so you have full flexibility once the rights revert.

2. Renewal Clauses: Keeping Your Options Open

A renewal clause outlines the terms under which you or the publisher can renew the contract after it expires. This clause is particularly relevant for series or multi-book deals, where both parties may want the option to continue the relationship beyond the initial agreement.

- **How Renewal Clauses Work**: In some cases, the publisher has the option to renew the contract if they meet certain conditions, such as maintaining a minimum level of sales or agreeing to pay an additional advance. Alternatively, you may have the option to renew the contract if you're satisfied with the publisher's performance and want to continue the partnership.

- **Why Renewal Matters**: Renewal clauses offer flexibility, allowing you to extend the relationship with your publisher if it's mutually beneficial. However, they also give you the opportunity to renegotiate the terms of the deal based on your book's success. For example, if your book performs well, you may be able to secure a higher advance or better royalty rates in the renewal agreement.

- **Strategy**: Negotiate for renewal terms that allow you to retain some control over the decision. For example, you might include a clause that allows you to refuse renewal if the publisher doesn't meet specific sales targets or marketing commitments. Additionally, ensure that the renewal includes the option to renegotiate key terms like advances, royalties, and subsidiary rights, rather than locking you into the same terms as the original contract.

3. Exit Clauses: Knowing When to Walk Away

An exit clause—also known as a termination clause—provides a way for you or the publisher to end the contract early under certain conditions. While it's not something you want to think about at the beginning of the publishing process, having a well-defined exit strategy can protect you if the relationship with your publisher sours or if they fail to meet their obligations.

- **Common Exit Triggers**: Exit clauses often come into play if the publisher doesn't fulfill key contractual terms, such as paying advances or royalties on time, meeting publication deadlines, or providing adequate marketing support. You may also be able to terminate the contract if the publisher breaches its obligations, such as failing to distribute the book as promised.

- **Why Exit Clauses Are Crucial**: Without an exit clause, you could be stuck in a contract with a publisher who isn't delivering on their promises, with no way to reclaim your rights. Exit clauses give you a safety net, allowing you to walk away if things go wrong and retain the ability to publish your book elsewhere.

- **Strategy**: Negotiate for an exit clause that includes specific performance benchmarks for the publisher. For example, you might require that the publisher release the book within a certain time frame, meet minimum marketing commitments, or ensure a certain level of sales within the first year. If the publisher fails to meet these benchmarks, you should have the right to terminate the contract and reclaim your rights.

4. Negotiating for Flexibility and Protection

When it comes to reversion, renewal, and exit clauses, the key is to negotiate for flexibility and protection. These clauses aren't just technicalities—they're tools that give you control over the future of your book and your career. Here are some final tips for protecting your long-term interests:

- **Be Specific**: Vague language in these clauses can lead to confusion or disputes later on. Ensure that all terms are clearly defined, including what constitutes "out of print," what sales thresholds trigger reversion, and what performance benchmarks the publisher must meet.

- **Set Reasonable Time Frames**: Whether you're negotiating reversion, renewal, or exit clauses, make sure the time frames work in your favor. For example, you don't want to wait five years for reversion rights to trigger if your book is no longer selling after the first year.

- **Get Professional Help**: These clauses can be complex, and their long-term implications can be difficult to predict. Working with a literary agent or publishing lawyer can help you navigate the fine print and ensure that your rights are fully protected.

- **Plan for the Future**: Always think long-term when negotiating these clauses. Your career as an author may evolve, and you want to make sure that you have the flexibility to move on to new opportunities, explore different markets, or republish your work if necessary.

Reversion, renewal, and exit clauses are essential tools for protecting your future in the publishing world. By negotiating clear, favorable terms for each of these clauses, you can ensure that your book—and your career—remain under your control, even as your publishing relationship evolves. With these safeguards in place, you'll have the flexibility to navigate any challenges that arise and continue building a successful, sustainable writing career.

Quick Tips and Recap

- **Understand Reversion Clauses**: Ensure your contract includes a clear reversion of rights clause that allows you to reclaim your book if it goes out of print or falls below a specific sales threshold.

- **Negotiate Renewal Clauses**: Include terms that allow you to renegotiate key elements like advances and royalties if the contract is renewed, giving you flexibility for future success.

- **Include Exit Clauses**: Protect yourself with exit clauses that let you terminate the contract if the publisher fails to meet their obligations, such as timely payments, publication deadlines, or marketing commitments.

- **Be Specific**: Avoid vague language in your contract. Clearly define terms like "out of print," sales thresholds, and publisher performance benchmarks to ensure clarity and protection.

- **Get Professional Help**: Work with a literary agent or lawyer to negotiate reversion, renewal, and exit clauses that best safeguard your long-term interests.

- **Think Long-Term**: Plan for your future as an author by ensuring your contract allows you to retain flexibility, reclaim your rights, and explore new publishing opportunities when necessary.

- **Keep an Eye on Time Frames**: Ensure that the time frames for reversion, renewal, and exit clauses are reasonable and work in your favor, giving you control over your work sooner rather than later.

CHAPTER THREE

Grant of Rights Clause: What You're Really Signing Away

"Understanding the grant of rights clause isn't just paperwork—it's the
blueprint to how your book lives in the world. Handle it wisely, and
you dictate the terms of your work's journey."
— STEPHEN KING, AUTHOR

Welcome to Chapter Three, "Grant of Rights Clause: What You're Really Signing Away," where we peel back the curtain on the most thrilling—or terrifying—part of a publishing contract. Get ready, because you're about to become a legal language linguist, deciphering the cryptic runes known as the 'Grant of Rights.'

In this arena, your pen is mightier than a sword, and signing your name can feel like launching a ship or potentially torpedoing your own fleet. We'll dissect what it means when you grant rights to a publisher: are you giving away the family silver or just loaning out the lawn mower? From exclusive rights that cling like a jealous ex to non-exclusive rights that are as casual as a Tuesday taco night, we'll cover them all.

By the end of this chapter, you won't just be nodding along to terms like "territorial rights" and "duration of rights"; you'll be wielding them like a seasoned contract warrior. So strap in and sharpen your understanding, because we're about to turn fine print into your best friend—or at least a frenemy you respect.

Understanding the Basics: What Is the Grant of Rights?

The Grant of Rights clause is the heart of any publishing contract. It's the section where you, the author, grant specific rights to the publisher, allowing them to distribute, market, and sell your book. Think of it as a permission slip: you're giving the publisher the legal authority to manage certain aspects of your work. The scope of this clause determines not only how your book will be handled but also how much control you retain over its future.

At its core, the Grant of Rights specifies what rights you're giving away, to whom, and for how long. These rights can include everything from print and digital publishing to audiobooks, translations, film adaptations, and more. In exchange for these rights, you typically receive an advance and royalties. However, the specific rights you grant—and the terms of that grant—can have a major impact on your long-term career and income potential.

1. What Does "Granting Rights" Really Mean?

When you "grant" rights to a publisher, you're giving them the legal ability to exploit those rights, usually in exchange for money. This means they can print your book, distribute it, and sell it in certain formats or territories. It also means they get a cut of the profits. The rights you grant can be broad or narrow, depending on the deal.

For example, a standard Grant of Rights clause might cover:

- **Print Rights**: The publisher can produce and sell physical copies of your book (hardcover, paperback, etc.).

37

- **Digital Rights**: The publisher can distribute your book in electronic formats (eBooks, Kindle, etc.).

- **Audiobook Rights**: The publisher can produce and sell an audiobook version.

- **Subsidiary Rights**: The publisher may have the right to sell or license your book for film, TV, or translation into other languages.

Each of these categories can be granted in full or partially, depending on the negotiation. This is why understanding exactly what you're agreeing to is critical. Once you grant rights to a publisher, you typically lose the ability to sell or manage those rights independently—unless the contract states otherwise.

2. Why the Grant of Rights Clause Matters

The Grant of Rights clause is one of the most crucial sections of your contract because it defines the extent of your partnership with the publisher. Get it wrong, and you could accidentally give away far more than you intended. This clause affects:

- **Your Control**: The more rights you grant, the less control you retain over how your book is sold, marketed, or adapted. For instance, granting worldwide rights could mean the publisher decides where and when your book is released in foreign markets, with little input from you.

- **Your Earnings**: The rights you retain are potential revenue streams for you in the future. If you give away audiobook, translation, or film rights as part of the initial deal, you might miss out on future earnings from those avenues.

- **Your Future Opportunities**: Once you grant rights, they are typically gone for the duration of the contract. If the publisher doesn't fully exploit those rights (e.g., they don't pursue foreign translations or audiobook deals), those opportunities could go unrealized for years.

3. Types of Rights You Might Grant

Every publishing deal is unique, but there are a few common categories of rights that authors typically grant as part of their contract:

- **Primary Rights**: These are the rights that allow the publisher to produce and sell your book in its primary form (print and digital).

- **Subsidiary Rights**: These refer to additional rights, such as adaptations (film/TV), translations, or audiobook productions. Subsidiary rights can be highly valuable, so be careful about giving them away too easily.

- **Territorial Rights**: This defines where the publisher can distribute your book—domestically, internationally, or globally. Retaining the rights to certain regions can open doors to other deals with foreign publishers.

4. Negotiating the Grant of Rights Clause

When negotiating the Grant of Rights clause, your goal should be to retain as much control over your work as possible while ensuring that your publisher can successfully bring your book to market. Some tips for navigating this negotiation:

- **Be Specific**: Ensure that the clause clearly defines which rights you're granting and which you're keeping. For example, you might grant the publisher the right to produce print and eBook editions but retain the audiobook rights for yourself.

- **Limit the Scope**: Don't feel pressured to grant all rights upfront. If you're not sure whether you want to give away audiobook or film rights, consider holding onto them or negotiating separate deals for those rights later.

- **Consider Territorial Rights**: If your publisher doesn't have strong international distribution, it might be better to retain foreign rights so you can sell them to a foreign publisher who specializes in those markets.

By understanding the fundamentals of the Grant of Rights clause, you'll be better equipped to make informed decisions about which rights to grant, how to limit the scope of the grant, and how to retain control over your work in the long term. In the next section, we'll dive deeper into the difference between exclusive and non-exclusive rights and how they can impact your contract.

Exclusive vs. Non-Exclusive Rights: Know the Difference

When negotiating the Grant of Rights clause, one of the key decisions you'll face is whether to grant exclusive or non-exclusive rights to your publisher. This distinction plays a pivotal role in determining how much control the publisher has over your work and what opportunities you retain to exploit those rights yourself or with other parties. Understanding the difference between these two types of rights is crucial for making informed decisions that align with your goals as an author.

1. What Are Exclusive Rights?

Exclusive rights give the publisher full control over the granted rights for a specific territory, format, or time period. This means that only the publisher can exploit those rights—you, as the author, cannot grant them to anyone else or use them independently while the contract is in effect.

For example, if you grant the publisher exclusive print rights for North America, they are the only ones who can print and distribute your book in that region. If you grant exclusive digital rights, only they can publish and sell eBooks based on your work.

Exclusive rights are the most common form of rights granted in publishing contracts, especially for the primary forms of distribution (print and eBook). Publishers often prefer exclusivity because it gives them a greater incentive to invest in marketing and distribution. However, granting exclusive rights means you're putting all of your eggs in one basket, so it's essential to understand what you're giving away.

- **Advantages of Exclusive Rights**:
    - **Stronger Publisher Commitment**: By granting exclusive rights, the publisher has full control, which often motivates them to invest more heavily in marketing, distribution, and

promotion since they are the sole beneficiary of the book's success.

 o **Higher Advances and Royalties**: Exclusive rights often come with higher upfront payments (advances) and better royalty terms because the publisher has more control and greater profit potential.

- **Disadvantages of Exclusive Rights**:

 o **Limited Flexibility**: Once you grant exclusive rights, you lose the ability to pursue other deals for that format or region. This can limit your options, especially if the publisher isn't fully exploiting those rights.

 o **Potential for Missed Opportunities**: If your publisher doesn't effectively promote or sell your book in a particular format or region, you could miss out on potential sales and revenue streams. With exclusive rights, you can't turn around and find another partner to pick up the slack.

2. What Are Non-Exclusive Rights?

Non-exclusive rights allow you to grant the same rights to multiple parties or use them yourself while still allowing the publisher to exercise those rights. For example, if you grant non-exclusive digital rights, your publisher can sell your eBook, but you are also free to distribute it yourself or sell it to other platforms.

Non-exclusive rights are less common in traditional publishing contracts, but they can be beneficial for authors who want to maintain greater control over certain aspects of their work. Non-exclusive rights are most often used for subsidiary rights, such as translations, serializations, or adaptations. In some cases, non-exclusive digital or audiobook rights might be negotiable, allowing you to explore self-publishing options alongside your publisher's efforts.

- **Advantages of Non-Exclusive Rights**:

 o **More Flexibility**: Non-exclusive rights give you the freedom to explore multiple opportunities for your book. You can work with different publishers or platforms in parallel, maximizing your reach and revenue.

- o **Control Over Key Aspects**: If you grant non-exclusive rights for certain formats (like audiobooks or translations), you retain control over how your book is adapted, marketed, and sold in those formats.

- **Disadvantages of Non-Exclusive Rights**:

  - o **Lower Publisher Incentive**: Publishers are often less motivated to invest heavily in promoting or distributing your book if they don't have exclusive control. Since they're sharing the profits with other parties, they might allocate fewer resources to marketing and sales.

  - o **More Complex Management**: Managing non-exclusive rights can be more complicated, as you'll need to coordinate between different parties, ensuring that there's no conflict in how your book is marketed or distributed. You'll also need to be vigilant about contract terms to avoid overlap or confusion.

3. When to Choose Exclusive vs. Non-Exclusive Rights

The decision to grant exclusive or non-exclusive rights depends on several factors, including your goals as an author, the type of rights in question, and the capabilities of your publisher. Here are a few scenarios to help guide your decision:

- **Primary Distribution Rights (Print and Digital)**: It's common to grant exclusive rights for print and digital publishing because these are the core formats that a publisher needs to control to bring your book to market effectively. In return for exclusivity, you should expect a larger advance and stronger marketing support. However, if you have strong self-publishing capabilities, you might negotiate for non-exclusive digital rights so you can distribute your own eBook while the publisher handles print distribution.

- **Subsidiary Rights (Film, TV, Audiobooks, Translations)**: For subsidiary rights, non-exclusive agreements are often more beneficial. For example, you might grant non-exclusive audiobook rights, allowing your publisher to produce and distribute an audiobook, but also retaining the right to sell that format to other platforms or produce your own. Similarly, retaining non-exclusive film or translation rights gives you the flexibility to negotiate separate deals with specialists in those areas.

- **Territorial Rights**: When it comes to territorial rights, exclusive rights can be useful if your publisher has a strong presence in certain regions. For example, granting exclusive rights for North America to one publisher while retaining non-exclusive rights for international sales allows you to explore foreign deals on your own. This gives you more control over the global reach of your book.

4. Negotiating the Best Deal for Your Rights

When negotiating exclusive or non-exclusive rights, it's important to strike a balance that aligns with your long-term goals. Here are some strategies for getting the best deal:

- **Be Selective About Exclusivity**: Don't feel pressured to grant exclusive rights across the board. For primary formats (like print or eBook), exclusivity can make sense, but for subsidiary rights like translations, audiobooks, or film adaptations, retaining non-exclusive rights can open more doors.

- **Limit the Scope of Exclusivity**: If you do grant exclusive rights, consider limiting the scope. For example, you could grant exclusive rights for a specific territory (like North America) but retain the rights for international distribution. You could also limit exclusivity to a specific format (such as print) while retaining non-exclusive rights for digital formats.

- **Include Reversion Clauses**: To protect yourself, include a reversion clause in your contract that allows you to reclaim rights if the publisher fails to exploit them within a certain time frame. This ensures that if your publisher doesn't follow through on marketing or sales efforts, you can take back control and pursue other opportunities.

Understanding the difference between exclusive and non-exclusive rights empowers you to make informed decisions about your publishing contract. By carefully considering which rights to grant and under what conditions, you can retain more control over your work while still giving your publisher the opportunity to succeed. In the next section, we'll dive into Territorial Rights—understanding where in the world your book can be sold and how to negotiate the best deal for international sales.

Territorial Rights: Where in the World Can Your Book Be Sold?

Territorial rights are a critical part of your publishing contract, as they define where and how your book can be sold across different regions of the world. When you grant territorial rights, you're giving the publisher control over distributing, marketing, and selling your book in specific countries or regions. Understanding how these rights work and negotiating them wisely can significantly impact the reach of your book and your potential earnings. In this section, we'll explore what territorial rights mean, why they matter, and how to strike the right balance between giving your publisher the power to succeed while retaining control over international opportunities.

1. What Are Territorial Rights?

Territorial rights refer to the geographic scope in which a publisher is allowed to distribute your book. When you sign a contract with a publisher, they will typically ask for the rights to sell your book in one or more territories. A territory can range from a single country to a global market.

The main types of territorial rights include:

- **Domestic Rights**: Rights to distribute your book in the publisher's home country. For example, a U.S. publisher might request exclusive rights to sell your book within the United States.

- **Foreign Rights**: Rights to sell your book in countries outside of the publisher's home territory. These could include the United Kingdom, Canada, Australia, or other international markets.

- **World Rights**: Rights to distribute your book globally, including all domestic and foreign markets.

The territorial rights you grant determine where your book can be sold, who controls those sales, and how much of the revenue you'll see from international sales.

2. Why Territorial Rights Matter

Territorial rights matter because they dictate the global reach of your book and affect how much control you have over its distribution. If you grant a publisher world rights, you're giving them the authority to sell your book anywhere in the world. This can be convenient, as the publisher may handle international sales for you, but it also means you lose the opportunity to negotiate separate deals with foreign publishers or license your book in specific territories.

On the other hand, if you grant territory-specific rights, you retain more control over how your book is distributed globally. You might give a U.S. publisher exclusive rights to sell your book in North America but hold onto the rights for Europe or Asia, allowing you to negotiate separate deals with foreign publishers in those regions.

The choice of whether to grant world rights or limit your territorial rights is a strategic decision that depends on several factors:

- **Publisher's Global Reach**: Does your publisher have a strong presence in international markets? If not, granting them world rights may limit your book's exposure in foreign countries.

- **Your Book's Appeal**: If you believe your book has strong potential in international markets, retaining foreign rights can allow you to explore separate deals with publishers who specialize in those regions.

- **Earnings Potential**: Retaining foreign rights can open the door to additional advances and royalties from multiple publishers. Instead of receiving a single advance for world rights, you could negotiate separate advances for each territory.

3. Exclusive vs. Non-Exclusive Territorial Rights

When negotiating territorial rights, you'll need to decide whether to grant exclusive or non-exclusive rights for each territory. The choice between exclusive and non-exclusive rights will depend on how much control you want the publisher to have over your book's distribution in each region.

- **Exclusive Territorial Rights**: Granting exclusive rights means that the publisher is the sole entity allowed to sell your book in that specific region. This is common for domestic rights (e.g., granting exclusive rights to a U.S. publisher to sell your book in North America), but it can also apply to international markets. Exclusive rights give the publisher more incentive to invest in marketing and distribution because they control all sales in that region.

- **Non-Exclusive Territorial Rights**: With non-exclusive rights, multiple publishers or platforms can sell your book in the same region. This can be beneficial if you want to distribute your book through various channels (such as self-publishing in certain regions while your publisher handles others), but it may reduce the publisher's motivation to heavily invest in those markets.

- **Strategy**: For domestic rights, it's common to grant exclusive rights to the publisher. For foreign or international rights, you might consider retaining non-exclusive rights or granting exclusive rights on a region-by-region basis to maximize your options.

4. Strategies for Negotiating Territorial Rights

Deciding how to structure territorial rights requires balancing the publisher's capabilities with your own long-term goals. Here are a few strategies for negotiating territorial rights that give your book the best chance for global success:

- **Assess the Publisher's Global Capabilities**: Before granting world rights, research your publisher's ability to effectively distribute and market books in international territories. Some publishers have extensive global networks, while others primarily focus on domestic markets. If your publisher doesn't have a strong presence in foreign markets, consider retaining those rights to negotiate separate deals with international publishers who specialize in those regions.

- **Negotiate for Territory-Specific Deals**: Instead of granting world rights upfront, consider dividing your rights by region. For example, you might grant exclusive rights to a U.S. publisher for North America but retain the rights for Europe, Asia, or Australia. This allows you to negotiate separate deals with foreign publishers who may offer better terms or stronger distribution in their home territories. Retaining foreign rights can also increase your overall earnings by securing advances and royalties from multiple publishers.

- **Work with Foreign Literary Agents**: If you retain foreign rights, you can partner with literary agents who specialize in foreign markets to help you secure deals with international publishers. These agents have the expertise and connections to navigate foreign publishing landscapes and can help you get the best possible terms for your book in each region.

- **Include Reversion Clauses for Unexploited Territories**: If you do grant world rights or international territorial rights, ensure that your contract includes a reversion clause for territories where the publisher fails to sell your book. This clause should allow you to reclaim the rights for specific regions if the publisher doesn't actively market or distribute your book there. This way, if the publisher isn't capitalizing on international opportunities, you can take back control and pursue other deals.

- **Don't Overlook Translation Rights**: When negotiating territorial rights, consider whether you want to include translation rights. Translation rights allow a publisher to translate and sell your book in other languages. If your book has international appeal, retaining translation rights can open the door to separate deals with foreign publishers who specialize in translated works. Alternatively, you can negotiate for higher royalties if the publisher handles the translations.

5. Maximizing Your Book's Global Reach

Successfully negotiating territorial rights can significantly expand the global reach of your book, ensuring that it's available to readers in key markets around the world. Here's how to maximize your book's global reach through territorial rights:

- **Identify Key Markets for Your Book**: Determine which regions are most important for your book's success. For example, if your book is a genre that has strong international appeal (such as fantasy or thriller), you'll want to focus on securing distribution in markets like the U.K., Australia, and Europe. If your book is a memoir or non-fiction work with a more localized focus, retaining domestic rights might be more appropriate.

- **Monitor International Sales and Opportunities**: Once your book is published, keep an eye on its performance in international markets. If you retain foreign rights, actively seek out foreign publishers or agents who can help you exploit those opportunities. If you've granted world rights, make sure your publisher is actively promoting your book in foreign markets.

- **Consider Digital-Only Rights for International Sales**: In some cases, you may want to retain print rights for specific territories while granting **digital-only** rights for international sales. This allows you to self-publish or find a foreign print publisher while the digital version of your book is available globally through platforms like Kindle or Apple Books.

Territorial rights determine how far your book will travel and how many readers it can reach. By negotiating these rights wisely—whether through exclusive or non-exclusive deals, region-specific grants, or retaining translation rights—you can ensure that your book finds its audience across the globe. In the next section, we'll cover Duration of Rights—how long the publisher controls your work and why limiting the timeframe is essential to your long-term success.

Duration of Rights: How Long Does the Publisher Control Your Work?

The duration of rights refers to how long the publisher retains control over the rights you've granted them. This part of the contract is crucial because it dictates how long the publisher has exclusive access to your book and its various formats, and when (or if) those rights revert back to you. Understanding and negotiating the duration of rights is key to ensuring you don't lose control of your work indefinitely, while still giving the publisher enough time to make your book a success.

In this section, we'll dive into the common durations found in publishing contracts, why they matter, and how to negotiate for a fair timeline that protects your long-term interests.

1. Common Durations for Publishing Rights

Publishing contracts typically define the duration of rights in one of two ways:

- **Term-Based Contracts**: The rights are granted for a specific period (e.g., 5 years, 10 years). After this period, the rights either revert back to you automatically or are renegotiated for renewal.

- **Life-of-the-Contract**: The rights are granted for as long as the book remains in print or continues to sell. In these contracts, the duration is tied to the commercial life of the book—meaning the rights stay with the publisher until certain sales thresholds are no longer met, or the book goes out of print.

While both terms have their benefits, it's important to negotiate a duration that gives you flexibility and ensures that the publisher is actively promoting and selling your book during this period. Let's explore both in more detail.

2. Term-Based Contracts: A Set Timeline for Rights

A term-based contract grants rights for a specific, predefined period. This could be five years, ten years, or even longer, depending on the agreement. Once the term ends, the rights revert back to the author, unless the contract is renewed or extended.

- **Advantages**:

  - **Clear End Date**: A set term provides a clear endpoint for when the publisher's control over your work expires. This means that if the publisher is no longer actively promoting or selling your book, you can regain control and explore other opportunities, such as self-publishing, republishing with another publisher, or creating a new edition.

  - **Renewal Opportunities**: Term-based contracts often come with the option to renegotiate at the end of the term. If the book is doing well, you can negotiate for better royalties or additional advances before extending the deal.

- **Disadvantages**:

  - **Limited Time for Success**: In some cases, a shorter term might not give the publisher enough time to maximize the potential of the book, particularly if the marketing and promotion efforts take time to ramp up.

- **Strategy**: If you're negotiating a term-based contract, aim for a duration that balances giving the publisher enough time to succeed with your need for control over your work. A common sweet spot is between five and ten years, but shorter terms might be appropriate for some projects. Be sure to negotiate renewal options that allow for better terms if the book becomes a success.

3. Life-of-the-Contract: Tied to the Commercial Life of the Book

A life-of-the-contract agreement ties the duration of the rights to the commercial life of the book. This means that the publisher retains control for as long as the book remains in print, available for sale, or continues to meet certain sales thresholds. If the book goes "out of print" or falls below a specified sales level, the rights can revert back to the author.

- **Advantages**:

  - **Potential for Longer-Term Success**: This type of agreement can work well if your book has long-term potential, as it allows the publisher to keep promoting and selling the book as long as there's demand. It ensures the book remains available to readers for a longer period without having to renegotiate a new contract.

- **Disadvantages**:
    - ○ **Unclear End Date**: Life-of-the-contract agreements can sometimes lead to a situation where the book remains "in print" indefinitely, even if it's not being actively promoted. In today's digital world, eBooks rarely go out of print, which means the publisher could theoretically hold onto the rights forever if there's no clear reversion clause tied to sales performance.

- **Strategy**: If you're working with a life-of-the-contract agreement, make sure there are clear triggers for when the rights will revert to you. Define what constitutes "out of print" and include sales thresholds that allow you to regain rights if the book isn't selling well enough. For example, you could negotiate that if your book sells fewer than 100 copies in a 12-month period, you can request that the rights revert back to you.

4. Negotiating Reversion Clauses: Protecting Your Future

Whether you're dealing with a term-based or life-of-the-contract agreement, one of the most important parts of the duration of rights is the reversion clause. A reversion clause allows you to take back your rights if certain conditions are met, such as the book going out of print or failing to sell a minimum number of copies.

- **Out-of-Print Clauses**: Traditionally, reversion clauses were tied to whether or not the book was in print. If the book was no longer available in physical form, the rights would revert to the author. However, in today's digital age, it's rare for a book to truly go "out of print" since eBooks and print-on-demand formats can remain available indefinitely. Be sure to include a clear definition of what "out of print" means, such as the book not being actively marketed or sold in a particular format.

- **Sales Thresholds**: Sales-based reversion clauses are becoming increasingly common. These clauses trigger reversion if the book's sales drop below a certain threshold, such as selling fewer than 100 copies in a year. This ensures that you can regain control of your book if the publisher is no longer putting in the effort to market it effectively.

- **Territorial Reversion**: If you've granted territorial rights, consider including clauses that allow you to regain rights for specific regions if the publisher doesn't exploit them. For example, if your book isn't being sold in certain foreign markets within a reasonable time frame, you could reclaim the rights for those regions and negotiate separate deals with other publishers.

5. Key Considerations for Negotiating Duration of Rights

When negotiating the duration of rights in your contract, here are a few key points to keep in mind:

- **Define What Happens When the Contract Ends**: Whether you're working with a term-based or life-of-the-contract agreement, ensure the contract clearly states what happens when the rights expire. Do they automatically revert back to you, or is there a renewal process? Make sure you understand how to reclaim your rights if needed.

- **Protect Your Long-Term Interests**: Be wary of contracts that grant the publisher indefinite control over your work. Make sure there are clear reversion clauses that allow you to take back control if the book isn't performing as expected.

- **Include Opportunities for Renegotiation**: If your book becomes a success, you'll want the opportunity to renegotiate for better terms. Include clauses that allow you to revisit key aspects of the contract—such as royalties, advances, or subsidiary rights—when the contract is renewed or if sales exceed certain milestones.

The duration of rights is a crucial aspect of any publishing contract, as it determines how long the publisher controls your book and its various formats. By negotiating clear timelines, reversion clauses, and opportunities for renewal, you can ensure that you maintain control over your work in the long term while still giving the publisher enough time to make your book a success. With these safeguards in place, you'll be well-positioned to protect your career and make the most of future opportunities.

Quick Tips and Recap

- **Understand the Grant of Rights**: Know exactly which rights you're granting to the publisher, whether they're print, digital, audiobook, or subsidiary rights like film and TV.

- **Exclusive vs. Non-Exclusive**: Be mindful of whether you're granting exclusive or non-exclusive rights. Exclusive rights give the publisher full control, while non-exclusive rights allow you more flexibility to pursue other opportunities.

- **Territorial Rights Matter**: Carefully consider where your book can be sold. Granting world rights may simplify things but could limit your international potential. Retaining territorial rights for specific regions can open the door to foreign deals.

- **Negotiate Duration of Rights**: Set clear timelines for how long the publisher controls your book. Whether it's a term-based agreement or tied to sales, ensure you know when and how your rights will revert to you.

- **Include Reversion Clauses**: Always negotiate for reversion clauses that allow you to reclaim rights if your book goes out of print, isn't selling well, or isn't being marketed in specific territories.

- **Monitor Sales and Rights**: Stay proactive about tracking your book's sales and the performance of rights you've granted. If your book isn't selling or the publisher isn't exploiting certain rights, you may be able to trigger reversion clauses.

- **Think Long-Term**: Protect your long-term interests by including opportunities for renegotiation when rights expire or sales targets are met. Make sure your contract leaves room for flexibility and future success.

Subsidiary Rights: Unlocking Additional Value

"Subsidiary rights are not just icing on the cake—they are layers of potential that can elevate a book from a single story to a multimedia franchise." — J. J. ABRAMS, FILMMAKER AND PRODUCER

Welcome to Chapter Four, "Subsidiary Rights: Unlocking Additional Value," where we dive into the treasure trove that lies beyond the basic book deal. Think of subsidiary rights as the hidden compartments in a magician's hat—just when you think you've seen all the tricks, out pops another rabbit, or in this case, another revenue stream!

In this chapter, we're exploring all the golden nuggets—film rights, foreign translations, audiobooks, merchandise, and yes, even that elusive dream of seeing your characters adapted into a binge-worthy TV series. Subsidiary rights can turn a modestly successful book into a cultural phenomenon (and a financial windfall).

So, sharpen your business acumen and prepare to learn how to leverage these rights to their fullest potential. By the time we're done, you won't just hope for your book to be picked up for a movie deal; you'll strategically position it to be the next big hit—because, who knows, the right deal might just make your literary work the star of its own show.

Film and TV Rights: Bringing Your Story to the Screen

For many authors, the ultimate dream is to see their book come to life on the big screen or as a binge-worthy TV series. Film and TV rights are one of the most lucrative and exciting aspects of subsidiary rights, offering the potential to turn a successful book into a full-blown media phenomenon. But navigating the world of film and TV adaptations requires a clear strategy and a good understanding of how these deals work. In this section, we'll explore how you can bring your story to the screen by negotiating film and TV rights, and how to ensure that your book is positioned to make the leap from the page to the screen.

1. Understanding the Basics of Film and TV Rights

When you sell or license film and TV rights, you're granting a producer, studio, or network the right to adapt your book into a movie or television series. This doesn't mean the adaptation is guaranteed to happen; often, it starts with an option, which gives the buyer exclusive rights for a period of time to develop the project. If the option is exercised, the producer then moves forward with adapting your work.

Here are the key elements involved:

- **Option Agreement**: The producer pays for the right to "option" your book, typically for 12-24 months. During this time, they work to develop the project (e.g., write a screenplay, secure funding, attach a director or actors). If they exercise the option, they proceed to production. If not, the rights revert to you.

- **Purchase Agreement**: If the option is exercised, the producer buys the full film or TV rights, usually for a higher fee than the initial option. This is where the real money can come in, depending on the scope of the project.

- **Creative Input**: Depending on the terms of the deal, you may have little or no input into how your book is adapted. Many authors opt to negotiate for some level of creative involvement, whether as a consultant, co-writer, or executive producer, though this is often difficult to secure unless you have significant leverage.

2. How to Position Your Book for Film or TV Adaptation

Not every book is suited for film or TV, but many genres and stories have the potential to transition well into visual media. If your book has cinematic qualities, here are a few strategies to increase its appeal to producers and studios:

- **Focus on Visual Elements**: Books that are highly visual, with rich settings, vivid action scenes, or compelling characters, tend to translate well to the screen. Whether it's a historical drama, a fast-paced thriller, or a magical fantasy world, books that provide strong visual cues are more likely to capture a producer's imagination.

- **Develop a Strong Narrative Arc**: Films and TV shows thrive on stories with clear beginnings, middles, and endings, as well as well-defined character arcs. If your book has a plot that builds to a satisfying climax, it can make for a strong pitch to screenwriters and directors.

- **Consider Serial Potential**: TV adaptations, especially in the age of streaming platforms like Netflix and Amazon Prime, often look for stories that can be stretched over multiple seasons. If your book is part of a series or has multiple subplots that could be expanded, it might have potential as an ongoing TV show rather than a standalone film.

- **Build a Fanbase**: Books that already have a dedicated readership, especially through social media, fan clubs, or strong sales, have a greater chance of being picked up for adaptation. Producers are more likely to invest in projects with a built-in audience.

3. Negotiating the Option Agreement: What to Know

The option agreement is often the first step in selling film and TV rights. While it's exciting to be approached with an option offer, it's important to understand the terms before signing. Here's what to consider:

- **Option Fee**: This is the payment you receive in exchange for granting the producer the exclusive right to develop your book. Option fees vary widely, depending on the interest in your book and the size of the production company, but a typical range is anywhere from a few thousand to tens of thousands of dollars. Larger studios might offer more, but it's essential to assess whether the producer has the means and connections to bring the project to fruition.

- **Option Period**: The option period is the length of time the producer has to develop the project. A standard option period is 12-24 months, though it can be extended if the producer needs more time. Make sure there are clear timelines in the contract, and consider negotiating for additional payments if the option period is extended beyond the initial term.

- **Reversion of Rights**: If the producer fails to exercise the option within the specified time, the rights should revert back to you. Make sure your contract has a clear reversion clause that allows you to reclaim the film and TV rights if the project doesn't move forward.

- **Creative Control**: While it's rare for authors to retain full creative control over the adaptation, you can negotiate for involvement in the process. This might include a consulting role, script review privileges, or an executive producer credit. Having some input can help ensure your story stays true to your vision, but it's important to recognize that film and TV adaptations often diverge from the source material.

4. Maximizing the Value of Your Film and TV Rights

Selling film and TV rights can bring a significant financial windfall, but it's also about maximizing the long-term value of your work. Here's how to ensure you get the best deal possible:

- **Work with an Agent or Entertainment Lawyer**: Negotiating film and TV rights can be complex, and it's essential to work with a literary agent or entertainment lawyer who specializes in media deals. They can help you secure the best possible terms and protect your interests.

- **Retain Other Subsidiary Rights**: If you're selling film or TV rights, make sure you retain other subsidiary rights, such as merchandising, gaming, or theme park rights. These can lead to additional revenue streams if your book becomes a hit. For example, if your story becomes a TV show, the merchandising rights (e.g., action figures, clothing) could bring in substantial income.

- **Consider the Long-Term Impact**: Beyond the financial aspects, think about how a film or TV adaptation could affect your book's reputation and legacy. A successful adaptation can boost book sales and introduce your work to new audiences, but a poorly executed version can tarnish your brand. Be cautious about who you partner with and ensure that the producers share your vision for the story.

Film and TV rights offer exciting opportunities for authors to see their stories brought to life in new ways. By understanding the basics of these deals, positioning your book for adaptation, and negotiating wisely, you can open up a whole new avenue of success beyond the printed page. In the next section, we'll explore audiobook rights, another rapidly growing market that can help expand the reach of your work and provide an additional stream of income.

Audiobook Rights: Tapping Into a Growing Market

Audiobooks have become one of the fastest-growing segments of the publishing industry, offering authors a dynamic new way to reach readers—or in this case, listeners. With platforms like Audible, Apple Books, and Spotify making audiobooks more accessible than ever, securing audiobook rights can be a lucrative way to expand the reach of your work. Whether you choose to partner with an audiobook producer or self-publish your audiobook, understanding how to negotiate and maximize your audiobook rights is key to tapping into this thriving market.

In this section, we'll explore the importance of audiobook rights, how to approach negotiations, and whether you should consider producing your own audiobook or working with a professional publisher.

1. Why Audiobook Rights Matter

Audiobooks provide an entirely new way for readers to experience your story, and they offer a unique set of advantages over traditional print and digital formats. Here's why audiobook rights matter:

- **Expanding Your Audience**: Audiobooks appeal to a broader demographic, including busy professionals, commuters, and multitaskers who prefer to listen rather than read. For many readers, audiobooks are their primary or preferred way of consuming content, meaning your book can reach a wider audience than just those who buy print or eBooks.

- **Revenue Potential**: Audiobooks have become a significant source of revenue for authors, particularly as the market continues to grow. With platforms like Audible, Google Play, and other streaming services offering audiobooks on subscription or a la carte models, the financial potential is substantial. The more formats your book is available in, the more income streams you create.

- **Increased Engagement**: Audiobooks tend to have a higher level of engagement, as listeners can immerse themselves in your world while commuting, exercising, or doing other tasks. A well-produced audiobook can elevate the reading experience, making your story more memorable and accessible.

2. Negotiating Audiobook Rights: What to Consider

When it comes to securing audiobook rights, you have a few options depending on your publishing agreement. Audiobook rights are often bundled into traditional publishing deals, but you can negotiate to retain these rights separately, giving you more flexibility over how they're produced and distributed.

- **Bundled Rights**: In many cases, publishers will request the rights to produce and distribute your audiobook as part of the overall book deal. This can be convenient if you're looking for a hassle-free way to get your audiobook produced, as the publisher will handle all the details, from hiring a narrator to distribution.

  - **Strategy**: If you're granting audiobook rights to a publisher, make sure to negotiate favorable royalty rates. Audiobooks typically have higher royalties than print books, so aim for a royalty rate of 25-50% of net sales. Be sure to also define how the audiobook will be marketed and distributed.

- **Retaining Audiobook Rights**: If your publisher doesn't have a strong audiobook division or if you want more control over the production process, you can retain your audiobook rights and either self-publish or partner with an audiobook producer. This option allows you to choose your narrator, oversee production, and control how the audiobook is marketed.

  - **Strategy**: When retaining audiobook rights, consider whether you want to produce the audiobook yourself (either independently or through a platform like ACX) or work with a third-party audiobook publisher. Retaining control gives you flexibility but also means you'll be responsible for production costs and marketing efforts.

3. Self-Publishing vs. Partnering with an Audiobook Publisher

Once you've decided to retain your audiobook rights, the next step is determining whether to self-publish or work with a dedicated audiobook publisher. Each option has its pros and cons, so it's important to weigh them carefully.

- **Self-Publishing an Audiobook**: Platforms like ACX (Audiobook Creation Exchange), Findaway Voices, and Kobo Writing Life allow authors to self-publish their audiobooks, much like self-publishing an eBook or print book. These platforms provide access to professional narrators and producers, making the process easier for authors without studio connections.

- Advantages: Self-publishing gives you full control over the creative process, allowing you to choose your narrator, oversee the production quality, and determine pricing. You also retain a larger share of the royalties (up to 40% on platforms like Audible if you go exclusive), and you're not tied to a publisher's timeline.

- Disadvantages: The downside of self-publishing is the upfront cost of production. Hiring a professional narrator and producer can be expensive, and you'll also need to handle your own marketing and distribution efforts to get your audiobook noticed in a competitive marketplace.

- **Partnering with an Audiobook Publisher**: If you prefer not to handle the production yourself, you can partner with an audiobook publisher or producer who will take care of the recording, editing, and distribution. These companies often have established relationships with narrators and distributors, giving your audiobook a professional edge.

  - Advantages: By partnering with an audiobook publisher, you gain access to their expertise and resources, ensuring a high-quality product without the upfront cost. The publisher handles production and marketing, freeing you to focus on other aspects of your career.

  - Disadvantages: Partnering with an audiobook publisher means giving up some creative control and a portion of the royalties. Additionally, you may be tied into an exclusive agreement that limits your ability to distribute the audiobook on multiple platforms.

4. Choosing the Right Narrator: The Voice of Your Book

One of the most critical aspects of producing an audiobook is choosing the right narrator. The narrator becomes the voice of your book, and their performance can make or break the listener's experience. Here's what to consider when selecting a narrator:

- **Voice and Tone**: Your narrator should match the tone and style of your book. For fiction, this might mean selecting someone who can bring your characters to life with distinct voices and emotional depth. For non-fiction, the narrator should sound authoritative, engaging, and easy to follow.

- **Auditions**: If you're self-publishing, platforms like ACX allow you to listen to auditions from professional narrators. This gives you the opportunity to find the perfect match for your book. Pay attention to how the narrator handles dialogue, pacing, and emotional scenes.

- **Experienced Narrators**: If possible, work with experienced narrators who have a proven track record of delivering high-quality performances. You can often find top-notch narrators through audiobook publishers or freelance platforms.

- **Narrator-Focused Marketing**: A well-known narrator can also help with marketing your audiobook. Audiobook fans often follow specific narrators, so selecting a popular or established voice can increase your book's visibility.

5. Maximizing Your Audiobook's Reach

Once your audiobook is produced, the next step is ensuring it reaches the widest possible audience. Here are some tips for maximizing your audiobook's reach:

- **Exclusive vs. Wide Distribution**: When distributing your audiobook, you can choose to go exclusive with one platform (like Audible) or opt for wide distribution across multiple retailers (such as Google Play, Apple Books, and Kobo). Exclusive agreements, like those on ACX, often offer higher royalty rates but limit your ability to sell on other platforms. Wide distribution can help you reach more listeners but may come with lower royalties.

- **Cross-Promote with Other Formats**: If your book is available in multiple formats (print, eBook, and audiobook), be sure to cross-promote them. Many listeners discover audiobooks after reading the print version and vice versa. Include links to your audiobook on your website, social media, and in your print and eBook versions to encourage readers to try the audio format.

- **Utilize Audiobook Reviewers and Influencers**: Reach out to audiobook reviewers, bloggers, and influencers who specialize in audiobook content. Reviews from these sources can increase visibility and attract dedicated audiobook listeners to your work.

- **Leverage Subscription Platforms**: Platforms like Audible offer subscription models where listeners can download a certain number of books each month. Being part of a subscription model can encourage readers to try your book without the upfront cost of purchasing it individually.

Audiobooks are a rapidly growing market with enormous potential for authors. By retaining control over your audiobook rights, choosing the right narrator, and strategically distributing your audiobook, you can unlock an additional revenue stream while expanding your audience. In the next section, we'll explore how foreign translation and international rights can take your book beyond borders and into new markets around the world.

Foreign Translation and International Rights: Expanding Your Global Reach

Selling foreign translation and international rights can take your book beyond borders, unlocking a vast global audience. While your primary market might be domestic, the opportunity to have your book translated into other languages and sold internationally can exponentially increase its reach and revenue potential. With the right strategy, your book can find new life in markets that you may not have initially considered. In this section, we'll explore how to navigate the world of foreign translation rights, how to sell international rights, and how to maximize your book's success in global markets.

1. What Are Foreign Translation and International Rights?

Foreign translation rights allow a publisher to translate your book into another language and distribute it in non-English speaking markets. International rights, on the other hand, refer to the distribution of your book in other countries, either in English or translated into local languages. These rights can be sold separately or bundled as part of a larger publishing deal.

The key categories of international rights include:

- **Translation Rights**: These rights allow a foreign publisher to translate your book into another language. For example, if you sell the translation rights for your novel to a French publisher, they would produce a French edition of your book.

- **Territorial Rights**: These refer to the geographic regions where your book can be sold. You may sell rights for specific countries (e.g., Germany, Japan) or larger regions (e.g., Europe, Latin America).

- **World English Rights**: This is when you sell the rights to publish your book in English-speaking markets outside your home country (e.g., Australia, the UK, Canada). This can be included in your primary publishing deal or sold separately.

2. How to Sell Foreign Translation and International Rights

Selling foreign and international rights is often best done with the help of a literary agent who specializes in foreign markets, or through partnerships with sub-agents and foreign publishers. The process typically involves offering these rights to foreign publishers who are interested in acquiring books that fit their market's preferences. Here's how to approach the process:

- **Work with a Foreign Rights Agent or Sub-Agent**: A literary agent who specializes in international markets can be invaluable in selling your translation and international rights. These agents often have established relationships with foreign publishers and know how to pitch your book to the right market. Sub-agents, who work in specific countries, can also help negotiate deals on your behalf.

- **Pitch at International Book Fairs**: Events like the Frankfurt Book Fair and the London Book Fair are prime opportunities for selling foreign rights. These fairs bring together publishers, agents, and authors from all over the world, making them ideal venues for introducing your book to international markets. Even if you're not attending in person, your agent can pitch your book to foreign publishers at these events.

- **Assess Market Demand**: Not every book will have the same appeal in every market. Genres like thrillers, fantasy, romance, and self-help tend to perform well in international markets, while niche subjects may be harder to sell. Work with your agent to assess which countries or regions are most likely to be interested in your book.

- **Bundle Translation Rights Separately**: If you've already sold world rights or international rights in English-speaking territories, you can still sell translation rights separately. Many foreign publishers are looking for well-received books that they can adapt to their local language and culture, especially if the book has already performed well in your home market.

3. Maximizing the Value of Foreign Translation Rights

Selling your book's translation rights is not just about landing a deal with a foreign publisher—it's about maximizing the value of that deal. Here's how to ensure you're getting the most from your foreign translation rights:

- **Negotiate Separate Deals for Each Territory**: If possible, avoid selling a blanket "world rights" deal to one publisher unless they have a strong global presence and proven international distribution. By selling rights to individual foreign publishers in different regions, you can negotiate separate advances and royalties for each market, which can significantly boost your earnings.

- **Focus on Key Markets**: Some countries have more robust publishing industries than others, and certain markets may offer higher advances or stronger sales potential. Focus on regions where your book has the best chance of success. Key translation markets include Germany, France, Italy, Spain, China, and Japan. Emerging markets in Latin America and Southeast Asia are also growing rapidly.

- **Maintain Control Over Quality**: When negotiating translation rights, ensure there are provisions in the contract that allow you to maintain some oversight of the translation quality. Poor translations can harm your book's reputation in foreign markets. Some authors request to approve the translator or see sample translations before the book goes to press.

4. Working with Foreign Publishers

Once you've sold your foreign rights, the foreign publisher will handle the translation, production, marketing, and distribution of your book in their respective markets. However, it's still important to build a good relationship with the foreign publisher to ensure your book is being marketed effectively in that region.

- **Collaborate on Marketing Strategies**: While foreign publishers will often have their own marketing strategies, they may welcome input from the author, especially if your book has been successful in its home market. Provide them with any marketing assets, such as press releases, interviews, or book trailers that can be adapted for their audience.

- **Support Local Promotion**: If your book gains traction in a foreign market, consider participating in local events, book fairs, or virtual author interviews. Engaging with your foreign readers can build your profile and encourage more foreign publishers to take notice of your work.

- **Monitor Sales and Performance**: Stay updated on how your book is performing in international markets. Depending on the terms of your contract, you may receive regular sales reports or have access to data about how your book is selling in each country. This information can help you make decisions about future deals or the possibility of extending contracts with foreign publishers.

5. The Long-Term Benefits of Foreign and International Rights

Selling foreign translation and international rights offers long-term benefits that go beyond the initial deal. Here are a few reasons why expanding your global reach can be a game-changer:

- **Revenue Diversification**: International rights create multiple streams of income, allowing you to earn royalties from several countries at once. Even if your book's performance fluctuates in one market, strong sales in another can provide a steady revenue source.

- **Global Recognition**: Having your book translated into multiple languages elevates your status as an author and opens the door to more prestigious opportunities, such as international awards, speaking engagements, or invitations to global literary events.

- **Cross-Promotion**: If your book gains popularity in a foreign market, it can lead to increased sales in your home country, as international success often raises your profile and visibility. A strong global presence can also attract media attention, leading to more offers for foreign adaptations or additional translation deals.

Selling foreign translation and international rights is a powerful way to extend the life of your book and reach new audiences around the world. By working with the right agents, targeting key markets, and negotiating smart deals, you can maximize the value of your book and enjoy the rewards of international success. In the next section, we'll explore how merchandising rights can transform your book into a brand, unlocking additional revenue streams through licensed products, gaming, and more.

Merchandising and Beyond: Licensing Your Book for Products and Experiences

Merchandising rights offer authors an exciting opportunity to transform their book into a broader brand, extending beyond the pages into the world of products, experiences, and media. From action figures and clothing lines to video games and theme park attractions, licensing your book's characters, settings, and intellectual property (IP) for merchandising can unlock new revenue streams and create a deeper connection with fans.

In this section, we'll explore how to leverage your merchandising rights, the types of products and experiences you can license, and the strategies for maximizing the long-term value of your book as a brand.

1. What Are Merchandising Rights?

Merchandising rights refer to the ability to license elements of your book—such as characters, titles, settings, and themes—to companies that create physical products or interactive experiences. These rights can cover a wide range of categories, including:

- **Apparel**: T-shirts, hats, and other clothing items featuring your book's cover, characters, or iconic quotes.

- **Toys and Collectibles**: Action figures, dolls, or collectible items based on your characters or storyworld.

- **Games**: Board games, card games, or video games that are adapted from your book's plot or setting.

- **Apps and Digital Products**: Mobile apps, interactive eBooks, or augmented reality experiences that allow fans to engage with your story in new ways.

- **Theme Parks and Attractions**: While rare, blockbuster franchises like Harry Potter or The Hunger Games have led to theme park attractions and live experiences, offering immersive adventures based on their fictional worlds.

Merchandising rights can be a standalone element of your publishing contract or part of a larger media deal that includes film, TV, or gaming rights. By carefully managing these rights, you can build a brand around your book that extends far beyond its pages.

2. Licensing Your Book for Merchandising

Licensing your book for merchandising involves granting a third party the right to use elements of your book (such as characters or artwork) in their products. In exchange, you typically receive a licensing fee upfront and royalties from the sale of merchandise. Here's how to approach the process:

- **Work with a Licensing Agent**: Licensing agents specialize in matching authors and IP holders with companies that create products based on their work. If your book has strong merchandising potential, a licensing agent can help you negotiate deals with toy manufacturers, clothing companies, or app developers. They'll also ensure that your intellectual property is properly protected.

- **Bundle Merchandising Rights in Media Deals**: If your book is being adapted into a film, TV show, or video game, merchandising rights are often included in the overall deal. Be careful when negotiating these rights, as bundling them with other media rights can limit your ability to license products independently. Make sure the licensing terms are clear, and consider retaining some control over how your characters are portrayed in merchandise.

- **Negotiate Royalties and Terms**: When licensing your book for merchandising, negotiate for a fair royalty rate, which is typically a percentage of the revenue from product sales. Royalties for licensed products can range from 5% to 15%, depending on the product category and the strength of your IP. Be sure to define how and where the products will be distributed, and consider adding clauses that allow you to approve the designs or marketing of the merchandise to ensure it aligns with your brand.

3. Maximizing the Value of Merchandising

Merchandising can significantly increase the visibility and profitability of your book, but it's important to approach it strategically to ensure it enhances your brand. Here's how to maximize the value of your merchandising rights:

- **Identify Key Elements for Licensing**: Not every book is suited for merchandising, but books with memorable characters, iconic visuals, or strong fan followings are ideal candidates. If your book has characters that resonate with readers or features a unique world, those elements can translate well into products like toys, clothing, or games. For example, characters with distinct looks, magical powers, or recognizable symbols are more likely to catch the attention of product manufacturers.

- **Build a Fanbase**: Merchandising is most successful when you have a dedicated fanbase. The more your readers are invested in your world and characters, the more likely they are to want physical reminders of their favorite story. Engage with your readers through social media, fan clubs, or special events to build a community around your book that will support future product releases.

- **Start Small with Selective Licensing**: Rather than licensing your entire book for merchandising, consider starting with a few select products to test the market. For example, you might begin by licensing T-shirts or mugs with key quotes or artwork from your book. As these products gain popularity, you can expand into more categories, such as toys, games, or collectibles. Starting small allows you to control quality and build demand over time.

- **Collaborate with Artists and Designers**: Merchandise featuring unique or artistic interpretations of your book can be especially appealing to fans. Collaborate with professional designers or fan artists to create visually striking products that go beyond simple logos or book covers. Limited-edition artwork or collectible items can generate buzz and add to the exclusivity of your merchandising line.

- **Leverage Popular Platforms**: Platforms like Etsy, Redbubble, and Zazzle allow you to create and sell merchandise based on your book, without needing to negotiate with large manufacturers. These platforms are ideal for authors who want to sell directly to their fans or offer exclusive products. You can create your own store with customized merchandise, ranging from apparel to home décor.

4. Exploring Beyond Products: Experiences and Live Events

Beyond physical products, merchandising can also include immersive experiences that bring your book's world to life. If your book has a strong narrative or rich setting, you may be able to license it for experiences such as:

- **Escape Rooms**: Interactive experiences where participants solve puzzles and complete challenges based on your book's story or setting. Escape rooms have become popular for books with mystery or adventure elements.

- **Live Shows or Immersive Theater**: Some authors have licensed their work for live shows or immersive theater performances, where fans can engage with the story in a real-world environment. These experiences can be a fun way to attract new audiences and create a buzz around your book.

- **Themed Events**: Book-themed events, such as murder mystery dinners or fan conventions, allow readers to interact with your story in a social setting. These events can be licensed to event planners or hosted by the author to engage with fans directly.

5. Protecting Your Intellectual Property

While merchandising can offer lucrative opportunities, it's important to protect your intellectual property (IP) when entering licensing agreements. Here are some key considerations for safeguarding your rights:

- **Trademark Your Characters or Logos**: If your book features recognizable characters, symbols, or catchphrases, consider trademarking them to prevent unauthorized use. This can protect your brand from knockoff products or unauthorized merchandise.

- **Set Approval Rights**: Always include clauses in your merchandising agreements that give you the right to approve product designs, marketing materials, and distribution strategies. This ensures that your book is represented accurately and that the merchandise aligns with your vision for the brand.

- **Monitor for Infringement**: Keep an eye out for unlicensed merchandise or unauthorized use of your characters or book elements. If you discover infringement, work with a licensing agent or legal professional to take action and protect your IP.

Merchandising opens the door to new and exciting ways to engage with your readers and monetize your book. From toys and apparel to immersive experiences, the possibilities are vast. By carefully managing your licensing deals, collaborating with the right partners, and protecting your intellectual property, you can turn your book into a broader brand that resonates with fans—and continues to generate revenue long after its initial release.

In the next chapter, we'll explore how to protect and secure the rights you've worked so hard to acquire, ensuring your book's long-term success in both the domestic and international markets.

Quick Tips and Recap

- **Understand Merchandising Rights**: Know what merchandising rights include, such as licensing your book for toys, clothing, games, and other products based on your characters or world.

- **Work with a Licensing Agent**: Partner with a licensing agent to help you secure deals with manufacturers, ensuring that your intellectual property is well-represented and protected.

- **Start Small**: Test the market with selective products like T-shirts, mugs, or limited-edition artwork before expanding into larger merchandising categories.

- **Negotiate Royalties and Terms**: Make sure to secure a fair royalty rate (typically 5-15%) and retain some control over product designs, marketing, and distribution.

- **Collaborate with Designers**: Work with professional or fan artists to create visually appealing, high-quality merchandise that resonates with your readers and fans.

- **Leverage Online Platforms**: Use platforms like Etsy or Redbubble to sell merchandise directly to fans, especially if you want to offer exclusive or custom products.

- **Consider Licensing for Experiences**: Beyond physical products, explore licensing your book for immersive experiences like escape rooms, live shows, or themed events.

- **Protect Your IP**: Trademark key characters, symbols, or phrases and ensure you have approval rights over how your book is represented in products.

- **Monitor for Infringement**: Keep an eye out for unauthorized merchandise and take action to protect your intellectual property if necessary.

By following these strategies, you can unlock additional value from your book and expand its reach into exciting new areas through licensing and merchandising.

Protecting Your Rights: Ensuring Long-Term Control

"Protecting your creative rights isn't just about safeguarding today's
work; it's about securing your legacy for tomorrow."
— SHERYL SANDBERG, COO OF FACEBOOK

Welcome to Chapter Five, "Protecting Your Rights: Ensuring Long-Term
Control," where we switch from offense to defense in the game of
publishing. Here, you'll learn how to guard your creative offspring like a dragon
hoards treasure—fiercely and without apology.

This isn't about building a moat around your work; it's about strategically placing
chess pieces to ensure your creations continue to serve your interests, even while
you sleep. We'll cover everything from copyright registration to dealing with

infringement in a way that would make even a seasoned lawyer raise an eyebrow in respect.

By the end of this chapter, you won't just feel empowered to protect your rights; you'll have a veritable fortress of knowledge at your disposal. Prepare to learn the ins and outs of intellectual property law as it pertains to publishing so you can stand your ground and keep your pen mightier than the sword—or any sneaky contract clause.

Copyright Basics: Securing Legal Protection for Your Work

Copyright is the foundation of your ability to control, protect, and profit from your creative work. As soon as you put pen to paper (or fingers to keyboard) and create an original piece of work, you automatically own the copyright. However, there's more to securing your rights than just writing the book—you need to understand how copyright works, why formal registration is important, and how to ensure your creative work is legally protected. In this section, we'll dive into the essentials of copyright, what it covers, and how to secure formal legal protection for your book.

1. What Is Copyright?

At its core, copyright is a legal framework that grants the creator of an original work exclusive rights to its use and distribution. It gives you control over how your book is reproduced, distributed, performed, displayed, and adapted. As the copyright holder, you're the only one with the legal authority to:

- Reproduce the work (make copies of your book).
- Distribute the work (sell, lend, or give away copies).
- Create derivative works (adapt your book into a film, audiobook, or translation).
- Perform or display the work publicly (this applies more to plays, performances, or visual works, but can include public readings).

Importantly, copyright is automatic the moment your work is fixed in a tangible medium. In other words, the instant your manuscript exists as a written document, whether on paper or in digital form, it is protected by copyright law. However, while copyright is automatic, taking steps to register your copyright can significantly strengthen your legal protection.

2. Why Should You Register Your Copyright?

Although copyright is automatic, formally registering your copyright with the appropriate government office (e.g., the U.S. Copyright Office) provides several key benefits:

- **Legal Evidence**: Registered copyright provides public documentation that you are the rightful owner of the work. This makes it easier to prove ownership in the event of a dispute or if someone tries to infringe on your rights.

- **Right to Sue for Infringement**: In many jurisdictions, you cannot sue for copyright infringement unless your work is registered. Registering your copyright gives you the legal standing to pursue damages if someone uses your work without permission.

- **Enhanced Legal Remedies**: If your copyright is registered, you may be entitled to statutory damages and attorney's fees if you win an infringement lawsuit. This can make legal action more feasible and rewarding, as you won't have to rely solely on proving actual damages.

- **International Protection**: While copyright laws differ by country, many countries recognize U.S. copyright registrations through international treaties. Registering your copyright can help protect your work in foreign markets.

Registering your copyright is relatively simple and inexpensive, making it a crucial step in securing full legal protection for your book.

3. How to Register Your Copyright

In the U.S., registering your copyright is a straightforward process that can be done online through the U.S. Copyright Office. Here's a basic overview of the steps involved:

- **Step 1: Prepare Your Manuscript**: Before registering, make sure you have a complete version of your manuscript. You can register at any point in the creative process, but it's usually best to register the final version that will be published.

- **Step 2: Complete the Online Application**: Visit the U.S. Copyright Office website and fill out the online registration form. You'll need to provide basic information about your work, such as the title, author(s), and publication status.

- **Step 3: Pay the Filing Fee**: There's a small fee for registering your copyright, typically ranging from $35 to $85 depending on the type of work and whether you're filing as an individual or a company.

- **Step 4: Submit a Copy of Your Work**: You'll need to provide a copy of your manuscript as part of the registration process. This can usually be submitted electronically, though physical copies may be required for certain types of works.

- **Step 5: Receive Your Certificate**: Once your application is processed, you'll receive a copyright certificate confirming your registration. Keep this certificate in a safe place, as it serves as proof of your ownership and registration date.

For authors outside the U.S., most countries have their own copyright offices or agencies where you can register your work, and the process is similar.

4. What Does Copyright Protect?

Copyright protection covers the expression of your ideas, but not the ideas themselves. This distinction is important to understand:

- **Protected**: Your specific wording, phrasing, characters, plot structure, and dialogue are protected by copyright. Essentially, the unique way you've expressed your story in your book is what's protected.

- **Not Protected**: General ideas, themes, or concepts are not protected. For example, if you write a book about a detective solving a mystery, the concept of a mystery or detective story isn't protected—only your specific execution of the story (characters, scenes, dialogue, etc.) is.

Copyright protection also lasts for a significant period of time. In most cases, copyright protection lasts for the life of the author plus 70 years. After this period, the work enters the public domain and can be used by others without permission.

5. Common Misconceptions About Copyright

It's easy to misunderstand copyright law, so here are a few common misconceptions to watch out for:

- **Myth: I need to include a copyright notice for protection**: In the past, works needed a copyright notice ("© [Year] [Author's Name]") to be protected. Today, copyright protection is automatic, and a notice is not required. However, adding a copyright notice to your work is still a good practice as it informs others that the work is copyrighted and who owns the rights.

- **Myth: Self-publishing or posting online weakens my copyright**: Whether you self-publish or post your work online, your copyright remains intact. However, you should still register your copyright if you plan to take legal action in the event of infringement.

- **Myth: I lose copyright if I sell my book rights**: Selling or licensing certain rights (e.g., print rights, eBook rights) to a publisher doesn't mean you lose copyright. You still retain ownership of the work itself and can control other uses of the book, such as film adaptations or foreign translations.

Securing your copyright is one of the most important steps you can take to protect your creative work. By understanding the basics of copyright law and formally registering your copyright, you gain the legal power to control how your book is used, sold, and distributed. In the next section, we'll discuss key contract clauses that affect your long-term control, including strategies for negotiating favorable terms that keep your rights protected.

Contract Clauses to Watch: Maintaining Control Over Your Rights

When you sign a publishing contract, you're entering into a legal agreement that defines how your rights as an author will be managed and shared with the publisher. While it's exciting to get a book deal, you need to carefully read and understand every part of the contract—especially clauses that impact your long-term control over your work. Some of these clauses can either protect your rights or, if left unchecked, allow the publisher to take more control than you intended. In this section, we'll cover the most critical contract clauses to watch for and provide strategies for negotiating terms that safeguard your creative and financial interests.

1. Grant of Rights Clause: What You're Really Giving Away

The Grant of Rights clause outlines what rights you're giving to the publisher and in which formats or territories. This is one of the most important clauses in your contract because it determines how much control you retain over your work.

- **Exclusive vs. Non-Exclusive Rights**: Most publishers will ask for exclusive rights to publish your book in specific formats (print, eBook, audiobook) and territories. This means the publisher has the sole right to distribute your book in those formats or regions. However, if you can, try to retain non-exclusive rights for certain aspects, such as translation or audiobook rights, so you can negotiate separate deals.

- **Territorial Rights**: Be mindful of which territories you're granting rights to. Some publishers may ask for worldwide rights, but if they don't have strong distribution channels in certain regions, you might be better off retaining those rights and selling them to foreign publishers who specialize in those markets.

- **Strategy**: Try to limit the rights you're giving to the publisher based on their strengths. For example, grant them exclusive rights to publish in print in North America, but retain foreign rights, translation rights, or film and TV rights. Always negotiate for specific terms regarding how these rights will be used and distributed.

2. Reversion of Rights Clause: Getting Your Rights Back

The Reversion of Rights clause dictates when and how the rights to your book will return to you if the publisher stops selling or promoting it. Without a strong reversion clause, you could lose control over your book indefinitely, even if the publisher is no longer actively marketing it.

- **Out of Print**: This is the most common trigger for reversion. If your book goes out of print or is no longer available in significant formats, the rights should automatically revert to you. However, with the rise of digital publishing, books rarely go out of print completely. Make sure the contract specifies what constitutes "out of print" (e.g., sales falling below a certain threshold for a specific period).

- **Sales Thresholds**: Negotiate for a clear sales threshold in the contract. For example, you might include a clause that says if your book sells fewer than 100 copies in a 12-month period, you can request that the rights revert to you. This prevents the publisher from holding onto your book without putting effort into marketing or selling it.

- **Strategy**: Include a specific timeline for reversion. For example, if your book hasn't sold a certain number of copies within two years, you can request the return of your rights. Also, ensure that the reversion applies to all formats and territories so you regain full control of your book.

3. Non-Compete Clause: Protecting Your Freedom to Write

A Non-Compete clause restricts your ability to publish works that might compete with the book you're selling to the publisher. While publishers want to protect their investment, a broad non-compete clause can severely limit your freedom to write and publish other works.

- **Narrow the Scope**: Some contracts contain overly broad non-compete clauses that prevent you from publishing any book that could be considered "competitive" or similar in theme, genre, or audience. You'll want to negotiate this clause to be as specific and narrow as possible. For example, the non-compete should only apply to books that are direct sequels or spinoffs of your current book, rather than anything you write in the same genre.

- **Time Limit**: Ensure that the non-compete clause has a clear time frame. Typically, this should only cover the period leading up to the publication of your current book, and a short period after (e.g., 6-12 months). Once that period ends, you should be free to write and publish other works.

- **Strategy**: Negotiate to limit the non-compete clause to direct competition (sequels, prequels, or books featuring the same characters) and keep the duration short. This ensures that you maintain the freedom to work on other projects without excessive restrictions.

4. Subsidiary Rights Clause: Unlocking Additional Revenue

The Subsidiary Rights clause covers rights beyond the traditional print and digital formats, such as film, TV, audiobook, translation, and merchandising rights. These can be extremely valuable, and how they're handled in your contract can significantly impact your potential earnings.

- **Retain Key Subsidiary Rights**: Whenever possible, try to retain control of high-value subsidiary rights, such as film and TV rights, audiobook rights, and merchandising rights. These rights can open up new revenue streams if your book becomes a hit, and you may prefer to negotiate separate deals for these rights.

- **Negotiating Subsidiary Splits**: If your publisher insists on controlling certain subsidiary rights, negotiate for a fair split of the revenue. For example, if they sell translation rights to a foreign publisher, ensure that you receive a significant percentage of the deal (usually 50% or more).

- **Strategy**: Retain as many subsidiary rights as possible, especially those related to film, TV, and merchandising. If you must grant these rights to the publisher, negotiate for a high percentage of any licensing deals and include a clause that allows you to take back those rights if they're not actively exploited within a certain period.

5. Termination Clause: When and How You Can End the Contract

The Termination Clause outlines the circumstances under which you or the publisher can terminate the contract. This is important because it allows you to end the agreement if the publisher isn't fulfilling their obligations.

- **Breach of Contract**: Ensure the contract includes a provision that allows you to terminate the agreement if the publisher fails to meet key obligations, such as timely payment of advances or royalties, or failing to publish the book within the agreed-upon timeframe.

- **Automatic Termination**: You might also negotiate for automatic termination if certain conditions are met, such as your book failing to meet a sales threshold or not being published within a specified period.

- **Strategy**: Negotiate clear terms that allow you to terminate the contract if the publisher is not delivering on their promises. Make sure you can retain the rights to your work if the contract is terminated due to breach or failure to perform.

By carefully negotiating these key contract clauses, you can maintain greater control over your book and your career. From the Grant of Rights to Reversion and Non-Compete Clauses, these provisions will determine how your book is sold, marketed, and controlled in the long term. In the next section, we'll cover how to handle infringement—what to do if someone uses your work without permission, and the steps you can take to protect your rights legally.

Handling Infringement: How to Protect Against Unauthorized Use

As an author, protecting your work from unauthorized use is critical. Infringement occurs when someone uses your copyrighted material without your permission, whether that's copying your text, selling pirated versions of your book, or adapting your work into other formats without consent. Fortunately, copyright law provides you with tools to combat infringement, but it's important to know how to handle these situations efficiently and effectively. In this section, we'll explore how to monitor for infringement, what steps to take if it happens, and how to protect your rights against unauthorized use.

1. How to Spot Copyright Infringement

Copyright infringement can take many forms, including direct copying, unauthorized distribution, and derivative works. Knowing how to recognize and monitor for infringement is the first step in protecting your rights.

- **Common Forms of Infringement**:

  - **Unauthorized Copying**: This occurs when someone directly copies part or all of your book and publishes it as their own. It can happen in both print and digital formats.

  - **Piracy**: Websites that offer illegal downloads of your book (often for free or at discounted prices) are a common form of piracy. These sites can significantly harm your sales and undercut legitimate distribution channels.

  - **Unlicensed Translations or Adaptations**: Infringement may occur if someone translates your book or adapts it into another format (such as a film, TV series, or stage play) without permission.

- **Monitoring for Infringement**:

  - **Regular Online Searches**: Periodically search for your book's title and key excerpts online to see if unauthorized copies or downloads are available. You can also search specific piracy sites or platforms where infringement is common.

  - **Set Up Google Alerts**: Setting up Google Alerts for your book's title or key phrases from your book can help you stay informed if someone posts your work online without authorization.

  - **Use Anti-Piracy Services**: Many companies offer anti-piracy services that monitor the web for unauthorized use of your work and help you remove infringing content. Services like Blasty or

DMCA.com can automate the process of finding and taking down pirated copies of your book.

2. Taking Action: What to Do If You Discover Infringement

If you discover that someone has infringed on your copyright, it's important to act quickly to minimize the damage. Here are the steps you should take:

- **Step 1: Document the Infringement**:
  - o Before taking any action, gather evidence of the infringement. This might include screenshots of the offending material, URLs where it's hosted, or copies of pirated versions of your book. Having this documentation will be important if you need to take legal action later.

- **Step 2: Issue a DMCA Takedown Notice**:
  - o The Digital Millennium Copyright Act (DMCA) provides a simple, legal mechanism to request the removal of infringing content from websites. A DMCA takedown notice is a formal request to the hosting provider or search engine to take down the unauthorized material. Most platforms (such as Amazon, Google, or YouTube) have systems in place to respond to these notices quickly.
  - o You can issue a DMCA takedown notice yourself, or work with an anti-piracy service to handle the process for you. Make sure the notice includes your name, the copyrighted work in question, the specific location of the infringing material, and a statement asserting that you have the legal right to request its removal.

- **Step 3: Contact the Infringer**:
  - o In some cases, a direct approach might resolve the issue without legal action. You can send a cease-and-desist letter to the infringer, demanding that they stop using your work and remove any unauthorized copies. This letter should clearly state your ownership of the copyright, outline the specific

infringement, and explain the actions you expect the infringer to take (e.g., removing content, stopping sales).

- o In many cases, infringers—especially those who don't fully understand copyright law—will comply with a cease-and-desist letter to avoid legal trouble. However, if the infringer doesn't respond or comply, you may need to escalate to legal action.

- **Step 4: Pursue Legal Action**:

  - o If the infringement is serious or the infringer refuses to comply with your requests, you may need to pursue legal action. Depending on your jurisdiction, you can file a lawsuit in federal court to seek damages for copyright infringement. If your copyright is registered, you can pursue statutory damages (which may be awarded even if you cannot prove actual financial loss) and recover attorney's fees.

  - o If the infringement is occurring in another country, international copyright treaties like the Berne Convention provide legal protections, allowing you to pursue action in foreign courts.

3. Preventing Future Infringement

Once you've dealt with an infringement issue, it's important to take steps to prevent future incidents. While it's impossible to eliminate the risk of copyright violations completely, you can reduce the likelihood of future infringements by following these strategies:

- **Register Your Copyright**: While copyright protection is automatic, formally registering your work with the U.S. Copyright Office (or your country's equivalent) strengthens your legal standing if you need to take action against an infringer. A registered copyright allows you to pursue statutory damages and attorney's fees in court, making legal action more viable.

- **Use Copyright Notices**: Although not required by law, adding a copyright notice to your work (e.g., "© 2024 [Your Name]") serves as a clear warning to potential infringers that your work is protected by copyright. Including a copyright notice in both digital and print versions of your book can help deter unauthorized use.

- **Watermark Your Digital Files**: For eBooks or other digital products, consider adding a watermark to your files. Watermarks are subtle but visible markings that indicate ownership and make it harder for unauthorized users to pass off your work as their own. Some digital distributors offer built-in watermarking services.

- **Leverage Digital Rights Management (DRM)**: Some publishers and platforms use Digital Rights Management (DRM) technology to prevent unauthorized copying and sharing of digital files. While DRM is not foolproof, it can serve as a deterrent by limiting the ability to share or duplicate eBooks and other digital products.

4. When to Seek Professional Help

While minor infringement cases can often be handled with a takedown notice or cease-and-desist letter, serious infringement may require professional legal help. Here's when to seek out an attorney or copyright specialist:

- **Complex Infringement Cases**: If the infringement involves multiple parties, significant financial loss, or a large-scale operation (e.g., widespread piracy), it's best to consult a copyright attorney. They can help you assess the situation, build a strong case, and pursue damages through the courts.

- **International Infringement**: Copyright laws vary by country, and pursuing legal action against infringers based in other jurisdictions can be complex. An attorney who specializes in international copyright law can help you navigate the legal framework in different countries and pursue remedies under international treaties.

- **Negotiating Settlements**: In some cases, the infringer may offer a settlement to avoid legal action. If this happens, a legal professional can help you negotiate favorable terms and ensure your rights are fully protected in any agreement.

Infringement is a serious issue that can harm both your financial interests and the integrity of your creative work. By staying vigilant, using tools like DMCA takedown notices, and knowing when to seek legal help, you can protect your rights and take action against unauthorized use. In the next section, we'll explore trademarking as a way to protect the branding elements of your work, such as titles, characters, or logos, ensuring that your intellectual property remains uniquely yours.

Trademarking Your Brand: Protecting Characters, Titles, and Logos

As an author, your book is more than just the words on the page—it's a brand that includes recognizable elements like your title, characters, and even logos or symbols associated with your work. Trademarking these elements can help protect your brand from unauthorized use and ensure that you maintain control over how they're used in merchandising, adaptations, and marketing. In this section, we'll explore when and why to consider trademarking, what elements can be trademarked, and how the trademark process works.

1. What Is a Trademark and Why Does It Matter?

A trademark is a form of intellectual property protection that applies to distinctive names, phrases, symbols, or designs that identify and distinguish your work from others. While copyright protects the creative content of your book, a trademark protects the branding elements that are tied to your book or series. This can be particularly valuable if your book gains popularity and you begin to explore merchandising, adaptations, or other uses beyond the written work.

Trademarks help you:

- **Protect Brand Identity**: By trademarking key elements of your book, you can prevent others from using your title, character names, or symbols in a way that confuses readers or dilutes your brand.

- **Open Merchandising Opportunities**: Trademark protection allows you to license these elements for merchandise or other products, ensuring that only authorized entities can use your branding.

- **Ensure Consistency**: If your book is adapted into a film, TV show, or video game, a trademark ensures that your brand is represented consistently across all platforms, protecting the integrity of your intellectual property.

2. What Can You Trademark?

Not all elements of your book are eligible for trademark protection, but there are several key aspects that may qualify. Here's what you might consider trademarking:

- **Book Title or Series Title**: While a single book title generally isn't eligible for trademark protection, the title of a series can be trademarked. For example, if you write a multi-book series, trademarking the series title ensures that no one else can use it in connection with their work. A unique title that becomes synonymous with your brand can be a valuable asset.

- **Character Names**: If your book features distinctive characters with names that could be commercially valuable (e.g., through merchandise, adaptations, or spin-offs), you can trademark those names. Characters like Sherlock Holmes or Harry Potter have become trademarked brands in their own right, allowing for exclusive use in a wide range of products.

- **Logos or Symbols**: Any logos, designs, or symbols that are associated with your book or series can be trademarked. This is especially important if you're planning to expand into merchandising, such as creating apparel, posters, or toys based on your book. A recognizable logo helps build brand recognition and ensures that only licensed products carry your mark.

- **Taglines or Catchphrases**: If your book or characters use a distinctive catchphrase or tagline, this can also be trademarked. For example, famous phrases like "Winter is Coming" from *Game of Thrones* are trademarked to prevent unauthorized use on merchandise or in marketing materials.

3. When Should You Consider Trademarking?

Not every author needs to trademark their book or characters, but it's a smart move if you believe your work has the potential to grow into a larger brand. Here are a few scenarios where trademarking makes sense:

- **You're Planning a Series**: If your book is part of a multi-book series, trademarking the series title can help protect its identity as you expand into future books and related media.

- **Your Book Has Commercial Potential**: If you're exploring opportunities for film or TV adaptations, merchandising, or licensing, trademarking key elements (like characters or logos) ensures that you maintain control over how those elements are used.

- **You're Expanding into Merchandising**: If you plan to create and sell merchandise based on your book, trademarking logos, titles, or character names ensures that only licensed products can use those elements, protecting you from counterfeit goods or unauthorized products.

4. The Trademark Process: How to Secure Your Brand

Trademarking is a legal process that involves filing an application with your country's trademark office (e.g., the U.S. Patent and Trademark Office (USPTO) or the Intellectual Property Office in the UK). Here's a step-by-step guide to how the process works:

- **Step 1: Conduct a Trademark Search**: Before filing your trademark application, conduct a thorough search to ensure that no one else is already using the name, character, or logo you want to trademark. This is important because if your proposed trademark is too similar to an existing one, your application may be denied. You can use the online databases provided by your country's trademark office, or hire a trademark attorney to conduct a more comprehensive search.

- **Step 2: File the Application**: Once you've confirmed that your trademark is available, file an application with the relevant trademark office. This application will require you to provide detailed information about the element you're trademarking (e.g., the series title, logo, or character name), the type of goods or services associated with it (e.g., books, merchandise), and how you plan to use it commercially.

- **Step 3: Pay the Filing Fee**: Trademark applications typically come with a filing fee, which can range from $200 to $500 depending on the country and the type of trademark. Be sure to include this fee with your application.

- **Step 4: Review and Approval**: After filing your application, the trademark office will review it to ensure that it meets all the legal requirements. If everything is in order and there are no conflicts with existing trademarks, your application will be approved. This process can take several months, so be prepared for a wait.

- **Step 5: Use Your Trademark**: Once your trademark is approved, you'll need to start using it in commerce (if you haven't already). Trademark protection typically requires that you actively use the mark in connection with your business or products, so be sure to apply the trademarked elements to your books, merchandise, or marketing materials.

5. Maintaining and Enforcing Your Trademark

Once you have secured a trademark, it's essential to maintain and enforce it to protect your brand over time. Here are a few key points to keep in mind:

- **Keep Using the Trademark**: Trademark protection requires that you continue to use the trademark in the way it was originally intended. If you stop using the trademark for a long period, it could become vulnerable to cancellation. Be sure to use the trademarked title, logo, or character name in your marketing, products, or promotional materials consistently.

- **Monitor for Infringement**: Just as with copyright, you'll need to monitor for potential trademark infringement. This can include unauthorized use of your book's title, character names, or logos in connection with other works or products. If you discover infringement, take action by sending a cease-and-desist letter or, if necessary, pursuing legal remedies.

- **Renew Your Trademark**: Trademark protection lasts as long as you continue to use the mark, but you'll need to renew it periodically. In the U.S., trademarks must be renewed after five years, and again every 10 years after that. Be sure to keep track of renewal deadlines to avoid losing protection.

Trademarking your book's title, characters, or logos is a powerful way to protect your brand and ensure that you maintain control over how your intellectual property is used. By securing a trademark, you create a legal shield around the most recognizable elements of your book, making it easier to expand into merchandising, adaptations, and other commercial ventures while protecting your brand from unauthorized use. With your copyright and trademark protections in place, you'll be fully equipped to safeguard your creative work for years to come.

Quick Tips and Recap

- **Register Your Copyright**: Copyright protection is automatic, but formal registration strengthens your legal standing, allowing you to sue for damages and enforce your rights.

- **Negotiate Key Contract Clauses**: Watch for Grant of Rights, Reversion of Rights, Non-Compete, and Subsidiary Rights clauses to ensure you retain control over your work and maximize your earning potential.

- **Monitor for Infringement**: Regularly check for unauthorized use of your work online, and be prepared to issue DMCA takedown notices or cease-and-desist letters if infringement occurs.

- **Act Fast on Infringement**: Document unauthorized use, issue a DMCA notice, and consider legal action if necessary to protect your rights from copyright violations.

- **Consider Trademarking**: Trademark series titles, character names, logos, or catchphrases to protect your brand identity and open opportunities for merchandising and adaptations.

- **Use a Trademark Search**: Before applying for a trademark, conduct a thorough search to ensure no one else is using a similar mark in your category.

- **Stay on Top of Trademark Use**: Actively use your trademark and monitor for infringement. Renew your trademark as required to maintain protection.

- **Seek Professional Help**: For complex infringement or international cases, consult a copyright attorney to ensure your rights are fully protected.

By following these strategies, you can safeguard your creative work and maintain control over your intellectual property for the long term.

PART TWO

Preparing for Publication

Welcome to Part Two: "Preparing for Publication," where the metamorphosis from aspiring writer to seasoned publishing warrior takes place. Here, your manuscript doesn't just evolve—it undergoes a glamorous transformation worthy of a reality TV reveal. We're not merely crossing Ts and dotting Is; we're suiting them up in armor, ready to battle it out in the fiercely competitive arena of book sales. Prepare yourself for a whirlwind journey through the intricate dance of editing, the strategic planning of marketing, and the precision alignment of distribution channels. This is where you fine-tune your labor of love into a sleek, market-ready prodigy, poised not just to enter the market, but to conquer it. Strap in and sharpen your pencils—and maybe your wits, too—as we lay down the tracks for your book's thrilling ride from manuscript to masterpiece.

Manuscript Preparation and Submission: Perfecting Your Draft

"Revising your manuscript is like preparing for a grand performance.
Every edit sharpens your story, ensuring it resonates with the audience
long after the curtain falls." — MARGARET ATWOOD, AUTHOR

Chapter Six, "Manuscript Preparation and Submission: Perfecting Your Draft," is where your literary baby learns to walk before it can run into the arms of eager readers. Think of this phase as the boot camp for your manuscript, where we whip those flabby sentences into shape and polish those paragraphs until they shine like a new recruit's boots.

Here, you're not just a writer; you're a sculptor chiseling away the unnecessary bits of marble to reveal the David beneath. We'll tackle everything from the Oxford comma debates to the existential crises over character arcs, ensuring every element of your draft performs push-ups in perfect form. Then, when it's time to send your manuscript off to the powers that be, you'll do so with the confidence of a general dispatching troops into battle, equipped with everything you need to know about formatting, cover letters, and the delicate art of not obsessively refreshing your email for a response.

Prepare to roll up your sleeves and dive deep into your narrative. By the end of this chapter, your draft won't just be better—it'll be battle-ready, set to charge the literary beaches and capture the hearts and minds of publishers and readers alike.

Polishing Your Prose: Editing and Revising Like a Pro

Once you've written "The End" on your manuscript, the real work begins: transforming your draft into a polished, professional piece of writing. Polishing your prose is about refining every sentence, tightening your narrative, and ensuring that your characters, themes, and plot shine. This stage involves a combination of self-editing, feedback from others, and perhaps the help of professional editors. In this section, we'll break down the steps you need to take to edit and revise your manuscript like a pro, turning a rough draft into a polished masterpiece.

1. Self-Editing: Becoming Your Own Best Critic

Before you send your manuscript to beta readers or professional editors, the first step is to self-edit. This phase is all about taking a critical eye to your work and identifying areas that need improvement. Here's how to approach self-editing:

- **Take a Break**: After finishing your draft, step away from it for a few days or even weeks. This allows you to return with fresh eyes and a more objective perspective on your writing.

- **Read Aloud**: Reading your manuscript aloud is one of the best ways to catch awkward phrasing, run-on sentences, or dialogue that doesn't flow naturally. You'll be surprised at how different your words sound when spoken.

- **Cut the Fluff**: Be ruthless when it comes to cutting unnecessary words, phrases, or even entire scenes. Every sentence should serve a purpose—whether it's advancing the plot, developing a character, or building tension. Look for filler words like "very," "just," "really," or excessive adverbs, and remove them wherever possible.

- **Focus on Consistency**: Ensure that your characters' personalities, motivations, and actions remain consistent throughout the book. Double-check the timeline of events, and verify that your world-building or setting details are cohesive and logical.

- **Watch for Common Pitfalls**: Overuse of passive voice, clichés, or repetitive sentence structures can weigh down your writing. Look for opportunities to use stronger verbs, varied sentence lengths, and fresh, original descriptions.

2. Beta Readers: Gaining Fresh Perspectives

Once you've done a thorough self-edit, it's time to get feedback from others. This is where beta readers come in. Beta readers are often fellow writers, friends, or members of your target audience who provide honest, constructive feedback on your manuscript.

- **Choose Your Beta Readers Carefully**: Look for people who are familiar with your genre or who fit the profile of your ideal reader. Ideally, beta readers should have experience giving critical feedback and be willing to provide both positive and negative insights.

- **Provide Specific Instructions**: When giving your manuscript to beta readers, ask them to focus on specific areas, such as character development, pacing, or plot structure. Ask open-ended questions like "Did any scenes feel too slow?" or "Were there any characters you didn't connect with?"

- **Be Open to Criticism**: Receiving feedback can be difficult, especially if it's negative, but remember that beta readers are helping you improve your manuscript. Take notes on common feedback themes, and focus on areas where multiple readers point out issues or confusion.

3. Professional Editing: When to Bring in the Experts

After incorporating feedback from beta readers, you may want to consider hiring a professional editor to help you take your manuscript to the next level. Professional editors can provide a fresh perspective and catch issues you may have missed during self-editing. There are different types of editing services, so it's important to understand what each one offers:

- **Developmental Editing**: This is a deep dive into the structure and content of your manuscript. A developmental editor will help you refine your plot, character arcs, pacing, and overall story structure. If you feel that your manuscript needs significant revision, this is the best type of editing to start with.

- **Line Editing**: A line editor focuses on the flow and style of your writing at the sentence and paragraph level. They'll help you improve the clarity, tone, and overall readability of your prose without changing the content itself.

- **Copyediting**: Copyediting is all about the details—grammar, punctuation, spelling, and syntax. A copyeditor will ensure that your manuscript is error-free and adheres to standard writing conventions.

- **Proofreading**: The final step before submission or publication is proofreading, where the editor checks for any remaining typos or minor errors. Proofreading is less about content and more about presentation and polish.

- **When to Hire an Editor**: You should hire an editor once you've done multiple rounds of self-editing and received feedback from beta readers. An editor will refine what you've already improved, so it's best to send them a manuscript that's as polished as possible.

4. Revising: Embrace the Process

Revision is an ongoing process that may require multiple rounds of editing. It's important to understand that revision doesn't mean failure—it's a crucial part of the writing journey. Here's how to approach the revision process without getting overwhelmed:

- **Focus on One Thing at a Time**: When revising, it's helpful to focus on one major element at a time. For example, you might start with revising plot structure, then move on to character development, and finally focus on sentence-level changes.

- **Don't Be Afraid to Make Big Changes**: Sometimes, revision requires cutting out entire scenes, adding new chapters, or rewriting significant portions of your manuscript. While it can be hard to part with sections you've worked hard on, remember that these changes will make your story stronger.

- **Track Your Progress**: Keep a log of your revisions to track what changes you've made and why. This helps you stay organized and ensures you don't accidentally undo important improvements during the editing process.

- **Know When to Stop**: While revision is crucial, at some point, you need to recognize when your manuscript is as polished as it can be. Perfection is an unrealistic goal, so aim for a manuscript that is the best representation of your story, knowing that future editors (especially if traditionally published) may still suggest changes.

Polishing your prose takes time, patience, and a willingness to be your own toughest critic. By mastering self-editing, seeking feedback from beta readers, and working with professional editors, you can transform your manuscript into a refined, publishable work. In the next section, we'll dive into the technical aspects of preparing your manuscript for submission, ensuring that it looks as professional as it reads.

Formatting Your Manuscript: Professional Presentation Essentials

Once you've polished your prose and feel confident about your manuscript, the next step is to make sure it's presented in a way that meets industry standards. Formatting your manuscript correctly is crucial for making a professional first impression with agents, publishers, or even when self-publishing. Poor formatting can distract from the quality of your writing, while a clean, polished presentation demonstrates that you're serious about your work and understand the publishing industry. In this section, we'll cover the essential elements of manuscript formatting, including how to prepare your document for submission and avoid common mistakes.

1. Basic Manuscript Formatting Guidelines

The publishing industry follows specific guidelines for manuscript formatting, and deviating from these standards can cause your submission to be overlooked. Here are the most widely accepted formatting rules:

- **Font and Size**: Use a standard, easy-to-read font like Times New Roman or Courier New, in 10-point or 12-point size. Avoid fancy fonts or creative styles—your manuscript should be clear and professional.

- **Line Spacing**: Double-space your manuscript. This provides ample room for editors or agents to make notes and helps with readability. Do not single-space or add extra spacing between paragraphs.

- **Margins**: Set your margins to 1 inch on all sides. This ensures that your text is evenly presented and provides room for comments or corrections from editors.

- **Indentation**: Use half-inch indents for the first line of each paragraph. Do not add extra spaces or tabs between paragraphs—consistent indentation is the industry standard.

- **Alignment**: Your text should be left-aligned, not justified. Justified text can create awkward spacing between words, making it harder to read.

- **Header**: Add a header to every page that includes your last name, the title of your book (or an abbreviated version), and the page number. This ensures that if your manuscript is printed or gets separated, it can easily be identified and put back together.

- **Page Numbers**: Page numbers should appear in the top right corner of each page, aligned with the header. Make sure the page numbering starts on the first page of your manuscript, not the title page.

2. Title Page Formatting

The title page is the first thing an agent, editor, or publisher will see, so it's important to format it professionally. Here's how to structure your title page:

- **Top Left Corner**: Include your name, address, phone number, and email in the top left corner of the page. This provides all the contact information needed to get in touch with you if they're interested in your manuscript.

- **Word Count**: On the right side of the title page, include your book's word count (rounded to the nearest hundred or thousand). For example, "Word Count: 75,000." This gives the publisher or agent an idea of the manuscript's length, which is important for marketability.

- **Title and Subtitle**: Center your book's title roughly halfway down the page in all caps. If your book has a subtitle, place it underneath the title in italics or regular capitalization.

- **Byline**: Below the title, include your byline (e.g., "by [Your Name]"). If you're using a pen name, this is where it should appear.

- **Genre or Category** (optional): Below your name, you can optionally include the genre or category of your book (e.g., "Science Fiction Novel" or "Memoir") to help clarify the book's market.

3. Chapter Headings and Scene Breaks

Each chapter in your manuscript should start on a new page, and the chapter headings should be formatted consistently to give your manuscript a professional appearance.

- **Chapter Headings**: Start each chapter on a new page, roughly one-third of the way down the page. Type "Chapter [Number]" in bold or all caps (e.g., "CHAPTER ONE"). You can also include a chapter title below the chapter number if your chapters are named (e.g., "CHAPTER ONE: The Beginning"). Ensure that chapter titles and headings are styled consistently throughout the manuscript.

- **Scene Breaks**: When you need to indicate a change in scene or time within a chapter, use a consistent symbol or marker to indicate the break. The most common is three asterisks (***) centered on a line. Make sure to leave one blank line above and below the scene break for clarity.

4. Submission-Specific Formatting

Different agents and publishers may have specific submission guidelines that deviate from standard formatting rules. Always check the submission guidelines on their websites before sending your manuscript, as failure to follow their rules can result in immediate rejection. Here's how to ensure your submission meets their standards:

- **Follow Submission Guidelines Exactly**: Each agent or publisher may have their own preferences for formatting and submission, so always read their guidelines carefully. They may request different font types, single-spacing, or specific file formats (e.g., .doc, .docx, or PDF). Be sure to adhere strictly to these rules to avoid being disqualified from consideration.

- **File Format**: Most agents and publishers prefer manuscripts to be submitted in Microsoft Word (.doc or .docx) format. Some may request PDFs, but Word files are usually the standard because they allow for easier editing and note-taking.

- **Electronic vs. Print Submissions**: If you're submitting electronically, ensure that your document is properly formatted for digital reading, but also check for any platform-specific quirks (such as how the document appears in a preview pane). For print submissions, make sure your document prints clearly and that the pagination remains consistent.

5. Common Formatting Mistakes to Avoid

To ensure your manuscript is professional and error-free, avoid these common formatting mistakes:

- **Inconsistent Fonts**: Stick to one font and size throughout the entire manuscript. Mixing fonts or changing sizes for emphasis can make your manuscript look unprofessional and difficult to read.

- **Overuse of Italics or Bold**: While italics are appropriate for emphasis or internal dialogue, using them excessively can distract from the narrative. Bold text is rarely used in manuscripts except for chapter headings.

- **Incorrect Scene Breaks**: Avoid simply leaving extra space between scenes without using a marker like asterisks (***) or a similar symbol. This can confuse the reader or editor, making it unclear when a new scene begins.

- **No Page Numbers**: Always include page numbers, especially if you're submitting a printed manuscript. Without page numbers, it's easy for your manuscript to become disorganized if printed or shuffled.

Properly formatting your manuscript is crucial to presenting your work in the most professional light possible. By following these industry standards and tailoring your submission to specific guidelines, you can increase your chances of making a strong first impression. In the next section, we'll explore how to craft a compelling cover letter and synopsis to accompany your manuscript submission, ensuring that your entire submission package stands out to agents and publishers.

Writing a Strong Cover Letter And Synopsis

Once your manuscript is polished and formatted, the next step is preparing the documents that will introduce your book to agents or publishers: your cover letter and synopsis. These are just as important as the manuscript itself because they provide a snapshot of your professionalism, the strength of your story, and why your book should stand out in a crowded market. A well-crafted cover letter and synopsis can grab the attention of an agent or editor, making them eager to dive into your manuscript.

In this section, we'll break down how to write an engaging cover letter and a concise, compelling synopsis that highlights the best aspects of your book.

1. Crafting an Engaging Cover Letter

Your cover letter is the first impression you'll make on an agent or publisher, so it needs to be clear, professional, and compelling. It should introduce your book, provide a brief overview of your qualifications, and explain why you're reaching out to this specific agent or publisher. Here's how to structure it:

- **Opening Paragraph: The Hook**

    o   Start by grabbing the reader's attention with a brief, engaging introduction. This could be a single line that gives a quick snapshot of your book's genre, premise, or unique selling point.

    o   Example: *"I'm seeking representation for my 80,000-word contemporary romance novel, 'A Second Chance at Paris,' where a high-powered New York executive unexpectedly finds herself rebuilding her life—and her heart—in the streets of the City of Light."*

- **Second Paragraph: The Book Summary**

    o   Provide a brief but compelling summary of your book's plot. Focus on the core of the story—its protagonist, their primary conflict, and what's at stake. Keep it concise (2-3 sentences) and aim to capture the essence of your story without going into excessive detail.

    o   Example: *"When Julia, a career-focused New Yorker, is passed over for a major promotion, she impulsively books a trip to Paris. What starts as a brief getaway turns into a year-long journey of self-discovery, as she rebuilds her life, reconnects with her estranged family, and opens her heart to love once more."*

- **Third Paragraph: Your Credentials**

    o   Briefly mention your writing background, relevant qualifications, or previous publishing experience. If you don't have formal writing credentials, you can include any personal experience that makes you the right person to write this story. Keep it relevant and succinct.

- o Example: *"I hold an MFA in Creative Writing from Columbia University, and my short stories have been published in several literary journals, including 'The New Yorker' and 'Ploughshares.'"*

- **Closing Paragraph: Why Them?**

  - o End by explaining why you're submitting to this particular agent or publisher. Show that you've done your research and are not just sending a generic query to multiple people. Mention something specific about their work or client list that resonated with you.

  - o Example: *"I'm reaching out to you specifically because of your representation of strong, character-driven romances like [Author's] 'The Paris Affair.' I believe my novel would be a great fit for your list."*

- **Sign Off**

  - o Conclude politely and professionally, thanking the agent or editor for their time. Be sure to include your contact information and a link to your website or social media profiles if relevant.

  - o Example: *"Thank you for considering my manuscript. I look forward to the possibility of working with you. Please don't hesitate to contact me at [email] or [phone number] for any further information."*

2. Writing a Compelling Synopsis

A synopsis is a concise summary of your book's entire plot, from beginning to end. Agents and publishers request synopses to gauge the structure, pacing, and overall storyline of your book, so it's crucial to write a clear, well-organized summary that gives them confidence in your narrative. Here's how to craft an effective synopsis:

- **Length and Structure**

  - Most agents and publishers request synopses that are between 1-2 pages in length, single-spaced, with clear breaks between paragraphs. Follow any specific guidelines provided by the agent or publisher (some may prefer shorter or longer synopses).

  - Unlike the blurb on the back of a book, the synopsis should include major plot points, character arcs, and the ending. Don't hold back spoilers—the purpose is to show the full story's progression and resolution.

- **Opening Paragraph: Introduce the Main Characters and Premise**

  - Start by introducing your protagonist(s) and setting up the main premise of the book. Focus on who they are, what they want, and the central conflict that drives the story.

  - Example: *"Julia Michaels, a 34-year-old high-powered executive in New York City, has always placed her career above all else. But when she's passed over for a major promotion, her carefully constructed world starts to crumble. On a whim, she buys a ticket to Paris, determined to escape the pressures of her life for a short time."*

- **The Middle: Develop the Plot and Character Arcs**

  - In the body of your synopsis, describe how the main plot unfolds. Highlight major events, turning points, and character growth. Focus on the cause-and-effect relationships between events and how they impact the protagonist's journey. Be concise but thorough—include the key conflicts and stakes without diving too deeply into minor subplots.

  - Example: *"In Paris, Julia reconnects with her estranged father and begins to understand the value of family and slowing down. She meets Marc, a charming Parisian chef, and despite her initial resistance to romance, the two fall in love. However, when an opportunity arises for her to return to New York and reclaim her career, Julia must decide between her old life and the new possibilities she's discovered."*

- **The Climax and Conclusion: Show How the Story Resolves**

  o   Make sure to include the climax and resolution of your story. The synopsis should make it clear how the central conflict is resolved, how your protagonist changes, and what the ultimate outcome of the story is.

  o   Example: *"In the end, Julia realizes that while her career is important, it's not the only thing that defines her. She turns down the job in New York and decides to stay in Paris, where she opens her own business and builds a new life with Marc. The novel closes with Julia embracing the balance she has found between her personal and professional life."*

- **Keep It Simple and Clear**

  o   Avoid getting bogged down with too many characters, subplots, or details. Focus on the main storyline and the character's journey. Use straightforward language—this is not the time to show off your prose style. Clarity is key.

- **Write in Third-Person, Present Tense**

  o   Even if your book is written in first-person or past tense, synopses should always be written in third-person, present tense. This is the industry standard, and it helps agents and publishers easily follow the narrative's progression.

3. Common Mistakes to Avoid

- **Being Too Vague**: In your synopsis, avoid being too general or mysterious. The agent or publisher needs to know exactly how your story unfolds. Phrases like "chaos ensues" or "secrets are revealed" don't give enough information about what actually happens.

- **Writing a Synopsis That's Too Long**: Stay within the requested length, usually one or two pages. An overly long synopsis can be a red flag that your plot isn't well-organized or that you've included too many unnecessary details.

- **Leaving Out the Ending**: It's tempting to leave the reader hanging, but this is a mistake when it comes to synopses. Agents and publishers need to know how your story resolves, so always include the ending.

A strong cover letter and synopsis are essential parts of your submission package. The cover letter introduces you and your work in a concise, professional manner, while the synopsis gives agents and publishers a clear understanding of your story's structure and appeal. With these documents in hand, you'll be well-prepared to submit your manuscript and increase your chances of success. In the next section, we'll explore the submission process itself, offering tips on how to navigate it with confidence and resilience.

Submitting Your Manuscript: Navigating the Process with Confidence

With your manuscript polished, formatted, and accompanied by a compelling cover letter and synopsis, you're ready to take the next step: submitting your work to agents or publishers. This process can be both exciting and nerve-wracking, but understanding how to approach it with confidence and professionalism can significantly improve your chances of success. In this section, we'll guide you through the submission process, from researching the right agents and publishers to handling rejections, ensuring that you stay focused and resilient.

1. Researching Agents and Publishers

Before you start submitting your manuscript, it's crucial to do your homework. Not every agent or publisher will be the right fit for your book, and submitting to the wrong ones can waste time and opportunities. Here's how to approach the research phase:

- **Identify Agents Who Represent Your Genre**: Agents typically specialize in specific genres, so it's important to find those who are actively seeking books in your category. Look for agents who represent books similar to yours in terms of style, tone, and subject matter.

- o Resources: Websites like QueryTracker, Manuscript Wish List, and Publisher's Marketplace are excellent resources for finding agents, viewing their preferences, and tracking their submissions.

- **Target Publishers Accepting Unsolicited Submissions**: If you're submitting directly to a publisher without an agent, be sure to identify publishers that accept unsolicited manuscripts. Some publishers only work with agents, while others, particularly small presses, may have open submission periods for unrepresented authors.

- **Read Submission Guidelines Carefully**: Each agent or publisher has specific submission guidelines that must be followed precisely. These might include word count limits, required documents (e.g., first three chapters, full manuscript, or a query letter), and preferred file formats. Failing to follow these guidelines can lead to immediate rejection.

- **Personalize Each Submission**: Tailor your submission package for each agent or publisher. Address your cover letter to the specific agent by name, and mention why you believe your book is a good fit for their list. Avoid generic submissions, as personalized ones demonstrate professionalism and attention to detail.

2. The Submission Process: Step by Step

Once you've done your research, it's time to start submitting your manuscript. Here's a step-by-step guide to help you navigate the process smoothly:

- **Step 1: Organize Your Submission Materials**: Make sure your cover letter, synopsis, and manuscript are formatted correctly and tailored to each agent or publisher. Double-check the submission guidelines to ensure you're including exactly what's requested.

- **Step 2: Send Your Submission**: Most submissions are now done electronically via email or through a submission platform. When submitting via email, include your cover letter in the body of the email, and attach the requested materials (manuscript, synopsis) in the format specified (e.g., .docx, PDF). For submission platforms, upload your materials directly as instructed.

- **Step 3: Track Your Submissions**: Keep a spreadsheet or list of the agents and publishers you've submitted to, along with the date, materials sent, and any responses you've received. This will help you stay organized and avoid submitting to the same place twice. You can also track how long it's been since you sent your submission to follow up if necessary.

- **Step 4: Be Patient**: The submission process can take time—sometimes weeks or even months. While waiting for a response, focus on other writing projects or tasks to keep your mind occupied. Resist the urge to follow up too soon, as most agents and publishers specify their response timeframes in their guidelines (often 6-12 weeks).

3. Handling Rejections with Resilience

Rejection is an inevitable part of the submission process, and even the most successful authors have faced multiple rejections. It's important to understand that rejection doesn't necessarily mean your book isn't good—it often comes down to factors like market trends, agent preferences, or a crowded inbox. Here's how to handle rejection with confidence:

- **Stay Positive**: Every rejection brings you closer to finding the right agent or publisher. Remember that publishing is subjective, and what doesn't resonate with one person may be exactly what another is looking for.

- **Learn from Feedback**: If you receive personalized feedback with your rejection, take it as a valuable learning opportunity. Agents don't always provide specific reasons for rejection, so when they do, it's worth considering their suggestions to strengthen your manuscript or query letter.

- **Don't Take It Personally**: Rejection is a normal part of every writer's journey, and it's important not to take it personally. Many great books were rejected multiple times before finding their home. Keep in mind that each rejection is just one step in the larger process.

- **Reevaluate and Revise (if needed)**: After several rejections, take a moment to reassess your submission materials. It may be worth revising your query letter, synopsis, or even certain parts of your manuscript if you're consistently getting rejections without feedback. However, don't feel pressured to revise after every rejection—trust your work and give it time.

4. What to Expect After Submission

Once your manuscript is out in the world, it's natural to wonder what happens next. Here's what you can expect as you wait for responses:

- **Positive Responses**: If an agent or publisher is interested in your manuscript, they may request a full manuscript after reviewing your initial submission (usually the first few chapters). This is a promising sign, but don't assume it's an automatic acceptance—there are still steps before an offer is made.

- **Offers of Representation**: If an agent decides to represent you, they'll make an offer of representation, which means they believe in your book and want to pitch it to publishers on your behalf. Be sure to ask questions and understand what the agent expects from you and how they plan to work on your behalf.

- **Multiple Offers**: If you receive offers from multiple agents or publishers, you'll need to carefully evaluate each one before making a decision. Consider their track record, communication style, enthusiasm for your book, and any contractual details. Don't be afraid to ask questions before making your final choice.

- **No Response**: Unfortunately, many agents or publishers only respond if they're interested, which means you may not hear back at all. Most guidelines specify this, so if a certain amount of time has passed (often 8-12 weeks) without a response, assume it's a pass and move on to the next submission.

Submitting your manuscript is both an exciting and challenging part of the publishing journey. By researching agents and publishers, following submission guidelines, and handling rejections with resilience, you can navigate the process confidently and professionally. Remember, every submission brings you closer to finding the right home for your book. With patience, persistence, and a polished manuscript, your literary dream is within reach.

Quick Tips and Recap

- **Polish Your Prose**: Before submitting, thoroughly revise and edit your manuscript. Use self-editing techniques, beta readers, and professional editors to refine your work.

- **Follow Industry-Standard Formatting**: Use a clear, professional font (Times New Roman, 12-point), double-space your manuscript, and include a proper header with your name, title, and page numbers.

- **Create a Compelling Cover Letter**: Personalize your cover letter to each agent or publisher, highlight the key elements of your book, and explain why you're submitting to them specifically.

- **Write a Clear, Concise Synopsis**: Your synopsis should summarize the entire plot, including the ending, in 1-2 pages. Focus on the main characters, conflict, and resolution.

- **Research Agents and Publishers**: Submit only to agents or publishers who represent your genre, and always follow their submission guidelines to the letter.

- **Track Your Submissions**: Keep a detailed record of where and when you've submitted, so you can manage follow-ups and avoid duplicate submissions.

- **Be Patient**: Publishing is a slow process. Don't follow up too soon and use the waiting time to focus on other projects.

- **Handle Rejection Gracefully**: Rejections are a normal part of the process. Learn from any feedback, stay positive, and keep submitting until you find the right fit.

By following these steps, you'll be well-prepared to submit your manuscript with confidence, increasing your chances of capturing the interest of agents and publishers.

Copyright Registration: Securing Your Work Legally

"Securing your work through copyright registration is not just a legal
formality; it's a critical step in safeguarding your creative investments
and ensuring your rights are protected in a competitive marketplace."
— RUTH BADER GINSBURG, ASSOCIATE JUSTICE
OF THE U. S. SUPREME COURT

Chapter Seven, "Copyright Registration: Securing Your Work Legally," is
where we don our legal caps (they're less stylish than berets, but far more
useful) and get down to the business of protection. It's not enough to create; you
must also defend! Consider this the fortress-building stage of your publishing
journey, where we lay down the legal groundwork to shield your creative empire
from marauders and copycats alike.

Think of copyright registration as putting a giant, "No Trespassing" sign on your intellectual property. It's like declaring to the world, "Yes, I made this, and yes, you'll hear from my lawyer if you try to claim otherwise!" We'll navigate the riveting world of forms, filings, and the occasional caffeine-fueled late-night submission dash. By the end, you'll not only have airtight legal protection but the peace of mind that allows you to say, "Go ahead, make my day," to anyone thinking of infringing on your creative turf.

Strap in, because we're about to turn your work into a legal fortress, impervious to the slings and arrows of outrageous fortune—or at least those of opportunistic plagiarists.

What Is Copyright and Why Is It Important?

Copyright is the legal foundation that protects your creative work from being used or reproduced without your permission. As an author, copyright gives you ownership over the original works you create, whether it's a novel, short story, poem, or any other literary creation. While copyright is often thought of as a technical legal concept, at its heart, it's a powerful tool that ensures your work remains under your control and enables you to reap the benefits of your creativity.

In this section, we'll dive into what copyright is, how it works, and why it's crucial for authors to understand and leverage its protection.

1. What Is Copyright?

Copyright is a form of intellectual property protection granted to authors, creators, and artists for their original works. It gives the copyright holder exclusive rights over their work, allowing them to:

- **Reproduce the work** (make copies or distribute it in any form).

- **Distribute copies** to the public by sale, transfer, or rental.

- **Perform or display the work** publicly (for performance-based works, like plays or music).

- **Create derivative works** based on the original (such as adaptations into films or translations into other languages).

- **License the work** to others for various uses, such as publishing or adapting it into another format.

For authors, this means that your book or any other written material you create is automatically protected by copyright the moment it is "fixed in a tangible form"—whether that's a Word document on your computer, a printed manuscript, or even a digital file. In other words, as soon as your story exists in a recorded form, it is legally copyrighted.

2. Why Is Copyright Important for Authors?

Copyright protection is crucial for authors because it allows you to maintain control over how your work is used, distributed, and adapted. Without copyright, your creative work could be freely copied, sold, or modified by others without your permission. Here's why copyright is so important:

- **Ownership of Your Creation**: Copyright establishes you as the rightful owner of your work, giving you the legal authority to control how it's used. You can decide who gets to publish it, how it's marketed, and whether it can be adapted into other formats.

- **Exclusive Rights to Profit**: Copyright ensures that you, as the creator, have the exclusive right to profit from your work. Whether you're selling books, licensing film rights, or adapting your book into audiobooks or merchandise, copyright protects your ability to generate income from your intellectual property.

- **Preventing Unauthorized Use**: Copyright gives you the power to prevent others from using your work without permission. If someone tries to copy, sell, or adapt your book without your approval, copyright law provides the framework to take legal action and stop them.

- **Building a Legacy**: Copyright protection extends beyond your lifetime. In most jurisdictions, copyright lasts for the author's lifetime plus an additional 70 years. This means your heirs and beneficiaries can continue to benefit from the work long after your passing, creating a lasting legacy for your creative contributions.

3. What Does Copyright Protect?

It's important to understand that copyright protects the expression of an idea, not the idea itself. For example, if your book is about a detective solving a crime, the general concept of a crime-solving detective isn't protected by copyright. What is protected, however, is the specific way you've expressed that idea: the characters you've created, the plot you've developed, the dialogue, and the unique twists and turns of your story.

Copyright protects:

- **Written works** (novels, short stories, articles, etc.).

- **Dramatic works** (plays, scripts, etc.).

- **Artistic works** (illustrations, maps, etc., included in the book).

- **Derivatives of these works** (film adaptations, translations, or sequels).

However, copyright does not protect:

- **Ideas** (general concepts or themes).

- **Facts** (historical events, data).

- **Titles or names** (though these may be protected by trademarks, not copyright).

4. The Limits of Copyright Protection

While copyright offers broad protection, it's not absolute. There are certain exceptions and limitations, such as fair use laws, which allow for limited use of copyrighted material without the author's permission. Fair use might include activities like criticism, commentary, parody, or educational use. However, these exceptions are narrow, and it's important for authors to understand that they still maintain control over most uses of their work.

Understanding copyright is the first step in protecting your creative work. By securing your rights as the owner of your intellectual property, you not only safeguard your ability to profit from your book but also establish a legal framework that allows you to take action if someone tries to infringe on your work. In the next section, we'll explore the benefits of formally registering your copyright and how it strengthens your legal position as an author.

The Benefits of Formal Copyright Registration

While copyright protection is automatically granted the moment your work is fixed in a tangible form, formally registering your copyright provides significant additional benefits that can strengthen your legal position and safeguard your rights as an author. Copyright registration is a relatively simple process that offers robust protection, giving you peace of mind as you navigate the publishing world.

In this section, we'll explore why formal copyright registration is a smart move and the advantages it brings, from enhanced legal protection to maximizing your ability to enforce your rights.

1. Public Record of Ownership

When you register your copyright, it creates an official public record of your ownership. This means that if there's ever a dispute over who owns the rights to your work, the registration serves as legal proof that you are the original creator and rightful copyright holder.

- **Why This Matters**: Without a registered copyright, it could be harder to prove ownership in the event of a conflict. Having a formal registration in place makes it much easier to resolve disputes and ensures that you're recognized as the legal owner of the work from the date of registration.

- **Example**: If someone claims they wrote a similar story and tries to assert ownership over your work, your registered copyright acts as indisputable evidence that you are the rightful creator.

2. Eligibility to Sue for Infringement

While you automatically hold copyright from the moment your work is created, you cannot sue for copyright infringement unless your copyright is formally registered. If someone uses your work without permission—whether by copying, selling, or distributing it—you need a registered copyright to pursue legal action.

- **Why This Matters**: Without a registered copyright, you lose the ability to take legal action against infringers, leaving you vulnerable to unauthorized use of your work. If your copyright is registered, you can file a lawsuit and seek damages or an injunction to stop the infringement.

- **Example**: Suppose a website illegally distributes copies of your book without your consent. If your copyright is registered, you can sue the infringing party, demand they cease distribution, and seek compensation for any financial losses.

3. Statutory Damages and Attorney's Fees

One of the most significant benefits of copyright registration is the ability to seek statutory damages and attorney's fees in an infringement lawsuit. If your copyright is registered before the infringement occurs (or within a certain time frame after publication), you are eligible to claim statutory damages—set amounts of money—without needing to prove actual financial harm.

- **Why This Matters**: Proving the exact financial loss caused by copyright infringement can be challenging. Statutory damages allow you to receive compensation without the burden of proving the exact amount of lost revenue. Additionally, you can have your legal fees covered, making it more affordable to take action against infringers.

- **Example**: If a person illegally copies and sells your book, and you sue them with a registered copyright, you could be awarded statutory damages even if it's difficult to calculate how much money you lost from the unauthorized sales. On top of that, the infringer may be required to pay your legal fees, reducing your financial burden.

4. International Protection

Many countries around the world are signatories to international treaties, such as the Berne Convention, which recognize and protect copyrighted works across borders. If you register your copyright in your home country, that registration may be recognized internationally, giving you broader protection.

- **Why This Matters**: In an increasingly global marketplace, your book may be distributed or adapted in other countries, potentially exposing you to international infringement. Having a registered copyright helps protect your work not only in your country but also in international markets.

- **Example**: If someone in another country translates and publishes your book without permission, your registered copyright can be used to assert your rights in that foreign jurisdiction, depending on the country's copyright laws and treaties.

5. Deterrence Against Infringement

Formal copyright registration acts as a deterrent to would-be infringers. When your copyright is registered, it signals to others that you've taken steps to legally protect your work and are prepared to enforce your rights. This can discourage individuals or companies from attempting to use your work without permission.

- **Why This Matters**: If someone sees that your work is registered with a copyright, they're less likely to risk using it without permission because they know you can easily take legal action. Registration strengthens your position and makes others think twice before infringing.

- **Example**: If you display a copyright notice on your book (e.g., "© 2024 [Your Name]. All rights reserved. Registered with the U.S. Copyright Office"), it serves as a clear warning that you've taken legal steps to protect your work, reducing the likelihood of infringement.

6. Peace of Mind

Finally, registering your copyright provides peace of mind. Knowing that you've taken the necessary legal steps to protect your work allows you to focus on your writing and publishing journey without constantly worrying about theft or unauthorized use.

- **Why This Matters**: Copyright infringement can be a stressful and time-consuming issue to deal with. By registering your copyright, you establish a solid legal foundation that can protect your work, giving you the confidence to pursue publishing, marketing, and distribution without fear of losing control over your intellectual property.

- **Example**: Whether you're submitting your manuscript to publishers, self-publishing, or licensing it for film adaptation, you can proceed confidently, knowing that your work is legally protected.

In summary, formal copyright registration is a crucial step in securing your rights as an author. From providing legal proof of ownership to enabling you to sue for infringement and claim statutory damages, registration strengthens your position and helps protect your work from unauthorized use. In the next section, we'll walk through the step-by-step process of registering your copyright, ensuring you're fully equipped to defend your intellectual property.

How to Register Your Copyright: Step-by-Step Guide

Registering your copyright is a straightforward process that provides essential legal protection for your work. While copyright is automatically granted the moment your work is created, formal registration adds a layer of protection that's crucial if you ever need to enforce your rights. In this section, we'll walk through the step-by-step process of registering your copyright, making sure your work is legally secured.

1. Prepare Your Materials

Before you begin the registration process, it's important to gather all the necessary materials related to your work. Here's what you'll need:

- **The Final Version of Your Manuscript**: Copyright protects the specific form of your work, so you'll want to register the final version of your manuscript. Whether it's a novel, short story collection, or nonfiction work, make sure it's in the state you intend to publish or distribute.

- **Title and Description**: You'll need to provide the title of your work and a brief description (usually no more than a sentence or two) when submitting the copyright registration.

- **Your Personal Information**: The registration will require your full name, mailing address, and email. If you're registering the work under a pen name or a business entity, you'll need that information as well.

- **Payment Method**: Registration fees are required to process your copyright application. Have a valid payment method ready (credit card, debit card, or PayPal).

2. Choose Your Method of Registration

There are two main ways to register your copyright: online or through a paper application. The online method is faster, more efficient, and generally less expensive, so it's the preferred method for most authors. Here's how to choose:

- **Online Registration**: This is done through the U.S. Copyright Office's eCO system (or your country's equivalent system, such as the UK's Intellectual Property Office). Online registration is quicker, with lower fees, and provides an easy-to-use interface to submit your materials.

  o Fee: $45 (subject to change).

  o Processing Time: Typically 3-8 months.

- **Paper Registration**: You can also register by mail using Form TX, which is specifically for literary works. While paper registration is still an option, it is more expensive, and processing times can be significantly longer.

  o Fee: $125 (subject to change).

  o Processing Time: 10-12 months.

Tip: For most authors, online registration is recommended due to its speed and lower cost. However, if you prefer physical paperwork or are registering a complex work, you may opt for the paper application.

3. Complete the Online Registration Form

If you choose the online method, follow these steps to complete your copyright registration:

- **Step 1: Create an Account**: Go to the U.S. Copyright Office's eCO website (https://eco.copyright.gov/) and create an account if you don't already have one. Once you've created your account, log in to start the registration process.

- **Step 2: Select the Type of Work**: You'll be prompted to choose the type of work you're registering. Since you're an author, you'll likely select "Literary Works" from the list. This category covers novels, short stories, articles, essays, poetry, and other written materials.

- **Step 3: Provide Your Title and Information**: Enter the title of your work and any additional information requested (e.g., subtitle, volume number if it's part of a series). Be concise but accurate in describing the work.

- **Step 4: Enter the Author Information**: Provide your personal information, including your legal name and, if applicable, your pen name or pseudonym. If the work was created by more than one author, you'll need to include information about all co-authors.

- **Step 5: Specify Publication Status**: Indicate whether your work has been published or is still unpublished. For copyright purposes, "publication" refers to the distribution of copies to the public. If your work is already published, provide the date and location of the first publication.

- **Step 6: Claim Rights**: Specify which rights you're claiming in your work. This is usually straightforward—most authors will claim all rights to their original work. If there are any exclusions (such as parts of the work being previously published or based on pre-existing material), you'll need to indicate that here.

- **Step 7: Review and Submit**: Review all the information you've entered for accuracy. Once you're satisfied that everything is correct, you'll be prompted to submit your application and pay the required fee.

4. Upload or Send Your Manuscript

After submitting your application, you'll need to provide a copy of your manuscript to complete the registration process. Here's how to do it:

- **For Online Submissions**: Upload your manuscript directly through the eCO system. The system will accept most standard formats, including

PDF, **Word**, or **text files**. Be sure to upload the final version of your manuscript, as this is the version that will be protected by copyright.

- **For Paper Submissions**: If you're registering by mail, you'll need to send a physical copy of your manuscript along with your Form TX. Be sure to follow the instructions carefully, as the U.S. Copyright Office requires specific formats for certain types of submissions (e.g., printed books vs. electronic works).

5. Pay the Fee and Confirm Submission

Once you've uploaded your manuscript or submitted your physical copy, you'll need to pay the registration fee to complete the process. After payment, you'll receive a confirmation of your submission, along with an official case number. Keep this confirmation for your records—it serves as proof that your work is in the process of being registered.

6. Wait for Approval

After you've submitted your application and manuscript, you'll need to wait for the Copyright Office to review and approve your registration. The approval process can take several months, depending on whether you submitted your application online or by mail.

Once your application is processed, you'll receive a Certificate of Registration, which serves as official proof that your work is copyrighted. This certificate will include the registration number, date of registration, and details about your work.

7. Display Your Copyright Notice

Although not required by law, displaying a copyright notice on your book or manuscript is a good practice. A standard copyright notice includes the following elements:

- **The © symbol** (or the word "Copyright").
- **The year of publication**.
- **Your name (or your pen name)**.

Example: © *2024 [Your Name]. All rights reserved.*

Including this notice serves as a deterrent to potential infringers and clearly states that your work is protected.

Registering your copyright is a simple yet powerful way to legally protect your creative work. By following these steps, you ensure that your work is protected from unauthorized use and that you have the legal tools needed to enforce your rights if necessary. In the next section, we'll discuss how to handle copyright infringement and what actions you can take to defend your work if someone tries to use it without permission.

Handling Copyright Infringement: Defending Your Rights

Even with copyright registration in place, there's always the possibility that someone may infringe upon your rights by using your work without permission. Copyright infringement occurs when someone reproduces, distributes, or adapts your work without your authorization, whether it's copying entire sections, selling pirated versions, or creating unauthorized adaptations. If you discover that your work has been infringed upon, it's important to know how to protect your rights and take action.

In this section, we'll walk through the steps you should take to handle copyright infringement and ensure that your intellectual property is defended.

1. Identifying Copyright Infringement

The first step in defending your rights is recognizing when copyright infringement has occurred. Copyright infringement can take many forms, including:

- **Unauthorized Reproduction**: Someone copies part or all of your work and distributes it without permission (e.g., pirated eBooks or printed copies sold on unauthorized platforms).

- **Public Display or Performance**: Your work is performed or displayed publicly without authorization (e.g., a dramatic reading or public performance of your story).

- **Derivative Works**: Someone adapts your work into another form, such as a movie, audiobook, or translation, without obtaining the proper licensing from you.

- **Plagiarism**: Someone claims your work as their own by copying sections or ideas without crediting you as the original author.

If you come across any of these situations, it's essential to act quickly and take appropriate steps to stop the unauthorized use.

2. Document the Infringement

Before taking any action, you need to gather evidence of the infringement. Documentation is crucial if you plan to take legal steps, as it provides the proof needed to assert your rights.

- **Take Screenshots or Copies**: If your work is being shared or sold on unauthorized websites, take screenshots or download copies of the infringing material. Make sure to capture the URLs, dates, and any other relevant information.

- **Save Correspondence**: If you've communicated with the infringing party (such as receiving an email about the unauthorized use), save all correspondence as evidence.

- **Keep Sales Records**: If the infringement involves selling pirated copies of your work, record where the sales occurred, including platforms, dates, and any information about the seller.

Having detailed evidence strengthens your case if you need to escalate the situation.

3. Issue a Cease-and-Desist Letter

A cease-and-desist letter is often the first step in stopping copyright infringement. This formal letter informs the infringer that they are violating your copyright and demands that they stop the unauthorized use immediately. Here's what the letter should include:

- **Your Ownership of the Copyright**: Clearly state that you are the owner of the work and that it is protected by copyright. Reference your registration if applicable (e.g., "My work is registered with the U.S. Copyright Office under registration number XXXXXX").

- **Details of the Infringement**: Provide a clear description of how the infringer is using your work without permission, whether it's copying, selling, or adapting it.

- **Demand for Action**: Specify what you want the infringer to do—usually, this involves stopping the use, removing the material from public view, and ceasing distribution.

- **Deadline**: Give the infringer a specific timeframe to comply with your demands (typically 10 to 14 days).

- **Legal Consequences**: Warn that failure to comply will result in legal action, including lawsuits for copyright infringement.

If the infringer complies with the cease-and-desist letter, you may be able to resolve the issue without needing to go further.

4. File a DMCA Takedown Notice

If your work has been illegally posted online (such as on a website, blog, or social media platform), you can file a Digital Millennium Copyright Act (DMCA) takedown notice to have the infringing material removed. The DMCA is a U.S. law that protects copyright holders by providing a streamlined process for removing unauthorized content from the internet.

- **How to File a DMCA Notice**: Most websites and platforms (such as Amazon, YouTube, or Facebook) have a process in place for filing a DMCA takedown request. Look for a "copyright" or "report infringement" link on the platform, and follow their instructions.

- **What to Include in Your Notice**: Your DMCA notice should include your contact information, a description of the copyrighted work, the location of the infringing material (URL or specific link), and a statement confirming that the material is being used without permission.

- **Timeframe for Removal**: Upon receiving a valid DMCA notice, the platform or website must remove the infringing material promptly. In most cases, the content is taken down within a few days.

DMCA takedown notices are an effective way to quickly remove infringing content from the internet.

5. Seek Legal Action for Damages

If the infringer does not comply with your cease-and-desist letter or DMCA takedown notice, or if the infringement has caused significant financial harm, you may need to escalate the situation by pursuing legal action. Here's how to move forward with a lawsuit:

- **Consult a Copyright Attorney**: Hiring an attorney who specializes in copyright law can help you navigate the complexities of filing a lawsuit. They will assess the situation, review your evidence, and advise you on the best course of action.

- **File a Lawsuit**: With your attorney's help, you can file a lawsuit against the infringer in federal court (or your country's equivalent). If your copyright is registered, you'll be able to seek statutory damages and attorney's feesas part of the lawsuit.

- **Seek Damages or Injunctive Relief**: You can seek compensation for the financial losses caused by the infringement or request an injunction, which is a court order that forces the infringer to stop using your work immediately.

- **Consider Settlement**: In some cases, the infringer may offer a settlement to avoid going to trial. Your attorney can negotiate favorable terms, such as financial compensation and the removal of all infringing content.

Lawsuits can be time-consuming and expensive, but they may be necessary if the infringement is significant and the infringer refuses to cooperate.

6. Preventing Future Infringement

While dealing with copyright infringement is never pleasant, there are steps you can take to prevent future unauthorized use of your work:

- **Register Your Copyright Early**: As discussed earlier, registering your copyright early on strengthens your legal position and gives you the ability to take action quickly in the event of infringement.

- **Display a Copyright Notice**: Including a copyright notice on your work (e.g., "© 2024 [Your Name]. All rights reserved.") makes it clear that your work is protected by copyright and deters potential infringers.

- **Use Digital Rights Management (DRM)**: For eBooks and digital content, consider using DRM tools to prevent unauthorized copying or sharing. Many online platforms offer built-in DRM options to protect digital files.

- **Monitor for Infringement**: Regularly search for your work online to catch unauthorized use early. Set up Google Alerts for your book's title or key excerpts to receive notifications if your work is being mentioned or shared online without permission.

Dealing with copyright infringement can be a frustrating experience, but by knowing how to respond and defend your rights, you can protect your work and hold infringers accountable. From issuing cease-and-desist letters to filing DMCA takedown notices or pursuing legal action, you have several tools at your disposal to stop unauthorized use and recover damages if necessary. With your copyright registered and a solid plan in place, you can confidently defend your creative work and ensure it remains under your control.

Quick Tips and Recap

- **Copyright Protection is Automatic**: Your work is copyrighted the moment it's created in a fixed form, but formal registration adds important legal benefits.

- **Register Your Copyright**: Formal registration provides a public record of ownership and allows you to sue for damages if your work is infringed upon.

- **Statutory Damages and Legal Fees**: Registered copyright holders can seek statutory damages and attorney's fees in an infringement lawsuit, even without proving actual financial loss.

- **Use a Cease-and-Desist Letter**: If someone is infringing on your work, issue a cease-and-desist letter demanding they stop the unauthorized use.

- **File a DMCA Takedown Notice**: For online infringements, use the DMCA to have unauthorized copies of your work removed from websites.

- **Document Infringement**: Always gather evidence of infringement (screenshots, URLs, copies) to strengthen your case if legal action is needed.

- **Consult a Copyright Attorney**: If infringement persists, seek legal advice to explore your options for pursuing compensation or stopping the unauthorized use.

- **Monitor for Unauthorized Use**: Regularly check for online misuse of your work and set up Google Alerts to catch unauthorized distributions early.

- **Use a Copyright Notice**: While not required, displaying a copyright notice helps deter potential infringers and clarifies that your work is protected.

By taking these proactive steps, you can defend your intellectual property and protect your creative rights from unauthorized use.

Marketing and Promotion: Spreading the Word

"Effective marketing and promotion go beyond spreading the word;
they involve crafting messages that resonate deeply, creating
meaningful connections with your audience and turning interest into
action." — SETH GODIN, AUTHOR AND MARKETING EXPERT

Welcome to Chapter Eight, "Marketing and Promotion: Spreading the Word," where your book goes from being a well-kept secret to the talk of the town. Think of this as the debutante ball for your manuscript, where it's all about making the right impressions with the right people at the right time.

Here, we dive into the exhilarating world of book launches, press releases, and social media campaigns, turning each page of your marketing playbook into a strategic step towards bestseller status. We'll explore the alchemy of turning buzz into gold, using everything from traditional book signings to the viral potential of digital platforms. You'll learn how to harness the power of influencers, captivate audiences with compelling book trailers, and perhaps even dabble in the dark arts of guerrilla marketing.

By the end of this chapter, you won't just be ready to market your book; you'll be poised to make it a phenomenon. So sharpen your hashtags, polish your press pitches, and get ready to put your book on the map. The literary world won't know what hit it!

Building a Book Marketing Plan: Setting the Foundation

Marketing your book effectively starts with a solid, well-thought-out plan. Just like writing a manuscript, promoting your book requires strategy, structure, and clear goals. A book marketing plan is your roadmap to success, guiding you through the process of generating buzz, reaching your target audience, and maximizing your book's visibility. In this section, we'll cover how to build a comprehensive marketing plan that sets you up for success from the very start.

1. Define Your Goals

Before diving into marketing tactics, it's essential to identify what you want to achieve. Your goals will shape your entire marketing strategy and help you stay focused on what's important. Common goals might include:

- **Boosting Book Sales**: Whether it's your debut novel or the latest in a series, driving sales is often the primary goal of any book marketing campaign.

- **Building Brand Awareness**: Especially for new authors, establishing your presence and making your name known in the literary community can be just as important as selling books.

- **Growing an Audience**: If you're aiming to build a loyal fan base or attract readers for future projects, focusing on long-term engagement can be a key goal.

- **Landing Media Coverage**: Gaining attention from media outlets, blogs, and book reviewers can help establish credibility and generate buzz around your book.

2. Identify Your Target Audience

Knowing who you're marketing to is critical to the success of your campaign. Your target audience consists of the readers who are most likely to be interested in your book. By identifying your audience, you can tailor your marketing efforts to reach them more effectively. Ask yourself these questions to help define your audience:

- **Who are my ideal readers?**: Think about the age, gender, interests, and reading habits of the people who are most likely to enjoy your book. Are they young adults, professionals, parents, or retirees?

- **What genres and topics interest them?**: Consider the themes, genres, and subjects your target audience is drawn to. For example, if your book is a dystopian novel, your audience might enjoy similar genres like sci-fi or fantasy.

- **Where do they spend time online?**: Identifying where your audience hangs out—whether it's on social media, book blogs, forums, or Goodreads—will help you decide which platforms to focus your marketing on.

Once you've identified your audience, create a reader persona that represents your ideal reader. This persona will help guide your marketing decisions and ensure your messaging resonates with the right people.

3. Set a Budget and Timeline

Your marketing plan needs to be realistic, which means considering both your budget and the timeline leading up to your book's release (or any promotional events). Start by establishing a budget for various marketing activities:

- **Advertising**: This includes social media ads, Google ads, or Amazon ads, which can boost your book's visibility online.

- **Promotional Materials**: Things like book covers, bookmarks, business cards, or book trailers require an investment in design and production.

- **PR and Media Outreach**: If you're hiring a publicist, running press releases, or sending out advance review copies (ARCs), you'll need to account for those costs as well.

Once you've outlined your budget, create a timeline for key marketing milestones. This might include:

- **Pre-launch activities**: Building anticipation for your book before it's released, such as revealing the book cover, launching a pre-order campaign, or running a giveaway.

- **Launch day**: Coordinating events like a virtual book launch, social media blitz, or signing events.

- **Post-launch**: Sustaining momentum with ongoing social media content, author interviews, blog tours, and more.

A well-planned timeline ensures that you're promoting your book consistently and at the right moments to capture readers' attention.

4. Define Your Unique Selling Points (USPs)

What makes your book stand out from the rest? Defining your unique selling points (USPs) will help you craft compelling marketing messages and highlight why readers should choose your book. Your USPs should answer these questions:

- **What sets your book apart?**: Whether it's a unique plot twist, an unconventional protagonist, or a fresh take on a popular genre, think about what makes your book different from others in the market.

- **Why should readers care?**: Focus on the emotional or intellectual connection your book offers. Does it provide readers with an escape, a relatable experience, or thought-provoking ideas? Tapping into the emotional core of your story will make your marketing more effective.

- **What's your personal story?**: Sometimes, your personal story as an author can be a major selling point. If your journey to becoming an author is inspiring or if your background lends credibility to the themes of your book, include that in your marketing materials.

By defining your USPs, you'll be able to craft stronger messaging across your social media posts, website, and press materials, making your book more attractive to potential readers.

5. Track Your Success and Adjust

Your marketing plan should be a living document—something you regularly update and adjust based on what's working and what's not. Establish key performance indicators (KPIs) to measure the success of your marketing efforts. These might include:

- **Book sales**: Tracking daily or weekly sales figures.

- **Social media engagement**: Monitoring likes, shares, comments, and follower growth on your social media platforms.

- **Website traffic**: Keeping track of how many people visit your author website and where they're coming from (e.g., social media, Google searches).

- **Newsletter sign-ups**: Measuring how many people are subscribing to your email list.

By regularly reviewing your KPIs, you'll be able to identify which strategies are most effective and where you might need to pivot. For example, if you notice that Instagram ads are driving more traffic than Twitter posts, you might allocate more of your budget to Instagram moving forward.

Building a book marketing plan is the foundation of a successful promotional campaign. By defining your goals, identifying your audience, setting a budget, and tracking your progress, you can craft a strategic and organized approach that maximizes your book's visibility and impact. In the next section, we'll explore how to leverage social media and digital platforms to amplify your marketing efforts and engage with readers around the world.

Leveraging Social Media and Digital Platforms

In today's digital age, social media and online platforms are powerful tools for promoting your book and building your author brand. With millions of potential readers spending hours on social networks, these platforms offer a direct line to your target audience. By leveraging social media effectively, you can create buzz, generate engagement, and reach a wider readership—all from the comfort of your laptop. In this section, we'll explore how to use social media and digital platforms to your advantage, turning likes, shares, and follows into book sales.

1. Choosing the Right Platforms

Not all social media platforms are created equal, and it's important to focus your efforts on the ones that align with your book's audience. Here's a breakdown of the major platforms and how they can serve your marketing goals:

- **Instagram**: A visually driven platform that's perfect for sharing book covers, character art, behind-the-scenes peeks, and announcements. Instagram's large book-loving community, known as Bookstagram, is highly active and provides excellent opportunities to connect with influencers and readers. Use hashtags like #Bookstagram, #AmReading, and #BookLover to increase your reach.

- **Twitter**: Twitter is all about conversation and engagement. It's ideal for connecting with readers, other authors, and industry professionals in real time. Use Twitter to share quick updates, participate in trending conversations, and join communities like #WritersCommunity or #AmWriting. Twitter is also great for book release countdowns and interacting with fans.

- **Facebook**: Facebook offers a more personal approach, with features like author pages, groups, and events. It's a good platform for building an author community, running targeted ads, and hosting virtual book launches or Q&A sessions. Facebook Groups for readers and writers can also help you connect with niche audiences.

- **TikTok**: TikTok's BookTok community has become a major influence in the publishing world. If you're comfortable with creating short-form videos, TikTok can be a goldmine for reaching younger readers and promoting your book in fun, creative ways. Share teasers, character profiles, or even behind-the-scenes writing vlogs.

- **Goodreads**: While not a traditional social media platform, Goodreads is essential for authors. It's a place where readers go to discover, review, and discuss books. By creating an author profile, you can interact with readers directly, run Goodreads giveaways, and use the platform's ad options to target avid readers.

Tip: You don't need to be on every platform—focus on one or two that best align with your strengths and where your readers are most active.

2. Creating Engaging Content

Effective social media marketing isn't just about posting for the sake of posting—it's about creating content that engages your audience and sparks conversation. Here are some ideas to help you create compelling content:

- **Book Teasers**: Share quotes, excerpts, or sneak peeks from your book to build anticipation before its release. This can be in the form of a graphic with a quote or a short video where you read a passage from the book.

- **Cover Reveals**: A book's cover is often one of its biggest selling points. A cover reveal on social media can be an exciting way to generate buzz before the book's release. Create a countdown or collaborate with influencers to help share your cover across platforms.

- **Behind-the-Scenes Content**: Take your audience behind the curtain by sharing your writing process, workspace, or even the inspiration behind your story. Readers love to feel connected to the author, so offering insights into your creative journey can build a loyal following.

- **Character Profiles and Artwork**: Introduce your characters to the world by sharing character profiles or commissioning fan art. If you have an artist's rendering of your characters, post it on Instagram or Twitter and ask your audience which character is their favorite.

- **Engage with Your Audience**: Social media is a two-way street, so be sure to respond to comments, ask questions, and interact with readers. You could run a poll about favorite book genres, host a Q&A session, or ask your followers for their thoughts on a specific book-related topic.

3. Running Social Media Ads

While organic reach on social media is important, running paid ads can help you get your book in front of a larger audience. Social media platforms like Facebook, Instagram, and Twitter offer targeted advertising options that allow you to reach people based on their interests, demographics, and behavior.

- **Facebook and Instagram Ads**: These platforms offer a powerful ad manager that lets you create ads targeting specific audiences, such as people who love reading in your genre or follow similar authors. You can run ads to promote your book launch, a special discount, or even a giveaway.

- **Boosted Posts**: If you don't want to create a full ad campaign, you can boost an existing post on Facebook or Instagram to increase its visibility. This is a simple way to get more eyes on your content, particularly during important milestones like cover reveals or book releases.

- **Twitter Ads**: Twitter also offers ad options, such as promoted tweets and promoted accounts, to help grow your following and increase engagement. You can use these ads to highlight a major announcement or promote a new blog post, book review, or feature.

Tip: When running social media ads, make sure to have clear calls to action (CTAs). Whether it's driving traffic to your Amazon page, getting people to sign up for your newsletter, or increasing engagement, a strong CTA will ensure your ad has a specific, measurable goal.

4. Collaborating with Influencers and Bloggers

Working with influencers, book bloggers, and BookTubers (YouTubers who focus on books) can be a game-changer for your marketing campaign. Influencers have established followings that trust their opinions, so a recommendation or review from them can significantly boost your book's visibility. Here's how to collaborate with them:

- **Research Influencers in Your Niche**: Look for influencers who are passionate about your genre and have an engaged following. Platforms like Instagram, TikTok, and YouTube are great places to find influencers who regularly feature book reviews or recommendations.

- **Reach Out with a Personalized Pitch**: When approaching influencers or bloggers, send a personalized message explaining why your book would be a good fit for their audience. Offer them an advance review copy (ARC) or free copy of your book, and explain how they can benefit from working with you (e.g., giveaways, affiliate commissions, or cross-promotion).

- **Host Blog Tours**: A blog tour involves getting multiple book bloggers to feature your book on their blogs over a set period of time. This could include interviews, book reviews, guest posts, or even giveaways. Blog tours help build sustained visibility for your book and provide valuable exposure to different reader communities.

5. Building an Email List

While social media is a fantastic way to engage with your audience, an email list gives you direct access to readers without relying on platform algorithms. By collecting email addresses from interested readers, you can build a long-term relationship through newsletters and special offers. Here's how to get started:

- **Offer a Free Incentive**: Give readers a reason to sign up for your email list by offering something of value—such as a free chapter, short story, or discount. Make sure to include a prominent signup form on your website and social media profiles.

- **Send Regular Updates**: Use your email list to send regular updates about your writing journey, book releases, promotions, and behind-the-scenes content. Keep your emails engaging and value-driven, so readers look forward to hearing from you.

- **Segment Your List**: Over time, you may want to segment your email list based on reader preferences (e.g., genre, frequency of updates) to ensure your messaging is as targeted as possible.

Leveraging social media and digital platforms is a vital part of modern book marketing. By choosing the right platforms, creating engaging content, and collaborating with influencers, you can build a loyal following and amplify your book's visibility. In the next section, we'll dive into how to find the right balance between traditional and digital marketing to create a comprehensive promotional strategy that maximizes your book's potential.

Traditional vs. Digital Marketing: Finding the Balance

In today's competitive publishing world, successful book marketing often requires a blend of both traditional and digital strategies. Each has its unique strengths, and when combined, they can create a well-rounded promotional campaign that reaches a wide range of readers. By understanding the benefits and limitations of both approaches, you can craft a marketing plan that maximizes exposure while staying true to your goals and budget.

In this section, we'll explore the pros and cons of traditional and digital marketing methods and how to strike the right balance to amplify your book's visibility.

1. Understanding Traditional Marketing

Traditional marketing refers to long-established promotional methods that typically involve physical materials and in-person events. While many authors today rely heavily on digital platforms, traditional marketing still plays a crucial role in reaching certain audiences and building credibility.

Examples of Traditional Marketing:

- **Book Signings and Launch Events**: Hosting physical book signings at local bookstores, libraries, or literary festivals can help you connect with readers in person and create a memorable experience.

- **Press Releases and Media Coverage**: Sending press releases to local or national media outlets can generate buzz and potentially lead to reviews, interviews, or feature articles about your book.

- **Print Advertising**: Advertising in newspapers, literary magazines, or book-specific publications can introduce your book to a more traditional audience.

- **Direct Mail**: While less common today, some authors use direct mail campaigns (postcards, flyers) to promote upcoming book releases or events.

- **Word-of-Mouth Marketing**: Traditional marketing relies heavily on word-of-mouth, whether it's through book clubs, library talks, or local reader groups.

Benefits of Traditional Marketing:

- **Credibility and Trust**: Traditional marketing methods like press coverage or in-store book signings offer credibility, as they're often seen as more formal and trustworthy.

- **Local Engagement**: Connecting with your local community can create loyal, long-term readers. Attending book fairs, literary events, or hosting readings allows you to build strong relationships with readers who may not be active online.

- **Reaching Non-Digital Audiences**: Certain reader demographics, particularly older audiences, may be less active on digital platforms. Traditional marketing can be a way to reach these readers.

Limitations of Traditional Marketing:

- **Cost**: Many traditional marketing tactics, such as print ads or book tours, can be expensive, particularly for indie authors or those with limited budgets.

- **Limited Reach**: Traditional marketing methods are often constrained to specific geographic areas, which can limit your ability to reach a global audience.

- **Time-Intensive**: Organizing in-person events or securing media coverage takes time and effort, often with no guaranteed results.

2. Understanding Digital Marketing

Digital marketing leverages the power of the internet and social media to reach readers directly through various online channels. It offers a more flexible, cost-effective way to promote your book and build an ongoing relationship with readers. Digital marketing can be highly targeted and allows you to measure results in real time.

Examples of Digital Marketing:

- **Social Media Campaigns**: Promoting your book through platforms like Instagram, Facebook, Twitter, and TikTok allows you to engage with a global audience, share updates, and run paid ads.

- **Email Marketing**: Sending newsletters and updates directly to your readers' inboxes through an email list helps you stay connected and build anticipation for new releases.

- **Book Trailers and Video Content**: Short videos and book trailers shared on YouTube or social media can capture attention and give readers a visual sense of your book's themes and tone.

- **Influencer and Blogger Collaborations**: Working with book bloggers, BookTubers, and social media influencers can help spread the word about your book to a broader, engaged audience.

- **Goodreads and Amazon Ads**: Advertising on platforms where readers actively browse for books can be highly effective in converting browsers into buyers.

Benefits of Digital Marketing:

- **Global Reach**: Digital platforms allow you to promote your book to readers around the world, extending your reach far beyond your local area.

- **Cost-Effective**: Many digital marketing strategies, such as social media and email marketing, can be done at little to no cost, making them accessible for authors with tight budgets.

- **Real-Time Analytics**: Digital marketing platforms offer analytics tools that let you track how well your campaigns are performing. You can monitor metrics like clicks, views, and sales conversions, allowing you to adjust your strategies as needed.

- **Targeted Marketing**: Digital ads can be highly targeted, allowing you to reach readers based on demographics, interests, and even specific genres they follow.

Limitations of Digital Marketing:

- **Time-Consuming**: Building an online presence and growing an engaged audience requires consistent effort over time. Maintaining social media accounts, responding to followers, and creating content can be time-consuming.

- **Saturated Market**: The internet is flooded with content, and standing out from the crowd can be a challenge. To succeed, your digital marketing needs to be strategic and engaging to capture attention.

- **Platform Algorithms**: Algorithms on platforms like Facebook and Instagram can limit the organic reach of your posts, making it harder for your content to be seen without running paid ads.

3. Striking the Right Balance

Now that we've covered the strengths and weaknesses of both traditional and digital marketing, the key is to find the right balance for your specific goals and audience. Blending the best of both worlds allows you to reach a wider range of readers while playing to the strengths of each method.

How to Blend Traditional and Digital Marketing:

- **Start Local, Expand Digital**: Begin with traditional marketing efforts in your local community, such as book signings, readings, or press coverage in local media. Then, use digital platforms to share these events and coverage with a broader audience, leveraging social media, email newsletters, and blogs to spread the word.

- **Leverage Local Credibility for Online Buzz**: When you land a media feature, press review, or participate in an event, use it to your advantage online. Share the media coverage on your social platforms, mention it in your newsletters, and post it on your website to build credibility.

- **Host Hybrid Events**: Consider hosting a hybrid book launch or event that combines an in-person book signing with a virtual live stream on social media. This allows you to engage with local readers while also reaching those who can't attend in person.

- **Combine Influencer and Traditional Media Outreach**: Alongside reaching out to book bloggers and influencers, send press releases to traditional media outlets, such as local newspapers, literary magazines, or radio shows. This ensures your book gets exposure through both modern and classic channels.

- **Budget Wisely**: Allocate a portion of your marketing budget to both traditional and digital efforts. For example, you might invest in local print ads for a bookstore event while also running a small Facebook ad campaign targeted at your book's genre.

4. Tracking and Adjusting Your Strategy

The best way to determine the right balance for your book marketing plan is to track your results and adjust as you go. Whether you're running a local campaign or a global digital strategy, monitoring key metrics like sales, engagement, and media coverage will help you understand what's working.

- **For Traditional Marketing**: Keep track of how many people attend your events, how much coverage you receive from media outlets, and whether these efforts lead to increased book sales or online engagement.

- **For Digital Marketing**: Use analytics tools on social media, email platforms, and ad services to measure the success of your campaigns. Track clicks, likes, shares, and conversions to see where your digital efforts are having the most impact.

By blending traditional and digital marketing strategies, you can maximize your reach and engagement, ensuring that you're connecting with readers both locally and globally.

Finding the right balance between traditional and digital marketing is key to a successful book promotion strategy. By combining the credibility and local impact of traditional methods with the global reach and cost-effectiveness of digital platforms, you can craft a comprehensive campaign that maximizes your book's potential. In the next section, we'll dive into creative ways to generate buzz for your book through book trailers, influencer collaborations, and guerrilla marketing techniques.

Creating Buzz: Book Trailers, Influencers, and Guerrilla Marketing

In a crowded book market, generating buzz is essential to capture attention and keep readers talking about your work. Beyond traditional and digital marketing, some creative and unconventional strategies can help you stand out and build excitement around your book. From engaging book trailers to partnering with influencers, and even using guerrilla marketing tactics, these methods can turn your book launch into a memorable event. In this section, we'll explore how to use these strategies to create a buzz that leads to lasting success.

1. Book Trailers: Bringing Your Story to Life

A book trailer is a short video that introduces your book in a visually compelling way, similar to a movie trailer. It's a powerful tool to hook potential readers by giving them a taste of the story, characters, and tone of your book, all within a matter of seconds. Book trailers work particularly well on social media, author websites, YouTube, and in email marketing campaigns.

How to Create a Book Trailer:

- **Plan the Script**: Think of your trailer as a mini story that teases the core conflict or theme of your book without giving too much away. A trailer for a mystery might hint at a central puzzle or a thriller might show glimpses of the danger. Keep it short (30 to 90 seconds) and focus on key scenes or emotions.

- **Choose Music and Visuals**: The visuals and music should match the mood and genre of your book. For example, a dark, eerie score works for a horror novel, while upbeat music fits a romantic comedy. If possible, use stock video footage or hire an animator to create custom visuals that reflect your story.

- **Include Key Information**: End the trailer with essential details such as the book's title, release date, and where readers can buy it. You might also want to include your website or social media handles.

- **Promote Widely**: Once your trailer is ready, share it everywhere—on your social media accounts, website, Goodreads, YouTube, and even run ads on platforms like Instagram or Facebook to extend its reach. Ask readers to share the video to spread the word.

Why Book Trailers Work:

- **Visual Impact**: A well-made book trailer grabs attention and engages viewers emotionally, enticing them to learn more about your book.

- **Easy to Share**: Trailers are perfect for social media and video-sharing platforms, where visual content tends to go viral more easily than text-based posts.

- **Creates Anticipation**: A trailer builds anticipation, especially when released as part of a pre-launch marketing campaign.

2. Influencers: Amplifying Your Reach

Partnering with influencers—people with a strong following in your book's genre or niche—can exponentially increase your book's visibility. Influencers on Instagram, TikTok, YouTube, and blogs have built loyal communities that trust their recommendations, making them ideal partners to help spread the word about your book.

How to Collaborate with Influencers:

- **Identify Relevant Influencers**: Look for influencers who are passionate about your book's genre or themes. For example, if you've written a young adult fantasy novel, seek out BookTubers, Bookstagrammers, and BookTokers who frequently review YA books and engage with a fan base that matches your target audience.

- **Send Advance Copies**: Offer to send influencers an advance review copy (ARC) of your book in exchange for an honest review or feature on their platform. You can also provide digital copies or offer exclusive content, like an interview or Q&A.

- **Run Giveaways**: Partner with influencers to host giveaways. For instance, ask them to run a contest where followers can win signed copies of your book, along with some book-related swag. This helps build excitement and increases engagement.

- **Collaborate on Content**: Work with influencers to create unique content such as Instagram live sessions, TikTok challenges, or YouTube interviews. The more interactive and engaging the content, the more likely it is to gain traction.

Why Influencers Are Effective:

- **Built-In Audience**: Influencers already have a dedicated audience that trusts their recommendations, so a mention of your book can quickly generate interest.

- **Targeted Reach**: By working with influencers in your book's genre, you're getting your book directly in front of readers who are already interested in similar content.

- **Social Proof**: Positive reviews or endorsements from influencers act as social proof, increasing the likelihood that new readers will give your book a chance.

3. Guerrilla Marketing: Creative, Unconventional Tactics

Guerrilla marketing is all about thinking outside the box and using unconventional methods to grab attention in a memorable way. These campaigns often rely on creativity rather than a large budget and can make a big impact by surprising and delighting potential readers. Guerrilla marketing is particularly effective in creating word-of-mouth buzz and drawing media attention.

Guerrilla Marketing Ideas for Authors:

- **Street Art or Installations**: If your book is set in a specific city or features iconic locations, consider creating a street art installation or temporary mural that ties into your book's theme. For example, if your novel takes place in a bustling city, a mural with quotes from the book could appear in key areas, encouraging passersby to look up your book online.

- **Flash Mobs or Themed Events**: Host a flash mob or an interactive event related to your book. For example, a mystery novel author might organize a public "detective hunt" where participants solve clues to win a copy of the book.

- **Pop-Up Bookstores or Booths**: Set up a temporary pop-up shop or booth in high-traffic areas such as festivals, malls, or subway stations. This could serve as a mini bookstore where people can pick up signed copies or learn more about your book in a unique setting.

- **Teaser Campaigns**: Run a teaser campaign where you leave cryptic messages, quotes, or clues related to your book around public spaces or online. For example, post mysterious posters with only a compelling quote from your book and a hashtag. Encourage curiosity and conversation by revealing the full story later on your social platforms.

Why Guerrilla Marketing Works:

- **Memorable and Shareable**: Guerrilla marketing campaigns are designed to surprise and engage people, making them more likely to talk about and share the experience with others.

- **Media Attention**: Creative, bold campaigns can often attract local or national media coverage, giving your book additional exposure.

- **Budget-Friendly**: Guerrilla marketing doesn't necessarily require a big budget—just creativity and a willingness to think outside the box.

4. Combining Strategies for Maximum Impact

To create maximum buzz, consider combining book trailers, influencer marketing, and guerrilla tactics into a unified campaign. For example, you might launch your book trailer across social media, host influencer giveaways, and tease the release with a guerrilla-style street art campaign. This multi-pronged approach ensures you're reaching your audience through multiple touchpoints and generating sustained excitement.

Building buzz for your book requires creativity, collaboration, and boldness. Whether you're using visually striking book trailers, tapping into the power of influencers, or engaging in unexpected guerrilla marketing stunts, these strategies can elevate your marketing campaign and make your book stand out. By thinking outside the box and staying true to your book's unique appeal, you can capture attention, ignite curiosity, and ultimately drive sales.

With these strategies in hand, you're now ready to launch your book into the world, creating a memorable marketing campaign that resonates with readers long after they've turned the final page.

Quick Tips and Recap

- **Build a Solid Marketing Plan**: Set clear goals, identify your target audience, establish a budget, and create a timeline for your marketing efforts.

- **Leverage Social Media**: Use platforms like Instagram, Twitter, Facebook, and TikTok to engage with your audience, share teasers, and build excitement for your book.

- **Use Book Trailers**: Create a short, visually appealing book trailer to hook potential readers and share it widely across digital platforms.

- **Collaborate with Influencers**: Partner with Bookstagrammers, BookTubers, and BookTokers to expand your reach and generate buzz through reviews, giveaways, and interactive content.

- **Blend Traditional and Digital Marketing**: Use a mix of in-person events, media coverage, and digital strategies to reach both local and global audiences.

- **Run Social Media Ads**: Use targeted ads on platforms like Facebook, Instagram, and Twitter to promote your book and drive sales.

- **Get Creative with Guerrilla Marketing**: Think outside the box with unconventional marketing tactics like street art, flash mobs, and pop-up events to create memorable experiences that people will talk about.

- **Track Results and Adjust**: Regularly monitor your marketing efforts and make adjustments as needed to maximize your campaign's effectiveness.

With these strategies, you'll be well on your way to creating buzz and excitement for your book, helping it reach a wider audience and build lasting momentum.

Distribution Strategies: Getting Your Book Out There

"Distribution is about making sure your product meets your customers
where they are, in the way they want to be met."
— JEFF BEZOS, FOUNDER OF AMAZON

Welcome to Chapter Nine, "Distribution Strategies: Getting Your Book Out There," where we turn the spotlight from creating your masterpiece to ensuring it finds its way into the eager hands of readers everywhere. This isn't just about casting a wide net—it's about making sure that net reaches every potential nook, cranny, and reading nook on the planet.

In this chapter, we'll navigate the complex channels of book distribution, from the traditional bastions of brick-and-mortar bookstores to the digital dominions of e-readers and audio platforms. You'll learn how to charm distributors, negotiate with retailers, and perhaps most crucially, sidestep the common pitfalls that could relegate your book to the dreaded realm of "best kept secret."

We'll explore how to balance print runs with demand, how to pitch to major book chains, and the secrets to mastering the online marketplace algorithms that decide whether your book becomes the next big page-turner or just another spine on the shelf. Get ready to push your book out of the nest and watch it soar across global markets—it's time to spread those pages and fly!

Understanding Traditional Distribution Channels

For decades, traditional distribution channels have been the backbone of the publishing industry, getting books into bookstores, libraries, and retail chains where readers can browse, discover, and purchase them. Navigating this system is a key part of any author's marketing plan, whether you're working with a traditional publisher or going the self-publishing route. While digital distribution has grown in popularity, traditional channels remain vital for reaching a broad and diverse audience, including readers who prefer physical books or don't engage much with online platforms.

In this section, we'll explore how traditional book distribution works, how to get your book into physical bookstores and libraries, and what you need to know about working with distributors and wholesalers.

1. How Traditional Distribution Works

Traditional book distribution relies on a network of distributors, wholesalers, and retailers to get your book into the hands of readers. Here's how the process typically works:

- **Distributors**: These companies act as the middlemen between publishers and retailers. They store large quantities of books in their warehouses and fulfill orders to bookstores, libraries, and other retailers. Major distributors include Ingram, Baker & Taylor, and Simon & Schuster. Distributors charge a fee (often a percentage of book sales) in exchange for handling the logistics of book distribution, including inventory management, order fulfillment, and returns.

- **Wholesalers**: Similar to distributors, wholesalers purchase books in bulk from publishers and resell them to bookstores and libraries. The key difference is that wholesalers tend to buy large quantities of books upfront, whereas distributors may act on a more flexible, order-by-order basis.

- **Retailers**: These are the bookstores, online platforms, and other outlets that sell books directly to consumers. In traditional distribution, retailers often buy books from wholesalers or distributors, though they can sometimes order directly from publishers or self-published authors.

In traditional distribution, books are typically sold to retailers at a discounted rate, allowing retailers to mark up the price for profit. For example, a bookstore might purchase a book at a 40% discount from the publisher and sell it at the full retail price.

2. Getting Your Book into Bookstores

For many authors, seeing their book on the shelves of a brick-and-mortar bookstore is a dream come true. However, getting your book stocked in physical stores—especially major chains like Barnes & Noble or Books-A-Million—requires effort, persistence, and a solid pitch.

Here's how to improve your chances:

- **Work with a Distributor**: Most major bookstores only work with established distributors like Ingram or Baker & Taylor, as they streamline the purchasing and return process. By working with a distributor, you make it easier for bookstores to order your book in bulk, increasing the likelihood that they'll stock it.

- **Pitch Directly to Bookstores**: Independent bookstores may be more willing to work directly with authors or small publishers. Research local or specialty bookstores that align with your book's genre or subject matter, and approach them with a professional pitch. Include information like:

- A compelling synopsis of your book.

- Your sales and marketing plan (how you plan to drive foot traffic to their store).

- Reviews, press mentions, or awards that highlight your book's quality.

- Information about events you can host (e.g., book signings, readings).

- **Offer Consignment**: Some bookstores will agree to stock your book on consignment, meaning they don't pay you upfront but will sell your book and share the revenue with you once it's sold. This reduces the financial risk for the bookstore and gives your book an opportunity to be discovered by readers. Be sure to have a clear agreement on the percentage split and the terms of unsold books.

- **Host In-Store Events**: Hosting events like book signings, readings, or launch parties can give bookstores an incentive to stock your book. Offer to do a book signing where readers can meet you and get signed copies. This can help drive traffic to the store and boost sales for both you and the bookstore.

Tip: When pitching to bookstores, having professional-looking marketing materials (such as a media kit, reviews, or endorsements) can help make a strong case for why they should carry your book.

3. Libraries: Another Vital Channel

Libraries are often overlooked as a distribution channel, but they can be a significant source of book sales and long-term readership. Unlike bookstores, libraries purchase books to loan out to many readers over time, which means that a single library copy can reach dozens or even hundreds of readers. Additionally, having your book in libraries can help establish your reputation and encourage word-of-mouth recommendations.

Here's how to get your book into libraries:

- **List with Distributors**: Many libraries purchase their books through large distributors like Baker & Taylor or wholesalers like Ingram. If you're listed with these distributors, libraries can easily order your book.

- **Get Reviewed in Library Trade Publications**: Librarians often rely on reviews from trade publications like Library Journal, Booklist, and Publishers Weekly to decide which books to purchase. Having your book reviewed in one of these publications can significantly increase your chances of getting into libraries.

- **Reach Out to Local Libraries**: Much like independent bookstores, local libraries may be willing to work directly with authors. Reach out to libraries in your area and offer to donate a copy of your book. You can also offer to host an author event, such as a reading or a discussion about your book, which can help introduce your work to the library's patrons.

4. The Role of Book Fairs and Trade Shows

Book fairs and trade shows provide excellent opportunities to connect with distributors, retailers, and librarians in person. Events like the BookExpo America (BEA) or London Book Fair bring together publishers, agents, authors, and buyers, making them ideal venues for networking and promoting your book to key decision-makers in the industry.

At book fairs, you can:

- **Showcase Your Book**: Many book fairs have dedicated spaces for self-published authors to exhibit their books. This can be a great way to get your book in front of bookstore buyers, librarians, and distributors who are looking for new titles to add to their catalog.

- **Network with Distributors and Wholesalers**: These events often include representatives from major distributors and wholesalers, giving you a chance to pitch your book and learn more about how to get it into their system.

- **Participate in Panels or Signings**: Some book fairs offer opportunities for authors to participate in panels, discussions, or book signings, which can increase your visibility and help you build connections with the industry.

Traditional distribution channels remain essential for reaching readers in bookstores and libraries, and understanding how they work is crucial for maximizing your book's exposure. Whether you're working with a distributor, pitching directly to bookstores, or building relationships with librarians, these strategies can help you get your book out into the world and into the hands of readers who are eager to discover it.

In the next section, we'll explore how to leverage digital distribution and the online marketplace to broaden your reach and capitalize on the growing demand for eBooks and audiobooks.

Digital Distribution: Selling Your Book Online

In the modern book marketplace, digital distribution is an essential part of any author's strategy. Whether you're self-published or traditionally published, the ability to sell your book online opens up access to a global audience and provides endless opportunities to connect with readers through platforms like Amazon Kindle, Apple Books, and more. Digital distribution is not only convenient for authors—it's also a powerful way to keep costs low, track performance in real-time, and reach readers across formats like eBooks and audiobooks.

In this section, we'll explore the world of digital distribution, from the major platforms available to key strategies for optimizing your book's visibility and sales.

1. The Big Players in Digital Distribution

When it comes to selling your book online, a few key platforms dominate the market. These platforms make it easy to upload, distribute, and sell your book in digital format, while offering powerful tools for reaching readers.

Here are the major digital distribution platforms:

- **Amazon Kindle Direct Publishing (KDP)**: As the largest online book retailer, Amazon KDP is a must for any author looking to distribute their eBook. KDP allows you to upload your manuscript, design a cover, and publish your book to the Kindle Store with just a few clicks. You can choose between enrolling your book in KDP Select (which gives you access to promotional tools like Kindle Unlimited) or publishing wide (making your book available on other platforms).

    - o **Royalties**: KDP offers two royalty options—35% or 70%, depending on factors like pricing and distribution exclusivity.

    - o **KDP Select**: Enrolling in KDP Select requires a 90-day exclusivity period with Amazon, but offers benefits like promotional deals and inclusion in Kindle Unlimited.

- **Apple Books**: Apple's eBook platform is another major player in the digital market. By distributing through Apple Books, you can reach millions of readers using iPhones, iPads, and Macs. Apple offers a simple self-publishing process, allowing you to upload your book, set the price, and track sales.

    - o **Exclusive Features**: Apple Books offers tools like Pre-Orders and Promotions to help you build anticipation for your release.

- **Kobo Writing Life**: **Kobo** is popular in many international markets, particularly in Canada and Europe. Kobo's self-publishing platform, Writing Life, makes it easy to upload your eBook and make it available worldwide. Unlike Amazon, Kobo doesn't require exclusivity, allowing you to sell your book on multiple platforms simultaneously.

    - o **Global Reach**: Kobo is integrated into the **OverDrive** system, which means your eBook can also be available for borrowing at libraries across the world.

- **Barnes & Noble Press**: This platform is for authors who want to sell their eBooks through Barnes & Noble's online store, NOOK. It's an easy-to-use platform for uploading and managing eBook sales.

- o **Exclusive Promotions**: Barnes & Noble Press offers opportunities for authors to participate in exclusive sales and promotions, particularly if you're targeting U.S. readers.

- **Google Play Books**: Google's digital book platform allows you to sell eBooks and audiobooks to millions of Android users. It's another great option for distributing your book without exclusivity requirements, and it integrates well with Google's search engine for visibility.

Tip: Many authors choose to publish "wide," meaning they distribute their books on multiple platforms (Amazon, Apple Books, Kobo, etc.) to reach the widest possible audience. Others opt to focus on a single platform, such as enrolling in KDP Select to take advantage of Amazon's marketing tools. The best choice depends on your goals and target audience.

2. Optimizing Your Book for Digital Platforms

Once your book is uploaded and available on digital platforms, the next step is ensuring that readers can find it. Digital platforms are crowded, so it's essential to optimize your book's listing to stand out and attract attention.

Here's how to optimize your book for maximum visibility:

- **Metadata and Keywords**: Your book's metadata—including the title, subtitle, description, and keywords—plays a critical role in how it's discovered by potential readers. Choose your keywords carefully, focusing on terms that readers are likely to search for when looking for books in your genre.

  - o Use Amazon's Kindle Keyword Tool or other keyword research tools to find popular search terms in your genre.

  - o Write a compelling book description that highlights the key selling points of your story—focus on intriguing hooks, character conflicts, and why readers will be drawn to your book.

- **Pricing Strategies**: Pricing your eBook competitively is crucial to driving sales. On platforms like Amazon, pricing in the $2.99 to $9.99 range qualifies you for the 70% royalty rate, making this the sweet spot for most indie authors. Experiment with promotional pricing, including free days or 99-cent deals, to attract readers and generate reviews.

- **Use Categories and Subgenres**: Selecting the right categories and subgenres ensures your book appears in the right places on online marketplaces. For example, if your book is a fantasy novel with elements of romance, choosing subcategories like Epic Fantasy and Fantasy Romance will help target readers who are specifically interested in these genres.

- **Leverage Reviews**: Reviews are a key factor in persuading potential buyers to purchase your book. Encourage readers to leave honest reviews after reading your eBook by including a call to action at the end of your book, reminding them to leave feedback on the platform where they purchased it. The more reviews your book has, the higher it will rank in search results.

- **Maximize Amazon's Algorithm**: Amazon's algorithm rewards books that consistently generate sales, reviews, and engagement. By launching a pre-order campaign, offering limited-time discounts, and encouraging reviews during the early weeks of release, you can build momentum that improves your book's ranking and visibility.

3. Using Social Media to Drive Digital Sales

Social media is one of the most effective tools for promoting your eBook and driving traffic to your digital listings. Use social media platforms to engage with your audience, share snippets of your book, and announce sales or promotions. Here's how to harness social media for digital distribution:

- **Create a Pre-Launch Buzz**: Use platforms like Instagram, Twitter, and Facebook to build anticipation for your book launch. Share **cover** reveals, excerpts, or character profiles in the weeks leading up to your release. Offer incentives, like exclusive content or giveaways, to readers who pre-order or share your posts.

- **Leverage Hashtags**: Use genre-specific hashtags (e.g., #AmReading, #BookLover, #FantasyBooks) to help potential readers discover your posts. Engage with reading communities like Bookstagram or BookTok to reach readers who are passionate about your genre.

- **Run Paid Ads**: Platforms like Facebook and Instagram allow you to run targeted ads that direct readers to your Amazon or Kobo listing. These ads can be targeted by interests, demographics, and behaviors, allowing you to reach readers most likely to enjoy your book.

4. Maximizing International Reach

One of the major benefits of digital distribution is the ability to reach readers across the globe, far beyond your local market. If you want to maximize your international reach, here are some strategies to consider:

- **Distribute Globally**: Platforms like Amazon, Kobo, and Google Play Books allow you to distribute your book worldwide. Make sure your book is available in multiple countries, not just the U.S., and price your book appropriately for each region.

- **Translations**: Consider translating your book into other languages to reach non-English-speaking markets. You can hire a professional translator or use services like Babelcube or Reedsy to find qualified translators. Offering your book in languages like Spanish, German, or French can help you tap into huge international markets.

- **Use Global-Friendly Platforms**: Some platforms, like Kobo and Google Play Books, have strong market penetration in regions outside the U.S., such as Europe and Asia. Make sure to optimize your listings on these platforms if you're targeting readers abroad.

5. Tracking and Analyzing Sales Data

One of the biggest advantages of digital distribution is the ability to track your sales data in real time. This gives you valuable insight into how your book is performing, allowing you to adjust your marketing strategies as needed. Here's what to keep an eye on:

- **Sales Reports**: Most platforms provide detailed sales reports that show how many copies you've sold, which formats (eBook, audiobook), and where your sales are coming from. Use this data to identify trends and adjust your pricing, promotions, or marketing efforts accordingly.

- **Conversion Rates**: If you're running paid ads, track your conversion rates—the percentage of people who clicked on your ad and purchased the book. If your conversion rates are low, consider tweaking your ad copy or targeting to better align with your audience.

- **Reader Engagement**: Monitor your reviews, ratings, and social media engagement to gauge how readers are responding to your book. Positive reviews and social shares can create a snowball effect, leading to more visibility and sales.

Digital distribution is a powerful way to reach readers around the world and make your book available in multiple formats. By optimizing your book's listing, leveraging social media, and tracking your sales data, you can maximize your book's potential in the online marketplace. In the next section, we'll explore how to use Print-on-Demand (POD) and self-publishing platforms to manage physical copies of your book without the need for large upfront costs.

Print-on-Demand (POD) and Self-Publishing Platforms

Print-on-Demand (POD) and self-publishing platforms have revolutionized the publishing world by allowing authors to publish physical books without the need for large print runs or upfront costs. These platforms enable authors to make their books available in print form, with copies being printed and shipped only when a customer places an order. This eliminates the risk of unsold inventory and provides a cost-effective way for independent authors to manage physical book sales.

In this section, we'll explore how POD and self-publishing platforms work, their benefits, and how to choose the right platform for your book.

1. What Is Print-on-Demand?

Print-on-Demand (POD) is a publishing model where books are printed only when an order is placed. Unlike traditional publishing, where thousands of copies may be printed upfront, POD allows you to print just one copy at a time. This flexibility makes it an ideal option for self-published authors or those who want to avoid the high costs and risks associated with traditional print runs.

Here's how POD works:

- **Upload Your Manuscript**: You upload your manuscript and cover design to the POD platform.

- **Set Pricing and Distribution**: You set the retail price of your book and decide where it will be distributed (e.g., online retailers like Amazon, bookstores, libraries).

- **Print and Ship**: When a customer orders your book, the platform prints a single copy and ships it directly to them. You don't have to manage inventory or shipping logistics.

- **Royalties**: After the platform deducts printing and distribution costs, you receive a royalty on each sale.

2. Popular Print-on-Demand Platforms

Several POD platforms dominate the market, each offering different features, pricing structures, and distribution options. Here's an overview of the most popular POD services:

- **Amazon Kindle Direct Publishing (KDP)**: KDP is one of the most popular POD platforms, particularly for authors looking to reach a global audience. KDP allows you to publish both eBooks and print books, making your book available on Amazon and its extensive distribution network.

  - o **Advantages**: No upfront costs, wide distribution on Amazon, and integration with KDP for eBooks. You can choose expanded distribution to make your book available through retailers beyond Amazon.

  - o **Drawbacks**: Amazon's royalty rates and print costs are lower than some other platforms, and physical bookstore distribution is limited.

- **IngramSpark**: IngramSpark is another major POD platform that offers wide distribution to bookstores, libraries, and online retailers. IngramSpark's parent company, Ingram Content Group, is one of the largest book distributors in the world, which gives your book access to a vast network.

  o **Advantages**: IngramSpark offers excellent print quality, global distribution, and the ability to set industry-standard discounts for retailers. Your book can be distributed to major chains like Barnes & Noble, independent bookstores, and libraries.

  o **Drawbacks**: There are small upfront costs for uploading and revising your book, and IngramSpark's setup can be more complex than KDP.

- **Lulu**: Lulu is a versatile POD platform that allows authors to print and distribute a wide range of formats, including paperback, hardcover, and photo books. Lulu also offers expanded distribution to online retailers, bookstores, and libraries.

  o **Advantages**: Lulu provides a wide variety of book formats, including custom options like coil-bound or hardcover with dust jackets. There are no upfront costs for publishing a book, though expanded distribution may require a fee.

  o **Drawbacks**: Lulu's distribution network is not as large as IngramSpark's, and royalty rates can be lower depending on your chosen distribution channels.

- **Blurb**: Blurb is known for its high-quality printing, particularly for visually driven books like photography, art, or cookbooks. It also offers distribution to platforms like Amazon and IngramSpark.

  o **Advantages**: Excellent for books with a strong visual element, such as photography or art books. Offers the option to create custom books with high-quality print and paper options.

    o   **Drawbacks**: Limited to certain types of books (e.g., picture-heavy books), and not as focused on fiction or general non-fiction as other platforms.

Tip: Many authors choose to use a combination of KDP for Amazon distribution and IngramSpark for broader retail and library distribution. This gives you the best of both worlds—access to Amazon's massive marketplace and IngramSpark's wider network.

3. Benefits of Print-on-Demand

POD offers several key advantages for self-published authors:

- **No Upfront Costs**: Since you don't need to print large quantities of books upfront, POD eliminates the risk of unsold inventory and hefty upfront investments. You only pay for the printing and distribution costs when a book is ordered.

- **Low Risk**: You don't need to estimate how many copies you'll sell. If demand increases, you can easily scale up without worrying about running out of stock.

- **Flexibility**: POD platforms allow you to make updates to your book at any time, whether it's fixing a typo, updating the cover, or adding new content. You're not locked into a single print run.

- **Global Reach**: Many POD platforms offer distribution through online retailers like Amazon, as well as brick-and-mortar bookstores and libraries. This gives your book the opportunity to reach readers worldwide.

- **Easier to Manage**: With POD, you don't have to worry about managing inventory, storage, or shipping. The platform handles the entire fulfillment process, allowing you to focus on marketing and promoting your book.

4. Managing Print Runs vs. Print-on-Demand

While POD offers flexibility and low upfront costs, some authors may still choose to do traditional print runs for specific situations—such as large events, book signings, or direct sales.

Here's how to decide between POD and a traditional print run:

- **When to Use POD**: POD is ideal for ongoing sales through online retailers, especially if you're unsure how many copies you'll sell or want to minimize financial risk. It's also perfect for reaching global readers without worrying about managing shipping or distribution yourself.

- **When to Use Traditional Print Runs**: A traditional print run might be the better option if you're planning to sell a large number of books at a specific event (like a book launch or signing). Print runs are typically cheaper per unit than POD, so if you know you'll need hundreds or thousands of copies at once, a traditional print run can save money in the long run.

Many authors choose to combine the two strategies—using POD for general sales and ordering traditional print runs for events, direct sales, or special editions.

5. Formatting and Designing for POD

To ensure your book looks professional when printed, it's important to follow the platform's guidelines for formatting and design. Here are some key steps:

- **Formatting Your Manuscript**: Most POD platforms require your manuscript to be formatted in a print-ready PDF. You'll need to adjust margins, set up appropriate page sizes, and ensure that elements like headers, footers, and page numbers are consistent throughout.

  o **Trim Sizes**: Choose the correct trim size (the size of your printed book) based on genre and industry standards. Common sizes include 5"x8" or 6"x9" for novels.

  o **Margins and Bleeds**: Ensure your manuscript follows the platform's guidelines for margins and bleeds (areas where the content extends to the edge of the page). This is especially important for full-page images or illustrations.

- **Designing a Professional Cover**: The cover is the first thing readers see, so it's important to make a great impression. POD platforms typically provide templates to help you design a cover that meets their specifications.

  o **Front, Back, and Spine**: Unlike eBooks, print books need a complete cover, including the front, back, and spine. Ensure that the spine thickness is adjusted based on the number of pages in your book.

  o **Hire a Designer**: If you're not experienced with graphic design, it's worth hiring a professional designer to create a polished, eye-catching cover. Platforms like Fiverr, Upwork, or Reedsy can connect you with qualified designers.

6. Distribution and Royalties with POD

One of the key decisions you'll make when using a POD platform is how to distribute your book. Most platforms offer the following distribution options:

- **Direct Sales on Amazon or Other Retailers**: Platforms like KDP and IngramSpark allow you to list your book directly on Amazon or other online retailers, where customers can purchase both print and eBook versions.

- **Expanded Distribution**: Some POD platforms, like IngramSpark, offer expanded distribution to bookstores, libraries, and academic institutions. Keep in mind that bookstores may be more likely to stock your book if you offer standard industry discounts (typically 40–55%) and allow returns.

- **Royalties**: Your royalties will vary depending on the platform, the format (paperback, hardcover), and the distribution channel. For example, Amazon's KDP pays royalties based on the book's price minus the printing cost, while IngramSpark deducts printing and distribution fees before paying royalties.

Tip: When setting your book's retail price, factor in printing and distribution costs to ensure you're earning a reasonable royalty. Use the platform's pricing calculator to see how pricing decisions affect your royalties.

Print-on-Demand (POD) and self-publishing platforms offer incredible flexibility for independent authors, allowing you to produce and sell physical books without the high upfront costs of traditional print runs. By choosing the right platform, designing a professional product, and managing your distribution strategically, you can reach readers around the world and make your book available in multiple formats. In the next section, we'll explore how to maximize your reach even further by creating audiobooks and alternative formats for different types of readers.

Maximizing Audiobook and Alternative Formats

In recent years, the demand for audiobooks and alternative book formats has skyrocketed, creating new opportunities for authors to expand their reach and tap into additional revenue streams. Audiobooks, in particular, are a fast-growing segment of the publishing industry, with millions of readers turning to audio as a convenient way to consume books while commuting, exercising, or multitasking. Offering your book in multiple formats—whether it's audio, large print, or translated editions—allows you to reach a wider audience and cater to different reader preferences.

In this section, we'll explore how to create and distribute audiobooks, as well as other alternative formats that can help you broaden your book's accessibility and appeal.

1. Creating an Audiobook: Why It's Worth It

Audiobooks have become a popular way for readers to engage with books, and offering an audiobook version of your work can dramatically increase your potential audience. With platforms like Audible and Spotify making audiobooks more accessible than ever, creating an audiobook is a valuable investment for authors looking to diversify their offerings.

Here's why creating an audiobook is worth considering:

- **Reach a Broader Audience**: Audiobooks attract readers who prefer to listen rather than read, whether it's for convenience or accessibility. Offering an audiobook allows you to cater to a growing audience that might not pick up a traditional print or eBook.

- **Generate Additional Revenue**: Audiobook sales can generate a significant stream of income. Many audiobook listeners are willing to pay a premium for high-quality audio productions, and subscription services like Audible can boost your book's exposure.

- **Stay Competitive**: As more authors and publishers offer audiobooks, not having an audio version of your book may put you at a disadvantage, especially if your competitors have both print and audio options available.

2. How to Produce an Audiobook

Creating an audiobook may seem like a daunting task, but with the right tools and resources, it can be a smooth process. You have two main options when it comes to audiobook production: narrating the book yourself or hiring a professional narrator.

Narrating Your Own Audiobook

- **Recording Equipment**: If you choose to narrate your audiobook, you'll need high-quality recording equipment, such as a good microphone, soundproofing materials, and audio editing software. It's essential to produce a professional recording with clear audio and minimal background noise.

- **Skill and Consistency**: Narrating a book requires skill, consistency, and the right tone to match the book's content. Make sure you're comfortable reading aloud for long periods and can maintain a consistent voice throughout the entire recording.

- **Post-Production**: Once you've recorded the audio, you'll need to edit the files, removing any mistakes, pauses, or background noise. You can either handle this yourself or hire an audio editor to ensure a polished final product.

Hiring a Professional Narrator

- **Platforms Like ACX**: One of the easiest ways to produce an audiobook is through platforms like ACX (Audiobook Creation Exchange), which connects authors with professional narrators. ACX allows you to post your book for auditions and choose a narrator that fits your story's tone and style.

- **Royalty Share vs. Upfront Payment**: ACX offers two payment models—you can either pay the narrator upfront for their services or agree to a royalty share, where the narrator receives a percentage of your audiobook's sales. Royalty share is a good option if you're on a tight budget, but paying upfront typically gives you access to higher-tier narrators.

- **Professional Quality**: Hiring a professional narrator ensures your audiobook is of high quality, which is crucial for attracting audiobook listeners who expect a polished and engaging experience.

3. Distributing Your Audiobook

Once your audiobook is produced, you'll need to distribute it to reach potential listeners. Just as with print and eBooks, there are several platforms where you can sell your audiobook:

- **Audible**: Audible is the largest audiobook platform and is owned by Amazon, making it a key player in audiobook distribution. If you publish through ACX, your audiobook will automatically be available on Audible, Amazon, and Apple Books.

- **Findaway Voices**: Findaway Voices is another popular audiobook distribution platform that offers broader reach beyond Audible. It distributes your audiobook to platforms like Google Play, Spotify, Kobo, and libraries.

- **Direct Sales**: You can also sell your audiobook directly from your website or through platforms like Payhip or Gumroad, which allows you to keep a larger percentage of the revenue.

When setting up your audiobook for distribution, consider pricing it competitively. Audiobooks are typically priced higher than eBooks, but offering discounts or promotions can help you attract listeners who are new to audiobooks or trying out your work for the first time.

4. Exploring Other Alternative Formats

In addition to audiobooks, offering your book in other alternative formats can help you reach readers with specific needs or preferences. These formats include:

Large Print Editions

- **Why Offer Large Print**: Large print editions cater to readers with visual impairments or those who prefer larger text for comfort. Many libraries, senior centers, and specialty bookstores stock large print books, which can increase your book's reach in underserved markets.

- **How to Create Large Print Editions**: You can create a large print version of your book using POD services like IngramSpark or Amazon KDP. These platforms allow you to select a larger font size (typically 16-point or higher) and adjust the layout accordingly.

Translations

- **Expanding Your Global Audience**: Offering your book in different languages can open the door to international markets. If you've identified demand for your book in a non-English-speaking region, translating your book can significantly expand your reader base.

- **How to Find Translators**: Platforms like Reedsy, Upwork, and Babelcube can connect you with professional translators. Make sure to hire a translator who understands the nuances of your book's genre and style to maintain the integrity of your work.

Ebook Box Sets

- **Why Box Sets Work**: If you've written a series or multiple books, bundling them into a **box set** for digital platforms can increase sales and exposure. Box sets often attract readers who prefer to buy complete series at a discounted price.

- **How to Create a Box Set**: Use platforms like KDP or Draft2Digital to bundle your books into a box set. You can offer the set as an exclusive deal, which can encourage readers to purchase multiple books at once, increasing your overall sales.

5. Maximizing Accessibility and Inclusivity

Creating alternative formats is about more than just expanding your market—it's about making your book accessible to all kinds of readers. Here are a few more ways to maximize your book's accessibility:

- **Braille and Accessible Formats**: Consider making your book available in Braille or other accessible formats for readers with visual impairments. Organizations like Bookshare or the National Library Service for the Blind and Print Disabled (NLS) can help distribute books in accessible formats.

- **Interactive Ebooks**: For children's books or educational material, interactive eBooks with clickable elements, audio, or animations can enhance the reading experience. Platforms like Apple Books offer tools for creating interactive content.

Expanding your book's reach through audiobooks and alternative formats allows you to connect with more readers and create a lasting impact. By tapping into the growing audiobook market, offering large print editions, and exploring translations, you can maximize your book's accessibility and sales potential. In the next chapter, we'll focus on managing your author responsibilities beyond writing and how to maintain control over your career as a published author.

Quick Tips and Recap

- **Explore Print-on-Demand (POD)**: Platforms like Amazon KDP and IngramSpark offer flexible, cost-effective options for printing books only when ordered, reducing upfront costs and inventory risks.

- **Combine POD and Traditional Print Runs**: Use POD for ongoing sales and order traditional print runs for events or bulk sales, balancing cost and availability.

- **Leverage Major Digital Platforms**: Distribute your eBook and audiobook through Amazon, Audible, Apple Books, Kobo, and other global platforms to maximize reach.

- **Consider Audiobooks**: Tapping into the growing audiobook market with platforms like ACX and Findaway Voices can significantly boost your book's exposure and revenue.

- **Hire a Professional Narrator**: For a high-quality audiobook, consider hiring a professional narrator, or use platforms like ACX to find talent and manage the process.

- **Create Alternative Formats**: Offer large print editions, translations, and eBook box sets to expand your audience and meet the needs of diverse readers.

- **Maximize Accessibility**: Consider making your book available in Braille, interactive formats, or through accessible platforms like Bookshare to reach readers with disabilities.

- **Track Audiobook and Print Sales**: Use real-time data from distribution platforms to adjust pricing, marketing strategies, and promotion efforts.

By embracing these distribution strategies, you can ensure that your book is available in multiple formats and reach a broad audience, increasing your overall sales and visibility.

Navigating Publication Delays: Keeping Your Launch on Track

"Every delay is a chance to refine and rethink. It's not about when you arrive but how well-prepared you are when you do."
— TIM COOK, CEO OF APPLE

Welcome to Chapter Ten, "Navigating Publication Delays: Keeping Your Launch on Track," where the patience of a saint meets the strategic acumen of a chess master. Here, we prepare for the inevitable hiccups that sprinkle extra 'spice' on the path to publishing—because what's a journey without a little unexpected detour?

Think of publication delays as the plot twists in your publishing saga. Whether it's a printing hiccup, a logistical labyrinth, or the mysterious disappearance of manuscripts (now where did we last see those?), we'll tackle them all with grace and a plan. You'll learn the ins and outs of proactive communication with your team, how to adjust your marketing strategies on the fly, and how to keep your cool—and your fanbase engaged—even when your book's debut seems more like a fantasy than an upcoming event.

By the end of this chapter, you won't just be waiting out the storm; you'll be dancing in the rain, ensuring that when your book finally hits the shelves, it makes a splash that's worth the wait. So, brew some patience-enhancing tea and get ready to turn those delays into opportunities that amplify anticipation rather than dampen spirits!

Identifying Common Causes of Publication Delays

In the world of publishing, delays are almost as common as deadlines. Understanding the root causes of these delays can help you prepare for potential setbacks and minimize their impact on your launch. By anticipating the challenges that may arise, you'll be better equipped to handle them calmly and keep your book launch on track. In this section, we'll explore the most common causes of publication delays and how you can navigate them with strategic foresight.

1. Printing and Production Issues

One of the most frequent causes of publication delays is printing and production problems. These issues can range from minor mishaps, like a misprinted cover, to more significant challenges, like a paper shortage or machine malfunction.

Common printing and production issues include:

- **Incorrect formatting or design errors**: Misalignments in the layout, color inaccuracies, or issues with the cover design can cause delays, especially if these errors are not caught early.

- **Supply chain disruptions**: Shortages of paper, ink, or other materials can slow down the printing process, especially during high-demand periods.

- **Production capacity limitations**: During peak publishing seasons (such as the holidays), printing facilities may be overbooked, causing delays in your book's print run.

- **Technical malfunctions**: Machinery breakdowns or failures at the printing facility can halt production and push back your release date.

How to prepare:

- **Order proofs early**: Request a printed proof of your book early in the process to catch any design or formatting issues before the full print run.

- **Work with reliable printers**: Choose a printing service with a strong reputation for reliability and communication. If possible, build a relationship with your printer and discuss potential bottlenecks or risks ahead of time.

- **Stay flexible with your timeline**: Build some buffer time into your launch schedule in case production issues arise, so you're not caught off guard by last-minute delays.

2. Editorial and Proofreading Delays

Even with the best-laid plans, the editorial process can stretch beyond initial expectations, leading to delays in finalizing the manuscript. Editors and proofreaders may need additional time to polish your book, especially if revisions are more extensive than expected.

Common editorial delays include:

- **Extended revision rounds**: Sometimes, the feedback from your editor or beta readers requires more extensive changes than initially anticipated, which can lengthen the timeline.

- **Missed deadlines**: Your editor, proofreader, or formatting team may miss their deadlines due to workload, personal issues, or unforeseen complications.

- **Proofreading oversights**: Even after the editorial process, there may still be errors or inconsistencies that require further corrections before the book goes to print, causing additional delays.

How to prepare:

- **Set clear expectations**: Ensure that everyone involved in the editing and proofreading process is aware of the deadlines and expectations from the start. Regular check-ins can help avoid last-minute surprises.

- **Plan for multiple rounds of edits**: Build time into your schedule for more than one round of edits and proofreading, especially if your manuscript undergoes significant changes during revisions.

- **Be proactive in communication**: Stay in close contact with your editor and proofreader throughout the process. If delays occur, address them quickly to minimize the impact on your overall timeline.

3. Distribution and Shipping Challenges

Even after your book is printed, it still needs to get to the hands of readers and retailers. Distribution and shipping issues can cause delays that impact your ability to meet launch deadlines, especially if you're dealing with international shipping or multiple distribution channels.

Common distribution challenges include:

- **Logistical delays**: Shipping delays, customs issues, or warehouse backlogs can slow down the distribution of your book, particularly if you're working with global distributors or shipping to multiple locations.

- **Inventory mismanagement**: Sometimes, books are not delivered to the right location or are miscounted, leading to a shortage of copies at key retailers or events.

- **Retailer delays**: Retailers, especially larger ones like Amazon or Barnes & Noble, may take longer to stock your book due to internal processing times or backlog during busy seasons.

How to prepare:

- **Work with reliable distributors**: Partner with distribution services known for their reliability and transparency in communication. Platforms like IngramSpark and Amazon KDP have established processes for managing distribution and inventory.

- **Track shipments**: Stay on top of shipping and inventory management by tracking shipments closely and ensuring that books arrive at retailers and distributors on time.

- **Have a backup plan**: In case of shipping delays, have a contingency plan in place, such as offering digital versions or pre-order bonuses to keep readers engaged while waiting for the physical copies.

4. Marketing and Promotional Misalignment

Another frequent cause of delays is misalignment between the marketing timeline and the actual publication schedule. You may be ready to launch a marketing campaign, but if the book isn't available, the momentum you build can fizzle out before the launch happens.

Common marketing misalignment issues include:

- **Pre-orders not aligning with release dates**: If there's a delay in the production or distribution of your book, pre-orders may not be fulfilled on time, which can disappoint readers and hurt your promotional efforts.

- **Event rescheduling**: Delays can cause you to miss scheduled events, such as book signings, virtual launches, or blog tours, requiring you to reschedule and communicate new dates to your audience.

- **Miscommunication with promotional partners**: Bloggers, influencers, and media outlets may have scheduled posts or features around your launch date, and any delays could result in lost opportunities if you don't communicate the new timeline.

How to prepare:

- **Align marketing and production timelines early**: Ensure that your marketing plan aligns with your production schedule from the outset, so you're not promoting a book that's delayed. Build some flexibility into your promotional timeline.

- **Prepare for delays**: Always have a backup marketing plan in case your book's release is delayed. You can extend pre-order campaigns, offer additional content (such as sneak peeks or exclusive materials), and keep your audience engaged while they wait.

- **Communicate proactively with partners**: Keep your promotional partners, including bloggers and media outlets, in the loop about any changes to your timeline. This will help them adjust their schedules and prevent any missed opportunities.

By identifying the common causes of publication delays, you can take proactive steps to address potential issues before they escalate. Whether the delay is due to printing errors, editorial setbacks, or distribution challenges, being prepared can help you stay on top of the situation and minimize disruptions to your book's launch. In the next section, we'll discuss the importance of communicating with your team and stakeholders to keep everything on track and ensure that everyone is aligned with your revised timeline.

Communicating with Your Team and Stakeholders

Effective communication is the key to managing publication delays without causing confusion or frustration among your team, stakeholders, and audience. When delays occur, whether in printing, distribution, or marketing, the ability to convey changes in a timely and transparent manner can make all the difference in keeping your project on track. In this section, we'll cover strategies for maintaining clear communication with everyone involved in your book's publication process—from editors and publishers to readers and media partners.

1. Establish Clear Communication Channels Early

Before any delays occur, it's important to have a strong communication plan in place. By establishing clear communication channels early on, you'll be able to address issues swiftly and ensure that all parties are kept in the loop.

Here's how to set up effective communication from the start:

- **Designate Point People**: Ensure that everyone involved in your book's production and marketing knows who to contact in case of delays or issues. Designate a primary point of contact for each team (e.g., editor, publisher, printer, marketer) to streamline communication.

- **Use Collaborative Tools**: Leverage project management or communication tools like Trello, Asana, Slack, or Google Docs to keep track of tasks, updates, and deadlines. These platforms allow for real-time updates, ensuring that everyone stays informed of any changes.

- **Set Regular Check-Ins**: Schedule regular check-ins with your team to discuss the project's progress, address potential delays, and troubleshoot any problems that arise. These meetings can help you spot potential roadblocks early and allow for proactive adjustments.

Tip: Establish a clear communication protocol that outlines how delays or issues will be reported and handled. This ensures that when challenges arise, there's a defined process in place for addressing them quickly and effectively.

2. Proactively Communicate Delays to Your Team

When a delay is identified, the first step is to notify your team—editors, designers, printers, distributors, and marketers—so that everyone is aware of the new timeline. By addressing delays head-on, you can work together to find solutions and minimize the impact on your launch.

Here's how to communicate with your team during delays:

- **Be Transparent and Honest**: Clearly explain the nature of the delay, whether it's a production issue, distribution bottleneck, or editorial setback. Transparency is key to maintaining trust and ensuring that your team feels prepared to adjust their schedules accordingly.

- **Offer Solutions, Not Just Problems**: When notifying your team of a delay, present possible solutions alongside the problem. For example, if the printing process is delayed, suggest shifting certain marketing tasks (like social media promotions) to keep momentum going while the issue is resolved.

- **Provide a Revised Timeline**: As soon as you become aware of a delay, work with your team to establish a revised timeline. Share the updated schedule with everyone involved so they can adjust their plans accordingly. Make sure the new deadlines are realistic, considering the nature of the delay.

Example: "Due to an unexpected production issue with our printer, we're facing a two-week delay in the release of the paperback edition. I've attached an updated timeline and have proposed shifting the start of our social media marketing campaign to next Monday to maintain engagement. Let's discuss during our next meeting how we can adjust the rest of the schedule to accommodate this change."

3. Keep Stakeholders and Partners in the Loop

Your stakeholders, including publishers, retailers, media partners, and promotional influencers, also need to be kept informed of any delays to avoid confusion and misalignment. Ensuring that these partners are in the loop helps maintain strong relationships and reduces the risk of losing promotional opportunities due to rescheduling.

Here's how to communicate with stakeholders during delays:

- **Update Promotional Partners**: If your launch is delayed, be sure to notify bloggers, influencers, or media outlets who may have scheduled promotional content around your original release date. Give them as much notice as possible and suggest new dates for when they can feature your book.

- **Reschedule Launch Events**: If you've planned book signings, virtual events, or tours around your original launch date, communicate with the venues, platforms, or hosts as soon as possible to reschedule. Offer alternative dates and ensure that new promotional materials reflect the updated schedule.

- **Be Professional and Courteous**: When informing stakeholders of a delay, be professional and courteous in your communication. Delays can be frustrating, but showing that you're on top of the situation and have a plan in place will build confidence in your ability to manage the issue.

Example: "We wanted to inform you that the release date for our book has been pushed back by two weeks due to production delays. We're rescheduling the virtual book launch for [new date] and will be sending updated marketing materials shortly. Thank you for your flexibility and understanding."

4. Engage with Your Audience and Keep Them Excited

Your audience—whether fans, readers, or newsletter subscribers—is often the most affected by publication delays, as they're eagerly awaiting your book's release. While delays can be disappointing, how you handle communication with your readers can determine whether their excitement fades or builds even more.

Here's how to engage with your audience during delays:

- **Make an Official Announcement**: Use your email newsletter, social media, and author website to announce the delay to your readers. Be upfront about the situation and explain why the delay occurred, but maintain a positive tone.

- **Emphasize the Benefits of the Delay**: Highlight the benefits of the delay, such as ensuring that the final product is of the highest quality. Reframe the delay as a necessary step to create something even better for your readers.

- **Offer Bonus Content or Incentives**: To maintain excitement and engagement, offer bonus content, sneak peeks, or exclusive material to tide readers over while they wait for the new release date. This could include:

  o A free chapter or excerpt from the book.

  o Behind-the-scenes insights into the writing or production process.

  o Exclusive artwork, author interviews, or Q&A sessions.

  o Special giveaways or promotions that reward patience and loyalty.

Example: "We've hit a slight delay with the release of [Book Title], but we're working hard to make sure it's perfect for you! The new release date is [new date], and to thank you for your support, we're offering an exclusive sneak peek of the first two chapters! Stay tuned for more updates and exciting content leading up to launch day."

5. Monitor and Adapt as Needed

Once you've communicated the delay and updated timelines, it's important to continue monitoring the situation and keep lines of communication open. Delays can have a domino effect, impacting other aspects of the publication process, so be prepared to adapt and update your team, stakeholders, and readers as needed.

Here's how to stay adaptable:

- **Check in Regularly**: Keep checking in with your team and stakeholders to ensure that the revised timeline is being met. If any new issues arise, communicate them immediately to prevent further delays.

- **Adjust Marketing Plans**: Work with your marketing team to adjust any promotional plans in light of the delay. For example, if you had planned to launch ads or content on a specific date, make sure those dates are updated to reflect the new timeline.

Example: "Just a quick update: everything is on track with the revised timeline, and we're looking forward to launching the book on [new date]. Thanks to everyone for your flexibility and support—let's keep up the great work!"

Clear communication is essential for managing publication delays smoothly. By keeping your team, stakeholders, and readers informed and engaged, you can navigate the challenges with grace and maintain momentum for your book launch. In the next section, we'll explore how to adjust your marketing and launch strategy when faced with delays, ensuring that your promotional efforts stay strong, even if your timeline shifts.

Adjusting Your Marketing and Launch Strategy

When publication delays strike, they can disrupt even the most carefully planned marketing campaigns and launch strategies. However, with flexibility and creative thinking, you can adjust your marketing efforts to keep the momentum going.

Delays don't have to mean lost opportunities—they can even provide a chance to enhance your campaign and engage with your audience in new ways. In this section, we'll explore how to recalibrate your marketing and launch strategy when delays occur, ensuring your book's release is still a success.

1. Reevaluate Your Marketing Timeline

One of the first steps in adjusting your marketing strategy is to reassess the timeline you've already set. Whether it's social media campaigns, newsletter announcements, or blog tours, you'll need to align these efforts with your book's new release date. A well-adjusted timeline ensures that your promotional activities continue building momentum without losing steam during the delay.

Here's how to realign your marketing timeline:

- **Pause and Reschedule Promotions**: If your book's release is delayed, pause any ongoing ads, pre-order announcements, or influencer campaigns that are tied to the original launch date. Work with your marketing team to reschedule these efforts so that they align with the new release timeline.

- **Use the Extra Time to Build Anticipation**: Instead of seeing the delay as lost time, use it as an opportunity to build even more excitement. Gradually roll out exclusive content, such as cover reveals, character teasers, or behind-the-scenes posts, to keep readers engaged and looking forward to the new release.

- **Leverage Pre-orders**: If your book is available for pre-order, extend the pre-order period to take advantage of the delay. This can give you additional time to collect pre-orders, which can boost your book's rankings on platforms like Amazon when the book finally launches.

Tip: Adjust your marketing timeline so that major promotional activities—such as ads, interviews, or partnerships—happen closer to the new release date to maximize their effectiveness.

2. Keep Your Audience Engaged

Keeping your audience excited during a delay is crucial to maintaining their interest in your book. Readers who were initially excited about your launch may lose enthusiasm if they're left in the dark about the new timeline. However, by providing consistent updates and offering engaging content, you can sustain their interest and even deepen their connection with your book.

Here's how to keep your audience engaged:

- **Offer Sneak Peeks and Bonus Content**: Share **exclusive sneak peeks**, such as excerpts, cover art, or special Q&A sessions with readers. This keeps your audience invested and gives them something to look forward to while they wait.

- **Run a Giveaway or Contest**: Hosting a giveaway or contest is a great way to generate excitement and reward your loyal audience for their patience. You can offer signed copies, merchandise, or even early access to a chapter as a prize.

- **Engage Through Social Media**: Stay active on social media by posting regular updates, sharing fun facts about the book, or even creating polls to engage your readers. This keeps your audience involved and reminds them that the launch is still coming.

Example: "While we're ironing out the final details for the launch, here's a special behind-the-scenes look at the inspiration behind [Character Name]. Plus, stay tuned for a giveaway next week where you can win a signed copy of the book and exclusive merch!"

3. Reframe the Delay in a Positive Light

When you announce a delay, it's essential to frame it in a way that keeps your audience's excitement high and shows that the extra time will lead to an even better final product. Rather than apologizing profusely, shift the narrative to focus on how the delay will enhance the book or give readers something extra to look forward to.

Here's how to reframe the delay positively:

- **Highlight the Benefit to the Reader**: Explain that the delay allows you to perfect the book and ensure it meets the high standards your readers expect. For example, you can mention that you're fine-tuning the cover design, adding more bonus content, or ensuring the best quality for the print edition.

- **Keep a Positive Tone**: Maintain a positive and upbeat tone in all your communications, focusing on how the delay will ultimately make the launch even more exciting. Show your readers that the wait will be worth it and that you appreciate their patience and support.

Example: "We know you're excited to dive into [Book Title], and we want to make sure it's absolutely perfect for you! That's why we're taking a little extra time to put the finishing touches on it. In the meantime, we've got some exciting surprises coming your way, so stay tuned!"

4. Reschedule and Realign Events

If you've planned events around your original launch date—such as virtual book tours, signings, or interviews—these will need to be rescheduled to fit the new timeline. Don't see this as a setback—in fact, rescheduling gives you more time to prepare and possibly attract a larger audience.

Here's how to handle rescheduling:

- **Contact Hosts and Partners Early**: If you've scheduled interviews, blog tours, or collaborations with influencers, reach out to them as soon as possible to reschedule the event. Offering new dates and times can help you lock in their participation without losing the opportunity.

- **Reschedule Launch Events**: If you had a physical or virtual launch event planned, work with the venue or host to reschedule. Promote the new date with just as much enthusiasm as the original one—use the extra time to build more anticipation for the event.

- **Align Marketing Efforts with New Dates**: Make sure your new launch date is reflected in all your marketing materials, from social media banners to email campaigns. This helps your audience stay informed about the updated timeline and avoids confusion.

Example: "Due to unforeseen production delays, we've had to push back the launch event to [new date]. But don't worry—we're using this extra time to make it even more special, and we can't wait to celebrate with you all!"

5. Use the Delay to Refine Your Marketing Strategy

A delay offers a unique opportunity to reassess and refine your marketing strategy. You can take the extra time to optimize your ads, tweak your social media posts, or enhance your promotional efforts to ensure a more successful launch when the time comes.

Here's how to optimize your marketing during the delay:

- **Evaluate the Performance of Pre-Launch Campaigns**: Use the delay to assess the effectiveness of any pre-launch marketing efforts you've already run. Did certain social media posts perform better than others? Did one ad generate more pre-orders? Use this data to optimize future campaigns and maximize their impact.

- **Fine-Tune Your Messaging**: With more time to think about your book's positioning, consider refining your marketing message. Can you better highlight the unique selling points of your book? Should you update your pitch to reflect any new developments, such as additional content or a revised cover?

- **Experiment with New Marketing Channels**: If the delay gives you extra time, use it to experiment with new marketing channels. This could mean running ads on platforms you haven't used before, creating a book trailer, or reaching out to influencers or bloggers you hadn't initially planned to collaborate with.

Example: "We're taking this time to perfect our launch strategy, and we can't wait to share more exciting news and content with you. In the meantime, keep an eye out for sneak peeks and special announcements!"

By adjusting your marketing and launch strategy in response to delays, you can keep your promotional efforts strong and your audience engaged. Whether it's rescheduling events, reframing the delay in a positive light, or offering bonus content, your ability to pivot and adapt will ensure that your book's launch remains successful, no matter the challenges. In the next section, we'll explore how to turn delays into opportunities, making the most of the extra time to further enhance your book's launch.

Turning Delays into Opportunities

While delays may initially seem like setbacks, they can be transformed into opportunities to further enhance your book's launch and connect with your audience in new ways. The extra time you gain from a delay can be used to fine-tune your marketing efforts, create additional content, or build even more anticipation for your release. In this section, we'll explore how to make the most of publication delays and turn them into opportunities that work in your favor.

1. Use the Extra Time to Perfect Your Book

A delay offers a valuable opportunity to revisit your book and make last-minute improvements that could elevate its quality. Whether it's refining the manuscript, improving the design, or adding bonus material, the extra time can be used to make your book even more compelling.

Here's how to use the delay to perfect your book:

- **Additional Editing or Proofreading**: If your book's release is delayed, take the time to do an extra round of proofreading or light editing. This ensures that your manuscript is as polished as possible before it goes to print.

- **Enhance the Cover or Interior Design**: Review the cover design and interior layout with fresh eyes. Does the cover align with the current market trends? Is the formatting flawless? Use the delay to make design tweaks that could help your book stand out.

- **Add Bonus Content**: Consider including bonus material, such as author's notes, deleted scenes, or discussion questions, that give readers something extra. This can enhance the reader's experience and give them more value when the book is finally released.

Example: "Thanks to the extra time, we've been able to include some bonus content that I think you're going to love—stay tuned for exclusive behind-the-scenes details on the writing process!"

2. Create More Buzz with Exclusive Pre-Launch Content

Delays provide an opportunity to build even more anticipation for your book. By releasing exclusive content or sneak peeks, you can keep your readers engaged and excited while they wait. This additional content not only sustains momentum but can also attract new readers who may not have heard of your book initially.

Here's how to use exclusive content to build buzz:

- **Release Teasers and Excerpts**: Share sneak peeks, such as an early chapter, character profiles, or artwork, that give readers a taste of what's to come. Teasers can generate excitement and encourage readers to share their anticipation with others.

- **Host a Countdown or Reveal Event**: Consider hosting a cover reveal or a countdown to the new release date. These events can be interactive, such as a live stream or Q&A session with readers, and help build excitement leading up to the launch.

- **Offer Pre-Launch Incentives**: Encourage readers to pre-order or engage with your book during the delay by offering special incentives, such as signed copies, limited edition swag, or exclusive content. This gives readers a reason to stay invested even while the release date is pushed back.

Example: "To thank you for your patience, we're offering a special bonus: everyone who pre-orders the book by the new release date will receive a free exclusive short story set in the same world!"

3. Engage More Deeply with Your Audience

Delays give you more time to connect with your audience on a personal level. Whether it's through social media, your email list, or virtual events, engaging deeply with your readers can foster loyalty and build a stronger community around your book. This connection can pay off on launch day, as engaged readers are more likely to spread the word and support your book's release.

Here's how to use delays to engage with your audience:

- **Host Interactive Events**: Use the delay as an opportunity to host interactive events, such as live Q&A sessions, virtual book club discussions, or interviews with fellow authors. This keeps your audience engaged while giving them more insight into your book and creative process.

- **Personalized Updates**: Send personalized email updates to your readers, sharing your journey through the delay and how it's impacting the final product. Readers appreciate transparency, and regular updates will keep them excited for the eventual release.

- **Run Polls or Contests**: Ask your readers for their opinions on certain aspects of the book, such as favorite characters or potential future storylines. You can also run contests where readers submit fan art or guesses about the plot, with winners receiving exclusive prizes.

Example: "Join me for a live Q&A this Saturday where we'll talk about the world-building behind [Book Title] and take a sneak peek at the first chapter. Plus, I'll be answering all your burning questions!"

4. Enhance Your Marketing Campaign

A delay gives you more time to refine and expand your marketing campaign. This extra time can be used to explore new marketing channels, reach out to more promotional partners, or build a larger presence on social media. By enhancing your campaign, you can ensure that your book's eventual release will be met with even more enthusiasm.

Here's how to strengthen your marketing campaign:

- **Experiment with New Platforms**: Use the delay to explore new marketing platforms you hadn't originally planned on using. This could include running ads on Goodreads, collaborating with Bookstagrammers on Instagram, or creating video content for TikTok. Expanding your reach can help attract more readers.

- **Reach Out to Additional Influencers and Reviewers**: With more time on your hands, you can reach out to more influencers, bloggers, or reviewers who can help promote your book. Send them ARCs (advance review copies) or request features on their platforms to build more pre-launch buzz.

- **Double Down on Social Media**: Leverage social media to continue building your book's presence. Post teasers, engage with readers, and participate in relevant conversations within your genre. The more visibility you build, the more momentum you'll have on launch day.

Example: "We're using this extra time to really amp up our marketing efforts, so expect to see even more exciting content leading up to the new release date— follow along on Instagram for exclusive behind-the-scenes updates!"

5. Reward Loyal Fans and Build a Stronger Connection

Delays are an excellent opportunity to reward your most loyal fans and build deeper relationships with your readers. Offering special perks or incentives to your biggest supporters not only shows your appreciation but also strengthens the bond between you and your audience. These loyal readers will be your best advocates when the book is finally released.

Here's how to reward your loyal fans:

- **Create Exclusive Offers for Early Supporters**: Offer something special to those who have pre-ordered or have been following your book closely, such as signed copies, exclusive merchandise, or early access to bonus content.

- **Give Personalized Shoutouts**: Publicly thank your most engaged readers through social media shoutouts or personalized email updates. This builds goodwill and shows that you appreciate their patience and support.

- **Host a VIP Event**: Consider hosting an exclusive virtual event for your most loyal fans, such as a private Zoom Q&A or a virtual book club. This can deepen your connection with readers and make them feel like part of the journey.

Example: "To thank everyone for sticking with us through this delay, we're hosting an exclusive VIP event where I'll be sharing the first three chapters of [Book Title]—and answering all your questions live!"

Publication delays don't have to be a roadblock—they can be an opportunity to enhance your book launch in ways you hadn't initially considered. By perfecting your book, creating engaging pre-launch content, deepening your connection with readers, and refining your marketing campaign, you can turn a delay into a positive force that builds anticipation and strengthens your launch. With the right mindset and strategy, you can ensure that your book's release is even more successful than you initially planned.

Quick Tips and Recap

- **Identify Common Causes of Delays**: Be proactive by understanding potential issues like printing errors, editorial delays, and distribution challenges to prevent or address them early.

- **Communicate Transparently**: Keep your team, stakeholders, and audience informed of delays, providing clear updates, solutions, and revised timelines.

- **Adjust Your Marketing Timeline**: Pause and reschedule promotions, realign launch events, and use the delay to build anticipation with sneak peeks and bonus content.

- **Reframe the Delay Positively**: Highlight how the extra time will enhance your book's quality and create additional buzz for its release.

- **Engage Your Audience**: Keep readers excited with exclusive content, interactive events, and giveaways during the delay.

- **Leverage the Delay for Marketing**: Take advantage of the extra time to refine your marketing strategy, experiment with new platforms, and expand your outreach to influencers and reviewers.

- **Turn Delays into Opportunities**: Use the extra time to perfect your book, build more buzz, engage with your audience, and strengthen your marketing efforts.

By staying flexible and proactive, you can turn publication delays into opportunities to enhance your book's success and make your launch even more impactful.

PART THREE

Understanding Your Commitments

Welcome to Part Three: "Understanding Your Commitments," where we navigate the often treacherous but always essential waters of contractual obligations. Think of this as your guide to the fine print that binds—the chains you willingly wear to ensure your book not only sees the light of day but also finds its place in the sun. Here, we're not just crossing Ts and dotting Is; we're decoding the arcane language of contracts to uncover what you've promised to whom, and what mythical beasts you'll need to slay to keep those promises. From author responsibilities to managing multiple contracts without cloning yourself, this section prepares you to juggle your commitments with the finesse of a circus performer spinning plates. So, grab your magnifying glass and your best balancing shoes—it's time to ensure those commitments don't end up committing you!

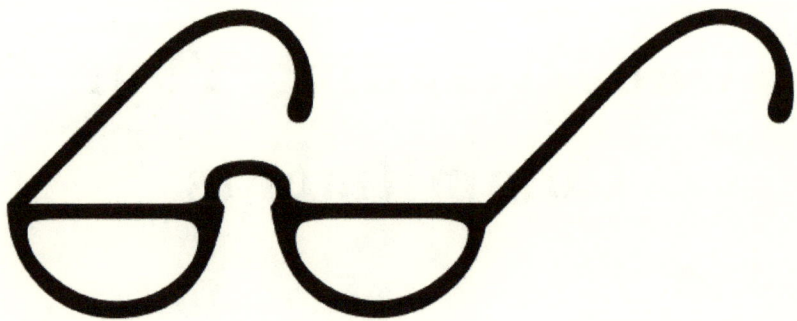

Author Responsibilities: Your Role Beyond Writing

"Being an author isn't just about writing; it's about throwing your whole self behind your work and engaging with your readers on every level." — NEIL GAIMAN, AUTHOR

Welcome to Chapter Eleven, "Author Responsibilities: Your Role Beyond Writing," where we explore the glamorous (and occasionally not-so-glamorous) life of an author after the final period is placed. Think of this as the behind-the-scenes tour where the real work begins—yes, Virginia, there's more to do than just penning your masterpiece!

Here, you're not just an author; you're a multitasking maestro, a promotional powerhouse, and a deadline-dueling dynamo. You'll learn how to wear multiple hats gracefully, from being your own biggest advocate during marketing

195

campaigns to potentially discussing character motivations in book clubs. We'll show you how to navigate interviews without breaking a sweat, how to read your work aloud without turning into a robot, and even how to handle the dreaded world of social media where every like is a high five and every troll is a test of patience.

Get ready to flex those muscles you didn't know you had, and prepare to step into the spotlight—it's not just about what you write, but how well you can juggle the flaming torches of responsibility that come with being an author in today's ultra-connected world.

Mastering the Art of Self-Promotion

As an author, writing the book is just the beginning. Once your manuscript is complete, one of the most critical responsibilities you'll have is promoting both your book and yourself. Self-promotion can feel daunting, but it's essential for building an audience, boosting sales, and establishing your author brand. In today's connected world, self-promotion is no longer optional—it's a necessity. The good news is that with the right tools and strategies, you can master the art of self-promotion without feeling overwhelmed.

In this section, we'll explore how to effectively promote your book and personal brand through various channels, from interviews and book signings to social media and author websites. Let's dive into how you can become your book's biggest advocate.

1. Create a Strong Author Brand

Your author brand is more than just your name—it's the identity you present to the world. It's how readers perceive you and your work, and it should reflect your values, style, and the themes of your books. Creating a consistent and memorable author brand is the foundation for all your promotional efforts.

Here's how to build a strong author brand:

- **Develop Your Author Persona**: Think about how you want to be perceived as an author. Are you approachable and humorous, or serious and thought-provoking? Align your social media tone, website content, and interviews with this persona.

- **Consistent Visual Identity**: Your book covers, website design, and social media profiles should have a cohesive look. Use consistent color schemes, fonts, and imagery that reflect the tone of your writing.

- **Craft a Memorable Author Bio**: Write a compelling author bio that captures your personality and highlights your accomplishments. This bio will be used across platforms, from your website to book jackets and interviews. Be sure to include what sets you apart as an author and any unique aspects of your journey.

Example: If you write whimsical fantasy, your author brand might lean into a playful, imaginative persona. You could use bright, magical imagery on your website, and your social media posts could reflect a sense of wonder, perhaps even featuring behind-the-scenes peeks into your creative process.

2. Leverage Social Media Effectively

Social media is a powerful tool for authors, providing a platform to engage directly with readers, share updates, and build a following. However, navigating social media effectively requires more than just posting occasionally—it's about building relationships and offering value to your audience.

Here's how to make the most of social media:

- **Choose the Right Platforms**: You don't have to be everywhere—choose the platforms where your target audience is most active. For many authors, Instagram, Twitter, and Facebook are effective, while platforms like TikTok (especially BookTok) and YouTube can also be valuable depending on your audience and content style.

- **Post Consistently**: Regularly post content that provides value, such as book teasers, writing tips, or insights into your writing process. Consistency is key to keeping your audience engaged and building a following.

- **Engage with Your Followers**: Social media is about interaction, not just broadcasting. Respond to comments, thank people for sharing your posts, and participate in discussions related to your genre or themes. Engaging with readers helps build loyalty.

- **Use Hashtags and Communities**: Hashtags like #AmWriting, #Bookstagram, and #BookTwitter help increase the visibility of your posts. Engage with communities of readers, writers, and reviewers who share your interests.

- **Host Giveaways or Contests**: A well-planned giveaway can generate excitement around your book. Offer signed copies, exclusive content, or book-themed merchandise as prizes to incentivize participation.

Tip: Make your social media posts more engaging by using visuals—book covers, photos of your writing space, or even short videos. Visual content tends to perform better and catch the attention of potential readers.

3. Build an Author Website

Your author website is your digital headquarters. It's where readers, media, and industry professionals will go to learn more about you, find your books, and connect with your work. A professional, user-friendly website is an essential part of your self-promotion strategy.

Here's what your author website should include:

- **About Page**: Share your author bio, your writing journey, and what inspires you. This page helps readers connect with you on a personal level.

- **Books Page**: Include a dedicated page for your books with links to purchase them. For each book, provide a synopsis, reviews, and any relevant bonus content, such as interviews or discussion guides.

- **Blog**: A blog can help keep your website active and give readers a reason to return. You can share insights about your writing process, upcoming projects, and book-related topics.

- **Newsletter Sign-Up**: Collect email addresses from visitors by offering a free newsletter. In exchange for signing up, you can offer exclusive content like a short story, early access to book updates, or writing tips.

Newsletters are a powerful way to maintain ongoing communication with your most engaged readers.

- **Media Kit**: If you plan to engage with the media, having a downloadable press kit—including your author bio, high-resolution photos, and book details—can make it easy for journalists or bloggers to feature you.

Example: If you write thrillers, your website design could reflect a dark, suspenseful aesthetic, with moody colors and a clean, professional layout. You could offer bonus chapters or deleted scenes to entice readers to sign up for your newsletter.

4. Maximize Book Launches and Signings

Your book launch is a major event, and it's an opportunity to create buzz, engage with readers, and sell copies. Whether it's an in-person signing or a virtual event, a well-executed book launch can generate significant momentum for your book's success.

Here's how to make the most of book launches and signings:

- **Plan Ahead**: Start planning your book launch well in advance. Promote the event through social media, your newsletter, and any partnerships with local bookstores or online platforms.

- **Host Virtual Events**: Virtual book launches and readings have become increasingly popular. Use platforms like Zoom, Facebook Live, or YouTube to engage with a wider audience. These events can include Q&A sessions, live readings, or even a behind-the-scenes tour of your writing process.

- **Prepare for In-Person Signings**: If you're hosting a physical book signing, ensure you have enough copies of your book available, and make the event interactive. Consider offering signed copies, personalized messages, or even small giveaways to attendees.

- **Partner with Bookstores and Libraries**: Partnering with local bookstores or libraries to host your launch or signing can increase visibility. They often help promote the event, bringing in more attendees.

Tip: For virtual launches, engage with the audience in real time by answering questions and interacting in the chat. Offering limited-time bonuses, like a discount on your book or an exclusive signed edition, can incentivize attendees to purchase during the event.

5. Utilize Media and Podcasts

Interviews with bloggers, podcasters, and journalists can significantly boost your visibility as an author. It's important to approach media outlets strategically and be prepared to speak about your book in a way that's engaging and informative.

Here's how to maximize media appearances:

- **Research Relevant Outlets**: Identify media outlets, blogs, and podcasts that cater to your book's genre or audience. Approach them with a personalized pitch that highlights why your book would be of interest to their readers or listeners.

- **Prepare Talking Points**: When preparing for interviews, have a few key talking points ready. These could include the inspiration behind your book, your writing process, or interesting details about your characters or world-building.

- **Be Authentic and Engaging**: Media appearances are an opportunity to showcase your personality and connect with a broader audience. Be genuine, stay on-topic, and make sure to mention where listeners or readers can purchase your book.

- **Leverage Appearances**: After an interview or media feature, share it across your social media and website. The more you promote these appearances, the greater the impact they'll have on your overall visibility.

Mastering the art of self-promotion is crucial to building a successful career as an author. By creating a strong author brand, leveraging social media, building a professional website, maximizing book launches, and utilizing media outlets, you can effectively promote your work and build a loyal readership. Remember, self-promotion is about engaging with your audience and presenting your work with authenticity and enthusiasm—it's your chance to showcase not just your book, but the unique voice behind it.

Engaging with Readers and Building a Community

Writing a book is often a solitary endeavor, but building a readership and fostering a community around your work is a collaborative effort. As an author, connecting with your readers goes beyond selling books—it's about creating meaningful relationships, offering value, and turning casual readers into dedicated fans. Engaging with your audience is one of the most fulfilling parts of being an author, and it plays a key role in your long-term success.

In this section, we'll explore strategies for engaging with readers, building a loyal community, and nurturing those connections so that your readers become your greatest advocates.

1. Be Accessible and Approachable

One of the best ways to engage with your readers is by being approachable. Today's readers love getting to know the person behind the words, and they appreciate authors who take the time to interact with them. Whether it's responding to comments on social media or replying to fan emails, showing that you value your readers' time and opinions can create strong bonds.

Here's how to make yourself more accessible:

- **Respond to Readers**: Whether it's through social media, email, or blog comments, make an effort to respond to readers who reach out. A simple "thank you" or a response to their questions can leave a lasting impression.

- **Host Q&A Sessions**: Consider hosting live Q&A sessions on social media platforms or through a virtual event. This allows readers to ask questions directly and get to know you better. You can offer insight into your writing process, characters, and upcoming projects.

- **Acknowledge Fan Contributions**: If readers create fan art, share reviews, or post about your book, take the time to acknowledge and share their contributions. It shows that you appreciate their support and encourages further engagement.

Example: "I'm so glad you enjoyed the book! Thank you for taking the time to share your thoughts. Stay tuned—I'll be hosting a live Q&A next week to discuss some behind-the-scenes details about the writing process."

2. Start an Author Newsletter

An author newsletter is one of the most direct and personal ways to communicate with your readers. Unlike social media, where posts can get lost in the shuffle, an email newsletter lands directly in your readers' inboxes. It allows you to provide exclusive updates, share personal stories, and keep your audience informed about upcoming releases.

Here's how to create an engaging newsletter:

- **Offer Exclusive Content**: Give readers a reason to sign up for your newsletter by offering something they can't get elsewhere. This could be a free short story, early access to chapters, or behind-the-scenes insights into your writing process.

- **Send Regular Updates**: Consistency is key. Whether you send your newsletter weekly, biweekly, or monthly, make sure you're delivering valuable content on a regular schedule. Share book updates, upcoming events, or personal reflections that keep readers interested.

- **Include a Call-to-Action**: Encourage readers to engage with your content by including calls-to-action. Ask them to reply with their favorite character, submit questions for your next Q&A, or share your newsletter with friends who might enjoy your books.

Tip: Keep your newsletter fun and personal. Readers enjoy feeling like they're part of an exclusive community, so share anecdotes, insights, or even photos of your writing space to make them feel connected to you as an author.

3. Create a Reader Community Online

Creating an online community around your work allows readers to connect not only with you but also with each other. A reader community can exist on social media platforms like Facebook, Goodreads, or Discord, where fans of your books can discuss your work, share ideas, and foster a sense of belonging.

Here's how to build a reader community:

- **Launch a Facebook Group or Goodreads Page**: Start a Facebook group or Goodreads author page where readers can join discussions about your books. In these groups, you can share updates, answer questions, and even offer sneak peeks of upcoming projects. The key is to foster interaction between members, so encourage them to share their thoughts and opinions.

- **Host Virtual Book Clubs**: Consider hosting a virtual book club where readers can gather to discuss your latest book. You can lead the discussion, offer insights, and take questions from readers, creating a more intimate and interactive experience.

- **Utilize Discord or Forums**: For more robust community-building, platforms like Discord allow you to create channels where readers can discuss different aspects of your work, from character development to fan theories. You can also pop into conversations, host live events, or share exclusive content with your most dedicated fans.

Example: "Join my exclusive reader community on Facebook, where we discuss everything from plot twists to character development. Plus, I'll be dropping some sneak peeks of my next book soon!"

4. Host Interactive Events

Interactive events are a fantastic way to engage with readers in real-time. Whether virtual or in-person, these events allow you to connect on a deeper level, share your passion for your work, and foster excitement about your projects. Virtual events, in particular, are accessible to readers worldwide and have become a go-to option for connecting with a larger audience.

Here's how to host successful interactive events:

- **Plan Virtual Book Launches**: Hosting a virtual book launch is a great way to engage readers from different parts of the world. You can do a live reading, host a Q&A session, and give readers an inside look at your writing process. Platforms like Zoom, Facebook Live, or YouTube are ideal for this.

- **Lead Writing Workshops or Webinars**: If you want to offer value beyond your books, consider leading a writing workshop or webinar where you share tips and tricks for aspiring writers. This positions you as an expert and deepens your connection with readers who may also be interested in writing.

- **Participate in Virtual Signings**: Virtual signings are another fun way to engage with readers. Platforms like Authorgraph allow you to sign eBooks digitally, or you can offer personalized signed bookplates to send to readers who pre-order or purchase your book.

Tip: Keep your virtual events interactive by taking audience questions, running live polls, or offering giveaways for those who attend. The more engaged your audience feels, the more likely they are to stay invested in your work.

5. Encourage Reader-Generated Content

When readers create their own content—such as reviews, fan art, or social media posts about your book—it helps spread the word about your work and builds a sense of community. Encouraging reader-generated content shows that you value your readers' creativity and opinions.

Here's how to encourage reader-generated content:

- **Host Fan Art or Fan Fiction Contests**: If you have a dedicated fanbase, consider running a contest where readers submit fan art or fan fiction based on your characters or world. Feature the winners on your website or social media and offer prizes like signed copies or exclusive merchandise.

- **Ask for Reviews**: Encourage readers to leave reviews on platforms like Amazon, Goodreads, or their personal blogs. Reviews help other potential readers decide whether to pick up your book and are a valuable form of word-of-mouth marketing.

- **Feature Reader Content on Social Media**: If readers post about your book on social media, share their posts and thank them publicly. This recognition not only makes readers feel appreciated but also encourages others to share their experiences with your book.

Example: "I'm hosting a fan art contest! Submit your artwork inspired by [Character Name] for a chance to win a signed copy of my book and be featured on my website. I can't wait to see what you create!"

Engaging with readers and building a community is about more than promoting your book—it's about fostering meaningful connections that can lead to lasting support. By being accessible, creating interactive events, encouraging reader participation, and offering value through newsletters and communities, you can turn casual readers into loyal fans who are excited to follow your journey as an author. Remember, building a community takes time, but the relationships you develop with your readers can have a profound impact on your success and fulfillment as an author.

Navigating the Media and Public Appearances

For many authors, engaging with the media and making public appearances can feel intimidating—but these opportunities are powerful tools for expanding your reach and building your brand. Whether you're giving an interview for a podcast, appearing on a panel at a book festival, or participating in a virtual book tour, these moments allow you to showcase your personality, discuss your work, and connect with readers in ways that go beyond the written word.

In this section, we'll explore how to navigate media interactions and public appearances with confidence, ensuring that you make a lasting impression while staying true to yourself.

1. Prepare for Interviews and Media Features

Media interviews are one of the most effective ways to reach new audiences. Whether it's a podcast, radio show, TV spot, or blog interview, being well-prepared is key to delivering a strong, engaging performance. Interviews can range from formal to casual, but in all cases, they offer a chance to introduce your book to potential readers.

Here's how to prepare for media interviews:

- **Know Your Key Points**: Before the interview, decide on a few key talking points you want to highlight about your book. These could include your inspiration, the book's central themes, or what makes your work unique. Having these points prepared will help you stay focused and ensure you mention the most important aspects of your book.

- **Anticipate Common Questions**: Interviewers often ask similar questions, such as "What inspired you to write this book?" or "Can you tell us about your main character?" Prepare thoughtful answers to these common questions in advance, so you can respond confidently and without hesitation.

- **Practice Speaking Clearly and Concisely**: Interviews often have time limits, so practice answering questions clearly and concisely. Keep your responses engaging but to the point, and avoid going off on tangents. Practicing your answers ahead of time can help you stay focused during the interview.

- **Share Personal Stories**: Audiences love to hear personal stories from authors. Share anecdotes about your writing process, funny behind-the-scenes moments, or challenges you faced while writing the book. These details make your interview more memorable and relatable.

Example: "One of the biggest challenges I faced while writing this book was balancing my full-time job with my writing schedule. I ended up waking up an hour earlier every day just to get some quiet time to work, and that routine eventually became part of my creative process."

2. Engage Confidently in Public Speaking and Panels

Public speaking, whether it's at a book signing, panel discussion, or literary festival, is another excellent way to showcase your work and connect with your audience. While many authors are more comfortable behind a keyboard than in front of an audience, public appearances offer a chance to build credibility and expand your fan base.

Here's how to prepare for public speaking events:

- **Know Your Audience**: Before the event, research who will be attending and what topics will resonate with them. A talk at a genre-specific convention might focus on your book's themes, while a panel at a writing conference may delve more into your creative process or writing advice.

- **Prepare a Loose Script**: You don't need to memorize an entire speech, but having a loose script or outline of what you plan to say can help keep you on track. Practice speaking out loud so you're comfortable with your pacing and tone.

- **Embrace Authenticity**: Public speaking is most effective when it feels genuine. Don't worry about being perfect—focus on being yourself. If you're passionate, a little humor or vulnerability can go a long way in making a connection with your audience.

- **Interact with the Audience**: Engaging with your audience can make the experience more interactive and enjoyable for everyone. Ask questions, invite audience members to share their thoughts, or leave time for a Q&A session at the end of your talk. This makes your event feel more like a conversation than a presentation.

Tip: If public speaking makes you nervous, start small by participating in local events or virtual panels where the audience may be smaller and more forgiving. Over time, your confidence will grow.

3. Leverage Virtual Appearances and Webinars

With the rise of virtual events, authors now have even more opportunities to engage with audiences from the comfort of their own homes. Virtual book tours, webinars, and online author events are all great ways to reach readers without the need for travel, and they allow you to connect with audiences across the globe.

Here's how to make the most of virtual appearances:

- **Choose the Right Platform**: Depending on the event, choose a platform that best suits the audience and format. Zoom, Facebook Live, and Instagram Live are great options for interactive events, while platforms like YouTube are ideal for pre-recorded webinars or book trailers.

- **Engage with Attendees**: Just like in-person events, it's important to engage with your virtual audience. Use the chat or Q&A features to interact with attendees in real time. Acknowledge questions, respond to comments, and create a sense of connection, even through a screen.

- **Promote Ahead of Time**: Virtual events often require extra promotion since people aren't attending physically. Share event details on your social media, website, and newsletter ahead of time, and send reminders on the day of the event to boost attendance.

- **Use Visual Aids**: Virtual events give you the chance to incorporate visual aids like slideshows, images, or videos. These can make your presentation more engaging and help break up the monotony of a typical talking-head format.

Example: "For my virtual book launch, I'll be doing a live reading from Chapter 1, followed by a behind-the-scenes look at how I developed the characters. I'll also be answering your questions live—so get ready to ask me anything about [Book Title]!"

4. Make the Most of Book Signings and Festivals

Book signings, whether virtual or in-person, are a great opportunity to connect with readers one-on-one. These events provide a personal touch that strengthens the bond between you and your audience, making your book's impact even more lasting.

Here's how to maximize book signings and festivals:

- **Be Personable and Engaging**: When readers approach you at a signing, they want to feel valued. Make eye contact, engage in brief conversations, and personalize each book with a message that resonates with the reader. Even a quick "Thank you for supporting my book!" goes a long way.

- **Prepare for Small Talk**: Many attendees will want to chat briefly while getting their book signed. Have a few go-to conversation starters, such as asking what they liked most about your book or if they've attended similar events before. This makes the interaction more memorable and personal.

- **Bring Promotional Materials**: Have promotional materials like bookmarks, postcards, or flyers on hand to give away. These items serve as a lasting reminder of your book and can help readers spread the word.

- **Network with Other Authors**: If you're attending a literary festival or group event, use the opportunity to network with fellow authors. Building relationships with other writers can lead to future collaborations, guest spots on blogs, or joint promotional efforts.

Tip: If you're nervous about large in-person events, start with smaller, local signings at independent bookstores or libraries before tackling bigger festivals or conferences.

5. Follow Up and Build Relationships

After a successful media appearance or public event, it's important to keep the momentum going by following up with the host or participants. Building relationships with media outlets, event organizers, and attendees can lead to repeat opportunities and ongoing support for your future projects.

Here's how to follow up effectively:

- **Thank the Host or Organizer**: Send a thank-you email to the host or organizer of the event. Express your gratitude for the opportunity, and offer to stay in touch for future projects or interviews.

- **Share the Event**: If your appearance was recorded (such as a podcast or virtual event), share it across your social media and website. Tag the host and encourage your audience to tune in.

- **Connect with Attendees**: If attendees reached out during the event or asked questions, consider sending a quick follow-up message thanking them for their participation. This adds a personal touch and keeps you top of mind for future book purchases.

Example: "Thank you so much for having me on your podcast! I had a great time discussing [Book Title] and would love to collaborate again in the future. I'll be sharing the episode with my audience today!"

Navigating the media and public appearances is an essential skill for authors who want to expand their reach and connect with new readers. By preparing for interviews, engaging confidently in public speaking, leveraging virtual appearances, and following up after events, you can build strong relationships with your audience and the media, all while promoting your work in an authentic and compelling way. With practice and preparation, you'll be able to shine in the spotlight and make the most of every opportunity.

Managing Deadlines and Balancing the Author Lifestyle

As an author, your responsibilities often extend far beyond writing. From juggling marketing efforts, public appearances, and social media engagements to managing multiple deadlines, it's easy to feel overwhelmed. Learning how to manage these various demands while maintaining a healthy balance between your writing career and personal life is essential to staying productive and avoiding burnout.

In this section, we'll explore strategies for managing deadlines, setting realistic goals, and creating a sustainable workflow that allows you to balance your author responsibilities with the rest of your life.

1. Set Realistic Goals and Deadlines

One of the biggest challenges authors face is managing the various deadlines associated with writing, editing, publishing, and marketing a book. It's important to set realistic goals for each stage of the process and ensure that your deadlines are achievable, not overwhelming.

Here's how to set and manage realistic goals:

- **Break Large Tasks into Smaller Steps**: Large projects, like writing a novel or preparing for a book launch, can feel overwhelming. Break them down into smaller, manageable tasks with mini-deadlines. For example, instead of setting a goal to "finish the manuscript," break it into "write 1,000 words a day" or "complete Chapter 5 by Friday."

- **Prioritize Your Tasks**: Not all tasks have the same level of urgency. Use a system like the Eisenhower Matrix to categorize tasks based on importance and urgency. Focus on the most important and time-sensitive tasks first, and tackle lower-priority tasks when you have the bandwidth.

- **Set Buffer Time for Unexpected Delays**: Life often throws unexpected curveballs, from personal obligations to unforeseen book delays. Build some buffer time into your schedule to accommodate these surprises without throwing off your entire timeline.

- **Celebrate Milestones**: When you reach a significant milestone, such as finishing a draft or launching a marketing campaign, take a moment to celebrate your progress. Acknowledging small wins along the way can boost your motivation.

Example: "This week, my goal is to write 5,000 words, draft a new blog post for my author website, and finalize the cover design with my illustrator. I'll tackle the writing first each morning, then work on the marketing tasks in the afternoon."

2. Create a Flexible Routine

While routines can be incredibly helpful in staying productive, it's also important to remain flexible—especially as an author, where creative inspiration and external obligations can fluctuate. Establishing a daily or weekly routine that balances writing time, promotion efforts, and personal activities helps you stay focused while maintaining enough flexibility to adjust when needed.

Here's how to create a flexible routine:

- **Dedicate Specific Time for Writing**: Whether you're a morning person or a night owl, dedicate specific time blocks to your writing. Treat this time as sacred, avoiding distractions like emails or social media. Even setting aside 30 minutes to an hour each day can make a big difference over time.

- **Incorporate Marketing and Promotion**: Just as you schedule time for writing, block off time for marketing activities, such as engaging on social media, sending newsletters, or reaching out to media outlets. Scheduling these activities ensures that you don't neglect the promotion side of your career.

- **Allow for Flexibility**: Life happens, and sometimes you'll need to adjust your schedule. Whether you need to respond to a media request, attend an event, or take a break, allow yourself flexibility within your routine to make those adjustments without guilt.

Tip: Experiment with different routines until you find one that works for you. Some authors prefer writing in short bursts with breaks, while others thrive with longer, uninterrupted writing sessions. Find what best fits your workflow and lifestyle.

3. Avoid Overcommitting and Know When to Say No

As an author, you'll face numerous opportunities—interviews, events, collaborations, and more. While it's exciting to participate in these activities, it's important to avoid overcommitting. Taking on too many responsibilities at once can lead to stress, burnout, and a decline in the quality of your work.

Here's how to manage your commitments:

- **Assess Each Opportunity**: Before saying yes to an event or collaboration, assess whether it aligns with your goals and whether you have the time to commit to it. Ask yourself if the opportunity will help you grow as an author or reach your target audience, and if it's worth the investment of your time.

- **Learn to Say No**: It can be difficult to turn down offers, but sometimes saying no is necessary to protect your time and energy. Politely declining an offer is better than overcommitting and risking burnout. You can also offer to revisit the opportunity at a later time when you have more availability.

- **Delegate When Possible**: If certain tasks, like social media management or administrative work, are taking up too much of your time, consider delegating them to a trusted assistant or freelance professional. This frees up more time for writing and other high-priority tasks.

Example: "I've decided to pass on this month's panel discussion because my deadline is approaching, but I'd love to participate in a future event. I'll reach out again when I have more time!"

4. Take Care of Your Physical and Mental Well-Being

Balancing your writing career with marketing, appearances, and other responsibilities can be draining. It's essential to prioritize your physical and mental well-being to maintain your productivity and avoid burnout. Remember that self-care is just as important as meeting deadlines.

Here's how to take care of yourself as you manage your author responsibilities:

- **Prioritize Breaks and Rest**: Working without breaks can lead to exhaustion and a decrease in creative energy. Schedule regular breaks during the day to recharge, whether it's a short walk, a stretch, or a few minutes of meditation. Also, ensure you're getting enough sleep to support your creativity and focus.

- **Practice Self-Care**: Make time for activities that relax and rejuvenate you, whether it's reading for pleasure, exercising, or spending time with loved ones. These activities will help you manage stress and keep a healthy balance between work and life.

- **Set Boundaries**: Setting boundaries with your time is crucial for protecting your well-being. This could mean turning off work notifications after a certain hour, scheduling "off" days where you focus solely on yourself, or setting limits on social media engagement.

- **Seek Support When Needed**: If you're feeling overwhelmed or struggling to balance your workload, don't hesitate to seek support. This could mean reaching out to fellow authors for advice, hiring professional help, or talking to a coach or therapist who can help you manage stress.

Tip: Use tools like the Pomodoro Technique, which encourages 25 minutes of focused work followed by a 5-minute break, to stay productive while also incorporating rest into your routine.

5. Track Your Progress and Adjust as Needed

Finally, it's important to regularly evaluate your progress and make adjustments to your schedule or goals when necessary. Life as an author is dynamic, and what works one month may not work the next. By tracking your progress and staying flexible, you'll be able to adapt to changing circumstances and continue growing in your career.

Here's how to track and adjust your progress:

- **Review Your Goals Regularly**: At the end of each week or month, take time to review your goals and progress. Have you met your writing targets? Are there any tasks that need more attention? This self-assessment helps you stay on top of your responsibilities and make any necessary adjustments.

- **Celebrate Achievements**: Recognize and celebrate your achievements, no matter how small. Whether you've met a writing goal or completed a successful interview, acknowledging your progress keeps you motivated.

- **Adjust When Needed**: If you find that a particular routine or strategy isn't working, don't be afraid to adjust. Whether it's changing your writing schedule, scaling back on commitments, or delegating tasks, staying adaptable will help you manage your workload more effectively.

Example: "This month, I'll shift my focus from marketing to completing the second draft of my manuscript. I've also decided to delegate social media management so I can focus more on writing."

Managing deadlines and balancing the author lifestyle requires careful planning, flexibility, and self-care. By setting realistic goals, creating a routine that works for you, avoiding overcommitment, and prioritizing your well-being, you can successfully navigate the many responsibilities of being an author. Remember that finding balance is an ongoing process, and adjusting your approach as needed will help you maintain both your productivity and your passion for writing.

Quick Tips and Recap

- **Break Tasks into Smaller Steps**: Manage big projects by breaking them into smaller, achievable tasks with clear deadlines.

- **Set Realistic Deadlines**: Plan achievable goals and allow buffer time to accommodate unexpected delays.

- **Create a Flexible Routine**: Dedicate time to writing, promotion, and personal activities, but be flexible enough to adjust when necessary.

- **Avoid Overcommitting**: Assess each opportunity and only commit to what aligns with your goals and capacity. Learn to say no when necessary.

- **Take Care of Your Well-Being**: Prioritize breaks, self-care, and setting boundaries to avoid burnout and maintain creativity.

- **Delegate When Possible**: Hand off administrative or time-consuming tasks to free up more time for writing and high-priority activities.

- **Track Your Progress**: Regularly review your goals and make adjustments to stay on track and maintain balance.

- **Celebrate Milestones**: Acknowledge and celebrate your achievements to stay motivated and maintain momentum.

By setting achievable goals, staying flexible, and prioritizing self-care, you can effectively manage the various responsibilities of being an author while maintaining a healthy work-life balance.

Contractual Commitments: What You've Agreed to Uphold

"Every contract you sign is more than a document; it's a promise. Understanding and upholding these commitments is fundamental to maintaining trust and credibility in your business dealings." — SIMON SINEK, LEADERSHIP EXPERT AND AUTHOR

Welcome to Chapter Twelve, "Contractual Commitments: What You've Agreed to Uphold," where we untangle the spaghetti bowl of promises and pledges you've served yourself with a side of contractual sauce. Here, it's less about creative prose and more about the prose of clauses that can dictate the next several years of your literary life.

Think of your contract as a marriage certificate between you and your publisher: for richer, for poorer, in sickness and in health, until the end of your rights do you part. We'll walk through the fine print with a fine-tooth comb, highlighting the 'I dos' and the 'I don'ts' that might slip past when the honeymoon phase of contract signing is over. You'll learn how to spot a bad deal from a mile away and the nuances of contract clauses that could make or break your authorial independence.

Prepare to don your legal eagle glasses and dive deep into the commitments that bind. By the end of this chapter, you'll not just understand your obligations—you'll own them, ready to navigate the contractual waters with confidence and maybe even a little swagger.

Key Contract Clauses: What You Need to Know

Signing a publishing contract is a significant milestone in your career as an author, but it's essential to understand exactly what you're agreeing to before putting pen to paper. Contracts can be dense and packed with legal language that may feel overwhelming, but certain clauses are especially important because they directly impact your rights, royalties, and responsibilities as an author. In this section, we'll walk through the key contract clauses you need to be familiar with and how they affect your relationship with the publisher.

1. Grant of Rights

The grant of rights clause defines which rights you are giving to the publisher and for how long. It's one of the most important parts of the contract because it determines what the publisher can do with your book and what rights you retain as the author.

Key points to consider:

- **Exclusive vs. Non-Exclusive Rights**: Most traditional publishers require exclusive rights to publish and distribute your book. However, pay close attention to whether you're granting exclusive rights to print, eBook, and audiobook formats, or if some rights remain non-exclusive, allowing you to pursue other avenues for those formats.

- **Territorial Rights**: This specifies where the publisher can sell your book. World rights give the publisher the ability to sell in any country, while territorial rights might limit sales to certain regions like North America or the UK. If world rights are granted, ensure you understand the financial implications of foreign sales.

- **Duration of Rights**: This section specifies how long the publisher holds the rights to your work. Often, rights revert to the author after a certain period of time or under specific conditions, such as if the book goes out of print.

Example: "You grant the publisher the exclusive right to publish, distribute, and sell the Work in all formats (including print, digital, and audio) worldwide for the duration of the copyright term."

Tip: Retaining some rights, such as film, merchandise, or translation rights, can allow you to explore other opportunities. Be sure to negotiate and understand which rights you're comfortable granting to the publisher.

2. Advances and Royalties

The advances and royalties clause determines how you will be paid for your work. This section covers the advance payment you receive upon signing the contract and how royalties are calculated once the book is published.

Key points to understand:

- **Advance Payment**: The advance is typically paid out in installments—often upon signing, upon delivery of the manuscript, and upon publication. Advances are against royalties, meaning you won't earn additional royalties until the publisher has recouped the advance through book sales.

- **Royalty Rates**: Royalties are usually a percentage of sales revenue and vary depending on the format. For example, you might receive a higher percentage for eBook sales compared to print. Understand the royalty structure for different formats—print, digital, audiobook, and foreign sales.

- **Earning Out the Advance**: Once your book's sales cover the amount of the advance, you begin to earn royalties. It's crucial to know when you can expect royalty payments and how often royalty statements are issued (e.g., quarterly or biannually).

Example: "Author will receive an advance of $10,000, payable in three equal installments: upon signing the contract, upon submission of the final manuscript, and upon publication. The royalty rate shall be 10% of the cover price for hardcover sales, 5% for paperback, and 25% for eBook sales."

Tip: If you receive a significant advance, remember that you won't earn additional royalties until your book's sales surpass the amount of the advance. Make sure you're comfortable with the royalty rates and payment schedule outlined in the contract.

3. Manuscript Delivery and Acceptance

The manuscript delivery and acceptance clause outlines your obligations for submitting the manuscript, including deadlines and revision requirements. This clause is important because it sets the timeline for when your book needs to be completed and what happens if the publisher requires revisions.

Key points to consider:

- **Delivery Deadline**: The contract will specify the deadline by which you must deliver the manuscript. Make sure this date is realistic based on your writing schedule and any other commitments you may have.

- **Acceptance and Revisions**: After you deliver the manuscript, the publisher has the right to request revisions before accepting the book for publication. It's important to understand the process for revisions and how many rounds of editing may be required.

- **Failure to Deliver**: The contract will include language about what happens if you fail to deliver the manuscript by the agreed-upon date. This could include the publisher terminating the contract or withholding further payments.

Example: "The Author agrees to deliver the completed manuscript by June 1, 2024. The Publisher shall review the manuscript and provide feedback within 60 days. Should revisions be required, the Author agrees to deliver a revised manuscript within 30 days of receiving editorial comments."

Tip: Don't hesitate to negotiate deadlines if the proposed timeline feels too tight. It's better to have a longer delivery schedule upfront than to miss a deadline later.

4. Marketing and Promotion

The marketing and promotion clause outlines what the publisher is responsible for when it comes to promoting your book—and what you, as the author, are expected to contribute. This section can vary widely between publishers, so it's important to clarify how much marketing support you'll receive.

Key points to consider:

- **Publisher's Marketing Efforts**: The contract may specify certain marketing activities the publisher will undertake, such as sending out review copies, arranging book signings, or investing in advertising. Understand the level of support you can expect.

- **Author's Responsibilities**: Some contracts include language that obligates the author to participate in promotional activities, such as attending events, maintaining a social media presence, or conducting interviews. Be clear on what's required of you and what expenses (like travel) the publisher will cover.

- **Cross-Promotions and Additional Marketing**: Some contracts may specify that the publisher can use your likeness or excerpts from your book for marketing purposes. Make sure you're comfortable with how your work and image will be promoted.

Example: "The Publisher agrees to undertake marketing efforts, including sending review copies to key industry publications, promoting the book on social media, and organizing book signings. The Author agrees to participate in promotional activities as reasonably requested by the Publisher."

Tip: Ask for specifics when it comes to the publisher's marketing efforts. A vague promise of "marketing support" might not mean much in practice. If marketing is important to you, request details about their strategy.

5. Termination and Reversion of Rights

The termination and reversion of rights clause outlines the circumstances under which the contract can be terminated and what happens to the rights to your book afterward. It's crucial to understand how and when you can regain control of your work if things don't go as planned.

Key points to understand:

- **Termination Conditions**: The contract will specify what happens if the publisher fails to meet certain obligations, such as failing to publish the book within a reasonable timeframe. This clause protects you if the publisher doesn't follow through.

- **Reversion of Rights**: If the book goes out of print or the publisher is no longer actively selling it, you may have the right to reclaim ownership. This allows you to seek new publishing opportunities or self-publish the work.

- **Exit Clauses**: Be aware of the conditions under which you or the publisher can terminate the contract early, and what financial or legal penalties may apply.

Example: "If the Publisher fails to publish the Work within 18 months of manuscript acceptance, all rights granted to the Publisher shall revert to the Author. In the event of a breach by the Author, the Publisher reserves the right to terminate the contract and retain the advance."

Tip: Negotiate for clear terms regarding reversion of rights. If the publisher no longer has interest in promoting your book, you should have the opportunity to reclaim it and explore other avenues.

Understanding these key contract clauses ensures that you're aware of your rights, obligations, and financial arrangements with the publisher. By familiarizing yourself with the grant of rights, royalties, manuscript delivery, marketing, and termination clauses, you'll be better equipped to negotiate a contract that supports your long-term success as an author. Always read the fine print carefully and seek legal advice if you're unsure about any aspect of the agreement.

Understanding Author Deliverables

When you sign a publishing contract, you're committing to more than just turning in a manuscript. As an author, you'll have various deliverables that go beyond writing, including revisions, marketing involvement, and sometimes even promotional materials. Understanding exactly what your publisher expects from you, and by when, is crucial to maintaining a healthy working relationship and ensuring that your book progresses smoothly from manuscript to publication.

In this section, we'll explore the different deliverables you may be responsible for under your contract and how to manage them effectively.

1. Manuscript Delivery and Revisions

The primary deliverable, of course, is the manuscript itself. But it's important to remember that the manuscript you submit may not be the final version your readers see. Most publishing contracts require that you not only submit the manuscript by a specific deadline but also complete revisions based on editorial feedback. This process could include multiple rounds of edits, and your ability to meet revision deadlines can impact the publication timeline.

Here's what to expect:

- **Submission Deadline**: Your contract will specify the date by which your manuscript must be submitted. This deadline is often tied to when you'll receive the second portion of your advance, so meeting it is important.

- **Editorial Revisions**: After submission, your editor may request revisions. The contract should outline how many rounds of revisions are expected and how long you'll have to complete them. Make sure the timeframe for revisions is realistic for you, given the scope of the edits and any other commitments you have.

- **Final Approval**: The publisher typically has the final say on whether the manuscript is considered "final." Once you and the editor have agreed on the manuscript, it moves into the next stages of production, such as copyediting and formatting.

Example: "The Author agrees to deliver the completed manuscript by June 30, 2024. The Publisher will provide feedback and revision requests within 30 days. The Author will submit revisions within 45 days of receiving editorial feedback."

Tip: Clarify in your contract the number of revision rounds expected and the time you'll have for each. This helps prevent surprises or rushed deadlines later in the process.

2. Ancillary Materials (Dedication, Acknowledgments, and Author Bio)

In addition to your manuscript, publishers often require ancillary materials that help round out the book's content and packaging. These include your dedication, acknowledgments, and author bio, all of which contribute to the reader's experience and how you are presented as an author.

Here's what to prepare:

- **Dedication**: This is a personal note at the front of your book, often addressing family, friends, or mentors. It's short but meaningful, and you'll likely need to submit this when your manuscript is finalized.

- **Acknowledgments**: The acknowledgments section gives you the opportunity to thank anyone who contributed to the creation of your book—editors, agents, beta readers, family, etc. Your contract might specify a deadline for this, often tied to the final stages of production.

- **Author Bio**: Most publishers will request a short author bio to include in the book's back matter or on marketing materials. This should be polished and professional, highlighting your credentials, previous works, and any relevant personal information.

Example: "The Author will submit the dedication, acknowledgments, and author bio no later than 60 days before the scheduled publication date."

Tip: Keep these deliverables in mind as you approach the final stages of manuscript preparation. Even though they seem minor, they can be important to both the book's presentation and your brand as an author.

3. Marketing and Promotional Materials

Many publishing contracts include clauses that obligate the author to participate in marketing and promotional activities. While the level of involvement can vary from publisher to publisher, it's important to understand what's expected of you when it comes to marketing your book.

Here are common promotional deliverables:

- **Press Kit**: Some publishers may require you to contribute to a press kit, which could include an extended author bio, interviews, or even Q&A content for media outlets. While they may draft the press kit for you, you might be responsible for reviewing or contributing to it.

- **Book Launch and Social Media**: You might be expected to play an active role in promoting your book, whether through participating in book launches, social media campaigns, or interviews. Make sure your contract outlines what your publisher will handle versus what's expected of you.

- **Interviews and Public Appearances**: Some contracts specify that you must make yourself available for interviews, book signings, or public appearances to promote the book. While this can be a great opportunity to engage with readers, make sure you understand how much of your time will be required.

Example: "The Author agrees to participate in reasonable marketing and promotional activities as requested by the Publisher, including interviews, social media campaigns, and virtual book launch events."

Tip: Discuss marketing expectations with your publisher ahead of time to ensure you're comfortable with the level of involvement. If you have a particular strength—such as social media engagement or podcast appearances—leverage that in the marketing plan.

4. Supplementary Content (Forewords, Afterwords, or Bonus Material)

Depending on the type of book you're writing, your publisher may request supplementary content, such as a foreword, afterword, or bonus material that adds value to the book. This is especially common in nonfiction works or special editions of novels, where extra content can enhance the reader's experience and give the book a competitive edge in the market.

Here's what to consider:

- **Foreword or Afterword**: A **foreword** is often written by another author or expert in your field, providing credibility and context for your work. In some cases, the author is asked to write their own afterword, reflecting on the book's themes or its journey from concept to publication.

- **Bonus Content**: Some publishers may request bonus content for special editions or eBook versions. This could include deleted scenes, character sketches, or additional essays related to your book. While not always mandatory, this content can serve as a valuable marketing tool and a way to engage your most dedicated readers.

- **Discussion Guides**: In some genres, particularly book club-friendly fiction or nonfiction, a discussion guide might be included at the back of the book. Publishers may ask you to provide questions or prompts to encourage deeper reader engagement.

Example: "The Author agrees to provide an afterword and discussion guide within 30 days of manuscript acceptance, to be included in the trade paperback edition."

Tip: Ensure any additional content requests are clearly defined in your contract. Knowing exactly what's required—and when—will help you avoid last-minute surprises and stress.

5. Managing Multiple Deliverables

With all the moving parts of a book deal, it's easy to feel overwhelmed by the various deadlines and deliverables you'll need to manage. A clear understanding of what's expected and effective organization is key to keeping everything on track.

Here's how to manage multiple deliverables:

- **Create a Timeline**: Break down all of your contract's deliverables into a timeline, starting with the manuscript deadline and working backward. Assign dates for when you'll work on ancillary materials, marketing content, and any additional writing required by the publisher.

- **Communicate with Your Publisher**: If at any point you feel that you won't be able to meet a deadline, communicate with your publisher as early as possible. Publishers can sometimes be flexible, especially if you keep them informed about your progress.

- **Stay Organized**: Use project management tools or even a simple calendar to keep track of your deliverables. Organizing everything in one place ensures you won't miss an important deadline or forget to submit necessary materials.

Tip: Consider creating a checklist for each stage of the process—manuscript delivery, marketing involvement, and additional content—to ensure you stay on top of each deliverable as you move toward publication.

Understanding author deliverables means recognizing that your role as an author extends beyond simply submitting a manuscript. From revisions and ancillary materials to marketing participation and supplementary content, your publishing contract will outline the various commitments you'll need to fulfill. By managing your time effectively and staying clear on what's required, you can meet these obligations confidently and keep your book's journey toward publication smooth and successful.

What Happens If You Miss a Deadline

Deadlines are an integral part of the publishing process, and while most authors strive to meet them, life sometimes gets in the way. Whether it's writer's block, personal emergencies, or unforeseen challenges, missing a deadline can happen. However, understanding the potential consequences of missing a deadline, and knowing how to communicate and negotiate with your publisher, can help you navigate this situation smoothly and protect your author-publisher relationship.

In this section, we'll explore what happens if you miss a deadline, how to mitigate the consequences, and strategies for avoiding serious setbacks.

1. The Contractual Consequences of Missing a Deadline

Every publishing contract outlines specific delivery deadlines for your manuscript and other obligations. Failing to meet these deadlines can trigger consequences, which are usually detailed in the contract's terms. It's crucial to understand what's at stake if you don't submit your manuscript or other deliverables on time.

Here's what could happen if you miss a deadline:

- **Delayed Payments**: If you're being paid in installments, your next payment might be tied to meeting your manuscript submission deadline. Missing that deadline could delay the payment until the manuscript is delivered and accepted by the publisher.

- **Termination of the Contract**: In some contracts, missing a deadline could give the publisher the right to terminate the agreement. While this is typically a last resort, it's important to know whether your publisher can take this action if deadlines aren't met.

- **Loss of Rights**: In extreme cases, missing a deadline might result in the publisher reclaiming the rights to the book. If the publisher chooses to terminate the contract, the rights granted to them might revert to you, but this can come with financial or legal penalties.

- **Reputational Impact**: Repeatedly missing deadlines or failing to communicate effectively about delays can damage your relationship with the publisher. This might make it more difficult to secure future contracts or maintain a strong working relationship.

Example: "If the Author fails to deliver the manuscript by the agreed-upon deadline, the Publisher reserves the right to terminate the contract and reclaim the advance, with the possibility of seeking reimbursement for any expenses incurred."

Tip: Review your contract carefully to understand the specific consequences of missing deadlines. Knowing the potential risks will help you prioritize meeting key dates or negotiating new ones if necessary.

2. Communicate Early and Often

The key to managing a missed deadline is communication. Publishers understand that unexpected circumstances arise, but it's your responsibility to communicate with them as soon as you realize you won't meet the deadline. Being proactive in your communication can prevent misunderstandings and allow for potential adjustments to the timeline.

Here's how to communicate effectively:

- **Notify Your Publisher Early**: As soon as you realize you may miss a deadline, notify your editor or publisher immediately. It's always better to communicate early and let them know about the situation rather than waiting until the last minute or missing the deadline without explanation.

- **Explain the Situation Honestly**: Be transparent about why you're unable to meet the deadline. Whether it's a personal issue, a creative block, or an unexpected revision challenge, providing context helps the publisher understand your circumstances.

- **Suggest a Revised Deadline**: When requesting more time, offer a realistic new deadline that you can commit to. Publishers are often open to granting extensions as long as the situation is communicated clearly and the new timeline is achievable.

- **Maintain Open Communication**: If your deadline is extended, keep the lines of communication open. Provide periodic updates on your progress to reassure the publisher that you're working toward the revised goal.

Example: "I wanted to reach out to let you know that I'm facing some delays with the manuscript and won't be able to meet the June 1 deadline. I've been revising key sections, and I believe I can deliver the completed manuscript by June 30. I apologize for the inconvenience and appreciate your understanding."

Tip: If you request an extension, be realistic about the time you'll need. Missing an extended deadline can be more damaging than missing the original one, so plan carefully.

3. Strategies for Negotiating Extensions

If you need to request more time to meet a deadline, it's important to negotiate effectively with your publisher. Publishers want to work with authors who deliver on time, but they also understand that creative processes and personal circumstances can be unpredictable.

Here's how to negotiate a deadline extension:

- **Offer a Concrete Solution**: When you request more time, propose a specific new deadline and explain why it's feasible. Offering a solution shows that you're committed to delivering the work and not just asking for an indefinite delay.

- **Outline a Revised Timeline**: In addition to the new delivery date, provide a timeline that shows your progress. For example, you might outline the sections of the manuscript you've completed and your plan for finishing the remaining parts. This reassures the publisher that you're making steady progress.

- **Be Flexible on Other Deliverables**: If extending the manuscript deadline will delay other parts of the process (e.g., marketing materials or edits), offer to be flexible on other deliverables to keep the overall timeline on track. This could include agreeing to faster turnaround times for revisions or promotional tasks.

- **Negotiate in Good Faith**: Publishers are generally willing to accommodate reasonable requests for extensions, but they need to know that you're serious about delivering. Negotiating in good faith means being honest about your situation, offering solutions, and showing that you're committed to meeting the revised deadline.

Example: "I'm requesting a 30-day extension for manuscript delivery to ensure the revisions are up to standard. I've already completed the first half of the edits and anticipate finishing the rest within the new timeframe. I'm also willing to adjust the revision turnaround times to keep the production schedule on track."

Tip: Be mindful of the publisher's overall production schedule. If your manuscript delay affects other areas—like cover design, marketing, or release dates—be open to helping expedite future tasks to minimize the impact.

4. Minimizing the Impact of a Missed Deadline

If you do miss a deadline despite your best efforts, it's important to minimize the impact on the rest of the publishing process. Being proactive and flexible can help mitigate any negative consequences and keep the project moving forward.

Here's how to minimize the impact:

- **Provide Partial Deliverables**: If you're unable to submit the entire manuscript by the deadline, consider submitting what you have completed. For example, you could deliver the first half of the book or a few polished chapters. This shows the publisher that you're making progress, and they can begin editing or preparing marketing materials while you finish the remaining sections.

- **Prioritize the Publisher's Needs**: Understand which parts of the manuscript are most critical for the publisher's production timeline. If they need specific sections for cover design, marketing, or pre-orders, focus on delivering those parts first, even if the rest of the manuscript isn't complete.

- **Work Efficiently with Editors**: If the publisher requests revisions after receiving your manuscript, be prepared to work quickly and efficiently with your editor to keep the rest of the process on track. Showing flexibility and commitment during the editing phase can help offset any delays caused by missing the original deadline.

- **Offer Solutions for Promotional Delays**: If missing the manuscript deadline affects promotional activities (e.g., interviews, marketing campaigns), suggest alternative solutions. You might offer to record an interview early or participate in additional promotional efforts to compensate for the delay.

Example: "While I'm still finalizing the second half of the manuscript, I've attached the first 10 chapters, which are ready for editing. I'll continue working on the remaining sections and expect to deliver them within two weeks. Thank you for your understanding."

Tip: Consider building a buffer into your own writing schedule to account for unexpected delays. By aiming to finish the manuscript ahead of the contract deadline, you'll have more flexibility to handle revisions or personal interruptions without missing the agreed-upon date.

Missing a deadline is not the end of the world, but it does come with consequences. By understanding the potential impact of a missed deadline and communicating effectively with your publisher, you can minimize the risks and keep the project on track. Proactive communication, realistic planning, and a willingness to collaborate with your publisher are key to handling missed deadlines gracefully and maintaining a positive working relationship.

Protecting Yourself: Amending or Exiting a Contract

While signing a publishing contract is an exciting step in your author journey, it's important to recognize that things don't always go as planned. Circumstances might change, making it necessary to renegotiate contract terms or, in some cases, exit the agreement entirely. Whether it's due to missed deadlines, changes in the publishing landscape, or other unforeseen challenges, knowing how to protect yourself and navigate these scenarios is critical.

In this section, we'll explore the process of amending a contract, how to exit a publishing agreement if necessary, and the steps you can take to safeguard your rights and interests.

1. When to Consider Amending a Contract

Sometimes, the terms of your contract may no longer suit the current situation— whether that's due to changes in your personal or professional life, the market, or the publisher's priorities. In these cases, amending a contract can help both parties adjust expectations while maintaining a positive working relationship.

Here's when to consider amending a contract:

- **Extended Deadlines or Revised Deliverables**: If unforeseen circumstances prevent you from meeting original deadlines or deliverables, you can request an amendment to extend the timeline or revise the scope of what you'll provide. This is especially useful when life events, like illness or family emergencies, disrupt your writing process.

- **Changes in Marketing or Promotion Requirements**: If the marketing landscape changes or the publisher requests additional promotional involvement, you may want to negotiate new terms for your marketing obligations. This ensures you're not overburdened with tasks that weren't part of the original agreement.

- **Royalties and Payment Adjustments**: Sometimes, you might need to revisit the financial terms of your contract. For example, if the royalty rates for eBooks or audiobooks have significantly changed since the contract was signed, or if your book performs unexpectedly well, you may wish to negotiate more favorable royalty terms.

Example: "Given the unforeseen delay in manuscript completion, I would like to request an amendment to extend the delivery deadline by 60 days. This will allow me to finalize the manuscript to the highest standard."

Tip: Always approach amendments with a spirit of collaboration. If the publisher agrees that adjustments are in the best interest of both parties, they'll likely be more willing to accommodate your requests.

2. How to Amend a Contract

If you need to amend your contract, the process typically involves a formal request followed by negotiation between you and the publisher. Both parties must agree to the changes, which should then be documented in writing and added to the original contract.

Here's how to amend a contract:

- **Identify the Specific Terms to Change**: Be clear about which clauses or terms need amending. For example, if you need more time to submit the manuscript, identify the deadline clause and propose a new, realistic date.

- **Communicate with Your Publisher**: Reach out to your editor or the publisher with a formal request. Explain why the amendment is necessary and offer a solution that benefits both parties, such as revised deadlines or adjusted obligations.

- **Negotiate the Terms**: Be prepared for a negotiation process. The publisher may request certain conditions in exchange for the amendments, such as faster turnaround times for revisions or additional marketing involvement.

- **Document the Amendment**: Once both parties agree, the changes must be documented in an official amendment or addendum to the original contract. This ensures the new terms are legally binding and prevent any confusion later.

Example: "I'm requesting an amendment to extend the manuscript delivery deadline from June 1 to August 1, due to [reason]. In exchange, I'm happy to expedite the revision process to keep the production schedule on track."

Tip: Always get amendments in writing. Verbal agreements can lead to misunderstandings, so ensure that any changes are documented and signed by both parties.

3. When to Consider Exiting a Contract

In rare cases, it may be necessary to exit a publishing contract. Whether the publisher has failed to meet their obligations, or you've encountered personal or professional challenges that prevent you from fulfilling your commitments, understanding your exit options is critical.

Here's when to consider exiting a contract:

- **Breach of Contract by the Publisher**: If the publisher fails to uphold their end of the agreement—such as not publishing the book within a reasonable time, failing to make payments, or not fulfilling their marketing promises—you may have grounds to terminate the contract. A breach of contract allows you to exit the agreement without penalty.

- **Creative or Professional Differences**: If there are significant creative differences or disagreements about the direction of the project, it may become difficult to continue working together. In such cases, you may negotiate an exit from the contract by mutual agreement.

- **Inability to Fulfill Obligations**: If personal circumstances make it impossible for you to meet your contractual obligations (e.g., severe illness or family emergencies), you may need to exit the contract. Some contracts include force majeure clauses, which allow either party to terminate the agreement in cases of extreme unforeseen events.

Example: "Due to unforeseen personal circumstances, I am unable to fulfill the obligations of the contract and would like to discuss the possibility of terminating the agreement on mutual terms."

Tip: Review your contract carefully for termination clauses. Many contracts outline the conditions under which either party can exit the agreement, as well as the consequences of early termination.

4. How to Exit a Contract

Exiting a publishing contract is a serious decision, and it's important to follow the correct process to protect your legal rights and minimize potential financial consequences. If you're considering terminating the contract, it's advisable to seek legal advice before proceeding.

Here's how to exit a contract:

- **Review the Termination Clauses**: Most contracts include specific clauses that outline the conditions for termination. Review these carefully to understand whether you're entitled to exit the contract and what the consequences might be (e.g., returning the advance or compensating the publisher for expenses).

- **Notify the Publisher**: If you believe you have grounds to terminate the contract, send a formal notification to the publisher explaining your intent to exit the agreement. Be clear about the reasons for termination and refer to the specific clauses that allow you to take this action.

- **Negotiate an Exit Strategy**: In some cases, you and the publisher may agree to a mutual termination of the contract. This might involve negotiating terms for returning the rights to the book, settling any financial obligations, and ensuring both parties can move forward amicably.

- **Get Legal Advice**: Terminating a contract can have legal and financial implications, so it's important to consult with a lawyer who specializes in publishing agreements. They can help you navigate the process, negotiate terms, and protect your rights.

Example: "As outlined in Clause 10 of the contract, the publisher has not fulfilled its obligation to publish the manuscript within 18 months of manuscript acceptance. I am therefore requesting the termination of the agreement and the reversion of all rights to the book."

Tip: If you're exiting a contract due to a breach by the publisher, keep detailed records of all communications and missed obligations. This documentation can support your case if there are disputes over the termination.

5. Reversion of Rights

If you exit a contract, or if the book goes out of print, the reversion of rights clause allows you to regain ownership of your work. Reverting the rights means you can either self-publish the book, seek a new publishing deal, or explore other opportunities such as film adaptations or foreign editions.

Here's what to know about reversion of rights:

- **Out-of-Print Clause**: Many contracts include a clause that allows the rights to revert to the author if the book goes out of print or if sales fall below a certain threshold. This ensures that if the publisher is no longer actively selling or promoting the book, you can regain control and potentially re-release it elsewhere.

- **Mutual Termination**: In some cases, the reversion of rights can be negotiated as part of a mutual termination agreement. This allows both parties to part ways while ensuring you retain the ability to use your work as you see fit.

- **Rights Reversion Process**: The process for reverting rights is typically outlined in the contract. If the book qualifies for reversion, you must formally request the rights back in writing, following the steps specified in the agreement.

Example: "As the book has been out of print for over 12 months, I am formally requesting the reversion of all rights to the work as outlined in Clause 12 of the contract."

Tip: Make sure your contract includes a clear reversion of rights clause that protects your ability to regain ownership of your book if the publisher stops promoting it or allows it to go out of print.

Amending or exiting a contract is sometimes necessary to protect your rights as an author or to adapt to changing circumstances. Whether you're renegotiating deadlines, adjusting marketing obligations, or exiting a contract due to breach or unforeseen challenges, it's essential to approach these situations carefully and with legal guidance. By understanding your options for amending or terminating a publishing agreement, you can navigate these decisions confidently and protect both your work and your career as an author.

Quick Tips and Recap

- **Understand Key Contract Clauses**: Familiarize yourself with the major contract terms, especially around rights, royalties, deadlines, and marketing obligations.

- **Communicate Early About Delays**: If you anticipate missing a deadline, notify your publisher immediately and propose a realistic new timeline.

- **Negotiate Amendments When Necessary**: Be proactive in requesting contract amendments for issues like extended deadlines, revised royalties, or changes in promotional expectations.

- **Exit Contracts Carefully**: If exiting a contract, review the termination clauses thoroughly and consult legal advice to protect your rights and minimize risks.

- **Reversion of Rights**: Ensure your contract includes a clear reversion of rights clause, allowing you to regain control of your book if it goes out of print or if the publisher fails to meet obligations.

- **Get Amendments in Writing**: Always document any contract changes or amendments in writing to avoid future disputes.

- **Seek Legal Advice for Major Contract Issues**: Consult a lawyer who specializes in publishing contracts before making significant decisions regarding amendments or exits.

By staying informed about your contractual obligations and rights, you can protect your work and navigate changes confidently, ensuring that your publishing journey stays on track.

Managing Multiple Contracts: Keeping the Plates Spinning

"Juggling multiple contracts is like conducting an orchestra; each has its part to play, and it's your job to ensure they harmonize perfectly to create a symphony, not a cacophony." — ELON MUSK, CEO OF TESLA AND SPACEX

Welcome to Chapter Thirteen, "Managing Multiple Contracts: Keeping the Plates Spinning," where you'll master the art of juggling not just your daily responsibilities but also a portfolio of contracts that could make a seasoned lawyer blink. If you thought multitasking was just for circus performers and stressed parents, prepare to join the league of extraordinary multitaskers: authors with more than one project on the go!

Here, each contract is a spinning plate, and your job is to keep them all whirling without crashing to the ground in a spectacular mess of legal and creative debris. We'll equip you with the strategies to keep your bearings, prioritize your commitments, and navigate the potential collisions of overlapping deadlines and conflicting rights. From synchronizing your calendars to syncing your legal understandings, you'll learn to choreograph a ballet of obligations that keeps your career moving gracefully forward.

Strap in, because we're about to turn you into a contractual virtuoso, conducting an orchestra of obligations with the finesse of a maestro and the cool command of a captain at sea. Let's keep those plates spinning!

Organizing Your Commitments: Creating a Master Plan

When managing multiple publishing contracts, the key to success is effective organization. With different deadlines, deliverables, and obligations to juggle, you need a clear strategy to keep track of everything without letting any important tasks slip through the cracks. By creating a master plan, you can streamline your commitments, prioritize your work, and ensure that you meet each contract's requirements efficiently.

In this section, we'll explore how to organize your commitments, set up a comprehensive timeline, and use tools to manage your tasks effectively.

1. Create a Master Timeline

The first step in organizing multiple contracts is to create a master timeline that lays out all of your deadlines and milestones in one place. Having a big-picture view of your commitments allows you to plan ahead, avoid conflicts, and make adjustments as needed.

Here's how to build a master timeline:

- **List All Deliverables and Deadlines**: Start by listing all the major deliverables from each contract, including manuscript deadlines, revision schedules, marketing commitments, and publication dates. For each deliverable, note the due date and the time you expect it will take to complete.

239

- **Identify Overlaps and Conflicts**: Look for any deadlines or commitments that overlap between your contracts. If you notice that two deadlines fall close together, flag them for further planning to ensure you can manage both without compromising quality.

- **Break Down Deliverables into Smaller Tasks**: Large deliverables, such as completing a manuscript, can feel overwhelming if they're left as a single line on your timeline. Break them into smaller, manageable tasks with mini-deadlines (e.g., "Finish Chapter 10 by April 15"). This will help you track progress and stay on schedule.

- **Build in Buffer Time**: Add buffer time between major deliverables to account for unexpected delays or extra revision rounds. This helps you stay on track even if something takes longer than expected.

Example: If you have a manuscript due in September and another project requiring revisions due in October, your timeline might look like this:

- July 15: Finish first draft of Project A
- August 1-15: First round of revisions for Project A
- September 1: Submit final manuscript for Project A
- September 5: Start revisions for Project B
- October 1: Submit revised manuscript for Project B

Tip: Use color coding in your timeline to differentiate between the various contracts and tasks. This helps you visually separate your commitments and keep everything organized.

2. Utilize Project Management Tools

Project management tools can make organizing multiple contracts much easier by providing a structured way to track deadlines, deliverables, and progress. Whether you prefer digital tools or more traditional methods, having a central location for managing your tasks is essential.

Here are a few options for managing your commitments:

- **Digital Project Management Tools**: Platforms like Trello, Asana, or Notion allow you to create boards or lists for each contract, organize tasks by due dates, and set reminders for important deadlines. These tools also let you visually track your progress as you move tasks from "To Do" to "Done."

- **Calendar Apps**: Use a calendar app, such as Google Calendar or Outlook, to schedule deadlines and block off time for specific tasks. Set reminders ahead of deadlines to ensure you stay on top of deliverables.

- **Task Lists**: If you prefer a simpler approach, a task list app like Todoist or Microsoft To Do lets you create checklists for each project and mark off tasks as they're completed. You can categorize tasks by project or due date for easy reference.

- **Physical Planners**: Some authors prefer the tactile nature of physical planners. Using a paper planner or wall calendar allows you to jot down deadlines, track progress, and physically cross off tasks. If you're someone who enjoys writing things down, this can be a helpful method for staying organized.

Tip: Whichever tool you choose, make sure to review it regularly. Update your timeline and task list at least once a week to stay on top of shifting deadlines or new commitments.

3. Set Priorities and Establish Workflow

Not all deadlines are created equal, and part of managing multiple contracts involves knowing which tasks take priority at any given time. Setting clear priorities allows you to focus on the most important work first, while managing less urgent tasks in the background.

Here's how to prioritize your tasks effectively:

- **Determine High-Priority Deadlines**: Identify which contracts or deliverables have the most urgent deadlines or the greatest impact on your career. For example, if a manuscript deadline is tied to a significant advance payment, that project should take precedence over less urgent tasks.

- **Batch Similar Tasks**: To stay efficient, batch similar tasks together. For example, if you're revising two different manuscripts, try to tackle them during the same workweek so you can stay in the editing mindset. Similarly, batch marketing tasks, such as writing social media posts or preparing interviews, to streamline your workflow.

- **Use Time Blocking**: Time blocking is an effective way to organize your day and avoid multitasking, which can reduce efficiency. Dedicate specific blocks of time to each project and focus solely on that task during the allotted time. For example, you might reserve your mornings for writing and your afternoons for editing or marketing.

Example: "This week, I'll prioritize finishing the final revisions for Contract A, and I'll spend two afternoons drafting marketing content for Contract B. I'll block off mornings for writing to make sure I stay on track with my next manuscript."

Tip: Consider using the Eisenhower Matrix to categorize tasks based on urgency and importance. This simple tool helps you focus on what needs immediate attention and what can be scheduled for later.

4. Review and Adjust Your Plan Regularly

Life as an author is dynamic, and your master plan may need adjusting as new contracts come in or timelines shift. Make it a habit to review your plan regularly and make updates as needed to ensure you're staying on track.

Here's how to stay flexible and adjust your plan:

- **Weekly Reviews**: Set aside time each week to review your progress and upcoming deadlines. If you notice any potential conflicts or bottlenecks, adjust your schedule to resolve them before they become issues.

- **Be Realistic About Your Time**: If you find that your original plan was too ambitious, don't hesitate to revise your timeline or request extensions from your publisher. It's better to adjust deadlines early than to scramble at the last minute.

- **Celebrate Small Wins**: Keep yourself motivated by celebrating progress along the way. Crossing off milestones, no matter how small, keeps you motivated and focused.

Tip: Always keep an eye on long-term projects or commitments that may be months away. Don't let them sneak up on you—by reviewing your plan weekly, you'll avoid any surprises.

Organizing your commitments through a master plan helps you manage multiple contracts efficiently, avoid deadline conflicts, and stay on top of your creative and business obligations. By creating a clear timeline, using project management tools, setting priorities, and regularly reviewing your plan, you can keep all your plates spinning and continue building your author career with confidence.

Balancing Overlapping Deadlines: Prioritizing Projects

When juggling multiple contracts, overlapping deadlines are often inevitable. Whether it's two manuscripts due within the same month or a marketing obligation conflicting with a revision deadline, knowing how to prioritize your projects becomes crucial to keeping everything on track. By balancing overlapping deadlines strategically, you can avoid feeling overwhelmed and ensure that you meet all your commitments without sacrificing the quality of your work.

In this section, we'll explore how to assess priorities, manage your time, and create a plan that allows you to navigate conflicting deadlines with ease.

1. Assessing the Importance of Each Deadline

Not all deadlines carry the same weight, so it's important to evaluate each one based on factors such as the financial impact, contractual obligations, and long-term career benefits. By assessing the importance of each deadline, you can prioritize your projects more effectively and allocate your time accordingly.

Here's how to assess your deadlines:

- **Financial Impact**: If a project is tied to a significant advance payment or a royalties agreement, it may take precedence over a project with lower immediate financial rewards. Focus on completing the projects that contribute most to your income.

- **Contractual Obligations**: Review the terms of each contract to understand the legal consequences of missing a deadline. If one contract has stricter penalties for delays or missed milestones, prioritize that project to avoid financial or reputational damage.

- **Career Impact**: Consider how each project fits into your long-term career goals. For example, a high-profile book deal or a project that opens doors to future opportunities may require more attention than a smaller, less impactful commitment.

- **Time Sensitivity**: Some deadlines might be tied to events or marketing campaigns (e.g., a book launch tied to a specific season or holiday). Deadlines tied to fixed dates or public events should be prioritized to avoid missing important windows for promotion or sales.

Example: "I have a manuscript deadline for a major publisher in six weeks and an article due for a blog in four weeks. The manuscript takes priority because it's tied to a larger advance, but I can't ignore the blog deadline either, so I'll work on both by devoting most of my time to the manuscript and scheduling smaller writing sessions for the article."

Tip: Keep a list of all your deadlines ranked by importance and time sensitivity. This will help you decide where to focus your energy each day.

2. Break Down Projects into Manageable Tasks

When multiple deadlines are looming, it's easy to feel overwhelmed by the sheer amount of work ahead. Breaking down large projects into smaller, manageable tasks can help you focus on completing one step at a time without getting lost in the bigger picture.

Here's how to break down your projects:

- **Create a Task List for Each Project**: Break down each major project into smaller tasks with individual due dates. For example, if you're working on a novel, you might divide the project into writing specific chapters, completing revisions, or formatting the manuscript. For marketing commitments, you could schedule time for writing blog posts, preparing for interviews, or designing social media content.

- **Estimate Time for Each Task**: Assign a realistic time estimate for each task. This helps you better allocate your time and prevents underestimating how long each task will take. Make sure to include buffer time in case certain steps take longer than expected.

- **Tackle One Task at a Time**: Avoid multitasking between different projects, as it can reduce productivity. Instead, focus on completing one task before moving to the next. For example, dedicate a morning to writing a chapter for one book, then spend the afternoon drafting marketing content for another project.

Example: "For Project A, my task list for this week includes writing two chapters and revising the outline. For Project B, I need to finalize three blog posts. I'll allocate my mornings to writing and reserve the afternoons for editing and blog work."

Tip: Consider using the Pomodoro Technique or other time management methods to stay focused. Set a timer for 25-30 minutes to work on one task, then take a short break before moving on to the next.

3. Stagger Your Workload

When deadlines are close together, one of the most effective strategies is to stagger your workload so that you're not tackling everything at once. By staggering tasks, you can spread out the work over a longer period, making it more manageable and reducing last-minute stress.

Here's how to stagger your workload:

- **Work Backwards from Each Deadline**: Start by looking at your deadlines and working backwards to create a schedule that gives you enough time to complete each project. For example, if one manuscript is due in four weeks and another in six weeks, prioritize the first project while gradually making progress on the second.

- **Overlap Phases of Different Projects**: Stagger different phases of your projects. For example, if you're in the drafting phase for one book and in the revision phase for another, alternate between the two. This keeps your mind fresh and allows you to make consistent progress on both.

- **Alternate High-Effort and Low-Effort Tasks**: Balance your schedule by alternating high-effort tasks (e.g., writing a new chapter) with lower-effort tasks (e.g., editing or marketing content). This prevents burnout and helps you maintain energy throughout the week.

Example: "This week, I'll focus on drafting two chapters for the manuscript due first. Next week, I'll switch to editing the second manuscript while continuing to write smaller sections of the first one. By alternating between writing and editing, I'll keep both projects moving forward."

Tip: Use overlapping phases of creativity and editing to stay productive. When you hit a creative block on one project, shift to a different type of work (such as revisions) on another.

4. Delegate or Outsource When Possible

If you're struggling to meet all your deadlines, consider delegating certain tasks or outsourcing parts of the process. While you'll need to handle the writing and creative aspects, there may be other tasks—such as administrative work, marketing, or formatting—that can be delegated to a professional or assistant.

Here's how to delegate or outsource effectively:

- **Identify Tasks That Can Be Outsourced**: Look at your workload and determine which tasks don't require your direct involvement. For example, you might outsource cover design, formatting, or website management, allowing you to focus on writing and editing.

- **Hire Freelancers or Assistants**: If budget permits, consider hiring a virtual assistant or a freelancer to handle tasks like managing your social media, scheduling interviews, or handling administrative work. This frees up more of your time to focus on writing.

- **Collaborate with Co-Authors**: If you're working on a collaborative project, divide the workload based on each person's strengths. For example, if you're stronger in outlining and character development, while your co-author excels in world-building or revisions, divide tasks accordingly to maximize efficiency.

Example: "I've hired a freelance editor to help with the initial proofreading of my second manuscript, and I'm working with a virtual assistant to schedule social media posts for the upcoming book launch. This allows me to focus on finishing the manuscript for my primary project."

Tip: Delegating tasks doesn't diminish your control over the project—it frees up your time to focus on what matters most. Just make sure to communicate clearly and set expectations with anyone you outsource work to.

Balancing overlapping deadlines requires strategic planning, prioritization, and sometimes delegation. By assessing the importance of each deadline, breaking down projects into manageable tasks, staggering your workload, and outsourcing when possible, you can stay on top of multiple projects without feeling overwhelmed. These strategies will help you maintain momentum and ensure that all your commitments are met on time, allowing you to continue building your career with confidence and professionalism.

Navigating Conflicting Contract Terms: Understanding Exclusivity and Rights

When managing multiple publishing contracts, one of the most important (and potentially tricky) aspects is navigating conflicting contract terms, especially around exclusivity and rights. Publishers often include clauses that limit what you can do with your work, which can lead to conflicts when you're juggling multiple projects or contracts. Understanding these clauses, knowing your rights, and negotiating favorable terms are crucial to ensuring you don't inadvertently breach an agreement or limit your career opportunities.

In this section, we'll explore how to navigate exclusivity clauses, understand different types of rights, and avoid conflicts between contracts.

1. Understanding Exclusivity Clauses

Exclusivity clauses are designed to protect the publisher's investment by ensuring that the author isn't working on projects that directly compete with the book they're publishing. However, these clauses can sometimes be overly broad or restrictive, making it difficult to pursue other projects or opportunities.

Here's what to know about exclusivity clauses:

- **Single-Project Exclusivity**: This type of exclusivity clause only applies to the specific book covered by the contract. It ensures that the publisher has the exclusive right to publish that particular work, but it doesn't limit your ability to work on other books or projects simultaneously. This is the most common and least restrictive form of exclusivity.

- **Broad Exclusivity**: Some contracts may include more expansive exclusivity clauses that prevent you from publishing any other works (especially in the same genre or market) while you're under contract. These clauses can be problematic if you're working on multiple books or have other commitments in the same genre.

- **First-Look or First-Option Clauses**: Some contracts may include a first-look or first-option clause, meaning the publisher has the right to review your next project and decide whether to publish it before you can take it elsewhere. While this can be beneficial in some cases, make sure the terms are clear and fair, and don't lock you into an agreement that limits your creative freedom.

- **Duration of Exclusivity**: Pay attention to the length of the exclusivity period. Some contracts only enforce exclusivity for a limited time—such as until the manuscript is delivered or the book is published—while others may extend exclusivity until certain sales or promotional goals are met.

Example: "The Author agrees to grant the Publisher exclusive rights to publish the Work in all formats. The Author further agrees not to publish any other work of a similar nature or genre until six months after the release of the Work."

Tip: If you find an exclusivity clause too restrictive, negotiate to limit it to just the project at hand or for a shorter time frame. Be sure to clarify whether the exclusivity applies to specific genres, formats, or markets.

2. Managing Conflicting Rights

In addition to exclusivity, contracts often outline the rights you are granting to the publisher. These include rights to publish your work in certain formats (e.g., print, digital, audio), as well as rights to foreign translations, film adaptations, or merchandise. When managing multiple contracts, it's essential to understand how these rights overlap or conflict with other agreements you may have.

Here's how to manage conflicting rights:

- **Primary vs. Subsidiary Rights**: Primary rights usually refer to the core publishing rights, such as the right to print and distribute the book in a particular market. Subsidiary rights include things like translation rights, audiobook rights, and film adaptation rights. Make sure you understand which rights are being granted to each publisher and which ones you retain.

- **Territorial Rights**: Territorial rights refer to where the publisher has the exclusive right to sell and distribute the book. For example, you might grant one publisher exclusive rights for North America, while retaining the right to license the book to other publishers in international markets. Ensure that your contracts don't grant conflicting rights in overlapping territories.

- **Format-Specific Rights**: Some contracts grant the publisher exclusive rights to certain formats (e.g., print or eBook), while others allow you to retain rights to other formats (e.g., audiobooks or merchandise). If you have multiple contracts, make sure the rights you grant to each publisher don't conflict. For example, you may grant one publisher the print rights to a book, while retaining the audiobook rights to license separately.

- **Reversion of Rights**: Pay attention to reversion clauses that allow you to reclaim rights if certain conditions are met (e.g., the book goes out of print). This can be helpful if you want to license the book to another publisher or explore other distribution avenues after the initial publication run.

Example: "The Publisher is granted exclusive print and digital rights to the Work in North America. All subsidiary rights, including foreign language translations and film adaptation rights, are retained by the Author."

Tip: Carefully review which rights you're granting and make sure there are no conflicts between contracts. If you're unsure, consult with a literary agent or lawyer to help you navigate these terms.

3. Avoiding Non-Compete Clauses

Non-compete clauses are designed to prevent you from publishing works that directly compete with the book under contract. While this can be understandable from the publisher's perspective, overly broad non-compete clauses can limit your ability to work on other projects in the same genre or market.

Here's how to avoid problematic non-compete clauses:

- **Limit the Scope**: If a contract includes a non-compete clause, try to limit its scope to the specific project covered by the contract. For example, you might agree not to publish another book in the same series or universe during the exclusivity period, but you shouldn't be restricted from working on unrelated projects or books in a different genre.

- **Define "Competing Work"**: Make sure the contract clearly defines what constitutes a "competing work." If the definition is too broad, you could find yourself unable to publish any other books in the same genre, even if they're unrelated to the current project. Negotiate for a more specific definition that only covers books with similar themes, characters, or settings.

- **Shorten the Non-Compete Period**: Many non-compete clauses extend for a period of time after the book's release (e.g., six months or a year). If this period is too long, it could prevent you from pursuing other opportunities. Negotiate to shorten the non-compete period or remove it entirely if it's not necessary.

Example: "The Author agrees not to publish or license any work that directly competes with the Work in the same genre or series for a period of six months following the release date."

Tip: Be careful with non-compete clauses that are vague or overly restrictive. If necessary, work with the publisher to clarify the language so you understand exactly what you're agreeing to.

4. Negotiating Flexibility in Your Contracts

If you're managing multiple contracts, negotiating flexibility is key to avoiding conflicts and maintaining creative freedom. Publishers may be open to more flexible terms, especially if you're transparent about your commitments and can demonstrate how other projects won't interfere with their work.

Here's how to negotiate more flexibility:

- **Retain Certain Rights**: When negotiating a contract, try to retain as many rights as possible—especially subsidiary rights like film, audiobook, or foreign translation rights. This gives you the freedom to license those rights to other publishers or explore other revenue streams without conflicting with your primary publishing contract.

- **Negotiate Exclusive Windows**: If the publisher insists on exclusivity, negotiate an exclusive window rather than open-ended exclusivity. For example, you might grant the publisher exclusive rights to the work for a limited period (e.g., six months to a year), after which you regain the ability to license the book in other formats or markets.

- **Clarify Terms in Writing**: Always get clear terms in writing. Verbal agreements or vague language can lead to misunderstandings down the line. If the publisher agrees to flexible terms or makes an exception to a clause, make sure it's documented in the contract.

Example: "The Author retains the exclusive right to license the audiobook and foreign translation rights to third parties. The Publisher shall have the first option to publish the Author's next work in the series, but the Author is free to pursue unrelated projects without restriction."

Tip: Approach negotiations with a collaborative attitude. If the publisher understands that flexibility benefits both parties, they're more likely to agree to terms that allow you to manage multiple projects without conflict.

Navigating conflicting contract terms requires a clear understanding of exclusivity clauses, rights management, and non-compete agreements. By reviewing your contracts carefully, negotiating for flexibility, and ensuring that your rights and commitments don't overlap, you can manage multiple contracts without running into legal or creative roadblocks. This approach allows you to protect your work, maximize your opportunities, and continue growing your career as an author.

Maintaining Your Creative Energy: Avoiding Burnout

Managing multiple contracts and juggling several projects can take a toll on your creativity and energy. The constant demands of writing, editing, promoting, and meeting deadlines can easily lead to burnout, especially when you're trying to keep up with everything at once. As an author, it's crucial to protect your creative energy, maintain a healthy work-life balance, and ensure that you stay inspired throughout your projects.

In this section, we'll explore strategies for avoiding burnout, preserving your creative energy, and finding a sustainable workflow that allows you to thrive even when your plate is full.

1. Establish a Sustainable Writing Routine

One of the best ways to prevent burnout is by establishing a sustainable writing routine that allows you to make steady progress without exhausting yourself. Consistency is key, but that doesn't mean you need to push yourself to the limit every day.

Here's how to create a sustainable routine:

- **Set Realistic Daily Goals**: Instead of aiming for marathon writing sessions every day, set smaller, more achievable goals. Whether it's writing 500 words, editing for an hour, or completing a specific task, small, consistent progress adds up over time without overwhelming you.

- **Prioritize Time Blocks for Creativity**: Dedicate certain blocks of your day or week to writing or creative work. Protect these blocks from distractions and non-creative tasks, like answering emails or handling administrative work. This ensures that your most creative energy is focused on producing quality work.

- **Take Regular Breaks**: Taking breaks throughout the day allows you to recharge and avoid mental fatigue. Whether it's a short walk, a few minutes of meditation, or simply stepping away from your desk, breaks help maintain your focus and productivity over the long term.

Example: "I'll write 1,000 words every morning for two hours, then take a break before moving on to other tasks. In the afternoon, I'll spend an hour editing or handling promotional tasks."

Tip: Experiment with different routines to find what works best for you. Some authors prefer short bursts of intense writing, while others thrive on longer, uninterrupted sessions. The key is finding a rhythm that feels sustainable.

2. Create Boundaries Between Work and Personal Life

When managing multiple projects, it's easy for work to bleed into your personal life. Setting boundaries is essential to protect your time and mental well-being, ensuring that you have the space to rest and recharge.

Here's how to set healthy boundaries:

- **Establish Clear Working Hours**: Set specific working hours for your writing and stick to them. Once your workday is done, resist the urge to continue working late into the evening or on weekends. This creates a clear separation between your professional and personal life, helping you avoid burnout.

- **Designate a Dedicated Workspace**: If possible, create a dedicated workspace for your writing and creative tasks. Having a physical space that's separate from your personal life helps reinforce boundaries. When you leave your workspace, you can mentally "clock out" from work.

- **Say No to Overcommitment**: It's tempting to take on every opportunity that comes your way, but overcommitting can quickly lead to burnout. Be selective about the projects you take on, and don't hesitate to say no if you're already at capacity.

Example: "I'll work from 9 a.m. to 4 p.m. on weekdays and take weekends off to spend time with family. Outside of my working hours, I'll avoid checking emails or thinking about work so I can fully disconnect and recharge."

Tip: Set clear expectations with clients, publishers, and collaborators about your availability. Let them know your working hours and when they can expect to hear back from you. This helps you maintain boundaries while managing multiple projects.

3. Incorporate Self-Care into Your Schedule

Taking care of your physical and mental health is critical to maintaining your creative energy. Incorporating self-care into your daily routine not only helps you avoid burnout but also ensures that you stay energized and inspired in the long run.

Here's how to prioritize self-care:

- **Exercise Regularly**: Physical activity is one of the best ways to boost your mood, relieve stress, and increase your energy levels. Even a short walk, yoga session, or quick workout can make a significant difference in how you feel and perform creatively.

- **Get Enough Sleep**: Lack of sleep can lead to poor focus, decreased creativity, and overall burnout. Aim for 7-8 hours of quality sleep each night to ensure that you wake up refreshed and ready to tackle your projects with clarity and enthusiasm.

- **Practice Mindfulness or Meditation**: Mindfulness and meditation practices can help you manage stress, stay focused, and maintain a positive mindset. Even a few minutes of deep breathing or meditation each day can have lasting benefits for your mental well-being.

- **Schedule Downtime**: Make time for activities you enjoy outside of work, whether it's reading, spending time with loved ones, or engaging in a hobby. Downtime allows your mind to rest and recharge, which can lead to bursts of creativity when you return to your writing.

Example: "I'll start each day with a 20-minute walk to clear my mind before sitting down to write. I'll also take regular breaks to stretch and move around to stay physically and mentally sharp."

Tip: Treat self-care as non-negotiable. Block off time for it in your schedule just as you would for writing or meetings, and honor that commitment to yourself.

4. Stay Connected to Your Creative Passion

One of the best ways to avoid burnout is to stay connected to the joy and passion that initially inspired you to write. When you're balancing multiple contracts and deadlines, it's easy to get bogged down in the business side of writing and lose sight of the creative spark. Reconnecting with that passion can help reignite your energy and keep you motivated.

Here's how to stay connected to your creativity:

- **Set Aside Time for Passion Projects**: In addition to your contracted projects, make time for writing that brings you pure joy, whether it's journaling, writing poetry, or working on a personal passion project. These creative outlets can reignite your love for writing and give you a break from the pressure of deadlines.

- **Inspire Yourself with New Ideas**: If you're feeling stuck or burned out, immerse yourself in new experiences or consume creative works that inspire you. Read books by authors you admire, watch films that spark your imagination, or visit new places to gain fresh perspectives.

- **Celebrate Your Accomplishments**: Take time to celebrate your achievements, whether it's finishing a chapter, completing a draft, or hitting a major milestone. Acknowledging your progress keeps you motivated and reminds you of why you started in the first place.

Example: "I'll spend one afternoon each week working on my personal writing project—something that's just for me. This helps me stay connected to the joy of storytelling without the pressure of deadlines."

Tip: Periodically reflect on your journey as a writer. Revisit old drafts or projects and remember how far you've come. This reflection can help you appreciate the progress you've made and renew your excitement for what's next.

Maintaining your creative energy while managing multiple contracts requires balance, boundaries, and self-care. By establishing a sustainable writing routine, setting clear boundaries between work and personal life, incorporating self-care into your daily schedule, and staying connected to your creative passion, you can avoid burnout and keep your inspiration alive. This approach not only helps you meet your deadlines but ensures that you continue to enjoy the writing process, even when your workload is demanding.

Quick Tips and Recap

- **Set Realistic Daily Goals**: Break large projects into manageable tasks to make consistent progress without overwhelming yourself.

- **Establish Boundaries**: Set clear working hours and protect your personal time to avoid burnout. Use a dedicated workspace if possible.

- **Incorporate Regular Breaks**: Take short breaks during work sessions to recharge and maintain focus.

- **Exercise and Rest**: Prioritize physical activity, sleep, and self-care to keep your body and mind energized.

- **Don't Overcommit**: Be selective about the projects you take on and avoid overloading yourself with too many responsibilities.

- **Schedule Downtime**: Make time for hobbies, relaxation, and activities that bring you joy outside of writing.

- **Reconnect with Creative Passion**: Work on passion projects or engage in creative activities that inspire and reignite your love for writing.

- **Celebrate Small Wins**: Acknowledge and celebrate your accomplishments to stay motivated and focused on your long-term goals.

By following these tips, you can manage your workload effectively while maintaining your creative energy and avoiding burnout, ensuring a sustainable and successful writing career.

CHAPTER FOURTEEN

Legal Implications of Non-Compliance: Avoiding Pitfalls

"Adhering to legal agreements isn't just about following rules—it's about establishing a reputation of reliability and trust in a world where your word is your bond."— WARREN BUFFETT, CEO OF BERKSHIRE HATHAWAY

Welcome to Chapter Fourteen, "Legal Implications of Non-Compliance: Avoiding Pitfalls," where we navigate the treacherous waters of what happens when you don't stick to the script—your contract, that is. Think of this chapter as the guide to avoiding booby traps in the jungle of legal obligations. It's less Indiana Jones running from a giant boulder, more Indiana Jones carefully navigating through a temple with a well-thought-out map.

Here, we'll uncover the horrors that lurk behind the bushes of non-compliance: fines, legal battles, and the dreaded breach of contract. You'll learn how to read the warning signs, sidestep common pitfalls, and what to do if you accidentally step into quicksand. From the gentle nudges of corrective actions to the sledgehammer of court proceedings, we'll ensure you have the know-how to avoid causing a legal landslide.

Arm yourself with knowledge, because in the world of contracts, ignorance is definitely not bliss—it's a recipe for disaster. Let's keep your legal journey as smooth as the pen that signed your contracts.

Breach of Contract: What It Is and How to Avoid It

A breach of contract occurs when one party fails to fulfill their obligations as outlined in the agreement. For authors, this can mean missing a deadline, failing to deliver the manuscript as specified, or not meeting marketing commitments. While some breaches can be minor and easily remedied, others can lead to serious legal and financial consequences. Understanding what constitutes a breach and how to avoid it is key to maintaining a healthy relationship with your publisher and protecting your career.

In this section, we'll explore what a breach of contract is, the common types of breaches authors encounter, and strategies to ensure you stay compliant with your agreements.

1. What Is a Breach of Contract?

A breach of contract occurs when one party fails to meet their obligations as specified in the contract. In the publishing world, this could involve missing deadlines, not delivering a manuscript, failing to participate in promotional activities, or violating exclusivity agreements.

Types of breaches include:

- **Minor Breach** (Partial Breach): This occurs when one party fulfills most of their obligations but fails in a small or less significant area. For example, submitting a manuscript slightly late but still within a reasonable timeframe may be considered a minor breach.

- **Material Breach** (Major Breach): This happens when one party fails to fulfill a fundamental obligation of the contract, significantly harming the other party. For example, if you fail to deliver the manuscript entirely, this could be considered a material breach, which may lead to legal consequences.

- **Anticipatory Breach**: If it becomes clear that a party will not be able to meet their contractual obligations, they may notify the other party ahead of time. This type of breach allows both parties to begin resolving the issue before the actual breach occurs.

Example: If your contract specifies that the manuscript is due on a certain date and you fail to deliver it by then without communicating with your publisher, you would likely be in breach of contract.

Tip: Always review your contract carefully and make sure you understand your specific obligations, including deadlines, deliverables, and any marketing commitments.

2. Common Causes of Breach for Authors

Authors can inadvertently breach their contracts in several ways. Knowing the most common causes of breaches can help you avoid falling into these traps:

- **Missed Deadlines**: One of the most common breaches is failing to deliver your manuscript or revisions on time. This can throw off the entire production schedule and result in penalties.

- **Failure to Meet Deliverable Standards**: Submitting a manuscript that doesn't meet the quality or length requirements specified in the contract can also constitute a breach.

- **Ignoring Marketing and Promotional Commitments**: Many contracts require the author to participate in marketing activities, such as interviews, book signings, or social media promotion. Failing to engage in these efforts, as outlined, can lead to a breach.

- **Violating Exclusivity Agreements**: Publishing another work that competes with your contracted book during the exclusivity period can breach the contract. This includes self-publishing or signing with another publisher for a similar project.

Example: If you sign an agreement that requires you to participate in a book tour or virtual events and you fail to attend or promote these events, you could be in breach of your contract.

Tip: Keep a detailed checklist of your contractual obligations, including all deliverables, deadlines, and marketing commitments. This will help you stay organized and avoid accidental breaches.

3. How to Avoid Breach of Contract

The best way to avoid a breach is to stay organized, communicate effectively, and plan ahead. Here are some strategies to help you stay compliant with your contracts:

- **Understand the Terms**: Before signing any contract, ensure that you understand all of the terms, deadlines, and obligations. If anything is unclear, ask for clarification or consult a lawyer.

- **Stay Organized with Deadlines**: Use tools like calendars, task management apps, or physical planners to track all of your deadlines and commitments. Schedule your work in advance to avoid missing important dates.

- **Communicate Early and Often**: If you're at risk of missing a deadline or encountering an issue, communicate with your publisher as soon as possible. Most publishers are willing to work with authors who provide advance notice and request reasonable adjustments.

- **Negotiate Realistic Terms**: When negotiating a contract, make sure the deadlines and deliverables are realistic based on your current workload. If a proposed timeline feels too tight, ask for more time up front rather than risking a breach later.

Example: You realize you're not going to meet your manuscript delivery deadline due to an unforeseen personal issue. You should reach out to your publisher as early as possible, explain the situation, and negotiate a new delivery date. By being proactive, you can avoid a breach.

Tip: Keep a copy of all communication with your publisher, including emails where deadlines are discussed or adjustments are made. This documentation can protect you in case of any disputes.

4. What to Do If You Breach Your Contract

If you realize that you've breached your contract, don't panic. While it's important to take the situation seriously, many breaches can be resolved with effective communication and corrective action. Here's what to do:

- **Acknowledge the Breach**: Be honest and upfront with your publisher if you've breached your contract or are at risk of doing so. Ignoring the issue will only make it worse.

- **Propose a Solution**: If possible, propose a solution to remedy the breach. This could involve delivering the manuscript late with a new deadline or offering to participate in additional promotional activities to make up for missed commitments.

- **Seek Legal Advice**: If the breach is serious or you're unsure of how to resolve it, consult a lawyer who specializes in publishing contracts. They can help you navigate the legal implications and negotiate a resolution.

- **Learn from the Experience**: Use this experience as a learning opportunity. Review what led to the breach and put systems in place to avoid it in the future, such as better time management or clearer communication.

Example: You miss your manuscript deadline but immediately notify your publisher and propose a revised timeline. By acknowledging the breach and taking corrective action, you may avoid legal or financial penalties.

Tip: If you anticipate future issues that could lead to a breach, be proactive in discussing potential solutions with your publisher before the problem escalates.

A breach of contract can have serious consequences, but it's often avoidable with careful planning, clear communication, and a proactive approach. By understanding what constitutes a breach and implementing strategies to stay compliant, you can protect yourself from legal and financial pitfalls and maintain a positive working relationship with your publisher.

Consequences of Non-Compliance: Penalties and Fines

When an author fails to comply with the terms of a publishing contract, the consequences can range from minor inconveniences to severe legal and financial penalties. Non-compliance, especially in the case of a material breach (a significant failure to fulfill the contract), can result in fines, loss of rights, damage to your reputation, and even costly legal battles. Understanding these potential outcomes is crucial to staying in good standing with your publisher and protecting your career.

In this section, we'll explore the most common consequences of non-compliance, including penalties, financial repercussions, and how these issues can affect your future opportunities as an author.

1. Financial Penalties

One of the most immediate and tangible consequences of non-compliance is financial penalties. These penalties can take many forms depending on the specific terms of your contract.

Common financial penalties include:

- **Return of Advance**: If you receive an advance payment from the publisher and fail to deliver the manuscript or fulfill other key obligations, the contract may require you to return the advance in full or in part. For many authors, this can be a significant financial burden, especially if the advance has already been spent.

- **Delayed or Withheld Payments**: If you miss deadlines or fail to meet deliverable standards, your royalty payments or remaining installments of your advance may be delayed or withheld. In some cases, publishers will refuse to make further payments until you have fully complied with your obligations.

- **Fines for Missed Deadlines**: Some contracts include clauses that impose fines for missing deadlines. These fines could be based on a daily or weekly rate, adding up the longer the delay continues.

- **Liability for Publisher Costs**: If your non-compliance causes the publisher to incur additional costs—such as hiring extra editors, extending marketing campaigns, or delaying production—you may be held liable for reimbursing those costs. This can happen if your breach forces the publisher to reschedule a book launch or pay for additional promotional efforts.

Example: If your contract states that you must return the advance if you fail to deliver the manuscript by a specified deadline, and you do not deliver, the publisher may demand repayment of the advance. Failure to repay could lead to further legal action.

Tip: Always review the financial terms of your contract closely, especially regarding advance payments, royalty structures, and potential penalties for non-compliance.

2. Loss of Rights

Another significant consequence of non-compliance is the **loss of rights** to your work. Publishing contracts typically grant certain rights to the publisher (e.g., print, digital, or subsidiary rights). If you breach your contract, the publisher may terminate the agreement and reclaim the rights you've granted them.

Here's how this can happen:

- **Reversion of Rights to Publisher**: In some cases, non-compliance can result in the rights to your manuscript or book being reverted to the publisher. This means you no longer have control over your work, and the publisher can determine its fate, such as whether or not it will be published.

- **Loss of Future Project Rights**: If your contract includes a first-option or first-look clause for future projects, non-compliance could result in the loss of that opportunity. The publisher may choose not to exercise these options, meaning you'll lose the chance to work with them on future books or series.

- **Forfeiture of Subsidiary Rights**: If your contract grants the publisher rights to translations, audiobooks, or film adaptations, non-compliance could result in the publisher reclaiming those rights and profiting from them without your further input or involvement.

Example: If you miss multiple deadlines for your manuscript and fail to communicate with the publisher, they may decide to terminate the contract and keep all rights to the book. You could lose control of your work and any future royalties tied to its publication.

Tip: Pay close attention to clauses related to the reversion of rights and termination of the contract. Know what rights you could lose if you fail to comply and what steps you need to take to avoid this.

3. Damage to Your Reputation

While financial penalties and loss of rights are serious consequences, the damage to your professional reputation can be even more long-lasting. Publishers, agents, and others in the industry are often wary of working with authors who have a history of non-compliance, as this can disrupt production schedules and create costly delays.

Here's how non-compliance can hurt your reputation:

- **Loss of Trust with Publishers**: If you consistently miss deadlines, fail to communicate, or don't fulfill your obligations, you may lose the trust of your publisher. This can make it harder to negotiate future contracts or receive favorable terms.

- **Negative Industry Perception**: Word travels fast in the publishing world, and a reputation for unreliability can make it difficult to secure new deals with other publishers or agents. Being known as an author who fails to deliver can limit your opportunities.

- **Limited Future Contracts**: If your breach of contract results in a legal dispute or a formal termination of the agreement, it may become part of your professional record. Future publishers may be hesitant to take a chance on an author with a history of legal issues or non-compliance.

Example: An author who repeatedly fails to deliver manuscripts on time or who engages in legal disputes with multiple publishers may develop a reputation for being difficult to work with. This could result in fewer offers or less favorable contract terms in the future.

Tip: Always strive to meet your obligations and maintain open, professional communication with your publisher. Even if issues arise, your transparency and willingness to resolve them can help preserve your reputation.

4. Legal Action and Court Proceedings

In cases of severe or unresolved non-compliance, publishers may resort to legal action to enforce the terms of the contract. This can lead to court proceedings, where both parties present their case, and a judge or arbitrator decides the outcome.

Legal consequences of non-compliance include:

- **Lawsuits**: If you breach your contract in a significant way, the publisher may file a lawsuit against you. This can be costly, both in terms of legal fees and potential damages you may be required to pay if you lose the case.

- **Damages and Compensation**: In some cases, the publisher may seek monetary damages to compensate for any financial losses they've incurred due to your non-compliance. This could include the return of the advance, reimbursement for marketing costs, or even punitive damages.

- **Contractual Enforcement**: A court may enforce the terms of the contract, requiring you to fulfill your obligations under the original agreement. This could mean being legally compelled to complete the manuscript or adhere to the terms you've agreed upon.

Example: If you sign a contract with a major publisher and breach the agreement by failing to deliver the manuscript or violating exclusivity clauses, the publisher may sue you for damages, seeking repayment of the advance and compensation for lost profits.

Tip: If you believe a legal dispute is on the horizon, consult a lawyer who specializes in publishing contracts as early as possible. They can help you navigate the situation, negotiate a settlement, or represent you in court if necessary.

Non-compliance with a publishing contract can have serious financial, legal, and reputational consequences. From fines and the return of advances to the loss of rights and legal battles, the stakes are high for authors who fail to fulfill their obligations. By understanding the penalties of non-compliance and taking proactive steps to meet your commitments, you can protect your career, avoid costly disputes, and maintain positive relationships with publishers and collaborators.

Resolving Contract Disputes: Mediation, Arbitration, and Litigation

When a contract dispute arises, authors and publishers are often faced with the challenge of resolving it in a way that minimizes damage to their relationship and avoids costly legal battles. Fortunately, there are several methods for resolving contract disputes, ranging from informal discussions to formal legal proceedings. The three most common paths are mediation, arbitration, and litigation—each offering different levels of formality, cost, and control over the outcome.

In this section, we'll explore the key differences between mediation, arbitration, and litigation, and how each approach can be used to resolve contract disputes effectively.

1. Mediation: A Collaborative Approach

Mediation is often the first step in resolving contract disputes and is a more collaborative and informal process. It involves a neutral third party, the mediator, who helps facilitate a discussion between the disputing parties to reach a mutually agreeable solution. Mediation is a voluntary process and typically focuses on finding a resolution that satisfies both parties without escalating the dispute to a formal legal setting.

Here's how mediation works:

- **Neutral Mediator**: A mediator, who is neutral and has no stake in the outcome, is selected by both parties. The mediator's role is to guide the conversation, help clarify the issues, and propose possible solutions, but they do not make a final decision.

- **Collaborative Discussion**: Both parties are encouraged to share their perspectives and negotiate in good faith. The mediator helps ensure that the conversation remains productive and that both sides are heard.

- **Non-Binding Outcome**: The outcome of mediation is non-binding, meaning that if both parties agree to a resolution, they can move forward. If no agreement is reached, they are free to pursue other methods, such as arbitration or litigation.

Example: If an author misses multiple deadlines but believes the publisher was not clear about their expectations, both parties may agree to mediation to discuss the issue and potentially revise the delivery schedule without resorting to legal action.

Tip: Mediation is often the least expensive and quickest method of resolving disputes. It's a great option if both parties are open to compromise and wish to preserve their working relationship.

2. Arbitration: A Formal but Private Resolution

Arbitration is a more formal process than mediation but is still less adversarial and time-consuming than litigation. In arbitration, a neutral third party, called an arbitrator, listens to both sides of the dispute and makes a legally binding decision. Arbitration can be voluntary, or it may be required by a clause in the contract.

Here's how arbitration works:

- **Selection of Arbitrator**: Both parties agree on an arbitrator (or a panel of arbitrators) who has expertise in the relevant field. The arbitrator acts similarly to a judge, reviewing evidence and hearing arguments from both sides.

- **Presenting Evidence**: Unlike mediation, where the goal is collaboration, arbitration is more structured. Both sides present their evidence, make arguments, and may have legal representation. The arbitrator reviews all of the information before making a decision.

- **Binding Decision**: The key difference between arbitration and mediation is that the arbitrator's decision is binding. Once the arbitrator rules on the dispute, both parties must comply with the decision, and there is limited room for appeal.

Example: If an author disputes the royalty calculations provided by the publisher and believes they are owed more, both parties might agree to arbitration, where an expert in publishing contracts would review the royalty terms and make a binding decision.

Tip: Many contracts include mandatory arbitration clauses that require both parties to use arbitration instead of going to court. Always review your contract to understand your options for dispute resolution.

3. Litigation: Taking the Dispute to Court

Litigation is the most formal and public way to resolve a contract dispute. It involves taking the matter to court, where both parties present their case to a judge (and sometimes a jury). Litigation is typically the last resort, as it can be time-consuming, costly, and damaging to relationships.

Here's how litigation works:

- **Filing a Lawsuit**: One party files a lawsuit against the other, formally initiating the legal process. Both parties may have legal representation, and they present evidence, call witnesses, and make legal arguments in court.

- **Court Proceedings**: Litigation follows strict legal procedures, and the dispute is resolved in a courtroom. A judge (or a jury in some cases) reviews the evidence and makes a ruling based on the facts of the case and the law.

- **Binding Judgment**: The court's ruling is legally binding, and both parties must comply with the decision. Depending on the nature of the dispute, the court may award damages, require specific actions, or enforce the terms of the contract.

Example: If an author believes that a publisher has breached their contract by failing to release a book as promised, the author may file a lawsuit seeking damages and a court order to enforce the contract.

Tip: Litigation should be considered a last resort due to its cost and length. However, if mediation and arbitration fail, or if the breach is serious enough, litigation may be necessary to protect your rights.

4. Choosing the Right Path for Dispute Resolution

When a contract dispute arises, the best path forward depends on the nature of the dispute, the relationship between the parties, and the terms of the contract. In most cases, it's preferable to start with mediation or arbitration to preserve relationships and avoid the costs of litigation.

Here's how to choose the right path:

- **Start with Mediation**: If the issue is relatively minor or based on a misunderstanding, mediation is a low-cost, low-stress option that can help resolve the dispute quickly.

- **Consider Arbitration for More Complex Disputes**: If the dispute involves significant financial or legal stakes, but both parties want to avoid the time and expense of court, arbitration is a good middle-ground option. It's formal and binding but less public than litigation.

- **Use Litigation for Severe Breaches**: If the breach of contract is serious, such as a major financial loss or violation of intellectual property rights, litigation may be necessary to enforce the terms of the contract or seek damages.

Example: If an author and publisher disagree about whether the author has met their promotional obligations, mediation may be a good first step. However, if the dispute involves royalty payments or a serious breach, arbitration or litigation might be more appropriate.

Tip: Review your contract for dispute resolution clauses that may require mediation or arbitration before litigation. Understanding these clauses will help you know what steps to take if a dispute arises.

Resolving contract disputes can be a complex process, but understanding the differences between mediation, arbitration, and litigation can help you navigate the situation effectively. Mediation is collaborative and non-binding, arbitration is more formal but binding, and litigation involves taking the dispute to court. By choosing the right path based on the severity of the dispute and the relationship with your publisher, you can resolve issues while protecting your rights and minimizing damage to your career.

Protecting Yourself: How to Stay Compliant and What to Do If You Slip

Navigating the complexities of publishing contracts requires careful attention to detail and proactive management. Staying compliant with your contractual obligations ensures that you avoid costly mistakes, maintain a positive relationship with your publisher, and protect your career. However, if you do slip up, understanding how to address the situation can minimize the damage and help you get back on track.

In this section, we'll explore strategies for staying compliant with your contract and the steps you should take if you find yourself at risk of breaching your agreement.

1. Stay Organized: Tracking Deadlines and Deliverables

One of the most effective ways to protect yourself from non-compliance is to stay organized and manage your commitments proactively. Keeping a close eye on your deadlines and deliverables ensures you meet your obligations and avoid misunderstandings with your publisher.

Here's how to stay organized:

- **Create a Master Calendar**: Track all your contract deadlines, including manuscript submission dates, revision periods, marketing commitments, and any other contractual obligations. Use digital tools like Google

Calendar, Trello, or Asana to set reminders and break larger tasks into manageable steps.

- **Prioritize Your Work**: If you have multiple projects or contracts, prioritize tasks based on urgency and importance. Focus on meeting the most pressing deadlines first, and be realistic about how much time you need to complete each task.

- **Review Your Contract Regularly**: Periodically review the terms of your contract to ensure that you understand your obligations. This helps prevent surprises and allows you to plan ahead for any upcoming responsibilities.

Example: You have a manuscript due in six months and promotional events scheduled two months before that. By creating a calendar and setting weekly writing goals, you can meet your manuscript deadline while also preparing for the promotional activities.

Tip: Use task management tools that allow you to set reminders for important deadlines, and regularly update your progress to stay on track.

2. Communicate Early and Often with Your Publisher

Communication is key to staying compliant with your contract. If you anticipate any issues—whether it's a potential delay or a misunderstanding about your obligations—communicating with your publisher early can prevent small problems from becoming major disputes.

Here's how to communicate effectively:

- **Address Issues Before They Escalate**: If you realize that you may miss a deadline or that you're unclear about a specific obligation, reach out to your publisher as soon as possible. Publishers appreciate transparency and are often willing to work with authors to adjust timelines or clarify expectations.

- **Set Clear Expectations**: From the beginning, ensure that both you and your publisher have clear expectations about your deliverables and deadlines. If there's any ambiguity, ask for clarification in writing to avoid confusion later.

- **Keep Records of All Communications**: Document all communications with your publisher, especially if any changes are made to your deadlines, deliverables, or other contractual terms. Having written records can protect you in case of any disputes down the road.

Example: If you know that a personal issue may affect your ability to meet a manuscript deadline, reach out to your editor early to explain the situation and request a new deadline. Clear communication shows professionalism and helps maintain trust.

Tip: Keep email records organized in a dedicated folder, and if any verbal agreements are made, follow up with a confirmation email to ensure you have everything in writing.

3. Know When to Negotiate Adjustments

Contracts are not always set in stone. If you find that you're struggling to meet the terms of your agreement, it's often possible to negotiate adjustments with your publisher. Whether it's extending a deadline or revising a marketing commitment, negotiating proactively can prevent a breach of contract and preserve your working relationship.

Here's how to negotiate adjustments:

- **Be Honest About Your Needs**: If a deadline or deliverable is no longer feasible, be upfront with your publisher about why you need an adjustment. Be prepared to explain how much extra time or flexibility you need and what you'll do to meet the revised commitment.

- **Offer Solutions**: When requesting adjustments, propose a concrete plan for how you'll meet the new terms. For example, if you need an extension on your manuscript, outline a new timeline with milestones to show how you'll stay on track.

- **Be Open to Compromise**: Publishers may agree to your request, but they may also suggest alternative solutions, such as reducing the scope of a promotional campaign or adjusting your marketing commitments. Be open to finding a compromise that works for both parties.

Example: If you've fallen behind on your manuscript due to an unexpected event, ask for a deadline extension and propose a revised timeline that includes additional check-ins with your editor to show progress.

Tip: When negotiating, remain professional and solution-oriented. Publishers are more likely to accommodate reasonable requests if they feel confident that you're committed to fulfilling your obligations.

4. What to Do If You Slip

Despite your best efforts, it's possible to make a mistake or miss a deadline. If this happens, the key is to take immediate action to mitigate the impact and resolve the issue.

Here's what to do if you slip:

- **Acknowledge the Issue Immediately**: Don't wait for your publisher to follow up. If you realize you've breached your contract or missed a deadline, take the initiative to inform your publisher right away. Acknowledge the mistake and explain the circumstances clearly.

- **Propose a Solution**: Once you've identified the issue, propose a specific solution to remedy the situation. This could involve offering a new deadline, agreeing to additional promotional efforts, or making up for the breach in other ways. Show your publisher that you're serious about fixing the problem.

- **Consult Legal Advice if Necessary**: If the breach is significant and you're unsure of how to proceed, consider seeking legal advice. An attorney who specializes in publishing contracts can help you navigate the situation, negotiate with your publisher, and protect your interests.

Example: If you've missed a major deadline, send a message to your publisher acknowledging the delay and proposing a new timeline for submission. Be prepared to offer additional support, such as increased promotional efforts, to make up for the missed deadline.

Tip: Act quickly to resolve any breach of contract, as waiting too long could escalate the issue and damage your relationship with your publisher.

Protecting yourself from non-compliance requires organization, clear communication, and proactive problem-solving. By tracking deadlines, maintaining regular communication with your publisher, negotiating adjustments when needed, and taking responsibility if you slip, you can stay compliant with your contract and avoid costly mistakes. If you do find yourself at risk of non-compliance, addressing the issue quickly and professionally is the best way to minimize damage and maintain a positive working relationship.

Quick Tips and Recap

- **Track Deadlines**: Use a master calendar or task management tools to stay on top of deadlines and deliverables.

- **Communicate Early**: If you anticipate a problem, inform your publisher as soon as possible to prevent issues from escalating.

- **Negotiate Adjustments**: If needed, proactively request deadline extensions or revisions to your obligations and offer clear solutions.

- **Keep Records**: Maintain documentation of all communications and agreements with your publisher for future reference.

- **Acknowledge Mistakes**: If you slip, acknowledge the issue immediately and propose a solution to remedy the situation.

- **Seek Legal Advice if Necessary**: For serious breaches or disputes, consult a legal expert to protect your rights and interests.

- **Be Proactive**: Taking early action when issues arise shows professionalism and helps preserve your relationship with your publisher.

By staying organized, communicating effectively, and addressing issues promptly, you can avoid non-compliance and maintain a positive, productive relationship with your publisher.

CHAPTER FIFTEEN

Future Works and Options: Planning Ahead

"Planning ahead for future works and options is about creating a
roadmap for success, enabling strategic flexibility and readiness to
capitalize on opportunities as they arise." — DANIEL PINK, AUTHOR
AND BEHAVIORAL SCIENCE EXPERT

Welcome to Chapter Fifteen, "Future Works and Options: Planning Ahead,"
where we equip you with a crystal ball to gaze into your literary future.
This isn't just about scribbling down ideas on napkins; it's about strategically
planting seeds today that will grow into towering trees of opportunity tomorrow.

In this chapter, we dive into the art of forecasting your writing career's trajectory
like a seasoned meteorologist predicts the weather. We'll explore how to secure
options that keep your options open, ensuring that every book deal or contract not
only meets your current needs but also lays the foundation for future projects.

You'll learn how to navigate clauses that talk about sequel rights, spin-offs, and all the other exciting possibilities that could extend the life of your work far beyond its initial publication.

Strap in and ready your planning tools, because we're about to turn you into a time-traveling strategist, adept at charting courses that lead to not just one successful publication, but a flourishing career filled with them. Let's make sure your next big hit is always just around the corner.

Sequel and Spin-Off Rights: Expanding Your Universe

One of the most exciting possibilities for an author is the chance to expand the world you've created through sequels and spin-offs. These projects can breathe new life into your existing work, allowing you to revisit beloved characters, explore new storylines, or dive deeper into different aspects of your fictional universe. But to fully capitalize on these opportunities, it's essential to understand and negotiate sequel and spin-off rights in your publishing contracts.

In this section, we'll explore what sequel and spin-off rights are, how to protect your creative control, and the strategies you can use to expand your universe while ensuring you maintain ownership over future works.

1. What Are Sequel and Spin-Off Rights?

Sequel rights give a publisher the ability to publish any future works that directly continue the story of your original book, while spin-off rights allow for the creation of related works that branch off from the original, such as prequels, companion stories, or books focusing on secondary characters. These rights are often included in your initial publishing contract and can play a crucial role in shaping the long-term success of your work.

Key distinctions:

- **Sequel Rights**: Typically refer to books that continue the storyline of your original work. For example, if your debut novel is part of a planned trilogy, your publisher may want the exclusive right to publish all subsequent books in the series.

277

- **Spin-Off Rights**: Cover works that take place in the same universe but may focus on different characters, timelines, or events. For example, a spin-off could explore the backstory of a supporting character or create a separate story within the same world as the original book.

Example: You write a fantasy novel, and it becomes a success. Your publisher might want to secure the sequel rights for any books that continue the story, but you also might have ideas for spin-offs based on minor characters that they'll be interested in.

Tip: Always clarify the scope of these rights in your contract. Make sure it's clear what constitutes a sequel versus a spin-off and whether you retain any control over future adaptations of your work.

2. Negotiating Sequel and Spin-Off Rights

When negotiating sequel and spin-off rights, it's important to ensure you have creative control and flexibility for future projects. Publishers often want to secure these rights upfront to lock in future revenues, but you should ensure that the terms work in your favor.

Here are some strategies for negotiating sequel and spin-off rights:

- **Limit the Scope**: If you're unsure about committing to a full series or spin-offs, negotiate for a more limited option. For instance, instead of granting the publisher the rights to all future books in the series, you could grant them an option for the next one or two books only, giving you the freedom to explore other publishing opportunities later.

- **Retain Spin-Off Flexibility**: If you want the freedom to create spin-offs or companion works independently, negotiate to retain control of spin-off rights. This allows you to potentially license those works to other publishers or develop them into other media formats, such as graphic novels or TV series.

- **Time-Limited Options**: Consider negotiating a time-limited option for sequels or spin-offs. For example, if the publisher doesn't commit to publishing the sequel within a certain time frame (e.g., two years after the first book's release), you regain the rights to publish it elsewhere.

- **Specify Payment Terms**: Make sure your contract outlines how royalties, advances, and other financial considerations will apply to future works. Sequels and spin-offs often come with different financial arrangements, so it's essential to clarify those terms upfront.

Example: Your publisher offers to publish the first book in your planned series but wants exclusive rights to all future sequels and spin-offs. You could negotiate to give them the rights to only the first sequel, with the option to renegotiate after the release, keeping your long-term options open.

Tip: Keep an eye on long-term creative freedom. While it's tempting to sign over all future rights to secure a deal, retaining some control over spin-offs and sequels can give you greater flexibility down the line.

3. Retaining Creative Control

One of the risks of granting sequel and spin-off rights is that you might lose some creative control over how these future works are developed. Publishers may have specific ideas for how they want the series to evolve, which could conflict with your vision. Therefore, it's essential to negotiate terms that allow you to maintain creative input over the direction of your future works.

Here's how to retain creative control:

- **Creative Approval Clauses**: Negotiate for creative approval clauses in your contract. This could give you the final say on major decisions regarding the storylines, characters, and tone of sequels and spin-offs.

- **Creative Collaboration**: Ensure that the publisher acknowledges your role as the primary creative force behind any sequels or spin-offs. If they want to bring in co-writers or other creatives, negotiate to remain involved in the development process.

- **Adaptation Rights**: If your book has potential for adaptations (e.g., film, TV, or games), negotiate to retain control over spin-offs in other media. Even if the publisher has sequel rights for the books, you may want to maintain control over adaptations into different formats.

Example: Your contract might include a clause that allows you to approve major plot developments or character changes in any sequels or spin-offs. This ensures that your creative vision is respected throughout the series.

Tip: Be cautious of giving away too much creative control in exchange for securing a deal. Maintaining input over your future works helps protect your artistic integrity and ensures that your universe evolves in the way you envision.

4. Planning for the Long Term

Securing sequel and spin-off rights is an important step in building a sustainable writing career. These projects allow you to continue benefiting from your existing work and can lead to additional opportunities, such as foreign editions, film adaptations, or merchandise.

Here's how to plan for the long term:

- **Think Beyond the First Book**: Even if you're focused on your current project, consider how sequels and spin-offs might fit into your larger career strategy. Do you envision an ongoing series, or do you want to explore different genres and storylines in spin-offs?

- **Build a Franchise**: If your work has franchise potential, sequels and spin-offs can help you create a long-term brand around your stories. This can open doors to other opportunities like merchandising, adaptations, or licensing deals.

- **Stay Flexible**: While planning ahead is important, leave room for flexibility. Your creative interests may evolve, and it's crucial to retain the freedom to explore new ideas or different projects even as you expand on your original work.

Example: After your first novel becomes successful, you start thinking about how you can expand the story world through sequels and spin-offs. By securing the rights and planning ahead, you're able to create a successful series and build a long-term career around your fictional universe.

Tip: Always consider the long-term implications of the rights you're granting. A well-negotiated contract for sequels and spin-offs can help you build a lasting legacy around your work, while also keeping your creative options open.

Sequel and spin-off rights provide authors with valuable opportunities to expand their creative worlds and build successful franchises. By negotiating these rights carefully, retaining creative control, and planning for the long term, you can maximize the potential of your existing work while ensuring that your future projects remain aligned with your vision. Whether it's a direct continuation of your story or a spin-off that explores new avenues, these rights are key to extending the life of your literary universe.

First-Option and First-Look Clauses: Understanding Your Publisher's Future Claims

When you sign a book contract, publishers often want the ability to review and potentially publish your future work—especially if your first book is successful. This is where first-option and first-look clauses come into play. These clauses allow your publisher the right to be the first to consider your next book or series, which can be beneficial but also potentially limiting if not negotiated carefully.

In this section, we'll break down what first-option and first-look clauses mean, how they impact your future projects, and how to negotiate terms that give you the flexibility to pursue other opportunities while maintaining a good relationship with your publisher.

1. What Are First-Option and First-Look Clauses?

First-option and first-look clauses are contractual agreements that give your publisher the right to evaluate and potentially publish your future works before you offer them to other publishers. These clauses can apply to direct sequels, books in the same genre, or even completely unrelated projects, depending on the terms.

Key distinctions:

- **First-Option Clause**: This gives your publisher the right to be the first to make an offer on your next book or project. If the publisher passes on the option, you are free to shop the book to other publishers. However, the option often requires you to provide detailed information or even a finished manuscript to the original publisher first.

- **First-Look Clause**: Similar to the first-option clause, but the first-look clause only gives the publisher the opportunity to review the work before others, not necessarily the first right to make an offer. The publisher has a limited time to decide if they're interested.

Example: You sign a contract with a publisher for your first book, and the contract includes a first-option clause for any future novels in the same genre. This means you're obligated to offer your next book to that publisher first, allowing them the chance to make an offer before you approach other publishers.

Tip: Read the fine print carefully—these clauses can apply to more than just sequels. Be clear on whether the option applies to all future works, specific genres, or certain types of projects.

2. Benefits and Risks of First-Option and First-Look Clauses

While these clauses can be advantageous in some situations, they also come with potential drawbacks. Understanding both the benefits and risks is key to negotiating the best terms for your future projects.

Benefits:

- **Guaranteed Interest**: If your publisher has invested in building your career, they may have a strong interest in publishing your next book, which can lead to a smoother transition for future works.

- **Continuity**: Having the same publisher for multiple projects can provide consistency in terms of marketing, branding, and editorial support.

- **Time-Saving**: First-option or first-look clauses can streamline the process of selling your next book, as you already have an established relationship with the publisher.

Risks:

- **Limiting Your Flexibility**: These clauses may restrict your ability to explore other publishing opportunities, especially if the option applies to all future works or is too broadly defined. You might find yourself locked into an arrangement that doesn't align with your evolving creative vision or career goals.

- **Delayed Projects**: If the publisher takes too long to decide on your next project, it can delay your ability to seek other offers, potentially slowing down your career momentum.

- **Less Competitive Offers**: If you're bound by a first-option clause, your publisher may make a less competitive offer than other publishers might, knowing that you're contractually obligated to offer them the work first.

Example: Your first-option clause requires that you submit your next manuscript to the publisher, but they take several months to make a decision. This delay could prevent you from pursuing other offers in a timely manner, leaving you stuck waiting.

Tip: Negotiate for a clear, short time frame during which the publisher must decide whether to take on your next project. This prevents unnecessary delays and allows you to move on if they aren't interested.

3. Negotiating Favorable First-Option or First-Look Clauses

First-option and first-look clauses can be powerful tools for both authors and publishers, but it's crucial to negotiate the terms carefully to ensure that they don't limit your future opportunities. Here are some key strategies for negotiating these clauses:

- **Limit the Scope**: One of the most important aspects to negotiate is the scope of the clause. Ensure that the clause only applies to specific types of works—such as sequels or books within the same genre—and not all future projects. This gives you the flexibility to explore other genres or formats without being tied to one publisher.

- **Time Frame for Review**: Negotiate a clear time frame for how long the publisher has to exercise their first option or review the work. Typically, this should be between 30 and 90 days. If the publisher doesn't respond within that period, you should be free to offer the work to other publishers.

- **Define Submission Requirements**: Clarify what you need to submit for the option or first-look clause. Does the publisher require a full manuscript, or would a proposal or outline suffice? The latter can give you more flexibility and reduce delays.

- **Specify Financial Terms**: Ensure that the option or first-look clause includes guidelines for the financial terms. For example, you may want to specify that the offer should meet or exceed the advance and royalty rates of your previous book. This protects you from receiving an uncompetitive offer.

Example: In your contract, you negotiate a first-option clause that applies only to sequels of your current book, giving you the freedom to shop other types of projects to different publishers. You also set a 60-day deadline for the publisher to decide whether to make an offer on your next project.

Tip: Always ask for clarity on how the publisher intends to handle the first option or first look. If possible, negotiate terms that don't overly restrict your creative freedom and career flexibility.

4. Balancing Creative Freedom with Publisher Relationships

One of the challenges of first-option and first-look clauses is balancing your creative freedom with the practical realities of maintaining strong publisher relationships. While you don't want to lock yourself into an unfavorable deal, maintaining a positive rapport with your publisher can help ensure future projects are welcomed and supported.

Here's how to find the balance:

- **Be Transparent**: If you're planning on writing works that fall outside of the first-option clause (for instance, a different genre or series), be upfront with your publisher. Clear communication about your career plans can help prevent misunderstandings and build trust.

- **Honor the Agreement**: If you've agreed to give your publisher the first option, be respectful of that commitment. Submit the manuscript within the agreed time frame and give them the opportunity to review it before seeking other publishers.

- **Know When to Walk Away**: If your publisher isn't meeting your needs or is consistently offering less competitive deals, it may be time to seek new opportunities once the option clause expires. Be prepared to walk away if the relationship isn't serving your long-term career goals.

Example: You've written a successful mystery novel and your publisher has first-option rights to any sequels. However, you're also interested in writing a fantasy novel. You make sure to notify your publisher that the fantasy project falls outside of the option clause, allowing you to pursue other publishing opportunities for that work.

Tip: Build a strong, professional relationship with your publisher by being communicative and reliable. This can make future negotiations easier and ensure that they're eager to work with you on future projects.

First-option and first-look clauses can provide valuable opportunities to work with the same publisher on future projects, but they also have the potential to limit your flexibility. By negotiating favorable terms, limiting the scope of these clauses, and balancing your creative freedom with your publisher relationships, you can protect your future projects while building a successful, long-term writing career. Always approach these clauses with a clear understanding of your goals and the potential impact on your future works.

Long-Term Career Planning: Balancing Current Contracts with Future Opportunities

As an author, you are not just working on your current book—you are also building a career. Long-term career planning requires thinking beyond your current projects and envisioning how each contract and opportunity aligns with your broader goals. It's about balancing the demands of your existing contracts with the potential for future opportunities, ensuring that you're not only successful today but also setting yourself up for ongoing growth.

In this section, we'll explore how to plan for long-term success, manage multiple projects, and make strategic decisions that keep your writing career moving forward, while avoiding the pitfalls of overcommitting or missing out on new opportunities.

1. Define Your Long-Term Career Goals

Before you can effectively balance your current contracts with future opportunities, it's essential to have a clear vision of what you want your writing career to look like in the years to come. Your goals will shape how you approach new opportunities and guide your decisions when negotiating contracts or taking on new projects.

Key questions to consider:

- **What genres or types of stories do I want to focus on long-term?** Are you building a career in a single genre (e.g., fantasy, romance), or are you interested in branching out into different genres?

- **Do I want to write for multiple publishers or stay with one?** Some authors prefer long-term relationships with a single publisher, while others enjoy working with multiple publishers to diversify their portfolio.

- **Am I open to writing in different formats (e.g., novels, short stories, screenplays)?** Consider how your writing might evolve over time and whether you want to explore other types of storytelling, such as TV writing, graphic novels, or podcasting.

- **What milestones do I want to achieve?** This might include hitting bestseller lists, winning awards, or adapting your work for film or television.

Example: You may start with a single fantasy series but plan to expand into science fiction in the future. Knowing this, you can ensure that your current contracts allow for creative flexibility in the genres you want to explore down the line.

Tip: Write down your long-term goals and refer to them when making decisions about new contracts. This will help you stay aligned with your vision and avoid taking on projects that don't support your career path.

2. Managing Current Contracts: Know Your Obligations

Your existing contracts are the foundation of your current work, but it's important to know how they affect your future projects. Staying on top of your contractual obligations—such as deadlines, deliverables, and promotional commitments—ensures that you meet your responsibilities without overextending yourself.

Here's how to effectively manage your current contracts:

- **Track All Deadlines**: Keep a detailed calendar of your contract deadlines, including manuscript submissions, revisions, and marketing efforts. Knowing your timeline allows you to plan your workload and avoid falling behind.

- **Understand Exclusivity and First-Option Clauses**: Be clear on whether your contracts include exclusivity clauses or first-option clauses (as discussed in the previous section). These clauses can impact when and how you take on new projects, so it's crucial to factor them into your planning.

- **Communicate with Your Publisher**: Keep your publisher in the loop about your progress, any delays, or potential scheduling conflicts. Publishers are more likely to accommodate adjustments if they're informed early and understand your overall workload.

- **Prioritize Workload**: If you're juggling multiple contracts, prioritize them based on deadlines and financial impact. For instance, if one contract includes a high advance or is for a high-profile project, it may require more of your attention than a smaller or lower-priority commitment.

Example: You're under contract for a series with one publisher, but you're also working on a standalone novel for another. Keeping track of deadlines and obligations for both projects ensures you don't miss any important milestones, allowing you to balance the demands of both contracts.

Tip: Use project management tools like Trello or Asana to stay organized, especially when balancing multiple contracts. Breaking tasks into manageable steps makes it easier to stay on top of your commitments.

3. Evaluating Future Opportunities: Choosing the Right Projects

As your writing career progresses, you'll likely be presented with new opportunities—whether it's the chance to write in a different genre, collaborate on a new project, or sign with another publisher. However, not every opportunity will align with your long-term goals, and it's important to be selective about which projects to take on.

Here's how to evaluate future opportunities:

- **Assess Alignment with Your Goals**: Does the opportunity move you closer to your long-term vision for your career? For example, if you want to be known for writing epic fantasy, taking on a project in a completely different genre might not be the best use of your time.

- **Weigh the Financial and Career Impact**: Consider the potential financial benefits of the project, but also weigh its impact on your career trajectory. A lower-paying project might be worth pursuing if it provides valuable exposure or helps you break into a new market.

- **Consider Time Commitments**: Ensure that the new project won't stretch your time too thin. If it interferes with your ability to meet current deadlines, you may need to reconsider. Overcommitting can lead to burnout or missed deadlines, which can hurt your reputation in the long run.

- **Factor in Creative Satisfaction**: Sometimes the best opportunities are the ones that reignite your creative passion. If a project excites you and aligns with your goals, it may be worth pursuing even if it's a departure from your current work.

Example: You're offered a contract to write a new series in a genre you're passionate about, but you're also finishing up your current series. Before committing, you evaluate whether you can realistically meet the deadlines for both projects and whether this new series aligns with your long-term career goals.

Tip: Don't be afraid to say no to opportunities that don't align with your career goals or current commitments. It's better to focus on a few high-quality projects than to stretch yourself too thin by taking on too many.

4. Balancing Short-Term Wins with Long-Term Strategy

Building a long-term writing career means balancing immediate success with your broader goals. While short-term wins, like signing a new contract or hitting a sales target, are important, they should always be weighed against how they contribute to your overall strategy.

Here's how to balance short-term wins with long-term planning:

- **Keep Your Eyes on the Bigger Picture**: When making decisions about new projects or signing contracts, always ask yourself how this move fits into your long-term career strategy. Does it help you build momentum toward your ultimate goals, or is it a short-term distraction?

- **Plan for Creative Evolution**: Your writing style and interests will likely evolve over time. Build flexibility into your career planning to allow for creative growth. Avoid locking yourself into contracts that limit your ability to explore new genres or formats down the road.

- **Build a Network for Future Opportunities**: Networking with other authors, agents, and publishers can help you discover new opportunities that align with your long-term goals. Attend industry events, engage in online communities, and foster relationships that will serve your career in the future.

- **Monitor Industry Trends**: Stay informed about changes in the publishing industry that could impact your career. Whether it's the rise of self-publishing platforms, shifts in reader preferences, or new opportunities in multimedia storytelling, being aware of trends allows you to adapt your strategy accordingly.

Example: You're offered a lucrative contract for a standalone novel that's outside your typical genre. While it's tempting in the short term, you decide to pass because it doesn't align with your long-term goal of building a series in your primary genre.

Tip: Set annual career goals to help balance short-term wins with long-term planning. This helps you stay focused on what matters most while still allowing for flexibility in pursuing new opportunities.

Long-term career planning is essential for building a sustainable, successful writing career. By defining your long-term goals, managing your current contracts effectively, evaluating future opportunities strategically, and balancing short-term wins with your broader vision, you can create a career path that not only meets your immediate needs but also sets you up for future success. The key is to stay flexible, be selective about new opportunities, and always keep your long-term goals in sight.

Rights Reversion and Future Publishing Opportunities

As an author, your rights to your work are one of the most valuable assets you own. When you sign a publishing contract, you typically grant certain rights to the publisher, such as the right to publish your book in print or digital formats. However, these rights are not always transferred permanently. Through rights reversion clauses, you have the opportunity to regain control over your work under certain conditions, opening the door to new publishing opportunities in the future.

In this section, we'll explore what rights reversion is, how to negotiate favorable reversion terms in your contracts, and how you can leverage reverted rights for new opportunities, such as reprints, digital releases, or adaptations.

1. What Is Rights Reversion?

Rights reversion is a clause in a publishing contract that allows an author to regain the rights to their book after certain conditions are met. This typically happens when the publisher is no longer actively promoting or selling the book, or after a specific period has passed. Once the rights revert to the author, you are free to republish the work in new formats, with different publishers, or even self-publish.

Key scenarios for rights reversion:

- **Out-of-Print**: One of the most common triggers for rights reversion is when a book goes out of print, meaning the publisher is no longer making physical copies available for sale. In this case, the author can request the reversion of their rights.

- **Sales Thresholds**: Some contracts allow for rights reversion if a book's sales fall below a certain threshold over a specific period. For example, if fewer than 100 copies are sold in a 12-month period, you may have the right to request reversion.

- **Time-Based Reversion**: In some contracts, rights may automatically revert to the author after a set number of years, regardless of the book's sales status. This allows the author to regain control after a fixed period.

Example: Your book has been on the market for five years, and sales have slowed significantly. The publisher decides to take it out of print. At this point, you could invoke the rights reversion clause in your contract, allowing you to explore new opportunities for the book.

Tip: Always include a clear rights reversion clause in your contract. Make sure the conditions for reversion are specific and easy to track, such as sales thresholds or out-of-print status.

2. Negotiating Favorable Rights Reversion Clauses

When negotiating your publishing contract, it's important to ensure that the reversion clause is favorable and gives you a realistic opportunity to regain control of your work in the future. Publishers may try to retain rights for as long as possible, so understanding how to negotiate this clause is key.

Here's how to negotiate favorable rights reversion terms:

- **Clear Definitions**: Ensure that the contract clearly defines what constitutes "out of print" or "low sales." For example, does "out of print" mean physical copies only, or does it include digital formats as well? The more specific the language, the easier it will be to trigger reversion when the time comes.

- **Low Sales Thresholds**: Negotiate for a reasonable sales threshold that allows for reversion if the book is no longer generating significant revenue. A common threshold might be fewer than 100 copies sold in a year, but this can vary depending on the type of book and the publisher.

- **Time-Based Reversion**: If possible, include a time-based reversion clause that allows you to regain rights after a set number of years, regardless of the book's sales or print status. This is particularly important for ensuring that you can repurpose your work even if the publisher keeps the book available in digital formats.

- **Triggering Reversion**: Make sure that the contract specifies how you can request reversion when the conditions are met. This typically involves sending a formal written request to the publisher. Negotiate a clear process for this, including timelines for the publisher's response.

Example: You negotiate a rights reversion clause that states if your book sells fewer than 50 copies in a 12-month period, the rights will revert to you. This gives you a concrete benchmark to track and ensures you can regain control when the book is no longer selling.

Tip: Revisit your contract every few years to check whether the conditions for reversion have been met. Being proactive about requesting reversion will give you more opportunities to repurpose your work.

3. Leveraging Reverted Rights for New Opportunities

Once your rights revert to you, you regain full control over your work, allowing you to explore a wide range of new opportunities. Whether you choose to republish the book yourself, find a new publisher, or adapt the work for different media, rights reversion gives you the flexibility to maximize the value of your book over the long term.

Here's how to leverage reverted rights:

- **Self-Publishing**: Many authors choose to self-publish their books after regaining the rights. This allows you to take full control over the marketing, pricing, and distribution of your work. You can release the book in new formats, such as eBooks or audiobooks, or even offer special editions.

- **New Publishers**: If your original publisher no longer wishes to publish the book, you may be able to find a new publisher who is interested in reprinting it. This is particularly useful if your book has gained a new audience or if it's relevant to a different market.

- **Revisions and New Editions**: Reversion gives you the opportunity to revise and update your book, creating a new edition for readers. You can add new chapters, update content, or even rebrand the book with a new title and cover design.

- **Foreign Markets and Translations**: Once you regain your rights, you can explore opportunities to license your book to foreign publishers or translate it into new languages. This opens up entirely new markets for your work.

- **Adaptations for Film, TV, or Stage**: With full control over your rights, you can explore opportunities to adapt your work for other media, such as film, television, or stage productions. This can significantly expand the reach and impact of your book.

Example: After your book goes out of print and you regain the rights, you decide to self-publish it as an eBook and audiobook, targeting a new generation of readers who prefer digital formats. You also explore the possibility of adapting it into a screenplay for a potential film deal.

Tip: If you regain the rights to multiple works, consider bundling them together into a box set or series collection to maximize sales. Offering your books as a package can attract new readers and increase the overall value of your work.

4. Planning for Future Publishing Opportunities

Rights reversion is a key element of long-term career planning, allowing you to continue benefiting from your work even after the initial publication run has ended. By planning ahead, you can ensure that you're in a strong position to capitalize on reverted rights and explore new publishing opportunities as your career evolves.

Here's how to plan for future opportunities:

- **Monitor Your Contract Status**: Keep track of your contracts and regularly review your sales figures, print status, and other conditions that could trigger rights reversion. By staying informed, you can act quickly when the opportunity arises.

- **Build a Strategy for Reverted Works**: As you approach the reversion of your rights, start building a strategy for what you want to do with the work. Will you self-publish, seek a new publisher, or pursue adaptation opportunities? Having a plan in place allows you to act quickly once the rights revert.

- **Stay Open to New Formats and Markets**: As technology and reader preferences evolve, new opportunities for republishing your work may arise. Keep an eye on emerging platforms, such as subscription services or new audiobook distributors, that could provide additional revenue streams for your reverted works.

- **Leverage Your Backlist**: As you gain more control over your backlist (previously published works), use them to cross-promote new releases or boost sales of your newer books. Offering discounted or free versions of reverted works can attract new readers to your current projects.

Example: You've had several books go out of print over the years, and the rights have reverted to you. You decide to launch a reprint campaign, releasing new editions of your backlist alongside your latest work, generating renewed interest in your entire catalog.

Tip: Keep a file of all your contracts and rights reversion conditions so that you can easily reference them as you plan future publishing opportunities. Knowing when and how to act is key to maximizing the value of your work.

Rights reversion is a powerful tool for authors, giving you the ability to regain control over your work and pursue new opportunities long after the initial publication. By negotiating favorable reversion clauses, planning for future republishing strategies, and leveraging reverted rights in creative ways, you can continue to benefit from your writing for years to come. Rights reversion allows you to maximize the longevity and profitability of your work, ensuring that your career remains dynamic and evolving.

Quick Tips and Recap

- **Understand Rights Reversion**: Rights reversion allows you to regain control over your work after certain conditions, such as low sales or going out of print, are met.

- **Negotiate Clear Reversion Clauses**: Ensure your contract clearly defines terms for reversion, such as sales thresholds, out-of-print status, or a fixed number of years after publication.

- **Track Your Contract Status**: Regularly review sales figures, print status, and contract conditions to know when you can request rights reversion.

- **Leverage Reverted Rights**: Once rights revert to you, explore self-publishing, new publisher partnerships, updated editions, or adaptations in new formats or markets.

- **Plan for Future Opportunities**: Build a strategy for your reverted works, whether it's reprinting, releasing digital versions, or expanding into foreign markets or media adaptations.

By staying proactive with rights reversion and planning strategically, you can unlock new opportunities for your books and extend the life of your creative work well beyond its initial publication.

PART FOUR

Managing Finances

Welcome to Part Four: "Managing Finances," where we transform authors from masters of metaphor to wizards of wealth management. Here, you'll learn to navigate the crucial, if less romantic, side of a writing career—finances. We demystify advances, royalties, and rights sales, equipping you with the skills to decipher royalty statements, manage cash flows, and tackle tax implications. As we delve into financial planning, contract negotiations, and efficient bookkeeping, you'll gain the tools to ensure your creative achievements not only enrich your spirit but also your bank account. This section is dedicated to making sure that your literary success translates seamlessly into financial stability, ensuring that both your creative and financial needs are met harmoniously.

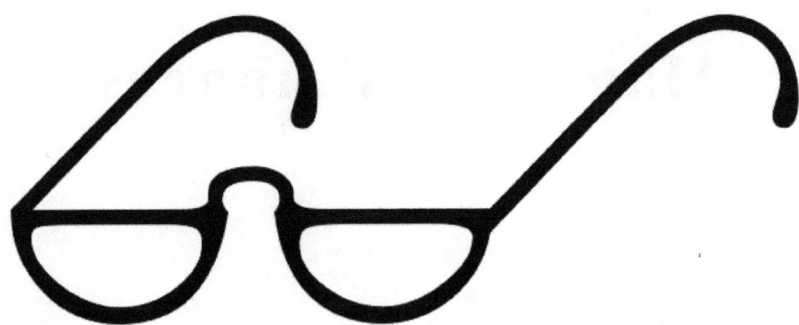

Understanding Advances and Royalties: The Economics of Your Work

"Understanding advances and royalties is essential for any creator. It's not just about the income, but understanding the economics of your work and how value is generated over time." — MICHAEL E. PORTER, ECONOMIST AND PROFESSOR AT HARVARD BUSINESS SCHOOL

Welcome to Chapter Sixteen, "Understanding Advances and Royalties: The Economics of Your Work," where we dive into the wallet-whispering world of literary finances. Here, you'll unravel the mysteries of advances and royalties—those delightful digits that make the life of letters worth living (and financing).

Advances: the upfront bounty for your brainchild, paid before your book graces the shelves. It's like a vote of confidence in your work, but in dollars, not just applause. And royalties? They're the gift that keeps on giving—percentages paid on sales, proving that your words keep pulling their weight long after the ink dries.

But beware, dear author, for the road to financial enlightenment is paved with contractual clauses and fine print. We'll decode these monetary codes, helping you understand what you're really earning and when to expect those precious pennies to ping your bank account. So, tighten your grip on your calculator—it's time to tally up your literary earnings with precision and a pinch of panache!

What Are Advances and How Do They Work?

An advance is the upfront payment an author receives from a publisher before the book is published. It's essentially a prepayment for future royalties, given as a gesture of confidence that the publisher believes your book will sell well enough to cover the amount advanced. For authors, an advance can serve as both financial support while writing and a sign that the publisher is invested in the success of the project.

In this section, we'll break down how advances work, how they are paid, and what they mean for your overall earnings as an author.

1. How Advances Are Calculated

Advances can vary significantly depending on factors like the publisher's budget, the author's previous track record, the anticipated market for the book, and the size of the publisher. Larger publishers tend to offer higher advances, but they are often more selective, while smaller publishers may offer lower advances but take on a wider variety of projects.

Here are some factors that affect how advances are calculated:

- **Author's Past Sales**: If you're a debut author, your advance may be more modest, since the publisher doesn't yet know how well your books will sell. If you're an established author with a proven track record of strong sales, your advance may be significantly higher.

- **Genre and Market**: Certain genres (like commercial fiction or self-help) tend to command higher advances, particularly if there's strong market demand. Literary fiction or niche genres may see lower advances, though there can be exceptions for highly anticipated works.

- **Publisher's Expectations**: The publisher's confidence in the potential success of your book plays a huge role. If they believe your book has bestseller potential or can be adapted for film or TV, they might offer a larger advance.

- **Foreign and Subsidiary Rights**: Publishers also consider the potential to sell foreign rights or adaptations, which can influence the size of the advance. If your book has strong global appeal, you might receive a higher advance upfront.

Example: A debut mystery novelist might receive an advance of $10,000, while a bestselling thriller writer might receive an advance of $200,000 or more based on their established sales history and market demand.

Tip: Advances are typically negotiable, so don't be afraid to discuss the offer with your agent or publisher to ensure you're getting a fair deal based on your work's potential.

2. How Advances Are Paid

Advances are rarely paid in one lump sum. Instead, they are typically paid in installments, often divided into two or three payments over the course of the publishing process.

Here's a common breakdown of how advances are paid:

- **Upon Signing**: The first payment (often one-third or one-half of the total advance) is paid when the contract is signed. This serves as a financial cushion while you work on your book.

- **Upon Delivery and Acceptance**: The second payment is made when the author delivers the manuscript, and the publisher formally accepts it. Acceptance means that the manuscript meets the publisher's standards and is ready to move forward in the publishing process.

- **Upon Publication**: The final portion of the advance is typically paid upon the book's publication, meaning when it officially goes on sale.

Example: If your advance is $30,000, you might receive $10,000 when you sign the contract, another $10,000 when you deliver the manuscript, and the final $10,000 when the book is published.

Tip: Be mindful of how the advance is split over time, as it's not an immediate lump sum. Budget accordingly to ensure financial stability through the various phases of the book's production.

3. What Happens If Your Book Doesn't "Earn Out"?

When you receive an advance, it's essentially a prepayment of your future royalties. Before you can receive additional royalty payments from your book's sales, you must first "earn out" the advance. This means your book's sales need to generate enough royalties to cover the amount of the advance.

Here's how the process works:

- **Royalties Deducted from Sales**: As your book sells, the royalties you would normally earn go toward paying back the advance. Once the total royalties from sales equal the advance, the book is said to have "earned out."

- **No Additional Payments Until Earned Out**: If your book doesn't earn out (meaning it doesn't sell enough copies to cover the advance), you won't receive additional royalties. However, you do not have to pay back the advance, even if the book doesn't earn enough to cover it. The advance is yours to keep.

- **Royalties After Earning Out**: Once your book earns out, you start receiving royalty payments for every sale beyond that point, which can add up to significant ongoing income if your book continues to sell well.

Example: If your advance is $20,000 and your royalty rate is 10% on a hardcover priced at $20, you'd need to sell 10,000 copies to earn out your advance (since you'd earn $2 per book sold). After selling those 10,000 copies, you would start receiving additional royalty payments for every book sold after that.

Tip: Don't be discouraged if your book doesn't earn out right away—earning out can take time, especially for debut authors. Focus on marketing efforts and building your readership to increase long-term sales.

4. The Impact of Advances on Your Career

Advances play an important role in shaping an author's career. A larger advance can provide financial security and boost an author's visibility, but it also comes with expectations for strong sales. If a book with a large advance doesn't earn out, it can affect the publisher's willingness to offer large advances for future projects.

Here's what to consider:

- **Higher Advances = Higher Expectations**: Publishers expect books with large advances to perform well in the market. If your book doesn't meet those expectations, it could impact your ability to negotiate future advances.

- **Building Trust with Publishers**: If your book earns out and continues to sell well, you build trust with your publisher, which can lead to more favorable contracts and higher advances in the future.

- **Balancing Financial Security with Career Growth**: While a large advance is appealing, it's important to balance the financial security it offers with the potential career risks if your book doesn't earn out. Sometimes, a more modest advance with more realistic sales expectations is a better long-term strategy.

Example: An author who receives a $100,000 advance may feel pressure to sell enough copies to meet the publisher's expectations. If the book falls short, the author might struggle to negotiate large advances for future books. In contrast, an author with a $20,000 advance might exceed sales expectations, leading to more lucrative offers in the future.

Tip: Consider the long-term impact of your advance on your career. A reasonable advance that's easier to earn out can help build a sustainable relationship with your publisher and lead to more opportunities down the line.

Understanding how advances work is crucial to managing your financial expectations as an author. From how they're calculated and paid to what it means if your book doesn't earn out, advances play a key role in shaping both your immediate income and your long-term career growth. By negotiating favorable terms and being mindful of how advances impact your future earnings, you can make informed decisions that support both your creative and financial success.

Royalties: Earning from Your Book Sales

Royalties are a significant part of an author's income, representing the ongoing payments you receive based on your book's sales. After your advance is earned out, royalties kick in, allowing you to continue profiting from your work for as long as your book is selling. However, royalty structures can vary widely depending on your contract, the format of the book, and where it's sold.

In this section, we'll dive into how royalties work, what percentage of sales you can expect to earn, and how different formats and markets impact your earnings.

1. How Royalties Are Calculated

Royalties are a percentage of the revenue generated from your book's sales. Typically, this percentage is calculated either based on the list price (the retail price of the book) or the net receipts (the amount the publisher receives after discounts to retailers). The royalty rate and calculation method will be outlined in your contract, and understanding these terms is essential for knowing how much you'll earn from each sale.

Here's how royalties are commonly structured:

- **List Price Royalties**: In this structure, your royalty is calculated as a percentage of the book's full retail price (e.g., 10% of a $20 hardcover book would be $2 per book sold). This is typically more straightforward and often used for physical books like hardcovers or paperbacks.

- **Net Receipts Royalties**: In this structure, your royalty is calculated based on the amount the publisher actually receives from retailers, after discounts. For example, if your book's retail price is $20 but the publisher sells it to a retailer at a 50% discount, your royalty would be calculated based on the $10 the publisher receives, rather than the full list price. This is more common for digital formats like eBooks and audiobooks.

Example: If your contract specifies a 10% royalty on the list price of a $15 paperback, you would earn $1.50 for every copy sold. If the royalty is based on net receipts, and the publisher receives $9 from a retailer, you would earn 10% of that amount, or $0.90 per book.

Tip: Always clarify in your contract whether your royalties are based on list price or net receipts. List price royalties are generally more favorable for authors, but they may not be available for all formats or markets.

2. Typical Royalty Rates for Different Formats

Royalty rates can vary depending on the format of your book. Physical books, eBooks, and audiobooks each have their own standard rates, and understanding the differences will help you set realistic expectations for your earnings.

Here's a breakdown of typical royalty rates by format:

- **Hardcover**: Royalty rates for hardcover books are generally higher than other formats, ranging from 10% to 15% of the list price. These rates may increase after a certain number of copies are sold (e.g., 10% for the first 5,000 copies, 12.5% for the next 5,000, and 15% for any additional copies).

- **Paperback**: For trade paperbacks, royalties typically range from 7.5% to 10% of the list price. Mass-market paperbacks often have lower royalty rates, usually around 5% to 8%.

- **eBooks**: Since production and distribution costs are lower for eBooks, royalty rates are generally higher. Authors can expect to earn 25% to 50% of the net receipts from eBook sales, with 25% being the industry standard for traditional publishing.

- **Audiobooks**: Royalties for audiobooks vary depending on whether the book is self-published or traditionally published. In traditional publishing, audiobook royalties are often 25% to 40% of net receipts. For self-published audiobooks, royalty rates can range from 40% to 75%, depending on the platform and distribution options.

Example: If you publish a hardcover book with a 12% royalty on a $25 list price, you would earn $3 per book. If that same book is available as an eBook with a 25% royalty on net receipts, and the publisher receives $10 per eBook sale, you would earn $2.50 per eBook sold.

Tip: Keep in mind that different formats may sell at different rates. For example, while eBooks offer higher royalties, paperbacks may sell in higher quantities, so it's important to consider both when estimating your total earnings.

3. International and Subsidiary Royalties

In addition to earning royalties from domestic sales, you may also earn royalties from international sales and subsidiary rights. These royalties can open up new revenue streams, especially if your book is translated into other languages or sold in foreign markets.

Here's how international and subsidiary royalties work:

- **Foreign Rights**: If your publisher sells the rights to publish your book in other countries, you will earn royalties from those sales. These royalty rates may differ from your domestic rates, and they are usually based on the net receipts the publisher receives from the foreign publisher or retailer.

- **Translation Rights**: If your book is translated into other languages, the translation publisher typically pays a percentage of royalties to the original publisher, which then passes a portion of those royalties to you. The percentage you receive will depend on the terms of your contract.

- **Subsidiary Rights**: Subsidiary rights include things like film and TV adaptations, audiobooks, or merchandise. If your publisher sells these rights to other companies, you will receive a portion of the proceeds. These payments may be structured as a lump sum or as ongoing royalties, depending on the deal.

Example: Your publisher sells the rights to publish your book in Germany. You receive 50% of the net receipts from the German publisher, which earns $5,000 in total from the sale. You would receive $2,500 as your share of the royalties.

Tip: Keep track of any international or subsidiary rights sales your publisher makes. These additional royalties can be an important part of your overall income, even if they take time to materialize.

4. When and How Royalties Are Paid

Royalties are not paid immediately after each sale but are typically distributed on a set schedule, often quarterly or semiannually. It's important to understand when you'll receive royalty payments and how to interpret royalty statements, which detail how much you've earned.

Here's what to expect regarding royalty payments:

- **Quarterly or Semiannual Payments**: Most publishers pay royalties either quarterly (every three months) or semiannually (every six months). Your contract should specify the payment schedule, and you can expect to receive a royalty statement detailing your earnings for that period.

- **Royalty Statements**: Royalty statements can be complex, as they detail the number of copies sold, returns, discounts, and any deductions that impact your total earnings. It's important to review these statements carefully to ensure that they align with your contract's terms.

- **Recouping the Advance**: Remember that royalties are only paid once your advance has been earned out. If you haven't earned enough in royalties to cover your advance, you won't receive additional payments until you do.

Example: Your contract specifies that royalties are paid semiannually. In your first royalty period, your book sells 1,000 copies at a 10% royalty rate on a $20 list price. Your royalty statement will show that you earned $2,000 in royalties for that period. If your advance was $5,000, you still have $3,000 to earn before receiving additional royalty payments.

Tip: Keep track of your royalty payments and statements over time. If anything seems unclear or incorrect, reach out to your publisher or agent for clarification.

Royalties are a vital part of an author's income, representing long-term earnings from book sales. By understanding how royalties are calculated, what typical rates are for different formats, and how international and subsidiary rights can increase your revenue, you can make informed decisions about your publishing contracts and future projects. Keep track of your royalty payments and review your statements carefully to ensure you're receiving the earnings you're entitled to.

Earning Out: What It Means and How It Affects You

"Earning out" is a crucial concept in the world of publishing and refers to when the royalties from your book sales have fully covered the amount of the advance you were paid. Once you "earn out," you begin receiving additional royalties for every sale going forward. For many authors, understanding the process of earning out is key to managing expectations and long-term financial planning.

In this section, we'll explore what earning out means, how it affects your income, and what happens after you've earned out your advance.

1. What Does It Mean to "Earn Out"?

When a publisher offers you an advance, it is essentially a prepayment of royalties—money given to you upfront based on the publisher's expectation of how many copies your book will sell. Before you can receive any further royalties from your book, your advance must be "earned out" through sales.

Here's how the process works:

- **Advances as Prepaid Royalties**: The advance is an estimate of the royalties your book is expected to earn. For example, if you receive a $10,000 advance and your royalty rate is 10%, you need to sell enough copies of your book to generate $10,000 in royalties before you receive any additional payments.

- **Sales Covering the Advance**: As your book sells, the royalties earned are applied toward recouping the advance. Once the total amount of royalties equals the advance, you've "earned out" and begin receiving royalties for each additional sale.

- **No Repayment of the Advance**: One of the most important things to remember is that, even if your book does not earn out, you do not have to repay the advance. The advance is yours to keep, regardless of how the book performs.

Example: If you receive a $20,000 advance and earn $2 per book in royalties, you would need to sell 10,000 copies to earn out the advance. After that point, any additional sales would generate royalty payments directly to you.

Tip: Don't stress if you don't earn out right away. Some books take time to gain momentum, and earning out can happen slowly over time as your book continues to sell.

2. How Earning Out Affects Your Income

Once you've earned out, your book begins generating additional income beyond the advance. This means that every sale after earning out translates into direct royalty payments, which can provide a steady stream of income as long as the book remains in circulation.

Here's how earning out affects your income:

- **Additional Royalties**: After earning out, each sale contributes directly to your income. If your royalty rate is 10% on a $20 hardcover book, you'll receive $2 for every copy sold after the advance is recouped.

- **Potential for Long-Term Income**: Books that continue to sell steadily over time can provide long-term royalties. Even if your book doesn't hit bestseller status, steady sales over years or decades can generate a significant stream of royalties.

- **Sales from Multiple Formats**: If your book is available in different formats—hardcover, paperback, eBook, audiobook—royalties from all formats contribute to your earnings. This diversification can help you earn out faster and generate more income once you've reached that threshold.

Example: After earning out a $15,000 advance with 7,500 book sales, you continue selling 1,000 copies per year. With a $2 royalty per book, that generates an additional $2,000 in income annually, providing ongoing royalties even years after the book's release.

Tip: Earning out can take time, but once you do, your book can become a consistent source of passive income. Keep an eye on your royalty statements to track your earnings as they increase after earning out.

3. Factors That Affect How Quickly You Earn Out

The time it takes to earn out your advance depends on several factors, including the size of the advance, the royalty rate, the book's price, and its sales performance. Some books earn out within months, while others may take years—or might never earn out at all.

Here are the key factors that affect how quickly you earn out:

- **Advance Size**: A larger advance means you need to sell more copies to earn out. For example, if your advance is $50,000, you'll need to sell more books to cover the advance than if your advance was $10,000. While a larger advance provides financial security upfront, it may take longer to earn out.

- **Royalty Rate**: Your royalty rate determines how much you earn per book sold. A higher royalty rate means you'll earn out faster, as each sale contributes more toward covering the advance.

- **Book Price**: The price of your book plays a significant role in how quickly you earn out. For example, earning a 10% royalty on a $30 hardcover will help you earn out faster than earning 10% on a $10 paperback. However, higher-priced books may sell fewer copies, which can slow down the overall earning process.

- **Sales Volume**: The number of copies sold is the most important factor. A high sales volume allows you to earn out more quickly, especially if your book is available across multiple formats (e.g., hardcover, eBook, audiobook).

Example: If you receive a $25,000 advance, earn $1.50 per paperback copy sold, and sell 2,000 copies in the first six months, you will have earned $3,000 in royalties toward your advance. You'll need to continue selling more copies to eventually earn out the full $25,000.

Tip: Keep promoting your book even after its initial release. Strong marketing efforts, ongoing publicity, and building a readership can help increase sales and accelerate the earning-out process.

4. What Happens If You Don't Earn Out?

Not all books earn out, and that's okay. If your book doesn't earn enough in royalties to cover the advance, you won't receive additional royalty payments, but you do not have to pay back the advance. The publisher assumes the risk when offering the advance, and it's their responsibility to recoup that money through sales.

Here's what happens if your book doesn't earn out:

- **No Additional Royalties**: If your book doesn't sell enough to earn out, you won't receive any further royalty payments. However, the advance remains yours, and you don't owe the publisher anything.

- **Impact on Future Advances**: If a book doesn't earn out, it may impact the size of the advance offered for your next book. Publishers may be more cautious about offering large advances if previous books didn't meet sales expectations.

- **Long-Tail Sales**: Even if your book doesn't earn out in the short term, it may continue to sell slowly over time. While this won't generate immediate income, steady sales can eventually lead to earning out in the long run.

Example: You receive a $40,000 advance, but your book only generates $25,000 in royalties over time. You won't receive any additional payments, but you don't have to repay the remaining $15,000 of the advance.

Tip: Focus on building a long-term career, even if some books don't earn out right away. Many authors have a mix of books—some that earn out quickly and others that take longer to reach that point.

Earning out is a key milestone in an author's financial journey. Once your book's sales have recouped the advance, you begin earning royalties on every additional copy sold. While earning out can take time, especially for larger advances, it's important to manage your expectations, stay proactive with marketing, and track your progress. Whether you earn out quickly or slowly over time, each sale brings you closer to generating long-term income from your writing.

Tracking Payments and Managing Your Literary Income

Managing your literary income effectively is key to building a sustainable writing career. From tracking advance payments to understanding royalty statements and planning for taxes, staying organized with your book earnings will help you navigate the financial side of being an author. This section will provide you with practical strategies for keeping tabs on your payments, understanding your royalty statements, and budgeting for the unpredictable nature of literary income.

1. Understanding Royalty Statements

Once your book is published and starts selling, you'll receive regular royalty statements from your publisher. These statements provide a detailed breakdown of how many copies of your book were sold, what formats were sold, any returns, and how much you've earned in royalties.

Here's what to look for on a royalty statement:

- **Sales Numbers**: The statement will show how many copies of your book were sold during the royalty period, broken down by format (e.g., hardcover, paperback, eBook).

- **Royalties Earned**: The royalty rate for each format (based on your contract) will be applied to the sales figures to calculate how much you've earned in royalties.

- **Returns**: If retailers return unsold copies of your book to the publisher, the value of those returns is deducted from your total sales, reducing your royalty payment.

- **Recoupment of Advance**: The royalties earned will be applied toward recouping your advance. The statement will indicate how much of the advance has been recouped and whether you have started earning additional royalties.

Example: Your royalty statement shows that 1,000 hardcover copies were sold at a 10% royalty rate on a $20 list price. This means you've earned $2 per book for a total of $2,000 in royalties. If your advance was $5,000, the statement will show that you have $3,000 remaining to recoup before you start earning additional royalties.

Tip: Review your royalty statements carefully, and if anything is unclear or appears incorrect, don't hesitate to ask your agent or publisher for clarification. Understanding these statements ensures you're aware of how much you're earning and how close you are to earning out.

2. Tracking Advance Payments and Royalties

Advances are typically paid in multiple installments, and royalty payments are distributed on a quarterly or semiannual basis. Keeping track of when these payments are due is essential for managing your cash flow as an author.

Here's how to track your advance and royalty payments:

- **Create a Payment Schedule**: When you sign your contract, note the key dates for when your advance payments are due. This typically includes an installment upon signing the contract, another upon delivery and acceptance of the manuscript, and a final payment upon publication. Add these dates to your calendar so you know when to expect payments.

- **Mark Royalty Payment Dates**: Royalty payments are often made quarterly or semiannually, and your contract will specify the exact schedule. Keep these dates in mind and track when you receive statements and payments from your publisher.

- **Record Payments**: Keep a detailed record of each payment you receive, whether it's an advance or a royalty. This will help you monitor your total earnings and ensure that payments align with what's outlined in your contract.

Example: If your contract states that you'll receive 50% of your advance upon signing and 50% upon delivery, you'll receive two separate payments. For a $10,000 advance, that would mean $5,000 when you sign the contract and $5,000 when the manuscript is delivered. If royalty payments are due semiannually, track each payment to ensure everything is on time and in the correct amount.

Tip: Use a spreadsheet or financial management software to track all your payments. This will help you stay organized, especially if you have multiple books or projects generating income.

3. Budgeting for Irregular Income

One of the challenges of being an author is managing an income that can be unpredictable and irregular. Advances may come in large chunks, but they are often spread out over a year or more, and royalties can fluctuate depending on how well your book is selling. Effective budgeting helps ensure that you can manage your finances during periods when income is less consistent.

Here's how to budget for irregular income:

- **Create a Monthly Budget**: Even if your income comes in sporadic payments, create a monthly budget to track your essential expenses. This helps ensure you live within your means during periods when you may not have a large payment coming in.

- **Set Aside a Buffer**: When you receive a large advance payment or a significant royalty check, set aside a portion of it in savings to cover future expenses. This creates a financial buffer for months when payments are lower or nonexistent.

- **Plan for Taxes**: Remember that advance payments and royalties are considered taxable income. Set aside a percentage of each payment (typically 25-30%) for taxes, and consider working with a tax professional to ensure you're meeting all of your tax obligations as a self-employed author.

Example: You receive a $20,000 advance split into two payments of $10,000 each. Instead of spending the entire amount, you allocate $5,000 for taxes and put another $5,000 into savings, leaving you with $10,000 to cover your living expenses over the course of the year. By creating a monthly budget, you can ensure that the advance lasts until your next royalty payment or book deal.

Tip: Avoid relying on a single payment or royalty check to cover all of your expenses. Spread your income over time to create financial stability, and always budget for taxes to avoid surprises when tax season arrives.

4. Managing Multiple Income Streams

As an author, your income may come from a variety of sources beyond book advances and royalties. These could include speaking engagements, freelance writing, teaching, or licensing subsidiary rights (such as film, TV, or foreign translations). Diversifying your income can provide more financial security and help smooth out the ups and downs of book sales.

Here's how to manage multiple income streams:

- **Track Each Income Stream Separately**: If you're earning income from several different sources (e.g., royalties, speaking fees, freelance projects), track each stream separately to get a clear picture of where your money is coming from. This helps you see which areas are most profitable and where you might want to focus more of your efforts.

- **Diversify Your Opportunities**: Look for ways to supplement your book earnings by exploring other related opportunities. For example, you could offer workshops, sign licensing deals for your book, or write articles for magazines or websites.

- **Allocate Income Wisely**: Whether you're receiving income from book royalties, freelance work, or speaking fees, allocate it according to your financial goals. Some income may go toward essential expenses, while other sources might be saved for future projects or invested in professional development.

Example: In addition to receiving royalty payments for your book, you're invited to give a keynote speech at a writing conference, which provides additional income. By tracking your income from both royalties and speaking fees, you're able to see which activities contribute most to your earnings and plan accordingly for the future.

Tip: Consider investing in your author platform (e.g., building a website, attending conferences) to create more opportunities for additional income streams, such as consulting, teaching, or speaking.

Tracking payments and managing your literary income is essential for building a sustainable and financially secure writing career. By understanding your royalty statements, keeping track of advance and royalty payments, budgeting for irregular income, and diversifying your income streams, you can create a financial plan that supports both your creative work and long-term goals. Staying organized and proactive will help you navigate the complexities of literary finances with confidence and clarity.

Quick Tips and Recap

- **Understand Your Royalty Statements**: Regularly review royalty statements to track sales, returns, and how much of your advance has been recouped.

- **Track Payments**: Keep a schedule of when to expect advance installments and royalty payments, and ensure they align with your contract.

- **Budget for Irregular Income**: Set up a monthly budget and save a portion of large payments to cover periods when income may be lower or inconsistent.

- **Plan for Taxes**: Set aside 25-30% of your advance and royalty payments for taxes, as these are considered taxable income.

- **Diversify Your Income**: Explore additional income streams like speaking engagements, freelance work, or licensing deals to supplement your book royalties.

- **Keep Detailed Records**: Use spreadsheets or financial management tools to track all payments and expenses, helping you stay organized and financially secure.

By keeping track of payments, managing your income smartly, and diversifying revenue streams, you can build a stable financial foundation for your writing career.

Negotiating Financial Terms: Maximizing Your Earnings

"Negotiating financial terms is more than a skill—it's an art that ensures the value of your work is fully recognized and rewarded in every contract." — ROBERT KIYOSAKI, AUTHOR AND BUSINESSMAN, FAMOUS FOR HIS BOOK "RICH DAD POOR DAD"

Welcome to Chapter Seventeen, "Negotiating Financial Terms: Maximizing Your Earnings," where you'll learn to tango with the titans of the publishing world. Here, the pen might be mightier than the sword, but a sharp calculator and a sharper mind are your best allies.

Negotiating isn't just about asking for more money; it's about understanding the value of your work and the mechanics of the market. It's a dance where every step, every pivot, and twirl could mean the difference between a decent deal and a fantastic one. We'll guide you through the rhythms of royalty rates, the swing of subsidiary rights, and the quickstep of advance payments.

Arm yourself with knowledge, confidence, and perhaps a strong cup of coffee. After this chapter, you won't just be ready to sit at the negotiation table—you'll be prepared to set it! Let's dial up your deal-making prowess and ensure your work pays off—literally.

Understanding the Value of Your Work: Setting Your Financial Expectations

Before stepping into any negotiation, it's crucial to have a clear understanding of the value your work holds in the marketplace. Whether you're a debut author or a seasoned writer, setting your financial expectations based on informed knowledge will help you confidently navigate the negotiation process and ensure that you're asking for what your book is truly worth.

In this section, we'll explore the factors that determine the value of your book, how to set realistic financial goals, and how understanding the market can help you maximize your earnings.

1. Assessing Your Platform and Marketability

The first step in understanding the value of your work is assessing your author platform and how marketable your book is to publishers. This involves evaluating your existing audience, social media presence, previous publications, and any industry connections you have that can support the success of your book. Your platform can directly influence how much a publisher is willing to invest in your book, including the size of your advance and the percentage of royalties you can expect.

Here's what to consider when assessing your platform:

- **Social Media Following**: Publishers may consider your reach on platforms like Twitter, Instagram, or YouTube. If you have a significant following, it can be a strong selling point that increases the value of your book.

- **Mailing List**: If you have a mailing list of subscribers who are engaged and ready to buy your book, this can make your proposal more attractive to publishers.

- **Previous Sales**: If you've published before, your past sales performance will play a significant role in how much publishers are willing to invest in your next book. Strong sales can justify a higher advance or better royalty terms.

- **Industry Reputation**: Are you known for speaking engagements, guest blog posts, or media appearances? Any visibility you've garnered within the industry can bolster your marketability and, consequently, the financial value of your work.

Example: You're a debut author with a strong social media presence of 50,000 engaged followers on Instagram, along with a blog that gets 10,000 views per month. This established platform shows publishers that you have a built-in audience ready to support your book, potentially increasing the size of your advance.

Tip: Highlight the strengths of your platform and marketability in your book proposal. This not only helps publishers see the potential for your book but also gives you leverage during negotiations.

2. Understanding the Genre and Market Trends

The financial value of your book is also influenced by the genre in which you write and current market trends. Some genres, such as commercial fiction, romance, and self-help, tend to have larger audiences and higher sales potential, which can justify higher advances. On the other hand, niche genres like literary fiction or experimental works may have smaller, more targeted audiences, resulting in more modest advances.

Here's how to evaluate the market value of your genre:

- **Research Sales Trends**: Take the time to research the sales trends of your genre. Are books in your category on the rise, or are they experiencing a downturn? Market trends can affect a publisher's willingness to invest heavily in a project.

- **Comp Titles**: Look at recently published books in your genre that are similar to your work. What kind of advances did those authors receive, and how are their books performing? Comp titles can provide valuable context for setting your own financial expectations.

- **Book Longevity**: Some genres may offer the potential for long-term sales. For example, self-help or evergreen nonfiction books may have steady sales over a long period, while commercial fiction might see a sales spike around the initial release but taper off more quickly. Understanding the longevity of your book can help you anticipate long-term earnings potential.

Example: You're writing a commercial thriller, and after researching similar titles in the genre, you find that many books in this category are receiving advances in the $50,000 to $100,000 range. Armed with this knowledge, you know that it's reasonable to expect an advance in this ballpark, depending on other factors like your platform and experience.

Tip: Stay current with market trends by reading industry reports, bestseller lists, and author interviews. Knowing what's hot in the market will help you frame your book's value during negotiations.

3. Considering Subsidiary and Foreign Rights Potential

In addition to advances and royalties from book sales, subsidiary rights—such as film, TV, audiobooks, and foreign translations—can add significant value to your work. Some publishers will handle these rights for you, while others may offer to split the proceeds. Understanding the potential for these additional revenue streams will help you assess your book's full financial potential.

Here's what to consider when evaluating subsidiary and foreign rights potential:

- **Adaptability**: Does your book have strong visual or cinematic elements that make it a good candidate for film or TV adaptation? If so, you may be able to negotiate favorable terms for film rights.

- **Foreign Appeal**: If your book has broad appeal beyond your home country, there's potential for foreign translations and international sales, which can add a significant boost to your earnings.

- **Audiobook Market**: Audiobooks are a growing segment of the publishing industry. If your book is well-suited for audio (e.g., nonfiction or narrative-driven fiction), this could be another source of revenue.

Example: You're writing a dystopian YA novel that features a visually striking world with high-stakes action. Given the rise of streaming adaptations for YA books, you could highlight the potential for film or TV rights during negotiations, increasing the perceived value of your work.

Tip: When negotiating with publishers, retain as many subsidiary and foreign rights as possible, or negotiate a favorable split. This can open additional streams of income beyond traditional book sales.

4. Setting Realistic Financial Goals

Once you've assessed your platform, genre, and subsidiary rights potential, it's time to set realistic financial goals for your book deal. Your goals should be informed by the research you've done on market trends and comparable titles, but it's also important to recognize that every book deal is unique. Having a realistic understanding of the market and your book's potential will help you negotiate from a position of strength and avoid disappointment.

Here's how to set realistic financial expectations:

- **Use Comp Titles**: Compare the advances and royalty rates of books similar to yours. This gives you a benchmark for what you can expect.

- **Consider Your Long-Term Strategy**: Think about how this deal fits into your long-term career. If you're a debut author, you might prioritize securing a reasonable advance and building a relationship with your publisher over demanding the highest possible upfront payment.

- **Weigh the Total Deal Package**: Remember that the advance is just one part of the deal. Royalties, subsidiary rights, marketing support, and creative control are all important factors that contribute to the overall value of your contract.

Example: After researching your genre and comparable titles, you determine that an advance of $40,000 would be fair for your first book. You also recognize that the real financial value will come from strong royalties and potential film adaptation rights, so you prioritize those terms during negotiations.

Tip: Be flexible and open to negotiation. It's not always about securing the largest advance but about striking the right balance between upfront payment, long-term earnings, and opportunities for additional revenue streams.

Understanding the value of your work is the foundation for successful financial negotiations. By assessing your platform, understanding market trends, and evaluating subsidiary rights potential, you can set realistic financial expectations and enter negotiations with confidence. With a clear picture of your book's worth, you'll be better equipped to secure a deal that maximizes your earnings while supporting your long-term career goals.

Maximizing Your Advance: How to Negotiate Upfront Payments

The advance is often one of the most exciting parts of a publishing deal—it's the upfront payment you receive before your book is even published. However, negotiating a higher advance requires more than just asking for more money. Publishers consider multiple factors when determining advance amounts, and understanding these can help you secure the best possible deal.

In this section, we'll explore the key elements of negotiating your advance, how to leverage your strengths, and when it makes sense to prioritize other aspects of your contract over a higher upfront payment.

1. Understanding How Advances Are Calculated

Before negotiating, it's important to understand how publishers calculate advances. Publishers consider several factors when determining how much to offer, including their projected sales for your book, your marketability, and the financial risks involved. Larger publishers typically offer higher advances, but they also have higher expectations for sales performance.

Here's what publishers consider when calculating advances:

- **Projected Sales**: Publishers make advance offers based on how many copies they believe your book will sell. This estimate is influenced by your platform, genre, and the market demand for your book. The higher the projected sales, the higher the advance.

- **Genre**: Some genres traditionally receive larger advances due to their broader appeal and higher sales potential. Commercial fiction, thrillers, and romance often command higher advances, while more niche genres like literary fiction or poetry may see smaller offers.

- **Author Platform**: If you have a strong platform, such as a large social media following, an engaged mailing list, or previous successful publications, publishers will factor this into their offer. A solid platform means built-in marketing potential, which reduces the publisher's financial risk.

- **Publisher's Budget**: The size of the publishing house and its budget can also affect the advance. Large publishers may have more resources to offer higher advances, while smaller, independent presses might provide lower advances but better royalty terms or more creative control.

Example: A debut author writing a commercial thriller may receive an advance of $50,000 if the publisher projects strong sales and sees potential for film or TV adaptations. On the other hand, a niche literary novel might receive a $10,000 advance from a smaller press.

Tip: Research advances in your genre and understand the publisher's typical range. This knowledge will give you a realistic starting point for negotiations.

2. How to Leverage Your Strengths

During negotiations, leverage your unique strengths to increase the size of your advance. Whether it's your existing platform, past sales, or market trends, showcasing your value to the publisher will help justify a higher upfront payment.

Here are some ways to leverage your strengths:

- **Highlight Your Platform**: If you have a large social media following, an active blog, or a loyal audience, emphasize this in negotiations. A strong platform makes you a more attractive investment because it suggests you'll be able to drive sales and support marketing efforts.

- **Showcase Past Success**: If you have a track record of successful book sales or notable achievements in your writing career, such as awards, bestsellers, or strong sales numbers, use this to your advantage. Publishers are more likely to offer a higher advance if they know you can deliver.

- **Use Market Trends**: If your book taps into a hot trend or a genre that's currently in high demand, use this to justify a higher advance. Publishers are often willing to invest more in books that align with current market demands.

Example: You're a nonfiction author with a podcast that has 100,000 monthly listeners. Highlighting your ability to reach this audience can help increase your advance, as the publisher will see the potential for strong pre-sales and engagement.

Tip: Provide concrete data about your platform or market potential during negotiations. Publishers are more likely to respond positively when they see clear evidence of your ability to drive sales.

3. When to Prioritize a Lower Advance

While it may seem counterintuitive, there are situations where accepting a lower advance could be the smarter choice for your long-term success. A lower advance can relieve the pressure of having to sell a large number of copies quickly to earn out, and it may give you more favorable royalty terms or other benefits that provide greater long-term value.

Here's when you might consider accepting a lower advance:

- **Better Royalty Rates**: In some cases, a lower advance might be accompanied by a higher royalty rate. If you expect your book to have strong long-term sales, prioritizing royalties over a high advance could result in greater earnings over time.

- **More Marketing Support**: Some publishers may offer a smaller advance but promise to allocate more resources toward marketing and promotion. If you believe that strong marketing will increase your book's visibility and sales, this trade-off can be worth it.

- **Long-Term Career Strategy**: If you're a debut author, you might choose a lower advance to build a strong relationship with a publisher and establish a track record of earning out your advance. This can lead to larger advances and better deals for future projects.

Example: You're offered a $15,000 advance with a 10% royalty on the list price, but the publisher is willing to increase the royalty to 12% if you accept a lower advance of $10,000. If you believe your book has strong sales potential, the higher royalty rate could lead to more earnings in the long run.

Tip: Look at the entire package when negotiating. Sometimes, securing better royalty rates, more marketing support, or other creative benefits can outweigh a higher upfront advance.

4. Negotiation Strategies for a Higher Advance

When you're ready to negotiate your advance, it's important to come prepared with specific strategies to maximize your offer. Negotiation is an art, and by using the right tactics, you can increase the publisher's willingness to offer a more favorable deal.

Here are some key strategies for negotiating a higher advance:

- **Work with an Agent**: A literary agent is one of your best assets when negotiating an advance. Agents have insider knowledge of what different publishers typically offer, and they can negotiate on your behalf to get the best possible deal. An experienced agent knows how to leverage your strengths and ensure you get a fair offer.

- **Be Willing to Walk Away**: One of the most powerful negotiation tactics is the willingness to walk away if the deal doesn't meet your expectations. If the advance offered is significantly lower than the value you've assessed for your work, letting the publisher know you're considering other offers can sometimes result in a better deal.

- **Negotiate in Ranges**: Instead of demanding a specific advance amount, suggest a range that you're comfortable with. This approach gives the publisher flexibility while signaling that you have a clear sense of your book's value.

- **Know When to Push and When to Concede**: Negotiations are about give and take. If you're pushing for a higher advance, you might need to be more flexible on other terms (such as royalty rates or delivery deadlines). Be strategic about where you push and where you're willing to concede to create a win-win situation for both you and the publisher.

Example: Your agent negotiates an advance range of $40,000 to $60,000 for your debut novel, citing the market potential and your strong platform. The publisher initially offers $40,000, but after further negotiation and highlighting the book's film rights potential, they agree to $50,000.

Tip: Negotiation is a two-way process. While it's important to advocate for yourself, maintaining a positive and collaborative attitude can help build a strong working relationship with your publisher.

Maximizing your advance requires a combination of understanding how advances are calculated, leveraging your strengths, and using smart negotiation tactics. By preparing thoroughly and knowing when to push for a higher advance or accept other favorable terms, you can secure the best possible financial deal for your book. Remember, a successful negotiation isn't just about the upfront payment— it's about creating a deal that sets you up for long-term success.

Negotiating Royalties: Getting the Best Rate for Long-Term Earnings

While the advance is the upfront payment you receive for your book, royalties represent the long-term earnings you can make over the life of your book. Royalties are the percentage of sales that you, as the author, earn from each copy of your book sold. Negotiating favorable royalty rates can significantly impact your income long after your advance has been earned out.

In this section, we'll explore how royalties work, the standard rates for different formats, and strategies for negotiating the best possible royalty rates to maximize your long-term earnings.

1. How Royalties Are Calculated

Royalties are typically calculated as a percentage of either the book's list price (the retail price of the book) or the net receipts (the amount the publisher receives after retailer discounts). It's important to understand the difference between these two models, as they can affect how much you earn from each sale.

Here's how royalties are typically structured:

- **List Price Royalties**: This is the most straightforward model, where your royalty is a percentage of the full retail price of the book. For example, if your royalty rate is 10% on a hardcover priced at $25, you would earn $2.50 for each book sold. This model tends to be more favorable for authors because it's based on the full sale price.

- **Net Receipts Royalties**: In this model, your royalty is based on the net amount the publisher receives from the retailer after discounts. For example, if your book's retail price is $25 but the publisher sells it to retailers at a 50% discount, your royalty would be based on the $12.50 the publisher actually receives, meaning you'd earn less per sale. This model is more common for eBooks and audiobooks.

Example: If you have a 10% royalty on the list price of a $20 hardcover, you'd earn $2 per book sold. However, if your royalty is 10% of the net receipts and the publisher sells the book to retailers at a 40% discount, you'd earn $1.20 per book.

Tip: Always aim for royalties based on the list price, especially for physical books. If net receipts are the only option, negotiate a higher percentage to compensate for the lower base price.

2. Typical Royalty Rates for Different Formats

Royalty rates can vary significantly depending on the format of your book (e.g., hardcover, paperback, eBook, audiobook). Understanding the typical royalty rates for each format will help you negotiate better terms during contract discussions.

Here's a breakdown of standard royalty rates for different formats:

- **Hardcover**: Royalty rates for hardcover books are generally the highest, typically ranging from 10% to 15% of the list price. Some publishers may offer tiered royalties, where the rate increases after a certain number of copies are sold (e.g., 10% for the first 5,000 copies, 12.5% for the next 5,000, and 15% for all copies beyond that).

- **Paperback**: For trade paperbacks, royalties are typically around 7.5% to 10% of the list price. Mass-market paperbacks usually have lower royalty rates, ranging from 5% to 8%.

- **eBooks**: Since eBooks have lower production and distribution costs, royalty rates for eBooks are generally higher than for print books. The industry standard for eBook royalties is around 25% of net receipts, though some authors may be able to negotiate higher rates.

- **Audiobooks**: Audiobook royalty rates vary, especially between traditional publishing and self-publishing platforms. Traditionally published audiobooks often offer royalties of 25% to 40% of net receipts, while self-published audiobooks through platforms like Audible can offer royalties as high as 40% to 75%.

Example: You're offered a 10% royalty on the list price of your hardcover book and 25% of net receipts for eBook sales. If the hardcover retails for $25 and the eBook is priced at $10, you would earn $2.50 per hardcover sale and $2.50 per eBook sale (assuming the publisher receives $10 from eBook retailers).

Tip: If you expect strong eBook or audiobook sales, prioritize negotiating higher royalties for these formats, as they can provide a significant portion of your long-term earnings.

3. Negotiating for Higher Royalty Rates

Once you understand the standard royalty rates for your book's formats, it's time to negotiate for the best possible terms. While it's often easier to negotiate higher royalty rates for eBooks and audiobooks, there's room to negotiate better rates for all formats if you have a strong platform or if the publisher is highly invested in your project.

Here's how to approach royalty negotiations:

- **Use Your Platform as Leverage**: If you have a strong platform, such as a large social media following or previous bestselling books, use this to negotiate higher royalty rates. Publishers may be more willing to offer better terms if they believe you have the potential to drive significant sales.

- **Push for Tiered Royalties**: If the publisher is unwilling to offer a higher flat royalty rate, negotiate for tiered royalties that increase as sales reach certain milestones. For example, you could negotiate for 10% royalties on the first 5,000 copies sold, 12.5% on the next 5,000, and 15% on any sales beyond that.

- **Negotiate Higher Rates for Digital Formats**: Since eBooks and audiobooks have lower production costs, publishers may be more flexible when negotiating these royalty rates. Push for higher percentages, especially if you expect digital formats to perform well.

- **Consider Self-Publishing for Audiobooks**: If you feel confident in your ability to produce and market an audiobook, self-publishing through platforms like Audible's ACX can yield much higher royalties, often in the **40% to 75%** range. If you retain audiobook rights, this could be a lucrative option.

Example: You're offered a standard 10% royalty on hardcover sales, but after discussing your social media reach and potential for strong sales, you negotiate a tiered structure that gives you 12.5% on sales after 5,000 copies and 15% on sales beyond 10,000 copies.

Tip: Focus on negotiating royalty rates for the formats you expect to perform best. If you anticipate eBook sales will outpace hardcover sales, prioritize negotiating higher eBook royalties.

4. Maximizing Long-Term Earnings Through Royalties

While the advance provides immediate income, royalties represent the long-term earnings potential of your book. Negotiating favorable royalty rates is essential for ensuring that you continue to earn money as your book sells over time. Even if your advance doesn't seem large, strong royalties can help you earn significantly more once you've earned out the advance.

Here's how to maximize your long-term earnings through royalties:

- **Consider the Long-Term Sales Potential**: Some books, especially in genres like nonfiction or children's literature, may sell steadily for years. If your book has long-term sales potential, prioritize royalties over a large advance, as this can lead to higher total earnings in the long run.

- **Protect Your Subsidiary Rights**: Royalties don't just apply to the primary book format. Make sure you're also negotiating royalties for subsidiary rights, such as foreign translations, film adaptations, and merchandise. Retaining as many of these rights as possible or negotiating favorable splits with your publisher can open additional streams of income.

- **Monitor Sales and Renegotiate for Future Books**: Keep track of your royalty statements and sales performance. If your book sells well and earns out quickly, use this success as leverage to negotiate even better royalty rates for future projects.

Example: Your book earns out its $20,000 advance after selling 10,000 copies. You begin receiving royalty payments for each additional sale, and since your book continues to sell steadily over the next few years, you earn significant income through royalties long after the book's initial release.

Tip: Pay attention to your royalty statements, and if you notice strong sales in certain formats (like eBooks or audiobooks), focus on negotiating even better rates for those formats in future contracts.

Negotiating royalties is a critical part of maximizing your long-term earnings as an author. By understanding the standard rates for different formats, leveraging your platform, and focusing on the formats with the most potential, you can secure the best possible deal. Remember, while the advance is a one-time payment, royalties provide ongoing income, making it essential to prioritize favorable royalty terms in your negotiations.

Subsidiary and Foreign Rights: Unlocking Additional Income Streams

While advances and royalties from book sales are significant, subsidiary and foreign rights can unlock valuable additional income streams. These rights include things like film and TV adaptations, audiobooks, foreign translations, and merchandise—all of which can add considerable earnings to your overall financial picture. Negotiating to retain control over these rights or securing favorable splits with your publisher is essential to maximizing your long-term profits.

In this section, we'll explore the various types of subsidiary and foreign rights, how to negotiate them, and how they can boost your income beyond traditional book sales.

1. What Are Subsidiary Rights?

Subsidiary rights refer to the rights to use your book in ways beyond the traditional print or digital publication. These rights open up opportunities for your work to reach new audiences and formats, providing additional streams of revenue. Publishers often seek to control these rights to maximize their own profits, but retaining control of them can benefit you financially in the long run.

Here are the most common types of subsidiary rights:

- **Film and TV Rights**: If your book has strong visual or narrative elements, it may be of interest to film or TV producers for adaptation. Selling the rights to adapt your book into a movie or TV series can generate significant one-time payments (option agreements) as well as ongoing royalties or profit shares.

- **Audiobook Rights**: Audiobooks are a growing market, and retaining the rights to produce and distribute your book in audio format can lead to a substantial revenue boost. Some authors prefer to self-publish their audiobooks to retain higher royalties, while others allow their publishers to handle distribution.

- **Foreign Language Rights**: Selling the rights to translate and publish your book in other languages can open up entirely new markets and audiences. These rights are typically licensed to foreign publishers, and you receive a percentage of the royalties or a flat fee from these deals.

- **Merchandising Rights**: If your book has strong branding or a loyal fanbase, there's potential to create merchandise like T-shirts, posters, or action figures. This is common for young adult series, fantasy novels, or children's books, but can apply to any genre with a passionate following.

- **Serial Rights**: First or second serial rights allow magazines, newspapers, or websites to publish excerpts of your book before or after it's published. These deals provide another revenue stream while increasing visibility for your book.

Example: A successful thriller novel is adapted into a popular Netflix series, earning the author a six-figure option agreement for the TV rights, plus a percentage of profits from the show's success.

Tip: When negotiating your contract, try to retain as many subsidiary rights as possible, especially if you believe your book has strong potential for adaptation or foreign publication.

2. Negotiating for Subsidiary Rights

When negotiating your publishing contract, one of the most critical discussions will be around who controls the subsidiary rights—whether you retain them or the publisher manages them. Publishers will often try to control these rights, as they represent significant potential earnings, but you may have more to gain by retaining them yourself, especially if you have the resources to explore these markets independently.

Here's how to approach negotiating subsidiary rights:

- **Retain as Many Rights as Possible**: If you have the option, try to retain the rights to film, TV, audiobooks, and foreign translations. This gives you the flexibility to explore these markets on your own terms or negotiate deals independently, potentially earning more in the long term.

- **Negotiate Favorable Splits**: If the publisher insists on controlling subsidiary rights, negotiate for a favorable split of the earnings. For example, you could negotiate for 50-75% of the earnings from foreign sales or film rights while allowing the publisher to manage the deals.

- **Use an Agent**: A literary agent is invaluable when negotiating subsidiary rights. They can help secure better terms and, if you retain these rights, can work to find deals for film, TV, audiobooks, and foreign sales on your behalf.

Example: You negotiate to retain the audiobook rights to your novel, allowing you to self-publish the audiobook through Audible's ACX platform. By retaining control, you earn 40-75% royalties from audiobook sales, significantly higher than what you would have received from the publisher.

Tip: Even if you allow the publisher to manage subsidiary rights, ensure that you're actively involved in the decision-making process. This ensures that the deals align with your vision and financial goals.

3. Foreign Rights: Expanding Your Book's Reach

Foreign rights deals allow your book to be translated and sold in other countries, expanding your readership and providing additional income. These deals are often managed by your publisher's foreign rights department, though you can retain control and sell these rights independently if you have an agent or foreign rights expert.

Here's how foreign rights deals work:

- **Licensing to Foreign Publishers**: When foreign rights are sold, the foreign publisher licenses the right to translate and publish your book in a specific language or country. You will typically receive an upfront payment (advance) from the foreign publisher, along with royalties on each sale.

- **Royalties from Foreign Sales**: Foreign rights deals often come with royalties similar to domestic book sales. You may receive a percentage of the list price or net receipts, depending on the contract, and these payments are typically managed through your primary publisher or agent.

- **Countries and Languages**: Some books do well internationally, leading to multiple foreign rights deals across different languages and countries. If your book has universal themes, a global appeal, or belongs to a genre popular in foreign markets (e.g., mystery, thriller, or romance), it's worth focusing on foreign rights negotiations.

Example: Your book is picked up by publishers in Germany, Brazil, and Japan, each paying an upfront fee to license the translation rights. You receive 50% of the advance and royalties for each sale in those countries, expanding your book's reach while earning additional income.

Tip: Keep track of your foreign rights deals and stay informed about the sales performance in each country. This will help you renegotiate better terms or expand into additional foreign markets with future projects.

4. Maximizing Your Subsidiary Rights Earnings

Effectively managing your subsidiary and foreign rights can lead to long-term financial success beyond traditional book sales. By retaining control over key rights or negotiating favorable splits, you can unlock additional revenue streams that have the potential to grow as your book gains popularity.

Here's how to maximize your earnings from subsidiary rights:

- **Build Relationships with Industry Professionals**: If you retain film or TV rights, build relationships with producers, agents, and industry insiders who can help pitch your book for adaptation. An agent with experience in film or TV rights can be especially helpful in navigating these complex deals.

- **Explore Multiple Foreign Markets**: Don't limit yourself to one or two foreign language deals. Work with your agent or publisher to explore multiple markets and languages, as the more countries your book is published in, the greater your potential earnings.

- **Stay Involved in the Process**: Whether you retain the rights or allow your publisher to handle them, stay informed and involved in the subsidiary rights process. Be aware of any film, TV, or foreign deals that may arise and ensure that the terms align with your long-term goals.

- **Diversify Your Opportunities**: Don't overlook smaller rights, such as merchandising or serial rights. Even though these may not generate the same level of income as a film deal, they can still add up over time and contribute to your overall financial success.

Example: After selling foreign rights for your novel in multiple countries, you work with your agent to negotiate a film option deal. While the project is in development, you also license merchandise based on your characters, expanding your income streams significantly.

Tip: Regularly revisit your subsidiary and foreign rights strategy as your career progresses. With each new book, you have the opportunity to explore additional markets and adaptation possibilities.

Subsidiary and foreign rights offer a wealth of opportunities for authors to expand their earnings beyond traditional book sales. By retaining control of key rights or negotiating favorable terms with your publisher, you can unlock additional income streams through film, TV, audiobooks, foreign translations, and more. Understanding and leveraging these rights can lead to long-term financial success and broaden the reach of your work across various formats and markets.

Quick Tips and Recap

- **Understand Subsidiary Rights**: Subsidiary rights include film, TV, audiobooks, foreign translations, merchandising, and serial rights, offering additional income streams beyond book sales.

- **Negotiate to Retain Rights**: Whenever possible, try to retain control of key rights, such as film, TV, and audiobook rights, to maximize your earnings or negotiate favorable splits with your publisher.

- **Work with an Agent**: A literary agent can help secure better terms for subsidiary rights and assist in selling foreign rights, film deals, or other adaptations.

- **Explore Foreign Markets**: Selling foreign translation rights can significantly expand your readership and income. Seek opportunities in multiple countries and languages.

- **Maximize Audiobook Potential**: Audiobooks are a growing market; consider self-publishing your audiobook or negotiating higher royalties if your publisher manages it.

- **Stay Involved**: Even if your publisher controls subsidiary rights, stay informed about potential deals to ensure they align with your financial and creative goals.

- **Diversify Your Income**: Look for opportunities to monetize your book through merchandising, serial rights, and adaptations, adding to your overall earnings.

By strategically negotiating subsidiary and foreign rights, you can unlock additional revenue streams and maximize the financial potential of your book across multiple platforms and markets.

Accounting and Payments: Tracking Your Income

"Effective accounting and diligent tracking of your income are not just about financial management; they're crucial for maintaining the fiscal health and sustainability of your business." — SUZE ORMAN, FINANCIAL ADVISOR AND AUTHOR

Welcome to Chapter Eighteen, "Accounting and Payments: Tracking Your Income," where we transform from literary geniuses to number-crunching ninjas. It's time to pull out those dusty calculators and dive deep into the thrilling world of debits, credits, and everything in-between.

Here, you'll learn the art of keeping tabs on your tabulations and ensuring that every dollar, euro, or yen earned from your literary labors is accounted for. Think of it as following the breadcrumb trail of your financial success, from the initial advance to the ongoing royalties that trickle in like a well-brewed espresso—slowly but richly.

This chapter will equip you with the tools to navigate the maze of accounting statements and payment schedules with the agility of a cat on a hot tin roof. We'll make sure that when it comes to your finances, you're not just literate; you're fluent. So sharpen your pencils—and possibly your wits—as we tackle the numbers game with gusto and a touch of humor. After all, who says accounting has to be dull?

Understanding Royalty Statements: Decoding the Numbers

Royalty statements are the key to understanding how much you're earning from your book sales, but they can often be confusing and packed with jargon. To ensure that you're receiving the correct payments and have a clear picture of your income, it's important to know how to decode these statements. In this section, we'll break down the key components of a royalty statement, explain the important terms, and help you understand how your earnings are calculated.

1. Key Components of a Royalty Statement

Every publisher formats royalty statements slightly differently, but most statements contain similar elements. Understanding these components will allow you to track how much your book is selling and how much you are earning from those sales.

Here's a breakdown of the main components of a royalty statement:

- **Sales Period**: This is the time frame covered by the royalty statement, typically quarterly or semiannually. It tells you which sales are being reported and when you can expect the next statement.

- **Units Sold**: This section details how many copies of your book were sold in different formats (e.g., hardcover, paperback, eBook, audiobook) during the reporting period. Units sold are often broken down by territory (e.g., U.S., UK, Canada) and channel (e.g., online retailers, bookstores).

- **Gross Sales**: The gross sales represent the total revenue generated by the sales of your book before any deductions. This is the amount your publisher has earned from selling your book.

- **Deductions and Returns**: Publishers account for returns, discounts, and other deductions before calculating your earnings. For example, if bookstores return unsold copies of your book, the revenue from those returns is subtracted from the gross sales. Understanding this section is crucial to tracking your true earnings.

- **Royalty Rate**: Your contract will specify the royalty percentage you earn on each sale. This section of the statement outlines the royalty rates applied to the different formats of your book (hardcover, paperback, eBook, audiobook, etc.).

- **Earnings**: This section shows how much you've earned in royalties during the reporting period. It's the result of applying the royalty rate to the net sales (gross sales minus deductions) for each format.

- **Advance Recoupment**: If you received an advance, your royalties will go toward repaying that advance before you start receiving additional payments. This section will show how much of your advance has been recouped and whether you've earned out.

- **Total Royalty Payment**: This is the final amount you will be paid for the sales reported during the period, after all deductions and recoupments have been applied.

Example: Let's say your royalty statement reports that 1,000 hardcover copies of your book were sold at a list price of $25, with a 10% royalty rate. Your gross earnings would be $2.50 per book, or $2,500 total. If 100 copies were returned, the returns would be deducted, leaving you with earnings on 900 copies, or $2,250. If you have not yet earned out your $10,000 advance, that $2,250 will be applied toward recouping your advance.

2. Understanding Deductions and Returns

One of the trickiest parts of understanding royalty statements is the deductions and returns section. Books are often sold to retailers at a discount, and bookstores may return unsold copies to the publisher, which reduces your overall earnings. Publishers also deduct fees for shipping, production, and marketing in some cases.

Here's what to look out for:

- **Returns**: In many cases, bookstores return unsold copies of your book to the publisher, and the value of these returns is deducted from your gross sales. Keep an eye on the returns section of your statement to see how much of your earnings are being offset by returned copies.

- **Discounts**: Publishers often sell books to retailers at a discount, which affects your earnings. For example, if your book's list price is $20, but the publisher sells it to retailers at a 50% discount, your royalty will be based on the discounted price of $10, not the full $20.

- **Reserve Against Returns**: Some publishers hold back a portion of your royalties to account for possible future returns. This is called a reserve against returns, and it can be frustrating because it reduces your immediate payment. However, these reserves are typically released after a certain period if the returns don't materialize.

Example: If your book sells 500 copies at a list price of $15 but the publisher sells them to retailers at a 40% discount, the gross sales will be calculated on $9 per copy, not $15. So, instead of earning 10% on $7,500, you would earn 10% on $4,500, resulting in $450 in royalties before deductions.

3. Tracking Your Advance Recoupment

If you received an advance, you won't start earning additional royalties until your advance is recouped. Your royalty statement will show how much of your advance has been earned out and how much remains to be recouped. This is an important section to track because it tells you how close you are to receiving direct royalty payments.

Here's how advance recoupment works:

- **Royalties Applied to Advance**: Until you earn out your advance, all of your royalty earnings are applied to repaying the advance. Once your royalties exceed the amount of your advance, you begin receiving payments.

- **Earning Out**: Once you've earned out your advance, you'll see payments reflected in the total royalty payment section of your statement. This is when you begin receiving additional income from your book sales.

Example: If you received a $5,000 advance and your royalties for the first quarter amount to $1,200, that $1,200 will be applied to your advance. You'll have $3,800 left to recoup. Once your royalties exceed $5,000, you'll start receiving payments.

4. Staying Organized with Your Royalty Statements

To ensure that you're receiving accurate payments and to keep track of your income, it's important to stay organized with your royalty statements. This will help you monitor trends in your book sales, spot any discrepancies, and plan for your financial future.

Here's how to stay organized:

- **Keep Digital Copies**: Store digital copies of all your royalty statements in a folder so you can easily reference them. This will help you track your earnings over time and quickly find past statements if needed.

- **Track Your Sales**: Create a simple spreadsheet to track your book sales and royalties over time. Include columns for sales by format (hardcover, paperback, eBook, etc.), gross sales, returns, deductions, and net earnings. This will give you a clear view of how your book is performing and whether sales are increasing or decreasing.

- **Review for Accuracy**: Always review your royalty statements for accuracy. Mistakes can happen, and you should verify that the sales numbers, royalty rates, and deductions align with your contract. If something looks off, don't hesitate to contact your agent or publisher for clarification.

Example: You track your royalty statements each quarter, noting that your eBook sales are increasing steadily while hardcover sales have leveled off. This data helps you make decisions about future marketing efforts and whether to prioritize eBook promotions.

Tip: Staying organized with your royalty statements not only helps you track your earnings but also gives you leverage when negotiating future book deals. If you can demonstrate strong sales and growth, you'll be in a stronger position to negotiate better terms.

Understanding royalty statements is essential for tracking your book's financial success and ensuring you receive accurate payments. By decoding the key components of these statements—sales figures, deductions, royalty rates, and advance recoupment—you can stay on top of your earnings and plan for the future. Stay organized, track trends, and always review your statements for accuracy to maximize your financial success as an author.

Payment Schedules: When and How You Get Paid

As an author, your income from a book deal is not paid all at once but rather spread out over time through advances and royalty payments. Understanding the payment schedule for your earnings is crucial for managing your cash flow and ensuring that you're receiving payments when you should be. In this section, we'll break down the typical payment schedules for both advances and royalties, explain how to track these payments, and offer tips on what to do if there are delays.

1. Advance Payments: How and When They're Distributed

An advance is a payment given to you upfront by the publisher as an advance against future royalties. This means that the publisher is betting on your book's success, paying you part of your anticipated earnings before the book even hits the shelves. However, the full advance isn't usually paid in one lump sum—it's often divided into multiple installments based on the milestones of your book's publication process.

Here's how advance payments are typically structured:

- **Upon Signing**: The first installment of your advance is usually paid when you sign the contract. This amount varies but can be anywhere from one-third to one-half of the total advance.

- **Upon Delivery and Acceptance**: The second installment is paid after you submit the final, polished manuscript to the publisher and it is accepted. This signals that your book is ready to move into the production phase.

- **Upon Publication**: The final installment of the advance is typically paid when the book is published and officially released to the public. Some contracts may include additional payments for publication in multiple formats (e.g., hardcover, paperback, or eBook).

Example: You sign a contract for a $30,000 advance. You receive $10,000 upon signing the contract, another $10,000 when you deliver and the manuscript is accepted, and the final $10,000 when the book is published.

Tip: Keep track of these milestones to ensure you receive each installment of your advance on time. If there are delays in the publishing process, this may also delay the release of your final payment.

2. Royalty Payments: How Often You're Paid

Once your book is published and starts selling, you begin earning royalties based on sales. However, royalty payments are typically not distributed immediately after each sale. Instead, they are paid on a regular schedule, such as quarterly or semiannually, depending on your contract and the publisher's policies. Understanding this payment schedule is important for planning your finances and knowing when to expect income.

Here's how royalty payments are structured:

- **Quarterly Payments**: Many publishers pay royalties on a quarterly basis. This means you'll receive payments four times a year, typically after the publisher closes its books for the quarter and calculates how much you've earned. Payments might arrive a few weeks or months after the quarter ends, as the publisher needs time to process the statements.

- **Semiannual Payments**: Some publishers, especially smaller or independent ones, may issue royalty payments semiannually (twice a year). In this case, you'll receive fewer but larger payments, and the statements will cover a longer sales period.

- **Annual Payments**: In rare cases, especially for older backlist books or less active publishing agreements, royalty payments may be made annually, meaning you'll receive one payment per year.

Example: If your contract states that royalties are paid quarterly, you might receive a payment for the January-March sales period in May or June. This gives the publisher time to calculate sales, handle returns, and issue your payment.

Tip: Review your contract carefully to understand how often you'll receive royalty payments. Mark these dates on your calendar so you know when to expect them, and follow up if there are delays.

3. Tracking and Monitoring Payments

To ensure that you're receiving all of your payments on time, it's important to track both advance installments and royalty payments. This will help you avoid surprises and ensure that you're being paid according to your contract. Here's how to stay on top of your payments:

- **Create a Payment Schedule**: When you sign your publishing contract, create a payment schedule based on the agreed-upon terms. Include advance installment dates and the royalty payment periods (quarterly, semiannual, or annual). This will serve as a roadmap to track when payments are due.

- **Check Your Royalty Statements**: With each royalty payment, you'll receive a royalty statement detailing the sales for the period. Review these statements carefully to ensure that the payment aligns with the sales figures. If you're nearing the end of your advance recoupment, track when you're likely to start receiving additional royalty payments.

- **Set Reminders**: Use digital calendars or reminders to alert you when payments should arrive. If you haven't received a payment by the expected date, follow up with your agent or publisher to inquire about the delay.

- **Track Multiple Streams of Income**: If you have multiple books, projects, or income streams (such as foreign rights sales, audiobooks, or merchandise), keep detailed records for each one. This will help you manage your overall earnings and ensure that no payments are overlooked.

Example: After signing a contract for a $20,000 advance, you set up a calendar with reminders for each milestone. You receive $10,000 upon signing and note the upcoming due dates for the manuscript submission and publication, ensuring you're paid on time for each milestone.

Tip: Organize your payment tracking with a spreadsheet or financial management software to help you stay on top of deadlines and income.

4. Handling Payment Delays

Unfortunately, delays in payment can happen in the publishing industry, whether it's due to slow processing, administrative issues, or other factors. It's important to be proactive about addressing delays and ensuring that you receive your money on time.

Here's how to handle payment delays:

- **Know Your Contract Terms**: Review your contract carefully to understand when payments are due and if there's any grace period for processing. This will help you identify whether a payment is truly late or just taking time to process.

- **Follow Up Promptly**: If a payment is delayed beyond the expected date, follow up with your agent or directly with the publisher's finance department. Be polite but firm in requesting information about the status of your payment.

- **Be Persistent**: Sometimes delays can take longer than expected to resolve. If necessary, continue following up regularly until the issue is addressed. If you're working with an agent, they can help push for timely resolution.

- **Stay Calm and Professional**: While it's frustrating to deal with delays, staying calm and professional will help you maintain good relationships with your publisher. Publishing is a long-term business, and keeping the communication lines open will benefit your career in the long run.

Example: You were expecting a royalty payment in early June for the January-March quarter, but it hasn't arrived by mid-July. After reviewing your contract to confirm the payment timeline, you contact your agent, who follows up with the publisher to resolve the delay and ensure you receive your payment.

Tip: Be proactive about following up on payments, but also understand that occasional delays may happen. Having a financial cushion in place will help you manage any disruptions in your cash flow.

Payment schedules in the publishing industry can vary, but by understanding how advances and royalties are paid, you can plan your finances effectively. Track each payment milestone, stay organized with royalty statements, and follow up promptly if there are delays. By staying on top of your payment schedule, you'll ensure that your income flows smoothly, allowing you to focus on your writing without unnecessary financial stress.

Tracking Your Earnings: Building a System for Financial Success

As an author, managing multiple income streams—advances, royalties, subsidiary rights, foreign deals, and more—can become overwhelming. Building an organized system for tracking your earnings will help you stay on top of your financial success, ensure accuracy in payments, and provide valuable insights for future negotiations. In this section, we'll cover the importance of tracking your earnings and provide practical strategies for building an efficient system that keeps your finances in check.

1. Why Tracking Your Earnings Is Essential

Whether you're a debut author or have multiple books under your belt, tracking your earnings isn't just about knowing how much you've made—it's about maximizing your long-term financial health. By maintaining clear records, you can:

- **Monitor Your Financial Progress**: Track how much you've earned over time, identify trends in your book sales, and assess which revenue streams (e.g., print vs. eBook vs. audiobook) are performing the best.

347

- **Ensure Accuracy in Payments**: With multiple royalty statements, advances, and subsidiary rights payments coming in, it's important to ensure that you're being paid correctly and on time. Keeping track of every payment helps you verify that you're receiving everything you're owed.

- **Prepare for Tax Season**: Having a system in place makes it easier to calculate your taxable income, track deductions, and prepare for self-employment taxes.

- **Plan for the Future**: Knowing your current financial situation allows you to budget for your expenses, reinvest in your writing career, and strategize for future book deals or projects.

Example: An author with three books may receive royalties from print, eBooks, and audiobooks, plus foreign translation rights. Tracking each of these revenue streams separately will help the author identify the most profitable format and focus their marketing efforts accordingly.

Tip: Treat your writing career like a business. Keeping accurate financial records gives you the data you need to make informed decisions and grow your career.

2. Setting Up a Simple System for Tracking Earnings

You don't need to be a financial expert to track your earnings effectively. With the right tools and habits, you can create a simple but powerful system that helps you stay organized and informed. Here are a few options for building your system:

- **Spreadsheets**: A basic spreadsheet program like Excel or Google Sheets is often sufficient for tracking your earnings. You can create a simple spreadsheet with columns for payment dates, payment sources (e.g., royalties, advances, foreign rights), amounts, and payment status. This allows you to easily monitor all your income streams in one place.

- **Financial Management Software**: For more complex finances, consider using financial management software like QuickBooks or FreshBooks. These tools offer features like income tracking, invoicing, and expense management, making it easy to keep track of your earnings and organize your finances for tax season.

- **Payment Trackers**: If you prefer more visual tracking, consider using apps or tools designed specifically for freelancers and self-employed individuals. These tools often provide payment dashboards, charts, and reminders, helping you track when payments are due and whether they've been received.

- **Dedicated Bank Account**: Consider setting up a separate bank account for your writing income. This makes it easier to track writing-related earnings and expenses without mixing them with your personal finances. It also simplifies tax preparation, as you'll have all your business-related income in one place.

Example: An author uses a spreadsheet to track earnings from different formats and countries. The columns include categories such as "Format" (print, eBook, audiobook), "Country" (U.S., UK, Canada), "Payment Source" (royalties, advance, foreign rights), and "Amount Received." Each row tracks a different payment, making it easy to calculate total income and spot any discrepancies.

Tip: Update your system regularly. By logging payments as soon as you receive them, you'll avoid falling behind and ensure that your records are always up to date.

3. Tracking Multiple Income Streams

As an author, your income may come from various sources beyond book sales. These might include speaking engagements, teaching gigs, freelance writing, or licensing deals. Creating a system that accounts for these diverse streams ensures that nothing slips through the cracks.

Here's how to track multiple income streams effectively:

- **Create Separate Categories**: Break down your earnings into categories based on the source of income. For example, have one category for "Royalties," another for "Advances," and additional categories for "Speaking Fees," "Merchandise Sales," "Foreign Rights," etc.

- **Track by Format**: If your book is sold in multiple formats—hardcover, paperback, eBook, and audiobook—track the earnings from each format separately. This will help you understand which formats are performing best and guide future contract negotiations.

- **Monitor Foreign Royalties**: If your book has been sold in foreign markets, track these earnings separately by country. Foreign rights deals can sometimes take longer to generate income, so tracking them helps you keep an eye on the timeline and payments from each country.

- **Include Non-Book Income**: If you regularly earn money from speaking, consulting, or freelancing, add these income streams to your tracking system. Keeping a holistic view of all your earnings will help you stay organized and informed.

Example: An author divides their spreadsheet into sections for "Royalties," "Speaking Fees," "Consulting," and "Foreign Rights." By categorizing each income stream, the author can quickly see which area is generating the most revenue and which needs more attention.

Tip: Use your income data to make strategic decisions. If foreign rights or audiobooks are outperforming other formats, you might prioritize those deals in future negotiations.

4. Evaluating Trends and Making Adjustments

Once you've established your system, tracking earnings over time can provide valuable insights into your career's financial trajectory. You'll be able to evaluate trends, spot inconsistencies, and make adjustments to your strategy based on the data.

Here's how to use your earnings data to inform your strategy:

- **Analyze Trends Over Time**: Regularly review your income records to spot trends. Are your royalties increasing or decreasing over time? Is a particular format, such as audiobooks, performing better than others? Identifying trends will help you adjust your marketing strategy or renegotiate contract terms for future projects.

- **Compare Earnings by Format or Source**: Break down your earnings by format (print, eBook, audiobook) or income source (royalties, advances, foreign rights) to see which are the most profitable. This can help you focus on the most lucrative areas of your career.

- **Plan for Slow Periods**: Writing income is often unpredictable, with royalties coming in bursts rather than regular intervals. Use your earnings data to plan for slower periods by setting aside money during high-earning months.

- **Adjust Marketing Efforts**: If you notice that sales for a particular format or market are slowing down, consider adjusting your marketing efforts to boost visibility and sales. Data from your earnings records can help guide these efforts.

Example: An author tracks their royalties for eBooks and notices a steady decline over the past three quarters. In response, the author shifts marketing efforts toward eBooks, investing in a targeted social media campaign to boost sales.

Tip: Set aside time at least once a quarter to review your earnings, evaluate trends, and make any necessary adjustments. Regular check-ins will keep you informed and help you make proactive decisions.

Tracking your earnings is essential for financial success as an author. By creating a system that organizes your income, you can monitor your financial progress, ensure accuracy in payments, and make informed decisions to grow your career. Whether you use spreadsheets, software, or simple financial tools, staying organized will give you greater control over your income and set you up for long-term success.

Managing Taxes: Preparing for Tax Season as a Writer

As an author, navigating taxes can be more complex than for a typical employee. With multiple streams of income, irregular payments, and a host of potential deductions, managing your tax responsibilities requires careful planning. In this section, we'll explore how to prepare for tax season, set aside money for taxes, track deductible expenses, and manage self-employment tax requirements. This will ensure that you're well-prepared, compliant, and able to make the most of the deductions available to you.

1. Understanding Self-Employment Taxes

As an author, you're considered self-employed, which means you're responsible for paying both income tax and self-employment tax (which covers Social Security and Medicare contributions). Unlike traditional employees, self-employed individuals don't have taxes automatically deducted from their paychecks, so it's essential to plan ahead.

Here's what you need to know about self-employment taxes:

- **Self-Employment Tax Rate**: The self-employment tax rate is currently 15.3%—this consists of 12.4% for Social Security and 2.9% for Medicare. You'll need to pay this tax on any net earnings (profit) you make as a writer, in addition to your regular income tax.

- **Quarterly Estimated Taxes**: If you expect to owe more than $1,000 in taxes for the year, you're required to pay quarterly estimated taxes to the IRS. These payments help you avoid penalties for underpayment when tax season arrives. Quarterly payments are typically due in April, June, September, and January.

- **Income Tax**: In addition to self-employment tax, you'll also owe income tax on your earnings. The amount you owe will depend on your tax bracket, which is determined by your total income for the year.

Example: If you earn $50,000 in a year from book sales, speaking engagements, and freelance work, you'll owe both income tax and self-employment tax. If your self-employment tax is 15.3%, that's $7,650, which you'll need to set aside along with your income tax.

Tip: Work with a tax professional or use tax software to calculate your self-employment tax liability and estimated tax payments throughout the year.

2. Setting Aside Money for Taxes

Because taxes aren't automatically deducted from your payments, it's crucial to set aside a portion of your income throughout the year to cover your tax obligations. This will help you avoid a big tax bill come April and ensure you can make quarterly payments on time.

Here's how to effectively set aside money for taxes:

- **Estimate Your Tax Rate**: Use your total expected earnings and tax bracket to estimate your income tax rate. Add this to your 15.3% self-employment tax to get a rough idea of your overall tax liability. For most authors, setting aside 25% to 30% of income is a good starting point.

- **Set Up a Separate Account**: To keep your tax money separate from your personal finances, open a dedicated savings account just for taxes. Each time you receive income, transfer a portion (e.g., 30%) into this account so you'll have the funds available when tax payments are due.

- **Stay Consistent**: Make it a habit to set aside money for taxes every time you receive a payment, whether it's from a royalty check, an advance, or freelance work. Consistently setting aside funds will help you stay on top of your tax obligations and avoid scrambling at the end of the year.

Example: You receive a $10,000 royalty payment and decide to set aside 30% of that amount for taxes. You transfer $3,000 into your dedicated tax account, leaving you with $7,000 to cover personal expenses and business costs.

Tip: Automate your savings by setting up an automatic transfer to your tax account each time you receive a payment. This will ensure you never forget to set aside money for taxes.

3. Tracking Deductible Expenses

One of the benefits of being self-employed is the ability to deduct certain business expenses from your taxable income, reducing the amount of tax you owe. As a writer, many of your work-related expenses are tax-deductible, but you need to track these carefully throughout the year to maximize your deductions.

Here are some common deductions for authors:

- **Home Office**: If you have a dedicated space in your home where you write and conduct business, you may be able to deduct a portion of your rent or mortgage, utilities, and internet expenses. The space must be used exclusively for work to qualify.

- **Supplies and Equipment**: Any tools or equipment you use for writing (e.g., computer, printer, software, notebooks) are deductible as business expenses.

- **Travel and Research**: If you travel for book research, conferences, or book signings, you can deduct travel costs, lodging, and meals. Keep receipts and records of your business-related trips.

- **Marketing and Promotion**: Expenses related to promoting your book, such as website hosting, social media ads, book trailers, and author events, are also deductible.

- **Professional Services**: Fees paid to agents, editors, cover designers, or legal services can be deducted as business expenses.

- **Educational Expenses**: Courses, workshops, or memberships to writing organizations that help you improve your craft are deductible.

Example: Over the course of the year, you spend $1,200 on office supplies, $500 on book marketing, and $2,000 on travel for a book tour. These expenses can be deducted from your taxable income, reducing the amount of taxes you owe.

Tip: Use an app or accounting software to track your expenses in real time. This will save you time when tax season arrives and ensure that you capture every possible deduction.

4. Working with a Tax Professional

While it's possible to manage your taxes on your own, many authors find that working with a tax professional who understands the nuances of self-employment is worth the investment. A qualified accountant can help you:

- **Maximize Deductions**: An experienced accountant can identify deductions you may not have considered and help you take full advantage of them, lowering your taxable income.

- **Ensure Compliance**: A tax professional will ensure that your tax filings are accurate and comply with IRS regulations, helping you avoid costly mistakes or penalties.

- **Plan for the Future**: If your income fluctuates from year to year, an accountant can help you create a financial plan that accounts for these variations and prepares you for future tax liabilities.

- **Handle Complex Situations**: If you have multiple income streams, foreign royalties, or complex business structures, a tax professional can navigate these situations with ease.

Example: You work with an accountant who helps you identify additional deductions related to a book tour you took last year. They also help you navigate paying taxes on foreign royalties, ensuring compliance with international tax treaties.

Tip: Find a tax professional who has experience working with authors, freelancers, or creative professionals. They'll be better equipped to understand your unique tax situation and provide tailored advice.

Managing taxes as a writer involves planning, organization, and staying informed about self-employment tax rules and deductions. By setting aside money for taxes, tracking deductible expenses, and working with a tax professional, you can navigate tax season with confidence and reduce your overall tax burden. The better you prepare, the more financial control you'll have over your writing career.

Quick Tips and Recap

- **Understand Self-Employment Taxes**: You'll need to pay both income tax and self-employment tax (15.3%) on your writing income. Set aside 25-30% of your earnings to cover your tax obligations.

- **Pay Quarterly Estimated Taxes**: If you expect to owe more than $1,000 in taxes, make quarterly payments in April, June, September, and January to avoid penalties.

- **Set Aside Money for Taxes**: Open a dedicated savings account for taxes and consistently set aside 25-30% of each payment you receive to cover taxes.

- **Track Deductible Expenses**: Deduct business-related costs such as home office expenses, supplies, travel, marketing, and professional services to reduce your taxable income.

- **Keep Detailed Records**: Use accounting software or spreadsheets to track income and expenses in real time, making tax season much easier.

- **Work with a Tax Professional**: Consider hiring an accountant with experience in working with authors or freelancers to help maximize deductions, ensure compliance, and handle complex tax situations.

- **Plan for Tax Season**: Regularly review your income and expenses, keep receipts for all deductible expenses, and stay proactive with tax planning throughout the year.

By staying organized and proactive with your tax preparation, you'll avoid surprises during tax season and ensure you're making the most of your tax deductions as a writer.

Audit Rights: Ensuring You Get What You're Due

"Understanding and exercising your audit rights isn't about mistrust; it's about due diligence and ensuring the accuracy that your hard work merits." — MICHAEL BLOOMBERG, BUSINESSMAN AND FORMER MAYOR OF NEW YORK CITY

Welcome to Chapter Nineteen, "Audit Rights: Ensuring You Get What You're Due," where we don our detective hats and magnifying glasses. It's time to channel your inner Sherlock Holmes, because we're diving into the riveting world of audits—a process as crucial as it is dreaded by many.

Think of audit rights as your backstage pass to the accounting rooms of the publishing world. This chapter isn't just about counting beans; it's about making sure every bean counted is in your jar. We'll explore how to exercise these rights without causing a stir or burning bridges, and how to tactfully ensure that every penny that should be rolling your way isn't stuck in someone else's piggy bank.

So, tighten your grip on those calculators and ready your most diplomatic smile. We're about to ensure that your financial reports are as spotless and accurate as your prose, proving that when it comes to ensuring you're paid your due, you're as relentless as any character from your novels. After all, the pen might be mightier than the sword, but the ledger is mightier still!

What Are Audit Rights? Understanding Your Contractual Protections

In the complex world of publishing, where your income depends on royalties, advances, and various subsidiary rights, audit rights are one of the most crucial protections included in your contract. These rights ensure that you can review your publisher's financial records to verify that your royalty payments are accurate and that you are receiving everything you're owed. Understanding what audit rights are and how they protect you is key to ensuring that your financial relationship with your publisher is transparent and fair.

1. Defining Audit Rights

Audit rights are a contractual provision that gives you, the author, the ability to request and review the financial records related to your book's sales and royalties. In simple terms, audit rights allow you to "double-check" the accounting practices of your publisher to make sure that the money you're supposed to be earning matches what you're actually receiving. These rights are not exercised often, but they provide a vital safeguard in case there are discrepancies or errors in your royalty statements.

Here's what audit rights typically allow:

- **Access to Financial Records**: You have the right to review the publisher's financial statements and accounting records related to your book's sales. This could include data on how many copies were sold, at what price, through which channels, and what deductions (like returns and discounts) were applied.

- **Requesting an Audit**: You can initiate an audit if you suspect an issue with the accuracy of your royalty payments. This is usually done by hiring an independent auditor or accountant who specializes in publishing finances.

- **Ensuring Fair Payment**: If the audit reveals that your publisher has underpaid you, the publisher is typically required to correct the error and pay you the full amount owed. Depending on your contract, they may also be responsible for reimbursing the costs of the audit.

Example: After reviewing your royalty statements, you notice that the eBook sales seem lower than expected compared to previous years, even though your book was promoted heavily during that period. You initiate an audit to confirm whether all eBook sales were accurately reported.

Tip: While audits are rare, simply having the right to audit provides a level of accountability and may encourage publishers to maintain accurate reporting, knowing that you can check their work if needed.

2. The Importance of Audit Rights

Having audit rights in your publishing contract is essential for several reasons. First and foremost, it gives you the legal authority to verify that you're being paid correctly, which is especially important when dealing with complex royalty calculations, foreign sales, or subsidiary rights (like audiobooks and film deals). Royalty statements can be difficult to interpret, and even the most honest publishers can make mistakes in accounting. Audit rights provide a safety net for ensuring that those mistakes don't affect your bottom line.

Here's why audit rights are important:

- **Transparency**: Audit rights ensure that there is transparency in the financial relationship between you and your publisher. It holds the publisher accountable for reporting sales accurately and paying you what you're owed.

- **Financial Security**: By having the right to audit, you are empowered to protect your income and make sure no royalties are slipping through the cracks. This is especially crucial if you rely on these earnings to support your writing career.

- **Negotiation Leverage**: If your contract includes strong audit rights, it can provide you with leverage during royalty disputes or renegotiations. The publisher knows you have the right to audit, which can incentivize them to maintain clear and accurate records.

Example: Your book has been selling well in foreign markets, but you notice that the foreign royalty payments are inconsistent. By exercising your audit rights, you can review the records from international distributors and verify that all foreign sales are being reported accurately.

Tip: Even if you never exercise your audit rights, having them in your contract gives you peace of mind. It ensures that you have recourse if something doesn't seem right with your payments.

3. How Audit Rights Work in Practice

While the idea of conducting an audit might seem intimidating, the process itself is fairly straightforward. Most contracts will specify how and when an audit can be requested, what records you are entitled to review, and the logistics of conducting the audit. Typically, audits are done by an independent auditor who specializes in publishing, and the process is handled professionally to avoid conflict between the author and the publisher.

Here's a general overview of how audit rights work in practice:

- **Initiating an Audit**: If you notice discrepancies in your royalty statements or suspect that something isn't adding up, you have the right to initiate an audit. This usually involves sending a formal request to your publisher, stating your intention to audit their records.

- **Hiring an Auditor**: You'll likely need to hire an independent auditor or accountant to conduct the audit. These professionals are experienced in reviewing publishing contracts, royalty statements, and financial records. They will analyze the publisher's books to ensure accuracy.

- **Reviewing the Records**: The auditor will review all relevant financial records related to your book sales. This could include sales reports, distributor statements, and other accounting documents that show how much your book has earned and how much you've been paid.

- **Resolving Discrepancies**: If the audit reveals that the publisher has underpaid you, they are typically required to pay the difference. Depending on the terms of your contract, they may also be required to cover the cost of the audit if the underpayment exceeds a certain threshold (e.g., 5% of total royalties).

Example: After noticing a discrepancy in your royalty statements, you hire an independent auditor to review your book's sales records. The audit reveals that the publisher accidentally underreported eBook sales by 8%, resulting in an underpayment of $3,000. The publisher pays the missing amount and covers the cost of the audit.

Tip: Before initiating an audit, it's a good idea to review your royalty statements thoroughly and consult with a literary agent or accountant to determine whether an audit is necessary.

4. How to Include Audit Rights in Your Contract

When negotiating your publishing contract, it's important to ensure that strong audit rights are included. While most standard publishing contracts include some form of audit rights, the details can vary, and you want to make sure the terms are favorable to you as the author.

Here's what to look for when negotiating audit rights in your contract:

- **Frequency of Audits**: Ensure that the contract allows you to conduct audits as needed, though many contracts limit how often audits can be conducted (e.g., once per year or once every two years). Make sure the frequency is reasonable.

- **Access to Records**: Clarify which records you'll have access to during an audit. You should be entitled to review all relevant financial documents, including sales reports, distributor agreements, and royalty calculations.

- **Audit Costs**: Negotiate who will cover the cost of the audit. Many contracts state that the author must cover the cost unless the audit reveals an underpayment above a certain threshold (e.g., 5% or more). In that case, the publisher may be required to cover the audit costs.

- **Timing**: The contract should specify how long after a royalty statement is issued you have to request an audit. Make sure the time frame is reasonable (e.g., 2-3 years after receiving a royalty statement).

Example: During contract negotiations, you include a clause that allows you to audit your publisher's records once every two years, with the publisher covering the audit costs if an underpayment of 5% or more is discovered.

Tip: Work with your literary agent or attorney to ensure that the audit rights in your contract are fair and protect your financial interests.

Audit rights are a crucial part of your contractual protections as an author, giving you the ability to verify that your royalties are being accurately reported and paid. By understanding how audit rights work, when to exercise them, and how to negotiate favorable terms, you can ensure that you are always receiving what you're due. Keeping your financial interests secure is just as important as crafting your next bestselling novel!

When to Exercise Your Audit Rights: Recognizing Red Flags

While **audit rights** provide a crucial safeguard, they aren't something you need to use with every royalty statement. However, there are certain red flags and situations where exercising your audit rights becomes necessary. In this section, we'll discuss how to recognize the signs that something might be off with your royalty payments and when to take action to ensure you're being paid correctly.

1. Inconsistent or Declining Sales Without Explanation

One of the most obvious red flags is a sudden and unexplained drop in sales reported by your publisher. If your royalty statements show a sharp decline in sales or earnings, but you know that your book has been actively promoted or received significant publicity, this could indicate an error or underreporting by your publisher.

Common scenarios where this red flag appears:

- **Promotional Efforts**: If your book has been featured in a major promotion (e.g., online book clubs, a social media campaign, or holiday sales) and you don't see a corresponding increase in sales, it's worth investigating.

- **Reviews and Exposure**: If your book has been receiving a lot of positive media coverage, strong reviews, or an uptick in reader engagement (such as on Goodreads or social media), and you notice a decrease in royalties, this discrepancy could be cause for concern.

- **Steady Decline Over Time**: While it's normal for book sales to taper off after a launch, a steep or sudden decline in sales without any clear reason could signal a reporting issue.

Example: Your book was featured on a popular book influencer's blog, and you noticed a significant increase in social media buzz. However, when you receive your next royalty statement, it shows a decrease in sales. This might be a sign that sales are being underreported or that there's an issue with distribution.

Tip: If you see a sudden dip in sales after a big promotional push, it's worth reaching out to your publisher first to ask for clarification. If their response doesn't satisfy your concerns, consider exercising your audit rights.

2. Discrepancies Between Formats or Markets

Another red flag is when you notice discrepancies between different formats of your book (e.g., hardcover, paperback, eBook, audiobook) or between various markets (e.g., domestic vs. foreign sales). These inconsistencies may suggest that one or more formats or markets are being underreported.

Key areas to watch for:

- **Inconsistent Sales Across Formats**: If one format of your book is performing significantly better or worse than others without a clear reason, it's worth investigating. For example, if your eBook sales are thriving but your audiobook sales seem unusually low, there could be an error in the reporting.

- **Foreign Market Sales**: Foreign rights sales can be particularly difficult to track, especially if you've sold the rights in multiple countries. If you're seeing consistent domestic sales but irregular or missing reports for international sales, this might be a red flag that your foreign royalties aren't being accurately reported.

- **Delayed Reports from Digital Platforms**: Some publishers may have delayed or incomplete reporting from digital platforms like Amazon, Apple Books, or Audible. If your digital royalties seem low, despite knowing your book is available on these platforms, it's worth investigating further.

Example: Your book is selling steadily in the U.S., but the foreign royalties from several key markets seem inconsistent or missing altogether. After noticing this pattern for several months, you decide to exercise your audit rights to investigate international sales more thoroughly.

Tip: Pay special attention to foreign rights deals and sales from less-transparent platforms like digital retailers or audiobooks. If these income streams seem inconsistent, consider conducting an audit.

3. Unexplained Deductions or Reserves Against Royalties

Your royalty statement might include deductions for returns, discounts, or reserves against returns. While some deductions are standard, unexplained or unusually large deductions can indicate an issue with how your earnings are being calculated. If you notice unfamiliar or disproportionate deductions, it might be time to look deeper.

Common issues to look out for:

- **Large or Unusual Deductions**: If you see a large percentage of your sales being deducted for returns or other reasons without an accompanying explanation, this could be a red flag. Returns are common in traditional book sales, but they should be proportional to the sales figures.

- **Unclear Reserve Amounts**: Publishers sometimes hold back a portion of your royalties as a "reserve against returns," especially with physical books. If this reserve seems too large or remains on your statement for an extended period, it's worth investigating to ensure it's necessary.

- **Hidden Fees or Deductions**: Look for any fees or deductions that are not clearly explained in your contract or royalty statement. These could include distribution fees, marketing costs, or other charges that you weren't expecting.

Example: Your royalty statement shows a significant deduction for returns, amounting to almost 50% of your sales. This seems unusually high, and your publisher doesn't provide a clear explanation. After seeing this pattern across multiple statements, you decide to audit the publisher's financial records.

Tip: Always review the deduction and reserve sections of your royalty statement carefully. If something doesn't add up, ask your publisher for more details. If they can't provide satisfactory answers, consider initiating an audit.

4. Long Delays in Royalty Payments

If you experience long delays in receiving your royalty payments, this could be a sign that something is amiss with your publisher's accounting process. While occasional delays can happen, consistent or unexplained delays are a red flag that warrants further investigation.

What to look out for:

- **Missed or Late Payments**: If your royalty payments are consistently late or missing altogether, this could be a sign that your publisher is struggling to manage its accounting or deliberately withholding payments.

- **Discrepancies Between Payment and Statement Dates**: If there is a significant gap between when your royalty statement is issued and when you receive payment, this could indicate a breakdown in communication or financial reporting within the publisher's accounting department.

Example: You receive your royalty statement in January, but the payment doesn't arrive until April, despite the statement indicating that the payment should have been issued in February. This has happened multiple times, raising concerns about whether your publisher is accurately managing royalty payments.

Tip: Keep detailed records of when royalty statements are issued and when payments are received. If there are recurring delays, ask your publisher for an explanation and document their response. If the delays persist, it may be time to request an audit.

5. Sudden Changes in Publisher Behavior

If your publisher's communication becomes infrequent, or they suddenly stop sending royalty statements or responding to your inquiries, this could be a sign of financial trouble or accounting issues. While some changes in behavior may have innocent explanations, sudden radio silence can be a red flag that warrants closer attention.

Signs to watch for:

- **Lack of Communication**: If your publisher stops responding to your emails or fails to send regular royalty statements, this could indicate internal issues or financial difficulties.

- **Sudden Changes in Reporting Practices**: If your publisher changes the way they report royalties (e.g., switching to a new accounting system or reporting less frequently), this might indicate potential problems with financial transparency.

- **Unexplained Changes in Terms**: If your publisher suddenly wants to change the terms of your contract, such as renegotiating royalties or extending deadlines for payments, it could signal that they are facing financial challenges.

Example: Your publisher has always sent quarterly royalty statements on time, but for the last two quarters, they've missed the deadlines and failed to respond to your inquiries. You notice that payments are also arriving later than usual. This change in behavior prompts you to consider exercising your audit rights.

Tip: Document all communication with your publisher, especially if you notice changes in their behavior or payment schedules. If these issues persist, an audit can help you get to the bottom of any discrepancies.

Knowing when to exercise your audit rights is essential for protecting your financial interests as an author. By recognizing red flags such as inconsistent sales, unexplained deductions, delayed payments, and changes in publisher behavior, you can take proactive steps to ensure that your royalty payments are accurate and timely. Auditing your publisher's records is a powerful tool for safeguarding your income and ensuring that you get what you're due.

How to Conduct an Audit: The Process and What to Expect

Once you've recognized the need for an audit, the next step is to understand how the process works and what you can expect. Conducting an audit of your publisher's financial records is not as daunting as it may seem, especially when you approach it with a clear plan and professional assistance. In this section, we'll walk you through the steps of conducting an audit, from notifying your publisher to reviewing their records and resolving any discrepancies.

1. Step 1: Review Your Contract and Royalty Statements

Before initiating an audit, it's essential to thoroughly review your publishing contract and past royalty statements. Your contract should specify the terms under which you can exercise your audit rights, including how often audits can be conducted, how long you have to request an audit, and any limitations on what can be reviewed.

Here's what to look for:

- **Audit Clauses**: Most contracts will outline when and how you can audit the publisher's financial records. This often includes details like how far back you can audit, how many times you can request an audit (typically once per year or every two years), and whether the publisher is responsible for covering the cost if significant discrepancies are found.

- **Royalty Statements**: Review your royalty statements carefully to identify any inconsistencies, missing payments, or unexplained deductions. This will help you pinpoint what you want the audit to focus on, such as eBook sales, foreign royalties, or subsidiary rights.

Example: Your contract allows you to audit your publisher once every two years, and after reviewing your royalty statements, you notice a significant discrepancy in foreign eBook sales. You decide to audit the publisher's foreign sales records for the last two years.

Tip: Keep a copy of your contract and royalty statements organized and easily accessible. This will make it easier to reference specific clauses and figures during the audit process.

2. Step 2: Notify Your Publisher of the Audit

The next step is to formally notify your publisher that you intend to conduct an audit. This is typically done in writing, with a letter or email that explains your concerns and states your intention to review their financial records. Be professional and clear in your communication, and be sure to reference the specific audit clause in your contract.

Here's how to notify your publisher:

- **Formal Request**: Send a formal letter or email to your publisher's finance department or royalties team, stating that you are exercising your audit rights as outlined in your contract. Specify the time period and records you intend to audit, such as all sales data for the past two years or a specific category like eBook royalties.

- **Maintain Professionalism**: While audits can feel confrontational, it's important to maintain a professional tone in your communication. Frame the audit as a standard business practice to ensure transparency and accuracy, rather than as an accusation.

- **Set a Timeline**: In your request, suggest a reasonable timeline for when the audit will take place and when you expect to receive the necessary documents. This helps to set expectations and ensures that the process moves forward efficiently.

Example: You send an email to your publisher's finance team, stating that you'd like to audit your book's foreign eBook sales from the last two years. You request access to the relevant financial records within the next 30 days and offer to coordinate with their team to facilitate the process.

Tip: If you work with a literary agent or attorney, it's often helpful to have them review your notification letter or send it on your behalf. This adds a level of formality and ensures that all the proper steps are followed.

3. Step 3: Hire an Auditor or Accountant

Conducting an audit usually involves hiring a professional auditor or accountant who is experienced in publishing finances. These professionals know what to look for in the publisher's records and can identify discrepancies that might not be obvious to someone without financial expertise. It's important to hire someone who understands the nuances of publishing contracts, royalty structures, and subsidiary rights.

Here's how to hire the right auditor:

- **Choose a Specialist**: Look for an accountant or auditor with experience in the publishing industry. They should be familiar with royalty statements, advances, subsidiary rights, and foreign sales. Ask for recommendations from your literary agent or fellow authors who have conducted audits.

- **Discuss Costs**: Before hiring an auditor, discuss their fees and how much the audit is likely to cost. Some contracts include a clause stating that if the audit reveals an underpayment above a certain threshold (e.g., 5% or more), the publisher is responsible for covering the cost of the audit. Otherwise, the cost may fall to you.

- **Provide Relevant Documents**: Once hired, provide your auditor with copies of your publishing contract, royalty statements, and any correspondence with the publisher. This will give them the context they need to conduct a thorough review.

Example: You hire an accountant who specializes in publishing audits. After discussing your concerns about foreign sales, they request a copy of your contract and the relevant royalty statements to review before contacting the publisher for additional records.

Tip: Ensure that the auditor you hire is impartial and professional. A neutral third party is more likely to foster cooperation between you and the publisher during the audit process.

4. Step 4: Review the Publisher's Records

Once your audit has been initiated, the publisher will provide access to the relevant financial records. These records will include detailed sales data, distributor agreements, and royalty calculations that show how your earnings were determined. Your auditor will review these records to verify their accuracy and ensure that all sales are properly accounted for.

Here's what to expect during the review process:

- **Detailed Sales Data**: The auditor will examine detailed sales reports for your book, breaking down sales by format (hardcover, paperback, eBook, audiobook), market (domestic and international), and distribution channels (bookstores, online retailers, etc.).

- **Distributor Agreements**: If there are concerns about foreign or subsidiary rights, the auditor may review the agreements between your publisher and foreign distributors or other partners to ensure that sales and payments were reported accurately.

- **Royalties and Deductions**: The auditor will also verify that the royalty rates applied to your sales match the terms in your contract. They will review deductions for returns, reserves, and discounts to ensure they are accurate and reasonable.

Example: Your auditor reviews the publisher's sales data for foreign eBook sales and discovers that sales from several key territories were underreported, resulting in an underpayment of royalties. They provide a detailed report outlining the discrepancies.

Tip: Be patient during the review process. Auditing financial records can take time, especially if you're reviewing multiple years of sales data or complex subsidiary rights agreements.

5. Step 5: Resolving Discrepancies

If the audit reveals discrepancies or underpayments, the next step is to resolve them with your publisher. Most publishers will correct any errors and pay the difference owed, especially if the underpayment was the result of an accounting mistake. In some cases, the publisher may also be required to cover the cost of the audit if the discrepancies are above a certain threshold (usually 5% or more of the total royalties).

Here's how to resolve discrepancies:

- **Present the Audit Findings**: Once the audit is complete, your auditor will provide a report outlining any discrepancies, underpayments, or errors they discovered. This report will be shared with the publisher, along with a request to correct the issue and pay any outstanding royalties.

- **Negotiate a Resolution**: In most cases, the publisher will agree to resolve the discrepancies and pay the additional royalties. If the underpayment exceeds the threshold outlined in your contract, the publisher may also be required to reimburse you for the cost of the audit.

- **Escalate If Necessary**: If the publisher disputes the audit findings or refuses to pay what is owed, you may need to escalate the issue. This could involve engaging your literary agent or attorney to negotiate a settlement or, in extreme cases, taking legal action.

Example: The audit reveals a $5,000 underpayment due to misreported foreign sales. Your publisher agrees to pay the additional royalties and covers the cost of the audit, as the underpayment exceeded 5% of the total royalties.

Tip: Keep the conversation with your publisher professional and solution-oriented. Most discrepancies are the result of honest mistakes, and publishers are usually willing to correct them once they are identified.

Conducting an audit is a straightforward process that involves reviewing your contract, notifying your publisher, hiring an experienced auditor, and carefully reviewing financial records. By following these steps, you can ensure that your royalty payments are accurate and that any discrepancies are resolved promptly.

Auditing is an essential tool for protecting your financial interests as an author, ensuring that you get what you're due from your hard-earned work.

Negotiating Audit Clauses: Setting Yourself Up for Success

When signing a publishing contract, the audit clause is one of the most important provisions to ensure you have the right to verify your royalties and sales data. A well-negotiated audit clause sets the foundation for transparency and accuracy in your financial relationship with the publisher. In this section, we'll explore the key elements of an audit clause, what to negotiate for, and how to set yourself up for success in case you ever need to exercise your audit rights.

1. The Importance of a Strong Audit Clause

An audit clause gives you the legal authority to review your publisher's financial records and ensure that your royalty payments are accurate. Without a clear and well-defined audit clause, you may face obstacles in getting access to important sales data or may be limited in your ability to check for discrepancies.

A strong audit clause ensures:

- **Access to Records**: You'll have the right to examine the publisher's financial records related to your book sales, royalties, and subsidiary rights.

- **Regular Audits**: The clause should allow you to conduct audits at reasonable intervals, ensuring that you can check your finances regularly without unnecessary restrictions.

- **Publisher Accountability**: Knowing that you can audit their records helps keep publishers accountable for accurate royalty reporting and payment.

Example: Your contract includes a well-defined audit clause that allows you to review financial records every two years. This ensures that if you ever notice a discrepancy, you have the legal right to access the necessary data and take action.

Tip: Make sure your contract includes an audit clause before signing. If there's no mention of audit rights, negotiate to have it added or clarified.

2. Key Elements to Include in an Audit Clause

When negotiating your contract, focus on key elements within the audit clause that will protect your rights and ensure fair access to financial records. The more comprehensive and clear the clause, the easier it will be to enforce your rights if you ever need to conduct an audit.

Here are the essential elements to include in an audit clause:

- **Frequency of Audits**: Specify how often you can request an audit. While most contracts limit audits to once every one or two years, ensure that the frequency is reasonable. For example, being able to audit your records once a year or every two years is standard.

- **Scope of the Audit**: Make sure the clause clearly defines the scope of the audit. You should be able to review all financial records related to your book's sales, royalties, advances, subsidiary rights, and deductions, including returns and reserves.

- **Cost of the Audit**: Negotiate who will cover the cost of the audit. A common provision is that if the audit reveals a significant underpayment (e.g., 5% or more), the publisher is responsible for covering the cost. If there are no discrepancies, you may be required to cover the audit expenses.

- **Access to Auditors**: The clause should allow you to hire an independent auditor or accountant of your choosing to review the publisher's financial records. Ensure that the publisher can't limit your choice of auditors.

Example: You negotiate a clause that allows you to audit the publisher's records once every two years and specifies that if the audit reveals an underpayment of 5% or more, the publisher will cover the audit costs. This ensures that you can protect your financial interests without bearing the full cost of the audit if discrepancies are found.

Tip: Be specific about the types of records you want access to during the audit, such as sales data by format (print, eBook, audiobook), returns, subsidiary rights income, and deductions. This will help avoid any confusion when the time comes to conduct an audit.

3. Negotiating the Costs of an Audit

Audit costs can vary depending on the complexity of the audit, the number of records being reviewed, and the auditor's fees. It's important to negotiate terms that protect you from covering the full cost of an audit if significant discrepancies are found. A well-structured clause can shift the burden of the audit cost to the publisher in certain situations.

Here's how to negotiate audit costs:

- **Threshold for Publisher to Cover Costs**: A common practice is to include a provision that states if the audit reveals underpayments exceeding a certain percentage (usually 5% or more), the publisher must cover the cost of the audit. This motivates the publisher to maintain accurate records and provides a safety net for you in case of significant discrepancies.

- **Cost-Sharing**: In some cases, you may negotiate a cost-sharing agreement, where you and the publisher split the audit costs if discrepancies are found below the threshold.

- **Reasonable Audit Fees**: Ensure that the contract allows for "reasonable" audit costs. This prevents the publisher from challenging your audit expenses if the cost is within industry standards.

Example: Your contract includes a clause stating that if the audit reveals an underpayment of 5% or more, the publisher will reimburse you for the audit costs. If the underpayment is less than 5%, you will cover the cost, which motivates you to only request an audit when necessary.

Tip: Clarify the cost threshold for the audit in your contract. Having clear terms upfront will help avoid disputes later on if discrepancies are found.

4. Setting a Reasonable Time Frame for Audits

When negotiating your audit clause, make sure it includes a reasonable time frame for requesting and conducting an audit. Some contracts impose strict limitations on how long after a royalty statement is issued you can request an audit, so it's important to set a time frame that works for you.

Here's what to consider:

- **Audit Time Limit**: Most contracts allow you to request an audit within a certain period after receiving a royalty statement, usually two to three years. Ensure that this time frame gives you enough opportunity to review your statements thoroughly before initiating an audit.

- **Duration of the Audit**: The contract should also specify how long the audit process can take. A reasonable time frame is key to ensuring that the audit is conducted efficiently and that you receive any owed payments promptly.

Example: Your contract allows you to request an audit within three years of receiving a royalty statement, giving you ample time to review your statements and address any concerns. The publisher is required to provide the necessary financial records within 30 days of receiving your audit request.

Tip: Ensure that the time frame for requesting an audit aligns with your ability to thoroughly review royalty statements. A two- to three-year window is typical and allows for flexibility in case discrepancies aren't immediately obvious.

Negotiating a strong audit clause is one of the best ways to protect your financial interests as an author. By focusing on key elements such as audit frequency, scope, costs, and time frames, you can set yourself up for success and ensure that your publisher remains transparent and accountable. A well-crafted audit clause gives you the peace of mind to know that if something doesn't seem right with your royalty payments, you have the power to take action and get what you're due.

Quick Tips and Recap

- **Understand the Importance of Audit Rights**: Ensure your publishing contract includes a clear audit clause that allows you to review financial records to verify the accuracy of royalty payments.

- **Recognize Red Flags**: Watch for signs like declining sales without explanation, discrepancies between formats, or delayed payments that may indicate a need for an audit.

- **Notify Your Publisher Professionally**: When initiating an audit, notify your publisher in writing, stating your concerns and referencing the audit clause in your contract.

- **Hire a Qualified Auditor**: Work with an independent auditor or accountant who specializes in publishing to ensure a thorough review of your publisher's financial records.

- **Negotiate Strong Audit Clauses**: Include terms that allow for regular audits, specify the scope of records, and require the publisher to cover the costs if significant discrepancies (5% or more) are found.

- **Set Reasonable Time Frames**: Ensure your contract allows ample time (two to three years) to request an audit after receiving royalty statements.

- **Resolve Discrepancies**: If an audit reveals underpayments, present the findings to your publisher and negotiate a resolution, including additional payments and audit cost coverage if applicable.

By securing well-negotiated audit rights and understanding when and how to exercise them, you can ensure transparency in royalty payments and safeguard your income as an author.

Financial Disputes: Resolving Money Matters

"Resolving financial disputes is an art—approach it with the right mix of facts, diplomacy, and firmness, and you can turn potential conflicts into opportunities for mutual gain." — INDRA NOOYI, FORMER CEO OF PEPSICO

Welcome to Chapter Twenty, "Financial Disputes: Resolving Money Matters," where we tackle the not-so-glamorous but utterly essential task of sorting out financial misunderstandings. Think of this as the cleanup crew after a lavish banquet—someone has to make sure everything is squared away, and that someone is you.

In this chapter, we're not just resolving disputes; we're navigating the choppy waters of financial disagreements with the finesse of a diplomat and the sharp acumen of a seasoned accountant. Whether it's a royalty miscalculation or a contractual misinterpretation, we'll arm you with the strategies to address and diffuse tensions without turning the negotiation table into a battlefield.

Prepare to sharpen your negotiation skills and dust off your diplomacy hat. We're about to turn every financial dispute from a potential disaster into a masterclass in resolution and relationships. After all, a well-resolved dispute can sometimes strengthen bonds, proving that even money matters can't shake your foundational integrity and commitment to fair play.

Identifying the Source of the Dispute: Pinpointing Financial Discrepancies

Before jumping into a resolution process, it's crucial to first understand the exact cause of the financial dispute. Financial disagreements between authors and publishers can arise from a variety of sources, including errors in royalty calculations, contract misunderstandings, or delayed payments. Pinpointing the root of the issue allows you to address it directly, making the path to resolution clearer and more efficient.

1. Common Causes of Financial Disputes

Understanding the most common sources of financial disputes can help you quickly zero in on the issue when something doesn't add up. Here are the most frequent areas where discrepancies arise:

- **Royalty Miscalculations**: One of the most common issues stems from incorrect royalty calculations. This could be due to misapplied royalty rates, miscounted sales figures, or inaccurate deductions (such as returns or reserves). It's important to review your royalty statements carefully to spot any inconsistencies.

- **Advances and Payments**: Delayed or missing payments are another common point of contention. This could involve a delay in receiving advance installments or royalties, or even a payment that doesn't reflect the amounts outlined in your contract.

- **Contract Misunderstandings**: Sometimes disputes arise from differing interpretations of the contract. You may believe you're owed more due to a particular clause, while the publisher has a different interpretation. This could involve issues like subsidiary rights payments, foreign sales, or audiobook royalties.

- **Deductions and Fees**: Discrepancies in deductions for returns, discounts, or marketing costs can also cause financial disputes. If the deductions seem unusually high or inconsistent with the sales figures, there may be an issue with how these deductions are being applied.

Example: After receiving your quarterly royalty statement, you notice that the percentage rate for your eBook royalties is lower than what was agreed upon in your contract. This leads you to believe there's been a miscalculation, prompting further investigation.

Tip: Keep copies of all your contracts, royalty statements, and payment schedules organized so you can easily reference them when discrepancies arise.

2. Reviewing Your Royalty Statements for Errors

The first step in identifying the source of a financial dispute is to review your royalty statements thoroughly. Royalty statements can be complex, with various line items for different formats, sales channels, and deductions. Look for any discrepancies between what was agreed upon in your contract and what's reflected in the royalty statement.

Here's what to look for:

- **Correct Royalty Rates**: Verify that the royalty rates in your statement match the rates in your contract for each format (eBook, hardcover, paperback, audiobook). If the rates don't align, this could indicate a miscalculation.

- **Sales Figures**: Check the sales numbers reported for each format and territory. If the sales figures seem unusually low or inconsistent with previous periods, it could be a sign that not all sales are being reported accurately.

- **Deductions and Reserves**: Review any deductions for returns, reserves against returns, or other fees. Ensure these deductions are reasonable and match the terms of your contract. If a large portion of your earnings is being deducted without a clear explanation, this could be a red flag.

- **Advance Recoupment**: If you received an advance, make sure that your royalties are being correctly applied toward recouping the advance. Once your advance is fully recouped, you should begin receiving additional royalty payments.

Example: You notice that your publisher has deducted a large sum for returns on hardcover sales, but you've received no explanation for this. This deduction seems disproportionately high compared to the previous periods, suggesting an issue with how returns are being reported.

Tip: Track your royalty statements over time and compare them against each other. This can help you spot unusual patterns or sudden changes in sales figures or deductions.

3. Cross-Referencing Your Contract

Once you've reviewed your royalty statements, the next step is to cross-reference the statement details with the terms of your contract. Your contract is the blueprint for how you're supposed to be paid, so it's crucial to ensure that the publisher is adhering to the agreed terms.

Here's how to cross-reference your contract:

- **Royalty Rates**: Double-check the royalty rates specified in your contract for each format and market (domestic vs. international). Ensure that the rates applied in your royalty statement are correct and match the contract.

- **Advance Payment Schedule**: Review the advance payment schedule in your contract to ensure that you've received all payments on time and in the correct amounts.

- **Subsidiary Rights**: If you've licensed subsidiary rights (e.g., foreign translations, film rights, or audiobooks), check that the royalties or payments for these rights are reflected in your statement and that they match the contract terms.

- **Deductions**: Ensure that any deductions for marketing, distribution, or returns are in line with the terms outlined in your contract. If your contract doesn't allow for certain deductions, this could be a point of contention.

Example: Your contract states that you're entitled to 25% of net receipts for eBook sales, but your royalty statement shows you're only being paid 20%. Cross-referencing your contract helps you identify this error and gives you the leverage to address it with your publisher.

Tip: If you have an agent, they can be a valuable resource for reviewing your contract and helping you pinpoint areas where the publisher may not be complying with the agreed-upon terms.

4. Gathering Evidence

Once you've identified the source of the dispute, it's important to gather all relevant evidence before approaching your publisher. Having clear documentation will make your case stronger and help facilitate a more productive conversation.

Here's what to gather:

- **Royalty Statements**: Collect all relevant royalty statements that show the discrepancy, including any supporting documentation (such as emails or communications about sales or payments).

- **Sales Data**: If possible, collect sales data from other sources, such as retailer reports (e.g., Amazon sales reports), to compare against the figures in your royalty statements.

- **Contract**: Have a copy of your contract on hand, highlighting the specific clauses related to royalty rates, payment schedules, and deductions.

- **Communication Records**: If you've previously raised concerns about payments or discrepancies with your publisher, gather any emails or correspondence that can support your case.

Example: You gather royalty statements from the past four quarters and notice a consistent underreporting of eBook sales. You also pull sales reports from Amazon's self-publishing dashboard, which shows higher sales than your royalty statement reflects. Armed with this evidence, you're ready to approach your publisher.

Tip: The more evidence you have to support your claim, the easier it will be to resolve the dispute. Be organized and methodical in your approach.

Identifying the source of a financial dispute is the first step in resolving it. By carefully reviewing your royalty statements, cross-referencing your contract, and gathering evidence, you can pinpoint where the discrepancy lies and prepare to address it with your publisher. Taking a methodical approach ensures that you're well-prepared to resolve the issue fairly and professionally.

Communicating Effectively: How to Approach Financial Disagreements

Once you've identified the source of the financial dispute, the next step is to address it with your publisher in a way that is both professional and effective. How you approach these conversations can make a significant difference in how quickly and amicably the issue is resolved. Maintaining clear, respectful communication, backed by evidence, will help you achieve a resolution without escalating tensions.

1. Be Clear and Professional

When addressing financial disagreements, it's essential to be clear and professional in your communication. Even if you feel frustrated or disappointed, keeping a calm and objective tone will set the stage for a constructive conversation. The goal is to resolve the issue, not to accuse or create conflict, so focus on the facts and avoid emotionally charged language.

Here's how to structure your communication:

- **State the Issue Clearly**: Begin by clearly outlining the issue at hand. Describe the discrepancy you've noticed (e.g., underreported royalties, a miscalculated payment, or unexplained deductions) without assigning blame.

- **Reference Your Contract**: Mention the specific section of your contract that relates to the dispute. For example, if the issue is with royalty rates, reference the clause that defines the agreed-upon rate.

- **Use Objective Language**: Stick to the facts and avoid making assumptions. Instead of saying, "You're not paying me correctly," say, "I've noticed a discrepancy between the royalty rate applied to my eBook sales and the rate outlined in our contract."

- **Request Clarification**: Frame your initial communication as a request for clarification. This gives your publisher the opportunity to explain or correct the issue without feeling defensive.

Example: Subject: Discrepancy in eBook Royalty Rate – Request for Clarification

Dear [Publisher/Editor's Name],

I hope this message finds you well. I'm writing to request clarification regarding the eBook royalty rate applied to my recent royalty statement for [Book Title]. My contract specifies a royalty rate of 25% of net receipts for eBook sales, but the statement reflects a 20% rate. Could you please help me understand why this difference occurred?

I've attached a copy of the relevant royalty statement and the section of the contract that outlines the agreed rate for your reference. I look forward to your clarification.

Best regards,
[Your Name]

Tip: Stay solution-focused. The tone of your communication should suggest that you are seeking a resolution, not trying to assign blame or escalate the conflict.

2. Present Your Evidence

To support your request for clarification, present the evidence you've gathered during your review of the royalty statements and contract. This strengthens your case and provides concrete details that your publisher can use to investigate the issue. When presenting your evidence, ensure that it is well-organized and easy to follow.

What to include:

- **Royalty Statements**: Attach the royalty statements that show the discrepancy. Highlight or reference specific figures that are in question.

- **Contract Clauses**: Include relevant sections of your contract that specify the terms you believe aren't being met. For example, if the issue is with subsidiary rights, highlight the clause that outlines your share of the profits.

- **Comparative Data**: If you have sales data from other sources (e.g., retailer sales reports), include this information as well. Comparing external sales data to your royalty statement can help illustrate the discrepancy.

Example: In your email, you attach a PDF of your last two royalty statements and include a scanned excerpt from your contract that outlines the eBook royalty rate. You also provide a summary of the discrepancies in a bullet point format, making it easy for the publisher to understand the issue.

Tip: Avoid overwhelming your publisher with unnecessary details. Stick to the most relevant facts and data, and present them in a way that's easy to digest.

3. Keep the Conversation Open and Collaborative

When addressing a financial dispute, it's important to keep the conversation open and collaborative. Financial disagreements can be resolved more effectively if both parties approach the issue with a willingness to work together. Make it clear that you're open to discussing the issue further and that you're looking for a solution that benefits both sides.

Here's how to keep the conversation open:

- **Invite Dialogue**: End your message with an invitation for further discussion. For example, you might say, "I'd be happy to discuss this in more detail if needed" or "Please let me know if there's any additional information you require from me."

- **Suggest Solutions**: If appropriate, offer suggestions for resolving the issue. This could be as simple as requesting a revised royalty statement or suggesting that the publisher review their sales reports for discrepancies.

- **Be Flexible**: Financial disputes may take time to resolve, especially if the publisher needs to conduct an internal review. Let your publisher know that you're open to working with them on a timeline that suits both parties.

Example: In your communication, you say, "I'd be happy to schedule a call to discuss this further if needed. I understand that these issues can take time to resolve, and I'm open to working together to find a solution."

Tip: Even if you feel the publisher is at fault, maintaining a collaborative tone will increase the chances of a quick and positive resolution.

4. Follow Up Respectfully

If you don't receive a timely response to your initial communication, it's important to follow up respectfully. Sometimes financial issues can slip through the cracks, especially if the publisher is busy with multiple projects. A polite follow-up email can help keep the conversation moving without appearing confrontational.

Here's how to follow up:

- **Wait a Reasonable Amount of Time**: Give your publisher enough time to review your request and respond. Depending on the complexity of the issue, one to two weeks is generally a reasonable amount of time to wait before following up.

- **Send a Polite Reminder**: If you haven't heard back after a couple of weeks, send a brief, polite reminder. Reiterate your request and let them know you're still available to discuss the issue.

- **Maintain a Professional Tone**: Keep your follow-up message professional and courteous. Avoid sounding impatient or accusatory, as this could hinder a constructive resolution.

Example: Subject: Follow-Up on eBook Royalty Discrepancy – [Book Title]

Dear [Publisher/Editor's Name],

I hope you're doing well. I wanted to follow up on my previous message regarding the discrepancy in the eBook royalty rate for [Book Title]. I understand these matters can take time, and I'm happy to discuss further if needed. Please let me know if there's any additional information I can provide.

Best regards,

[Your Name]

Tip: Keep track of your communication. If the issue remains unresolved after several follow-ups, you'll have a record of your efforts to address the problem, which can be useful if you need to escalate the matter.

Communicating effectively is essential when addressing financial disagreements with your publisher. By staying clear, professional, and solution-focused, you can keep the conversation constructive and increase the chances of resolving the issue quickly. Present your evidence in a well-organized manner, maintain an open dialogue, and follow up respectfully to ensure that both you and your publisher can work together toward a fair resolution.

Negotiating a Fair Resolution: Strategies for Finding Common Ground

Once you've identified the source of the financial dispute and communicated effectively with your publisher, the next step is negotiating a fair resolution. Resolving financial disagreements often requires a balance between standing up for what you're owed and maintaining a positive working relationship with your publisher. In this section, we'll explore strategies for finding common ground, ensuring that both parties are satisfied with the outcome.

1. Be Prepared with Facts and Solutions

When entering into a negotiation, preparation is key. Having your evidence and potential solutions ready will help you steer the conversation toward resolution. Be clear about your goals and what you need to achieve, but also be open to compromise if necessary.

Here's how to prepare for the negotiation:

- **Know Your Numbers**: Make sure you fully understand the financial discrepancy, whether it's an underpayment, incorrect royalty rate, or overcharged deduction. Have all relevant documents, such as royalty statements, contract clauses, and sales data, readily available.

- **Define Your Ideal Outcome**: Before negotiations begin, know what resolution you're aiming for. This could be as straightforward as requesting a corrected royalty statement, reimbursement for missed payments, or future adjustments to how royalties are calculated.

- **Consider Compromises**: Be realistic about what's achievable and think about potential compromises. For example, you might accept a lower repayment amount if the publisher offers to make adjustments in future payments.

Example: You've identified that the publisher underpaid you by $3,000 due to a miscalculation of eBook royalties. Your ideal outcome is to receive the full amount owed, but you're willing to negotiate a partial payment now with the remainder spread over future royalty periods if necessary.

Tip: Stay solution-oriented. Instead of focusing on what went wrong, guide the conversation toward how both parties can move forward and resolve the issue.

2. Focus on Collaboration, Not Confrontation

While it's natural to feel frustrated in a financial dispute, approaching the negotiation with a collaborative mindset is more likely to lead to a positive resolution. Keep the tone of the negotiation respectful and professional, and make it clear that you're looking for a mutually beneficial solution.

Here's how to keep the negotiation collaborative:

- **Avoid Blame**: Focus on finding a solution rather than assigning blame. Instead of saying, "You made a mistake with the royalties," try framing it as, "I noticed a discrepancy in the royalties and would like to work together to resolve it."

- **Use "We" Language**: Using inclusive language like "we" and "our" reinforces the idea that you and your publisher are on the same team. For example, "I'd like to work with you to ensure our royalty calculations are correct" sounds more collaborative than "I need you to fix this mistake."

- **Acknowledge Their Position**: Show that you understand the publisher's perspective and workload. This creates goodwill and makes them more likely to consider your concerns seriously. You might say, "I understand that managing multiple books and formats can be complex, and I appreciate your efforts in reviewing this issue."

Example: During the negotiation, you say, "I understand how busy things can get and that managing multiple royalty accounts is challenging. I really appreciate your willingness to take another look at the numbers so we can resolve this together."

Tip: Keep emotions in check. Even if you feel wronged, a calm, professional demeanor will help move the negotiation forward.

3. Present Alternative Solutions

If the publisher is unable or unwilling to meet your ideal resolution, it can be helpful to have alternative solutions in mind. Offering multiple options for resolving the dispute shows that you're flexible and willing to work with them to find a compromise.

Here's how to offer alternatives:

- **Suggest Payment Plans**: If the publisher can't pay the full amount owed immediately, suggest a payment plan where the underpayment is made up over future royalty periods. This can be a win-win if the publisher is facing cash flow issues.

- **Future Adjustments**: If there's a miscalculation in your royalties, but the publisher can't correct past payments, suggest adjusting future payments to ensure accuracy going forward. For example, you could ask for a higher royalty rate on future sales to compensate for past discrepancies.

- **Offer to Share Costs**: In some cases, you might suggest sharing the cost of resolving the dispute, especially if it involves a third-party audit. This shows that you're committed to resolving the issue fairly and are willing to meet the publisher halfway.

Example: You might say, "If it's difficult to issue the full amount owed right away, I'd be open to receiving partial payments over the next two royalty periods. Alternatively, we could adjust my eBook royalty rate going forward to make up for the shortfall."

Tip: Offering solutions makes you seem cooperative and pragmatic, which can increase the chances of reaching an agreement that works for both parties.

4. Know When to Stand Firm

While compromise is important, there may be times when you need to stand firm on certain issues—especially if the financial impact is significant or the publisher isn't responding appropriately. If your publisher refuses to acknowledge the issue or offers an unfair resolution, it's important to defend your position confidently.

Here's when to stand firm:

- **Significant Financial Impact**: If the underpayment or discrepancy has a substantial impact on your earnings, don't hesitate to stand firm on receiving full repayment. For example, if you've been underpaid by a significant amount over a long period, compromising too much could set a precedent for future disputes.

- **Contractual Violations**: If the issue involves the publisher failing to honor specific terms in your contract (such as royalty rates or payment schedules), it's important to insist that the contract be upheld as agreed.

- **Unreasonable Offers**: If the publisher offers a resolution that doesn't fairly address the issue, don't be afraid to push back. For example, if they offer to pay only a small portion of what's owed or request unreasonable deductions, it may be time to assert your position more strongly.

Example: The publisher offers to resolve the $3,000 underpayment by increasing your royalty rate slightly over the next year, but the amount wouldn't make up the full discrepancy. You stand firm and say, "I appreciate the offer, but I believe the full amount should be repaid as outlined in the contract."

Tip: Be assertive but respectful. There's a difference between standing firm and becoming confrontational. Clearly state your position, backed by facts and evidence, without escalating the situation.

5. Document Everything

Throughout the negotiation process, it's important to keep detailed records of all communications and agreements. This ensures that you have a paper trail in case the issue isn't resolved quickly or if further disputes arise in the future. It also protects you if the dispute escalates to legal action or mediation.

Here's how to document the negotiation:

- **Record All Communication**: Save all emails, letters, and notes from phone calls or meetings. If agreements are made verbally, follow up with an email summarizing what was discussed and agreed upon.

- **Request Written Confirmation**: Once a resolution is reached, request a written confirmation from the publisher outlining the agreed-upon terms. This could include a revised royalty statement, payment schedule, or contract amendment.

- **Track Payments**: If the resolution involves repayment over time, keep track of when and how much you've been paid to ensure the publisher follows through on their commitment.

Example: After negotiating a repayment plan for the $3,000 underpayment, you send an email confirming the terms: "As discussed, the publisher will repay the $3,000 underpayment over the next two royalty periods, with $1,500 to be paid in each statement. Please confirm that these terms are correct."

Tip: Keep your records organized and accessible. If further issues arise, you'll have a clear history of the negotiation process.

Negotiating a fair resolution requires a balance of preparation, collaboration, and assertiveness. By being clear about your goals, staying open to alternative solutions, and maintaining a professional tone, you can work toward a resolution that benefits both you and your publisher. Whether it involves repayment, contract adjustments, or future changes, the key to success is finding common ground while ensuring your financial interests are protected.

When to Escalate: Mediation, Arbitration, and Legal Action

In most cases, financial disputes between authors and publishers can be resolved through communication and negotiation. However, there are times when negotiations stall or when the publisher is unwilling to resolve the issue fairly. If you've exhausted all other options and the dispute remains unresolved, it may be time to escalate the situation through mediation, arbitration, or even legal action.

This section will guide you through when and how to escalate a financial dispute and what to expect if it reaches the point of mediation, arbitration, or legal proceedings.

1. Recognizing When to Escalate the Dispute

Before deciding to escalate the dispute, it's important to recognize the signs that further negotiation may not lead to a resolution. Escalating the dispute should be a last resort after attempts at direct resolution have failed.

Here's when escalation might be necessary:

- **Unresponsive Publisher**: If the publisher fails to respond to your requests for clarification or resolution after multiple follow-ups, it may indicate that they are unwilling or unable to resolve the issue voluntarily.

- **Inadequate Resolution Offers**: If the publisher offers a resolution that is clearly inadequate or doesn't address the core issue, and they refuse to negotiate further, it may be time to escalate.

- **Repeated Issues**: If the same financial discrepancies or disputes continue to arise over time, despite previous attempts to resolve them, this could suggest a systemic problem that requires more formal intervention.

- **Contract Violations**: If the publisher is in breach of your contract and refuses to comply with its terms, escalating may be necessary to enforce your rights.

Example: After several months of communication and negotiation, the publisher continues to underpay royalties and is unresponsive to your requests for corrections. You decide that escalation is the only remaining option to recover what you're owed.

Tip: Keep detailed records of all communications and attempts to resolve the issue before deciding to escalate. This documentation will be crucial if the dispute moves into mediation, arbitration, or legal proceedings.

2. Mediation: A Collaborative Approach

Mediation is often the first step in escalating a dispute. Mediation involves bringing in a neutral third-party mediator to facilitate discussions between you and the publisher. The goal of mediation is to help both parties reach a mutually acceptable resolution without going to court.

Here's what to expect from mediation:

- **Voluntary Participation**: Both you and the publisher must agree to participate in mediation. It is a voluntary process, and the mediator helps guide the conversation without imposing a solution.

- **Neutral Mediator**: A professional mediator acts as a neutral party to help both sides communicate more effectively and explore potential solutions. The mediator doesn't take sides or make decisions, but rather facilitates the negotiation.

- **Informal Process**: Mediation is less formal than arbitration or litigation and can be quicker and less expensive. It allows both parties to discuss their concerns in a more collaborative and flexible environment.

- **Non-Binding**: Mediation is typically non-binding, meaning that neither party is legally required to accept the outcome. However, if both parties agree to a resolution, a written settlement agreement can be created.

Example: You and the publisher agree to mediation after several unsuccessful attempts to resolve a royalty discrepancy. With the help of a mediator, you both reach a compromise where the publisher agrees to pay part of the amount owed now and the rest in future royalties.

Tip: Mediation is often a good option if you want to maintain a positive working relationship with your publisher while resolving the issue. It allows for a more amicable discussion and often leads to quicker resolutions.

3. Arbitration: A Binding Resolution

If mediation doesn't lead to a resolution, or if the dispute is more serious, arbitration may be the next step. Arbitration involves presenting your case to an arbitrator or arbitration panel, who will make a binding decision on the dispute. Unlike mediation, arbitration results in a legally enforceable outcome.

Here's how arbitration works:

- **Binding Decision**: The arbitrator (or panel) listens to both sides of the dispute and then makes a decision that is binding on both parties. This means that once the arbitrator's decision is made, it must be followed, and there is little room for further negotiation.

- **Less Formal than Litigation**: While arbitration is more formal than mediation, it is still less formal than going to court. It usually involves submitting documents and evidence, and there may be a hearing where both parties present their case.

- **Arbitration Clauses**: Some publishing contracts include an arbitration clause, which requires both parties to use arbitration to resolve disputes instead of taking the issue to court. If your contract includes this clause, you may be obligated to resolve disputes through arbitration.

- **Costs and Fees**: Arbitration can be more expensive than mediation but is typically less costly than full legal proceedings. Costs are often shared between the parties unless otherwise agreed.

Example: Your contract includes an arbitration clause, so after failing to resolve the dispute through negotiation, you enter into arbitration. The arbitrator reviews your royalty statements, contract, and communication records before ruling that the publisher must pay the full amount owed, with interest.

Tip: If your contract includes an arbitration clause, familiarize yourself with the specific terms and conditions regarding how disputes will be handled. Arbitration decisions are legally binding, so it's important to present your case clearly and thoroughly.

4. Legal Action: Taking the Dispute to Court

If all other avenues fail or the dispute is severe, legal action may be the final option. This involves filing a lawsuit against the publisher for breach of contract or other financial grievances. While litigation can be time-consuming and costly, it may be necessary to recover the money you're owed or to enforce the terms of your contract.

What to consider before taking legal action:

- **Consult an Attorney**: Before filing a lawsuit, consult with an attorney who specializes in publishing contracts and intellectual property. They can help you assess whether legal action is the best course and whether you have a strong case.

- **Prepare for a Lengthy Process**: Litigation can take months or even years to resolve, depending on the complexity of the case. Be prepared for a potentially lengthy legal battle, and weigh the costs and benefits of pursuing legal action.

- **Costs of Litigation**: Legal action can be expensive, especially if the case goes to trial. Consider whether the potential recovery is worth the costs of legal fees and court expenses. Many cases are settled before going to trial, but there are no guarantees.

- **Public Nature of Lawsuits**: Unlike mediation and arbitration, which are private processes, litigation is part of the public record. Consider the impact this may have on your reputation and your future relationships in the publishing industry.

Example: After months of failed negotiations and an unsuccessful arbitration, you and your attorney file a lawsuit against the publisher for breach of contract. The case goes to court, where the judge rules in your favor, requiring the publisher to pay damages and legal fees.

Tip: Legal action should always be a last resort. It can be expensive, time-consuming, and may strain your professional relationships. Consider all other options before pursuing litigation.

Escalating a financial dispute to mediation, arbitration, or legal action is sometimes necessary when negotiations fail to resolve the issue. Mediation is a collaborative, non-binding process that can help you find a solution while maintaining a positive relationship with your publisher. Arbitration offers a binding decision that is less formal than litigation but still legally enforceable. If all else fails, legal action may be required to recover what you're owed or enforce your contract. Understanding when and how to escalate a dispute will help you navigate these processes effectively, ensuring that you protect your financial interests while seeking a fair resolution.

Quick Tips and Recap

- **Identify the Source of the Dispute**: Review royalty statements and cross-reference them with your contract to pinpoint discrepancies before initiating any further action.

- **Communicate Clearly**: Approach your publisher with a professional, solution-oriented tone, presenting the facts and requesting clarification.

- **Be Prepared to Negotiate**: Enter negotiations with a clear understanding of the issue, your ideal outcome, and potential compromises. Stay collaborative while standing firm on key issues.

- **Know When to Escalate**: If direct negotiations fail, consider mediation or arbitration to resolve the dispute before turning to legal action.

- **Mediation**: A voluntary and non-binding process that brings in a neutral third party to help you and your publisher reach a mutual agreement.

- **Arbitration**: A more formal, binding resolution where an arbitrator reviews the evidence and makes a legally enforceable decision.

- **Legal Action**: The last resort if all other efforts fail, involving taking the dispute to court to recover what you're owed or enforce your contract.

- **Document Everything**: Keep detailed records of all communications, royalty statements, and agreements throughout the process for reference in case of escalation.

By following these strategies, you can navigate financial disputes effectively, protect your rights as an author, and work towards a fair resolution that preserves your professional relationships.

PART FIVE

Concluding the Relationship

Welcome to Part Five: "Concluding the Relationship," where we gracefully navigate the art of the amicable split. This isn't just about ending contracts; it's about wrapping up with such finesse that even a Hollywood goodbye seems lackluster in comparison. Here, we tie up loose ends with the elegance of a master weaver, ensuring that every party walks away not just satisfied, but ready to pen glowing recommendations or, who knows, perhaps return for a sequel. From rights reversion to contract termination, this section is about closing chapters on a high note, proving that all good things come to an end, but they don't have to end messily. Buckle up, because we're about to turn farewells into art forms, ensuring your professional goodbyes are as smooth and polished as your literary openings.

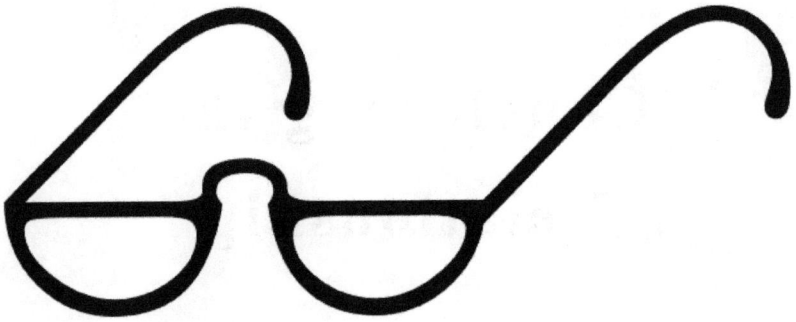

Rights Reversion: Taking Back Control

"Rights reversion is about taking back control of your creative work, enabling you to rejuvenate its presence and explore new opportunities in an ever-evolving market." — CORY DOCTOROW, AUTHOR, BLOGGER, AND JOURNALIST

Welcome to Chapter Twenty-One, "Rights Reversion: Taking Back Control," where we embark on the noble quest of reclaiming what was once yours. Picture this as a dramatic scene in a medieval saga—only instead of storming castles, you're storming the formidable gates of publishing agreements to seize your rightful intellectual property.

In this chapter, we're not just discussing rights reversion; we're planning a strategic coup to win back your creative sovereignty. You'll learn how to wield your contract clauses like a sword, cutting through the red tape to liberate your works from the clutches of expired deals. We'll guide you through the when, why, and how of requesting your rights back, ensuring you do so with the poise of a diplomat and the precision of a surgeon.

Prepare to don your armor (metaphorically speaking, of course) and rally your courage. By the end of this chapter, you'll be ready to march up to the negotiation table with a clear battle plan, ensuring that your creations return home to roost under your banner once more. After all, every author deserves to be the master of their destiny—and their manuscripts.

Understanding Rights Reversion: What It Is and Why It Matters

Rights reversion is a powerful tool for authors who want to regain control of their creative work. Simply put, it's the process by which the rights to a book or other intellectual property revert from the publisher back to the author. This allows you to decide what to do with your work next—whether that's republishing, self-publishing, or exploring new markets.

1. What Is Rights Reversion?

Rights reversion occurs when the rights to your book, which you granted to a publisher, return to you. When you sign a publishing contract, you typically grant the publisher specific rights to produce, distribute, and market your work for a certain period or under specific conditions. Once those conditions are met, or the contract term expires, you can request the reversion of your rights, effectively taking back control over how your book is managed going forward.

Rights reversion can apply to:

- **Print and Digital Editions**: If your publisher no longer prints or sells physical copies, or if digital sales have dropped significantly, you may be able to get those rights back.

- **Subsidiary Rights**: These are rights the publisher may have licensed to third parties (like for audiobooks, translations, or film adaptations). If these rights are not being actively used, you can request their reversion too.

- **Territorial Rights**: If your publisher has rights to distribute your book in certain regions but has failed to do so, you may be able to reclaim the rights for those territories.

Example: Your book has been out of print for years, and the contract states that if a book goes out of print, you can request a reversion of rights. By invoking this clause, you can regain full control over your manuscript and decide whether to republish or explore other formats like audiobooks or digital versions.

2. Why Rights Reversion Matters

Reclaiming your rights is not just a formality—it's a crucial step in extending the life of your work and giving you greater control over its future. Here's why rights reversion matters:

- **Creative Control**: Once the rights revert to you, you're free to update, revise, or republish your book in any format or through any platform you choose. You are no longer tied to the terms of your original contract.

- **Financial Benefits**: Rights reversion can open new revenue streams. You can republish your book through a new publisher or self-publish it, potentially earning higher royalties or reaching new audiences. Additionally, if your publisher didn't pursue certain rights (e.g., audiobooks or translations), you can now explore these options independently.

- **Reintroduce Your Work**: Sometimes, a book's life cycle with a publisher ends prematurely. By reclaiming your rights, you have the opportunity to reintroduce your work to the market, perhaps with a fresh marketing campaign, a new cover, or even updated content.

- **Freedom from Unused Subsidiary Rights**: If your publisher hasn't pursued opportunities for foreign translations, audiobook adaptations, or other subsidiary rights, reversion gives you the chance to take those avenues into your own hands.

Example: After reclaiming the rights to your book, you decide to self-publish a new edition on Amazon Kindle. You add a few updates, refresh the cover design, and launch a digital marketing campaign. This gives your book a second life and potentially opens up new streams of income.

3. The Advantages of Being Proactive

Understanding rights reversion empowers you to be proactive about your career. Waiting for your publisher to take action could mean your book remains stagnant, gathering dust in the backlist with little attention. By actively seeking rights reversion, you can:

- **Seize New Opportunities**: Whether it's self-publishing, partnering with another publisher, or exploring audiobooks and foreign markets, having your rights back gives you the flexibility to act on new opportunities.

- **Maintain Momentum**: Especially in today's fast-paced publishing environment, you want to keep your work relevant. Reversion allows you to refresh your book and stay engaged with your audience.

- **Safeguard Your Legacy**: If you have multiple books or a series, regaining rights to older works ensures that you maintain control over your entire portfolio. This is especially important for authors who want to manage the future of their body of work.

Tip: Even if your book isn't a top seller at the moment, reclaiming your rights gives you the chance to repackage, remarket, and breathe new life into your work. You can relaunch the book with new materials or promote it alongside new releases.

Rights reversion is an essential part of an author's long-term strategy for managing their work. It allows you to take back control of your creative property, explore new markets, and reintroduce your work to readers. Whether your book is out of print, underperforming, or simply at the end of its contract, rights reversion gives you the opportunity to make the most of your work and continue its journey under your control.

When to Request Rights Reversion: Timing and Conditions

Timing is everything when it comes to rights reversion. Knowing when and under what conditions you can request your rights back is essential to regaining control of your work at the right moment. Each publishing contract is different, so it's important to understand the specific terms that govern when your rights can revert and what triggers the reversion process.

1. Common Conditions for Rights Reversion

Most publishing contracts will specify the conditions under which you can request a reversion of rights. These conditions can vary widely, but here are the most common scenarios where you can ask for your rights to revert:

- **Out-of-Print Status**: One of the most common triggers for rights reversion is when a book goes out of print. If your publisher is no longer producing new copies of your book, this typically gives you the right to request the return of your publishing rights. The definition of "out of print" can vary, so make sure your contract specifies what this means (e.g., no longer available in physical bookstores or out of stock for a certain period).

- **Low or No Sales**: Many contracts include a sales threshold clause, which allows you to request rights reversion if sales drop below a certain number over a set period (for example, fewer than 200 copies sold in a year). If your book is no longer generating significant sales, you can often invoke this clause to take your rights back.

- **End of Contract Term**: If your contract has a set expiration date, the rights to your book may revert to you automatically or at your request once the term ends. This is often the case with older contracts that don't have an automatic renewal clause.

- **Digital Availability Only**: In some cases, a book may remain available in digital formats (eBook, audiobook), but the publisher has stopped producing physical copies. If your contract specifies that reversion is possible when physical sales cease, you may be able to reclaim the rights to the print version while the digital rights remain with the publisher.

- **Subsidiary Rights Not Exercised**: If your publisher holds certain subsidiary rights (such as film, foreign translation, or audiobook rights) and hasn't exercised them within a specific time frame, you may have the right to request their reversion. This allows you to explore other opportunities, such as selling those rights independently.

Example: Your book has been out of print for over a year, and your contract specifies that if the book is unavailable for more than six months, you can request rights reversion. You send a formal request to your publisher, citing the out-of-print clause, and ask for the rights to be returned to you.

2. Monitoring Your Book's Performance

To know when to request rights reversion, it's important to keep an eye on your book's performance. This means regularly reviewing sales reports, royalty statements, and the book's availability in both physical and digital formats. If you notice a significant drop in sales or if the book is no longer available in certain channels, this may indicate that it's time to explore reversion.

Here's how to monitor your book's status:

- **Check Royalty Statements**: Regularly review your royalty statements for signs of declining sales or minimal earnings. If sales have fallen below the threshold outlined in your contract, you may be able to request a reversion.

- **Monitor Availability**: Periodically check online retailers and bookstores to see if your book is still available for purchase. If it's difficult to find or only available in limited formats (such as eBook only), this could be a trigger for requesting rights reversion.

- **Communicate with Your Publisher**: If you're unsure about the book's current status, don't hesitate to reach out to your publisher for clarification. Ask about their plans for reprinting or continuing promotion, and inquire about the availability of subsidiary rights like audiobooks or translations.

Example: You notice that your royalty statements show declining sales over the last two years, with fewer than 100 copies sold annually. Your contract specifies that if sales fall below 200 copies in a year, you can request rights reversion. Based on this information, you decide to approach your publisher to initiate the reversion process.

3. Timing Your Request for Maximum Benefit

The timing of your request for rights reversion can be strategic. You want to make sure that reclaiming your rights aligns with your future plans for the book. Here are a few factors to consider when deciding when to request reversion:

- **New Opportunities**: If you're considering republishing the book with another publisher, self-publishing, or releasing it in a new format (e.g., audiobook, foreign translation), it makes sense to request rights reversion as soon as the opportunity presents itself. This ensures you can act quickly and take advantage of new revenue streams.

- **Anniversaries or Special Events**: If your book has an anniversary coming up or is tied to a particular theme or event, reclaiming the rights in time for a new release or promotion can be a smart move. You can use the anniversary or event to relaunch the book and generate buzz.

- **Ending Publisher Support**: If your publisher is no longer actively promoting your book or investing in its success, it may be time to request reversion. This way, you can take over promotion and potentially relaunch the book with a fresh marketing campaign.

Example: You've recently been approached by a foreign publisher interested in translating your book into Spanish. However, your current publisher holds the foreign translation rights but hasn't done anything with them. You decide to request the reversion of those rights so you can move forward with the new opportunity.

4. Understanding the Fine Print

Before requesting rights reversion, make sure you understand the fine print of your contract. Every contract is different, and the specific terms and conditions for reversion will vary. Here are a few key things to look for in your contract:

- **Sales Thresholds**: If your contract includes a sales threshold clause, check the specific number of copies that need to be sold (or not sold) before you can request reversion. Make sure you understand the time frame over which sales are measured (e.g., annually, quarterly).

- **Out-of-Print Clauses**: Review the definition of "out of print" in your contract. Some contracts may define it as no longer available in any format, while others may only apply to physical copies.

- **Subsidiary Rights**: If your publisher holds rights to formats or territories they haven't utilized, check for any clauses that allow you to reclaim those rights after a certain period of inactivity.

- **Automatic Renewal**: Some contracts have automatic renewal clauses that extend the publisher's control over your book for additional terms unless you actively request reversion. Be aware of these clauses so you don't miss an opportunity to reclaim your rights.

Example: Your contract specifies that the book is considered "out of print" if no new copies are printed for a period of six months. However, it also states that the publisher has the right to release a limited number of digital copies to keep the book "in print." Understanding this clause helps you time your request carefully and negotiate for a full reversion of both print and digital rights.

Knowing when to request rights reversion is all about understanding your contract, monitoring your book's performance, and identifying the right moment to take back control. By keeping an eye on sales figures, the book's availability, and any new opportunities for the work, you can time your request for reversion strategically to maximize your future success. Rights reversion is a powerful tool that gives you the flexibility to manage your work on your own terms and unlock new revenue streams as your career progresses.

How to Initiate the Rights Reversion Process: Steps and Strategies

Once you've determined that it's the right time to request rights reversion, the next step is to formally initiate the process with your publisher. The key to success is following a clear, professional approach that aligns with the terms in your contract while negotiating the best possible outcome. This section will guide you through the steps and strategies needed to navigate the reversion process smoothly.

1. Review Your Contract for Reversion Clauses

Before making any formal request, it's critical to thoroughly review your contract for reversion clauses or any terms that specify when and how you can reclaim your rights. Your contract may outline the exact conditions under which reversion is allowed, such as low sales, out-of-print status, or the expiration of a certain term.

Here's what to look for in your contract:

- **Reversion Triggers**: Identify the specific triggers that allow for rights reversion, such as out-of-print status, low sales, or the end of a contract term. These are your starting points for requesting the reversion of your rights.

- **Time Frames**: Check if there are any time frames associated with reversion requests. Some contracts may allow you to request reversion only after a specific period has passed since the book was published or after it has been out of print for a certain number of months.

- **Sales Thresholds**: If your contract includes a sales threshold clause, ensure that you've met the conditions. For example, if the contract allows reversion when annual sales fall below 200 copies, make sure your sales figures meet this criterion.

Example: Your contract states that you can request rights reversion if your book sells fewer than 300 copies annually for two consecutive years. After reviewing your royalty statements, you confirm that your book has met this condition and you're eligible to request reversion.

2. Prepare a Formal Rights Reversion Request

Once you've confirmed that your book meets the criteria for reversion, the next step is to prepare a formal rights reversion request. This request should be clear, professional, and based on the specific terms of your contract.

Here's what to include in your request:

- **Reference Your Contract**: Start by referencing the specific clause or condition in your contract that allows for rights reversion. This shows that your request is legitimate and based on agreed terms.

- **Provide Supporting Evidence**: Include any relevant evidence, such as royalty statements or sales figures, that support your request. For example, if your contract allows for reversion due to low sales, attach the royalty statements that show the decline in sales.

- **Specify the Rights You Want to Revert**: Be clear about which rights you're requesting to revert. This could include print rights, digital rights, foreign rights, or subsidiary rights like audiobooks or film adaptations.

- **Keep the Tone Professional**: Even if you've had frustrations with your publisher, maintain a professional tone throughout your request. Remember that your goal is to reach an amicable agreement and reclaim your rights without conflict.

Example: Subject: Request for Rights Reversion – [Book Title]

Dear [Publisher's Name],

I hope this message finds you well. I am writing to formally request the reversion of rights for my book, [Book Title], as outlined in the reversion clause of our publishing agreement. Specifically, my contract allows for rights reversion if annual sales fall below 300 copies for two consecutive years, a condition that has now been met based on the royalty statements provided by your team.

I am requesting the reversion of all print and digital rights for [Book Title], effective immediately. I have attached copies of the relevant royalty statements and the reversion clause for your reference. Please confirm receipt of this request and let me know the next steps to finalize the reversion process.

Thank you for your time and consideration. I look forward to your response.

Best regards,
[Your Name]

Tip: Keep your communication concise and to the point. Clearly state your request and provide any necessary documentation without overwhelming the recipient with too much information.

3. Negotiate Terms, if Necessary

While many reversion requests proceed smoothly, there may be instances where the publisher wants to negotiate the terms of reversion. For example, they may propose a limited reversion (returning only certain rights) or suggest that you wait until a specific time period has elapsed.

Here's how to handle negotiations:

- **Be Flexible**: If the publisher offers a compromise, consider whether it aligns with your goals. For example, they might propose reverting print rights while retaining digital rights for a limited time. If this works for you, it can be a good compromise.

- **Stand Your Ground**: If the publisher tries to deny your request without a valid reason, refer back to the terms of your contract. Be firm but respectful in asserting your rights, especially if you've met the conditions outlined in the agreement.

- **Consider Partial Reversion**: In some cases, a partial reversion may benefit both parties. For instance, if your publisher has no plans to release a new edition but wants to continue selling digital copies, you might agree to revert the print rights while they retain digital rights for a limited time.

Example: Your publisher agrees to revert print and foreign rights but asks to retain eBook rights for an additional six months due to ongoing digital sales. You agree to this compromise, as it still allows you to move forward with plans for a print re-release while waiting for the eBook rights to revert.

Tip: Always get any negotiated terms in writing. If you agree to a partial or delayed reversion, make sure the publisher provides a formal amendment to the contract that outlines the new terms.

4. Follow Up and Finalize the Reversion

Once your reversion request has been accepted, follow up to ensure that the process is completed smoothly. Make sure all necessary paperwork is finalized and that the publisher provides written confirmation of the rights that have been returned to you.

Here's what to do:

- **Request Written Confirmation**: Ask your publisher for written confirmation of the reversion, including a list of the specific rights that have been reverted and the effective date of the reversion.

- **Amend the Contract**: If necessary, ask for a formal contract amendment that reflects the reversion of rights. This helps protect you legally in case any issues arise later.

- **Update Your Records**: Once the reversion is complete, update your records to reflect that you now own the rights to your book. This will be important if you decide to republish or sell those rights to another party.

- **Keep Communication Open**: Even after reversion, maintaining a positive relationship with your publisher can be beneficial, especially if you plan to work with them again in the future.

Example: After your request is approved, you receive an email from the publisher confirming that the print and digital rights for [Book Title] have been reverted to you, effective immediately. They also send a formal amendment to your contract for your records.

Tip: Make sure that the effective date of reversion is clearly stated in the confirmation. This will help you know when you can begin taking action with your reverted rights, such as self-publishing or approaching new publishers.

Initiating the rights reversion process requires a careful review of your contract, clear communication, and sometimes negotiation. By following these steps, you can successfully reclaim control over your work and prepare for the next phase of its life. Whether you plan to republish, self-publish, or explore new opportunities with your reverted rights, initiating reversion with professionalism and clarity will ensure a smooth transition back into your creative control.

Maximizing the Potential of Reverted Rights: Republish, Self-Publish, and Beyond

Once you've successfully reclaimed the rights to your book, it's time to explore the new opportunities that come with having full creative control again. Maximizing the potential of your reverted rights can breathe new life into your work, allowing you to republish, self-publish, or explore alternative formats and markets that may not have been accessible before. This section will guide you through the various ways you can leverage your reverted rights to open new revenue streams and expand your audience.

1. Republish with a New Publisher

One of the most straightforward options after reclaiming your rights is to find a new publisher interested in re-releasing your book. This can be especially appealing if your book has continued relevance, or if you feel another publisher might be better suited to promote and market your work.

Here's how to approach republishing:

- **Revise and Update**: Consider revising or updating the content of your book before seeking a new publisher. Adding fresh material, updating outdated references, or even creating a new cover can make your book more appealing to a new audience.

411

- **Target Specialized Publishers**: If your original publisher was broad-market, you might consider approaching smaller, more specialized publishers who focus on your book's genre or subject matter. This can help you reach a more targeted and engaged audience.

- **Use Sales and Reviews**: If your book had decent sales or strong reviews in its initial release, use those as selling points when pitching to new publishers. Highlight any awards, endorsements, or media coverage the book received.

Example: After reclaiming the rights to your mystery novel, you update the plot with a modern twist and approach a publisher that specializes in crime fiction. They agree to re-release the book, and you secure a new contract with updated terms and better promotional support.

Tip: Before signing with a new publisher, review the contract carefully to ensure it addresses your needs, especially regarding marketing efforts, subsidiary rights, and payment terms.

2. Self-Publish for Greater Control

If you want full control over your book and its distribution, self-publishing is an excellent option. With platforms like Amazon Kindle Direct Publishing (KDP), IngramSpark, and others, you can easily re-release your book as an eBook, paperback, or even hardcover, without the need for a traditional publisher.

Here's how to succeed with self-publishing:

- **Format for Multiple Platforms**: Prepare your book for different formats, including eBooks, print-on-demand paperbacks, and even audiobooks. This will allow you to reach a wider audience across multiple platforms.

- **Create a New Marketing Strategy**: Self-publishing requires you to take charge of your own marketing. Develop a solid promotional plan, including social media campaigns, email marketing, and collaborations with influencers or book bloggers. Consider using services like Amazon Ads or Facebook Ads to target your ideal readership.

- **Update the Cover and Blurb**: A refreshed cover design and a catchy new blurb can reinvigorate interest in your book. Investing in professional cover design and editing services can help your book stand out in a competitive self-publishing marketplace.

Example: You self-publish your book on Amazon KDP, offering it in both eBook and paperback formats. By creating an engaging marketing campaign and running targeted ads, your book quickly gains traction, and you enjoy the higher royalty rates that self-publishing offers.

Tip: Self-publishing platforms like Amazon KDP and IngramSpark allow for wide distribution, but be sure to read the fine print regarding exclusivity clauses. For example, if you enroll your eBook in Amazon's KDP Select program, it must remain exclusive to Amazon for a set period.

3. Explore New Formats: Audiobooks, Foreign Translations, and More

Reverting rights allows you to explore new formats and markets that may not have been part of your original publishing contract. This is particularly valuable if your original publisher didn't pursue these options or if new opportunities have emerged since the book's initial release.

Here are some formats to consider:

- **Audiobooks**: The audiobook market is growing rapidly, and creating an audiobook version of your book can introduce your work to a whole new audience. Platforms like Audible's ACX allow you to produce and distribute audiobooks easily, whether you narrate the book yourself or hire a professional narrator.

- **Foreign Translations**: If your book has international appeal, consider translating it into other languages. You can sell the foreign language rights to international publishers or use platforms like Babelcube or PublishDrive to arrange translations and self-publish in foreign markets.

- **Special Editions**: Releasing a special edition of your book—such as a hardcover collector's version, an illustrated edition, or a limited signed print run—can help generate buzz and reach collectors or die-hard fans of your genre.

Example: After reclaiming your rights, you produce an audiobook version of your book through Audible's ACX platform. The audiobook attracts a new audience of listeners, and the additional revenue from audiobook sales significantly boosts your overall earnings.

Tip: Research your options for audiobook production and foreign translations carefully. Hiring professionals to handle the narration or translation will ensure that the quality of your book remains high across all formats.

4. Leverage Subsidiary Rights: Film, TV, and Merchandising Opportunities

Once your rights have reverted, you can also explore subsidiary rights, which can unlock significant additional revenue streams. Subsidiary rights include options like film or TV adaptations, merchandise deals, or even licensing your book for graphic novels or interactive content.

Here's how to pursue subsidiary rights:

- **Film and TV Adaptations**: If your book has strong visual storytelling potential, consider pitching it to production companies or literary agents who specialize in selling film and TV rights. Platforms like Coverfly or Stage 32 offer opportunities to connect with industry professionals looking for new material.

- **Merchandising**: If your book has a strong fan base or memorable characters, you can explore merchandising options. This could include anything from selling branded merchandise (e.g., T-shirts, mugs, posters) to licensing your characters for games or toys.

- **Graphic Novels and Interactive Content**: Graphic novels are increasingly popular, and your book might lend itself to visual storytelling. Consider partnering with an illustrator or working with a publisher that specializes in graphic novels. Additionally, interactive books or apps are growing in popularity, and your book could be adapted for digital storytelling formats.

Example: After regaining the rights to your fantasy series, you pitch the idea to a film production company, which shows interest in optioning the rights for a TV series adaptation. Additionally, you collaborate with an illustrator to release a graphic novel version of your book, further expanding your audience.

Tip: When pursuing subsidiary rights, consider working with a literary agent or entertainment attorney to navigate the complexities of contracts and negotiations, especially when dealing with film, TV, or merchandising deals.

Maximizing the potential of reverted rights opens up exciting opportunities to give your book a new life. Whether you choose to republish with a new publisher, self-publish for greater control, or explore subsidiary rights like audiobooks and film adaptations, reclaiming your rights gives you the freedom to expand your creative reach. By strategically planning your next steps, you can tap into new revenue streams, reach new audiences, and take your book on an entirely new journey.

Quick Tips and Recap

- **Understand Your Contract**: Before requesting reversion, carefully review your contract for specific reversion clauses, sales thresholds, and time frames.

- **Monitor Sales and Availability**: Keep an eye on your royalty statements and the availability of your book in various formats to know when it's time to request reversion.

- **Prepare a Formal Reversion Request**: Reference your contract, provide supporting evidence, and clearly state which rights you are requesting to revert in your formal request.

- **Negotiate, if Necessary**: Be open to negotiating partial reversion or specific terms, but always ensure any agreements are confirmed in writing.

- **Explore Republishing**: Once your rights are reverted, consider revising your book and approaching new publishers or specialized markets for a fresh release.

- **Self-Publish for Control**: If you want full control over your book's future, use platforms like Amazon KDP to self-publish, maximizing your royalties and creative decisions.

- **Explore New Formats**: Use reverted rights to tap into new markets like audiobooks, foreign translations, graphic novels, or special editions.

- **Leverage Subsidiary Rights**: Pitch your book for film and TV adaptations, or explore merchandising opportunities to extend the reach and profitability of your work.

By strategically managing your reverted rights, you can breathe new life into your book, unlock additional revenue streams, and take full control of your creative property.

Termination of Contract: Ending Your Agreement

"Termination of a contract should be approached with the same careful consideration as its inception, ensuring that ending an agreement is as respectful and strategic as its formation." — HENRY MINTZBERG, MANAGEMENT EXPERT AND PROFESSOR

Welcome to Chapter Twenty-Two, "Termination of Contract: Ending Your Agreement," where we learn the art of the elegant exit. Think of it as the graceful finale of a well-choreographed ballet, rather than a door-slamming soap opera breakup. Here, ending a contract becomes less about cutting ties and more about tying up loose ends with style and professionalism.

This isn't just about saying goodbye; it's about ensuring the goodbye is as beneficial and as amicable as possible. We'll navigate through the legal labyrinths and emotional minefields to help you part ways without drama, ensuring that your professional reputation remains as immaculate as your prose. You'll learn how to identify the right time to wave adieu, how to negotiate the terms of your departure, and how to exit stage left leaving applause in your wake, not debris.

So, dust off your negotiating hat and straighten your bow tie. It's time to close this chapter of your contractual relationship with the panache of a seasoned author penning the perfect ending to a beloved novel.

Recognizing When It's Time to End the Contract

Deciding to end a publishing contract can be a difficult and emotional choice. However, recognizing when it's time to part ways with your publisher can be crucial for your career and creative control. This section will help you assess whether it's the right time to terminate your agreement, offering key signs and considerations that indicate it may be time to move on.

1. Poor Sales and Lack of Promotion

One of the most common reasons authors consider terminating a contract is poor sales, especially when coupled with a lack of promotional support from the publisher. If your book isn't selling as expected and the publisher has done little to market or promote it, you may find yourself questioning the value of staying under contract.

Here's how to evaluate this situation:

- **Check the Publisher's Commitment**: Review your contract and communications with the publisher to assess how much marketing or promotional effort was promised versus how much has been delivered. If they have failed to meet these commitments, it might be time to consider your options.

- **Assess Sales Trends**: If your book is underperforming despite its potential, and the publisher seems to have given up on pushing sales, you may want to explore other avenues that offer more active promotion and support.

- **Lack of Communication**: If your publisher isn't communicating with you about plans for future marketing efforts or new strategies to boost sales, it may be a red flag that they're no longer invested in your success.

Example: Your book was released a year ago, but despite strong initial reviews, sales have been disappointing. You've repeatedly reached out to the publisher for marketing support or promotional campaigns, but their responses have been lukewarm or nonexistent. This could be a signal that it's time to move on.

Tip: While poor sales alone may not be a reason to terminate, it's important to weigh whether the lack of promotion or effort from the publisher is holding your career back.

2. Unmet Expectations and Contract Violations

Another clear sign that it may be time to end your contract is when your publisher consistently fails to meet the terms of the agreement. This could include anything from late royalty payments to not fulfilling marketing or distribution promises. If the publisher is not holding up their end of the bargain, you may have grounds to terminate the contract.

Common issues to look out for:

- **Breach of Contract**: If your publisher is in breach of specific contractual obligations—such as failure to pay royalties on time, underreporting sales, or not delivering on promised marketing support—you may have legal grounds to terminate the contract.

- **Lack of Transparency**: If the publisher is not providing you with royalty statements, sales reports, or clear communication about the status of your book, it's a red flag that they may not be managing your work properly.

- **Failure to Distribute**: If your book isn't available in key markets, either in print or digital formats, despite promises made in the contract, this could be another sign that the publisher isn't fulfilling their obligations.

Example: Your contract states that you will receive quarterly royalty statements, but it's been over six months since your last report. Despite multiple inquiries, your publisher has not responded or provided the required documentation. This could be considered a breach of contract and a valid reason to seek termination.

Tip: If you believe your publisher is in breach of contract, document all communications and missed obligations. This will help you if the issue escalates or if you need legal advice.

3. Creative Differences or Loss of Trust

Sometimes, a relationship with a publisher can deteriorate due to creative differences or a loss of trust. If you and your publisher no longer see eye to eye on how your work should be presented, marketed, or developed, it can lead to frustration and dissatisfaction. In cases where these differences are irreconcilable, it may be in your best interest to end the contract.

Signs of creative incompatibility:

- **Lack of Editorial Support**: If your publisher isn't providing the level of editorial support you need or is pushing for changes you strongly disagree with, this can create friction and lead to a strained relationship.

- **Disagreements on Direction**: If your vision for your book or career doesn't align with the publisher's strategy or goals, it may become difficult to work together. For example, if they want to take your work in a commercial direction that you're uncomfortable with, or if they are unwilling to explore new avenues for your book, this can stifle your creativity.

- **Loss of Trust**: If you feel that the publisher is not transparent, reliable, or communicative, it can erode the trust needed for a successful partnership. A breakdown in communication or trust can be a significant factor in deciding to part ways.

Example: Your publisher insists on making significant changes to your manuscript that go against your creative vision. After multiple discussions, it's clear that you're not on the same page about the direction of your book. This creative disconnect might indicate that it's time to explore other publishing options.

Tip: Creative differences can often be resolved through open communication. However, if the relationship has soured to the point of affecting your work's quality or your peace of mind, termination may be the best course of action.

4. Out-of-Print Status or End of Contract Term

In some cases, a contract naturally reaches its end when the book goes out of print or when the contract term expires. If your book has gone out of print, or if the contract's initial term is ending, it may be an opportunity to reassess your relationship with the publisher and decide if it's time to move on.

When this situation arises:

- **Out-of-Print**: If your book is no longer being actively printed or distributed, most contracts will allow you to request rights reversion. This can be a good time to terminate the contract and explore new opportunities, such as self-publishing or signing with a new publisher.

- **End of Term**: If your contract has a defined term (e.g., five years), and that term is nearing its end, you can evaluate whether the publisher has met your expectations. If not, this could be a natural exit point where both parties agree to part ways without further complications.

Example: Your contract with a publisher was for a five-year term, which is now coming to an end. Sales have slowed down, and your book is no longer available in print. Rather than renewing the contract, you decide it's a good time to regain control of your rights and explore new publishing options.

Tip: If you're nearing the end of your contract term, start thinking ahead about what you want to do with your book next. This is an opportunity to negotiate new terms or take your work in a different direction.

Recognizing when it's time to end a contract is essential for maintaining control over your career and creative vision. Whether it's due to poor sales, unmet expectations, creative differences, or the natural conclusion of your agreement, understanding the signs will help you make a confident decision to move on. By addressing the issue with professionalism and foresight, you can exit gracefully and set yourself up for future success.

Understanding Termination Clauses: Key Contract Terms

Before you can terminate a publishing contract, it's crucial to understand the termination clauses and key terms that are typically outlined in these agreements. Termination clauses dictate the conditions under which you or the publisher can legally end the contract, so knowing your rights and obligations will help you navigate the process with confidence.

This section will walk you through the most common termination clauses and how they can be used to end your agreement amicably and legally.

1. Breach of Contract Clauses

One of the most common grounds for terminating a publishing contract is when one party breaches the agreement. A breach occurs when the publisher or the author fails to fulfill their contractual obligations, which can include issues like failure to meet deadlines, not paying royalties on time, or failing to adequately promote the book.

Here's how to approach breach of contract clauses:

- **Material Breach**: This is a significant failure to perform duties outlined in the contract. If a publisher commits a material breach, such as failing to pay royalties or failing to distribute your book, you may have grounds to terminate the contract. In many cases, the contract will require that you provide the publisher with written notice of the breach and give them a specific period (often 30 to 60 days) to rectify the issue.

- **Repeated Minor Breaches**: While minor breaches alone might not justify termination, repeated minor breaches (such as frequent late payments) can accumulate into a larger problem. Document these issues and reference them when discussing termination with your publisher.

Example: Your publisher has failed to provide royalty statements for the last two quarters, a clear breach of the contract's terms. After sending a formal notice and giving them 60 days to correct the issue, they still have not complied. At this point, you may be entitled to terminate the contract.

Tip: Before taking action, review your contract for specific notice requirements. Always give the publisher an opportunity to correct the breach, as this is often a prerequisite for legal termination.

2. Out-of-Print Clauses

Many contracts include out-of-print clauses, which allow for termination if the publisher is no longer actively printing or distributing the book. This is often tied to specific sales figures or availability in key markets. If your book goes out of print, you may be able to request rights reversion and terminate the contract.

Understanding out-of-print clauses:

- **Define Out-of-Print**: Contracts often define "out of print" differently. Some may consider a book out of print if it is no longer available in physical stores, while others may include digital availability as a factor. Make sure you understand how your contract defines this term.

- **Request Reversion**: Once the book is considered out of print, many contracts allow you to request the reversion of rights. This typically initiates the termination process and allows you to take control of your book's future.

Example: Your book hasn't been available in bookstores for over a year, and sales on digital platforms have dropped significantly. According to your contract, this qualifies as "out of print," and you send a formal request to the publisher for rights reversion and contract termination.

Tip: Keep an eye on your book's availability and sales, as this will help you determine when it's time to invoke the out-of-print clause.

3. Mutual Termination Clauses

Some contracts include provisions for mutual termination, which allows both the author and the publisher to agree to end the contract at any time. This type of clause can be especially useful if both parties are dissatisfied or want to move on to other projects without any animosity.

Here's how to approach mutual termination:

- **Open Communication**: If you feel that the relationship with your publisher is no longer beneficial, initiating a discussion about mutual termination can be a respectful and amicable way to end the agreement. Be honest about your concerns and frame the conversation as a mutually beneficial solution.

- **Negotiation of Terms**: Even in mutual termination, there may be financial or legal obligations to settle. Discuss any outstanding royalties, advances, or obligations to ensure that both parties are satisfied with the termination terms.

Example: You and your publisher both acknowledge that your book hasn't performed as well as expected, and the marketing efforts aren't delivering results. You suggest terminating the contract by mutual agreement, allowing both parties to move on without hard feelings.

Tip: Ensure that mutual termination is confirmed in writing, and that any financial or contractual obligations are clearly outlined in the termination agreement.

4. Termination for Convenience

Termination for convenience is a rare but important clause that allows one or both parties to end the contract for any reason, without needing to prove breach or fault. This type of clause provides flexibility but often requires advance notice and may involve penalties or repayment of advances.

Understanding termination for convenience:

- **Advance Notice**: Most termination-for-convenience clauses require that one party provide written notice of intent to terminate the contract, usually 30, 60, or 90 days in advance. This gives the other party time to prepare for the end of the agreement and fulfill any remaining obligations.

- **Penalties or Repayment**: In some cases, terminating for convenience may involve penalties or the repayment of certain financial advances. For example, if your publisher paid you an advance that hasn't yet been earned out, you may be required to repay a portion of that advance upon termination.

Example: After two years under contract, you feel that the partnership with your publisher is no longer aligned with your career goals. Your contract includes a termination-for-convenience clause, allowing you to exit the agreement with 60 days' notice. You decide to exercise this option and prepare a formal termination notice.

Tip: If your contract includes termination for convenience, review the terms carefully to ensure that you understand any financial implications or penalties before initiating termination.

5. Force Majeure Clauses

A force majeure clause allows for the termination of a contract in the event of unforeseen circumstances beyond the control of either party, such as natural disasters, war, or other major disruptions. While rare in publishing, these clauses can be relevant in extreme cases where continuing the contractual obligations is impossible.

Here's what to know about force majeure:

- **Unforeseen Circumstances**: If a force majeure event occurs (e.g., a global pandemic), both parties may be excused from fulfilling their contractual obligations, and the contract may be terminated without penalty.

- **Review the Clause**: Not all contracts will have a force majeure clause, and the language can vary widely. Review the specific terms to understand how and when it applies.

Example: A major event disrupts the supply chain for physical books, and your publisher can no longer fulfill its obligations to distribute and market your book. The force majeure clause in your contract allows for the termination of the agreement without penalty.

Tip: Force majeure clauses are highly specific to the circumstances outlined in the contract. Always consult with legal counsel if you believe this clause may apply.

Understanding termination clauses in your contract is key to ending the agreement legally and protecting your rights as an author. Whether due to a breach of contract, out-of-print status, or mutual agreement, knowing the terms that allow for termination gives you the confidence to navigate the process effectively. By understanding these clauses, you can ensure a smooth and professional exit from your publishing contract, setting yourself up for future success.

Negotiating Your Exit: Strategies for a Smooth Termination

Ending a publishing contract can be a delicate process that requires careful negotiation. The goal is to exit the agreement on favorable terms while maintaining professionalism and protecting your rights. In this section, we'll explore strategies for negotiating a smooth termination, focusing on maintaining positive relationships, managing financial obligations, and securing your creative future.

1. Maintain Professionalism and Open Communication

The key to negotiating a smooth exit is maintaining professionalism throughout the process. Whether you're terminating the contract due to dissatisfaction or mutual agreement, keeping the lines of communication open and respectful will help facilitate a positive outcome.

Here's how to maintain professionalism:

- **Start the Conversation Early**: Don't wait until tensions have escalated to begin discussing termination. If you feel the relationship with your publisher isn't working, start the conversation early to give both parties time to explore options and negotiate an amicable exit.

- **Be Clear About Your Reasons**: When discussing termination, be upfront and honest about your reasons. Whether it's poor sales, unmet expectations, or creative differences, transparency can help prevent misunderstandings and resentment.

- **Focus on Solutions**: Instead of dwelling on the problems, frame the conversation around finding solutions that benefit both parties. This approach can lead to a smoother and more collaborative termination process.

Example: You notice that your book hasn't been performing well, and your publisher hasn't been able to provide the level of promotion you expected. You initiate a conversation with your publisher, explaining your concerns and suggesting that terminating the contract may be the best solution for both sides.

Tip: Always communicate in writing when it comes to official discussions about contract termination. This creates a clear record of your conversations and agreements.

2. Address Financial Obligations

One of the most important aspects of negotiating a contract termination is managing financial obligations. Depending on your contract, there may be financial issues to resolve, such as royalty payments, advances, or the repayment of unearned advances. Addressing these obligations early on will help prevent conflicts down the line.

Here's how to handle financial matters:

- **Review Royalties and Payments**: Before terminating the contract, review all royalty payments, advances, and other financial transactions to ensure that both parties are clear on what's been earned and what's owed. If there are unpaid royalties or advances, negotiate how these will be handled during the termination process.

- **Unearned Advances**: If your advance hasn't been fully earned out, your publisher may ask for a portion of it to be repaid. Be prepared to negotiate how much, if any, of the advance you'll need to return. In some cases, publishers may be willing to write off unearned advances to facilitate a smoother exit.

- **Final Royalty Statements**: Request a final royalty statement that covers all sales and earnings up until the date of termination. This ensures you're fully paid for any outstanding royalties, and both parties can move forward with a clean slate.

Example: Your book has sold fewer copies than anticipated, and your advance hasn't been earned out. During the termination negotiations, you and your publisher agree that a portion of the advance will be waived in exchange for an amicable exit, allowing you to retain your rights without having to repay the full advance.

Tip: Keep all financial discussions transparent and well-documented. Make sure any agreements regarding royalties or advance repayment are included in the termination agreement.

3. Negotiate Rights Reversion and Future Use

When terminating a publishing contract, one of the most important aspects to consider is the reversion of rights. You'll want to ensure that the rights to your work revert to you so that you can republish or explore new opportunities with your book in the future.

Here's how to negotiate rights reversion:

- **Request Full Rights Reversion**: Make sure that the termination agreement clearly states that all rights to your book—print, digital, audio, foreign, and subsidiary rights—will revert to you. This ensures that you retain full control over your work after the contract ends.

- **Negotiate Remaining Obligations**: If your publisher still holds certain rights (such as foreign translation or film adaptation rights), negotiate the timeline for those rights to revert. Be clear about when you will regain control of all subsidiary rights.

- **Clarify Reprint and Inventory Clauses**: If the publisher still has physical copies of your book in inventory, negotiate how these will be handled. Will the publisher be allowed to sell off remaining stock, or will those copies revert to you for resale or personal use? Make sure the agreement specifies what happens to any unsold inventory.

Example: During termination negotiations, you request the full reversion of rights for both the print and digital editions of your book. You also negotiate that any remaining copies in the publisher's warehouse will be sold at a discounted rate, with royalties paid to you on those final sales.

Tip: Carefully review the termination agreement to ensure that all rights are clearly addressed. If certain rights are still tied up, negotiate a timeline for when they will fully revert to you.

4. Plan for a Positive Exit

A successful contract termination doesn't have to mean the end of a professional relationship. If handled well, it can set the stage for future collaboration or at least preserve your reputation within the publishing industry. Always aim to leave on good terms, even if the relationship hasn't been as successful as you'd hoped.

Here's how to plan for a positive exit:

- **Express Gratitude**: Even if things didn't work out as planned, thanking your publisher for their efforts can go a long way in maintaining goodwill. This can be especially important if you want to leave the door open for future projects or partnerships.

- **Maintain Professional Contacts**: Publishing is a small world, and maintaining your professional contacts can benefit you in the long run. Whether it's with your editor, marketing team, or other staff members, keeping those relationships positive can lead to new opportunities.

- **Set Clear Boundaries**: Make sure that both you and the publisher are clear on what happens next. This includes ensuring that all obligations are met, rights are reverted, and the contract is officially terminated.

Example: As you finalize the termination of your contract, you send a thank-you note to your editor, expressing appreciation for their work and support during your time with the publisher. You end the relationship on positive terms, leaving the door open for future collaboration.

Tip: A graceful exit can protect your reputation and open the door for future opportunities. Even if the relationship wasn't ideal, leaving on good terms demonstrates professionalism and foresight.

Negotiating your exit from a publishing contract requires a combination of professionalism, clear communication, and attention to detail. By addressing financial obligations, securing rights reversion, and maintaining a positive relationship with your publisher, you can ensure that your departure is smooth and sets you up for future success. The key is to handle the termination with the same care and professionalism you put into your writing, ensuring that you leave on the best possible terms.

Moving Forward: What Comes After Contract Termination

Terminating a publishing contract can feel like the end of a chapter, but in reality, it's the beginning of a new phase in your writing career. After you've successfully negotiated your exit, it's essential to have a plan in place for what comes next. Whether you choose to republish, self-publish, or explore new formats, managing your creative future is entirely in your hands. This section will explore how to move forward after contract termination and make the most of your regained rights.

1. Regain Control of Your Rights

Once your contract is terminated, one of the most critical steps is to regain full control over your rights. With your publishing rights back in your hands, you're free to decide the next steps for your book. This newfound control allows you to explore different opportunities and ensure your work is managed according to your vision.

Here's what to do:

- **Ensure All Rights Revert to You**: After the termination process, confirm that all rights—print, digital, audiobook, foreign, and subsidiary—are officially reverted to you. This should be clearly outlined in the termination agreement. Keep a record of the formal reversion of rights to protect your legal standing.

- **Reevaluate Your Book's Potential**: With the rights to your book fully restored, you can now reevaluate its potential. Consider whether your book has opportunities for re-release, whether it could reach new audiences in different formats, or whether you might want to develop related works such as sequels or spin-offs.

Example: After terminating your contract, you receive confirmation that all rights to your book, including print and digital formats, have reverted to you. This means you are now free to republish the book or pursue new deals without any restrictions from your former publisher.

Tip: Once you regain your rights, keep a detailed record of your intellectual property, including dates and documentation of the rights reversion. This will help ensure that you maintain control over your work in future endeavors.

2. Consider Republishing or Self-Publishing

With your rights back, one of the first decisions you'll need to make is whether to seek a new publisher or to self-publish. Each option has its own benefits and challenges, so it's essential to weigh them based on your career goals, the current state of the book, and the potential for new markets.

Here's how to approach your options:

- **Seek a New Publisher**: If you still prefer the support of a traditional publisher, you can now shop your book around to other publishing houses. Be sure to update your manuscript if necessary and present it as a fresh opportunity. Highlight any strong sales figures, reviews, or other positive aspects that might appeal to new publishers.

- **Self-Publish for Greater Control**: If you want full control over your book's future, self-publishing can be a great option. Platforms like Amazon Kindle Direct Publishing (KDP) and IngramSpark make it easier than ever to publish your book as both an eBook and a print-on-demand paperback or hardcover. Self-publishing allows you to retain higher royalties, control pricing, and directly manage marketing strategies.

Example: After reclaiming your rights, you decide to self-publish your book on Amazon KDP. You release both eBook and paperback versions and use social media marketing to promote the new edition. You enjoy higher royalties than you received with your traditional publisher, and you have complete control over the book's presentation and marketing.

Tip: If you choose to self-publish, invest in professional services like cover design, formatting, and editing to ensure your book looks polished and professional.

3. Explore New Formats and Markets

Now that you have full control over your book, you can explore formats and markets that may not have been part of the original contract. This opens up opportunities to reach new audiences and potentially generate additional income streams.

Consider the following options:

- **Audiobooks**: The audiobook market continues to grow, and producing an audiobook version of your work can attract a new audience. Platforms like Audible's ACX allow you to produce and distribute audiobooks with ease, and you can choose to narrate the book yourself or hire a professional narrator.

- **Foreign Markets**: If your book has international appeal, consider selling foreign translation rights or self-publishing translated editions in new markets. You can work with freelance translators or use platforms like Babelcube to manage translations and global distribution.

- **Special Editions**: With the rights back in your hands, you can also explore the possibility of releasing special editions of your book, such as collector's editions, illustrated versions, or hardcover print runs.

Example: After self-publishing your book, you decide to create an audiobook version through Audible's ACX platform. By narrating it yourself, you connect with a new audience of audiobook listeners and increase your overall earnings from the book.

Tip: When exploring new formats, focus on quality. Whether it's translating your book, producing an audiobook, or releasing a special edition, make sure the end product reflects the same high standard as the original work.

4. Plan for Future Projects

Terminating a contract doesn't just mark the end of one project—it opens the door for future opportunities. Now that you've regained control of your work, you can plan your next steps with more freedom and creativity. Whether it's developing a new series, writing a sequel, or expanding into other genres, this is your chance to shape the next phase of your career.

Here's how to move forward with future projects:

- **Develop New Works**: With the experience of managing your rights and publishing your book, you're now in a stronger position to develop new works. Consider leveraging your existing fan base to promote future releases and expand your reach in your genre or niche.

- **Negotiate Better Terms in Future Contracts**: If you choose to work with a new publisher in the future, use what you've learned from your previous contract to negotiate better terms. Pay attention to rights clauses, royalty structures, and termination options to ensure you maintain more control over your work.

- **Build a Long-Term Strategy**: Think about your long-term goals as an author. Whether it's writing multiple books, creating a series, or expanding into new formats, having a clear plan will help you stay focused and continue to grow your career.

Example: After successfully self-publishing your reclaimed book, you begin developing a sequel. You use the feedback and insights from your first release to refine your writing and marketing strategies, setting yourself up for even greater success with the new book.

Tip: Keep building your author brand by engaging with your audience on social media, running promotions, and maintaining an active blog or newsletter. This will help you grow a loyal readership and support future projects.

Moving forward after contract termination is a time of opportunity and renewal. With your rights fully in your control, you can explore new ways to publish, expand into different formats and markets, and plan for the future of your writing career. By leveraging the experience gained from your previous contract and being strategic about your next steps, you can create exciting new opportunities and continue to grow as an author. Whether you choose to republish, self-publish, or develop entirely new works, the future is now in your hands.

Quick Tips and Recap

- **Regain Control of Your Rights**: Ensure that all rights—print, digital, audiobook, and subsidiary—are formally reverted to you. Keep documentation for future reference.

- **Consider Republishing or Self-Publishing**: Evaluate whether to seek a new publisher or self-publish to maintain full control and higher royalties.

- **Explore New Formats and Markets**: Expand your book's reach by creating audiobooks, foreign translations, or special editions to tap into new revenue streams.

- **Plan for Future Projects**: Use the termination as a springboard for future work. Develop new books, sequels, or series, and leverage what you've learned for better future contracts.

- **Negotiate Better Contracts**: When entering future publishing agreements, pay close attention to rights clauses and termination options to ensure you retain more control over your work.

- **Keep Relationships Positive**: Maintain professionalism and goodwill during the termination process to leave the door open for future opportunities with your former publisher.

By following these steps, you can move forward confidently after contract termination, with the tools and strategies to take your career to the next level.

Post-Contract Rights Management: Your Rights, Post-Publishing

"Managing your rights post-publishing is crucial for maintaining control over your work's future, ensuring you can continue to benefit from it under changing circumstances." — NAOMI KLEIN, AUTHOR, SOCIAL ACTIVIST, AND FILMMAKER

Welcome to Chapter Twenty-Three, "Post-Contract Rights Management: Your Rights, Post-Publishing," where the end of one adventure marks the beginning of another. Just because the ink has dried on one contract doesn't mean your vigilance should dry up too! Think of this as the after-party for your book's initial release—now it's time to keep an eye on who's spinning your tunes.

In this chapter, we're playing the long game, ensuring that the rights you've worked so hard to protect continue to be respected, used, and compensated for appropriately long after the initial deal has concluded. You'll learn the ins and outs of monitoring your rights like a hawk without crossing into scary stalker territory. From tracking royalties to renegotiating terms for reprints or sequels, we'll arm you with strategies to keep your rights robust and revenue rolling in.

So, put on your detective hat and polish that magnifying glass. It's time to ensure that every use of your work continues to bring in the bucks and the kudos it deserves. Let's make sure that your post-publishing rights journey is as rewarding and hassle-free as the first draft was thrilling to write!

Tracking and Managing Royalties: Ensuring Fair Compensation

Even after your publishing contract has ended, ensuring that you continue to receive fair compensation for your work is critical. Tracking and managing royalties effectively is essential for ensuring you are paid for all sales, reprints, and licensed uses of your book. This section provides strategies for monitoring royalty payments, reviewing royalty statements, and addressing discrepancies to make sure you get what you're owed.

1. Understanding the Royalty System Post-Contract

When your publishing contract ends, your book may continue to generate revenue through ongoing sales, reprints, or licensed formats like audiobooks and foreign translations. Even if you've regained the rights to your book, it's important to ensure that any remaining sales or royalties owed under the original contract are properly tracked and paid.

Here's what to keep in mind:

- **Ongoing Royalties**: Depending on your contract, you may still be entitled to royalties for sales made during the term of the agreement or for any licensed versions that continue to sell, such as foreign editions or audiobooks.

- **Residual Income**: If your publisher still holds inventory of your book, they may continue to sell off remaining stock after your contract ends.

You are entitled to royalties on those sales, even if the contract has been terminated.

Example: Your book is still being sold in some international markets under a foreign licensing agreement that was established before your contract ended. Even though your contract with the publisher has concluded, you are still entitled to royalties from those foreign sales.

Tip: Review the specifics of your contract to understand the timeline for when royalties must be paid and how long you can expect payments after the contract's conclusion. This ensures you don't miss any owed income.

2. Reviewing and Interpreting Royalty Statements

To ensure fair compensation, it's essential to regularly review and understand your royalty statements. Publishers are required to provide detailed reports on sales, royalties, and other income-generating activities related to your book. Here's how to effectively review these statements:

- **Verify Sales Figures**: Cross-check the sales figures reported in your royalty statements with any other data you have, such as reports from distributors, online retailers, or personal sales records. Make sure the numbers align, and look for any discrepancies in sales totals or earnings.

- **Understand Different Royalties**: Your royalty statement may break down earnings by different formats, such as hardcover, paperback, eBook, and audiobook sales. Ensure that you are receiving royalties for all formats, especially if your book has been licensed for multiple versions.

- **Keep a Calendar**: If your contract requires quarterly or bi-annual royalty payments, keep a calendar of when you should expect those payments and statements. Following up promptly when payments are late or missing helps you avoid long-term payment issues.

Example: After receiving a quarterly royalty statement, you notice that the sales numbers for the audiobook version of your book seem lower than expected. You request clarification from the publisher and discover that there was a reporting error, which is later corrected in your next payment.

Tip: If interpreting royalty statements feels overwhelming, consider working with an accountant or financial advisor who has experience with publishing contracts and royalties. They can help you navigate complex statements and ensure you're receiving accurate payments.

3. Addressing Discrepancies and Late Payments

In some cases, you may encounter discrepancies in your royalty statements or experience late payments. When this happens, it's important to address the issue swiftly and professionally to ensure you receive fair compensation.

Here's how to handle these situations:

- **Identify Discrepancies**: If you spot a discrepancy between reported sales and actual sales, gather all the relevant documentation, such as previous royalty statements, sales records, and communications with the publisher. Present this information clearly when you raise the issue.

- **Follow Up on Late Payments**: If a royalty payment is late, don't hesitate to contact the publisher's accounting or rights department to follow up. Reference the payment terms outlined in your contract and ask for an update on when you can expect your payment.

- **Negotiate for Better Terms**: If you encounter recurring issues with royalty payments, you may want to consider renegotiating the terms for future contracts or projects to ensure that royalties are paid in a more timely and transparent manner.

Example: You notice that one of your royalty payments is several weeks late, and after contacting the publisher, you discover that there was a delay in their accounting process. By addressing the issue promptly, you're able to receive the payment before the next royalty period begins.

Tip: Always communicate in writing when addressing payment discrepancies or late royalties. This creates a paper trail that can help protect you if the issue escalates or if legal action becomes necessary.

4. Using Tracking Tools and Resources

To keep better track of your royalties and payments, consider using tracking tools and resources that help you stay organized. From basic spreadsheets to more sophisticated software, these tools can streamline the process of monitoring your income and ensuring you're compensated fairly.

Here are a few options:

- **Spreadsheets**: Create a simple spreadsheet where you can log each royalty payment, sales figures, and any other relevant financial information. This will help you track patterns over time and spot discrepancies more easily.

- **Royalty Tracking Software**: Some authors use specialized royalty tracking software to manage their earnings from different formats and markets. These tools often offer real-time insights into sales data and provide automatic alerts for missing or delayed payments.

- **Hire an Accountant**: If your income from book sales is significant, it may be worth hiring an accountant who specializes in working with authors. They can help you organize your royalties, manage taxes, and ensure that all income is properly tracked.

Example: You use a basic spreadsheet to track your royalties and sales across different platforms (Amazon, Audible, international editions). This allows you to spot inconsistencies more easily and provides a clear record of your total earnings over time.

Tip: Keep digital and physical copies of all royalty statements, contracts, and payment confirmations. Having organized records will make it easier to resolve any disputes and ensure you're receiving the royalties you're owed.

Tracking and managing royalties is essential for ensuring fair compensation for your work post-publishing. By reviewing royalty statements regularly, addressing discrepancies promptly, and using tracking tools to stay organized, you can protect your financial interests and continue to earn from your creative work. Stay vigilant, and you'll be able to maximize your revenue long after the initial contract has ended.

Renegotiating for Reprints, Sequels, and Adaptations

Once your publishing contract has ended and you've regained control of your rights, opportunities for renegotiating terms for reprints, sequels, and adaptations become important avenues for keeping your book relevant and profitable. Whether your book gains renewed popularity or you see potential for expanding its universe, renegotiating new deals can offer fresh revenue streams and creative possibilities. This section explores strategies for approaching publishers, negotiating favorable terms, and capitalizing on your work's potential.

1. Timing Your Renegotiation: When to Approach Publishers

The timing of renegotiations is crucial to securing favorable terms. Ideally, you want to approach publishers or production companies when interest in your book is at its peak, such as after a notable sales surge, critical acclaim, or the release of related projects (like a movie adaptation). Here's how to assess the right time for renegotiation:

- **Renewed Interest**: If your book has experienced a resurgence in popularity—whether through word of mouth, a viral moment on social media, or favorable reviews—this is an ideal time to approach publishers about reprints or special editions.

- **Anniversaries or Milestones**: Consider leveraging anniversaries (e.g., 5-year or 10-year mark) or significant milestones (e.g., bestseller status) as a reason to renegotiate a reprint deal. Publishers are often more open to releasing special or commemorative editions tied to these moments.

- **Expanded Opportunities**: If your book has strong potential for adaptation, such as a sequel, film, or TV series, use that momentum to negotiate a broader deal. This could include new editions of the book, sequel rights, or merchandise opportunities.

Example: Your book's 10th anniversary is approaching, and you've noticed a steady uptick in sales on digital platforms. You approach your former publisher with a proposal to release a special anniversary edition with new cover art, additional content, and an exclusive author's note.

Tip: Stay connected to your audience and monitor sales trends to identify the best moments to initiate negotiations for reprints or adaptations. A well-timed approach can result in better terms and stronger promotional efforts.

2. Negotiating for Reprints and Special Editions

If you decide to pursue reprints or special editions of your book, renegotiating the terms with a publisher can open up new revenue streams. Reprints, anniversary editions, and special releases (such as hardcovers, illustrated editions, or boxed sets) can breathe new life into your book. Here's how to negotiate for the best deal:

- **Royalty Rates and Advances**: Since reprints are often tied to previous sales performance, use that data to negotiate better royalty rates or advance payments. If your book has maintained strong sales or gained new popularity, you have leverage to request higher royalties for the new edition.

- **Creative Control**: Ensure that you retain more creative control over aspects like cover design, marketing strategies, and any new content added to the reprint (e.g., forewords, additional chapters, or bonus material). This helps maintain the integrity of your work while offering something fresh to your audience.

- **Marketing and Promotion**: Negotiate a strong marketing push for the reprint. Make sure the publisher commits to promoting the new edition through traditional media, digital marketing, or special events. The success of a reprint often hinges on the effort invested in promotion.

Example: You negotiate a reprint deal with your publisher for a deluxe hardcover edition of your book, which includes new cover art and a special introduction. As part of the deal, you secure a higher royalty rate and ensure that the publisher will launch a targeted marketing campaign around the release.

Tip: Use any success from the original publication (e.g., awards, positive reviews, or bestseller status) as a bargaining chip in your negotiations. Demonstrating the book's value will help you secure better terms.

3. Developing and Pitching Sequels or Spin-Offs

Sequels and spin-offs offer a natural way to extend the life of your book and its universe, keeping readers engaged and opening up new storytelling possibilities. Here's how to approach developing a sequel or spin-off and pitching it to publishers or producers:

- **Expand on Popular Characters or Themes**: If readers have responded strongly to particular characters, themes, or settings, consider developing a sequel or spin-off that focuses on those elements. This can reinvigorate interest in your work and draw in both returning and new readers.

- **Prepare a Strong Pitch**: When pitching a sequel or spin-off to a publisher, come prepared with a compelling story outline, character arcs, and a clear vision for how the new project expands on the original. Be sure to include any market research or data that supports the demand for a follow-up (e.g., reader reviews, sales figures, or fan engagement).

- **Negotiate Improved Terms**: Since this is a new project, you have the opportunity to negotiate better terms than you had in your original contract. Push for higher royalty rates, a larger advance, and more control over creative decisions, especially if the original book was successful.

Example: After the success of your fantasy novel, readers have been clamoring for more stories from the same world. You develop a spin-off series focusing on a secondary character and pitch it to your publisher. With the success of the original book as leverage, you negotiate higher royalties and more input into the marketing plan for the new series.

Tip: Engage with your readers through social media or fan communities to gauge their interest in sequels or spin-offs. Their enthusiasm can be used to build a case when negotiating with publishers or producers.

4. Negotiating Adaptation Rights: Film, TV, and Beyond

In the world of modern publishing, adaptation rights can be a gold mine. If your book has potential for film, TV, or digital adaptation, renegotiating adaptation rights can significantly boost your book's exposure and revenue. Here's how to negotiate for the best terms when it comes to adaptations:

- **Retain Creative Control**: If possible, negotiate for a degree of creative input into the adaptation process. While you may not be able to oversee every decision, maintaining some involvement ensures that the adaptation remains true to your original vision.

- **Option and Purchase Agreements**: Be mindful of option agreements, which give a producer the exclusive right to purchase the adaptation rights within a set timeframe. When negotiating, ensure that the option period is reasonable (usually 12-18 months), and that the purchase price for the rights is clearly defined.

- **Maximizing Financial Benefits**: Negotiate not only for an upfront payment for the adaptation rights but also for backend participation (a percentage of profits from the film or TV series). Additionally, retain the rights to produce sequels, merchandise, and other spin-offs based on your original work.

Example: A film production company approaches you to option the film rights to your book. You negotiate an upfront payment for the option period, as well as a guaranteed purchase price if the film moves forward. You also ensure you'll receive a percentage of box office profits and retain the right to approve the screenplay.

Tip: Work with an entertainment attorney or literary agent when negotiating adaptation rights. The complexity of these deals requires expert advice to ensure you don't sign away key rights or miss out on valuable financial opportunities.

Renegotiating for reprints, sequels, and adaptations allows you to capitalize on your book's success long after its initial release. By timing your negotiations strategically, preparing strong pitches, and securing favorable terms, you can expand your creative universe and maximize your earnings. Whether you're reissuing your book, developing sequels, or exploring film adaptations, thoughtful negotiation will set you up for continued success.

Exploring New Revenue Streams: Audiobooks, Foreign Markets, and Merchandising

After your publishing contract has ended, there are numerous opportunities to expand your book's reach and tap into new revenue streams. By exploring formats such as audiobooks, foreign language translations, and merchandise, you can breathe new life into your work and continue generating income long after its initial release. This section will guide you through the process of leveraging these opportunities and maximizing the financial potential of your book.

1. Creating and Marketing Audiobooks

Audiobooks are a rapidly growing market, offering a fantastic opportunity to reach a broader audience. Whether your book was previously released as an audiobook or not, creating and marketing a high-quality audio version can help you tap into a new revenue stream. Here's how to explore this format:

- **Self-Produce or License to a Publisher**: You can either license your audiobook rights to a company like Audible, which will produce and distribute the audiobook, or you can self-produce through platforms like Audible's ACX (Audiobook Creation Exchange). Self-producing allows for more control and a higher share of royalties, but it requires an investment in production and narration.

- **Choose a Narrator Wisely**: Whether you're self-producing or working with a publisher, selecting the right narrator is crucial. A great narrator can elevate your story and engage listeners. If your book has multiple points of view or distinct characters, you may want to consider hiring multiple narrators to bring those voices to life.

- **Market Your Audiobook**: Once your audiobook is produced, make sure it receives the promotion it deserves. Leverage social media, newsletters, and partnerships with audiobook reviewers or platforms to build buzz around the release. Consider offering samples or snippets of the audiobook to give potential listeners a taste of the content.

Example: After your book's rights revert to you, you decide to self-produce an audiobook using ACX. You hire a professional narrator, release the audiobook on Audible, and promote it through your social media channels. The audiobook reaches a new audience of listeners who prefer audio formats, and your earnings increase accordingly.

Tip: Audiobook listeners are often different from traditional book readers. Tailor your marketing efforts to reach these audiences by partnering with audiobook influencers or running promotions on audiobook platforms.

2. Expanding into Foreign Markets with Translations

Foreign markets represent a massive opportunity to reach readers in new regions and languages. Translating your book can unlock new revenue streams, especially in markets where certain genres (e.g., romance, mystery, or self-help) are highly popular. Here's how to approach foreign translations:

- **Work with Translation Services or Publishers**: You can either license your foreign rights to a foreign publisher or self-publish translated versions of your book. If you're self-publishing, platforms like Babelcube and PublishDrive offer translation services and international distribution to help you reach foreign readers.

- **Focus on High-Demand Markets**: Do some research to identify which foreign markets might have the highest demand for your genre. Popular markets for certain genres may include Germany, Japan, Brazil, and China. Targeting the right markets ensures that your book finds its ideal audience.

- **Negotiate Licensing Deals**: If you choose to license your foreign rights to a publisher, negotiate favorable terms. Make sure the contract outlines how royalties will be paid and what marketing efforts will be made to promote your book in the foreign market.

Example: After gaining back the rights to your book, you decide to license your foreign rights to a German publisher. The deal includes translation services and distribution in the German market, which opens up a new stream of royalties. With strong sales, the publisher later approaches you for rights to produce a sequel.

Tip: When working with foreign publishers, negotiate to retain certain rights, such as the ability to self-publish digital editions or control merchandising, so you can explore additional revenue opportunities in those regions.

3. Merchandising: Turning Your Book into a Brand

If your book has a dedicated fan base or features memorable characters, themes, or imagery, there may be potential for merchandising. From branded merchandise like clothing and accessories to limited-edition collectibles, turning your book into a brand can create new revenue streams and help build your audience's connection to your work. Here's how to get started:

- **Identify Key Themes or Characters**: Consider what elements of your book resonate most with readers. Are there iconic quotes, characters, or visuals that lend themselves to merchandise? Focus on what could appeal to your audience, whether it's character-driven (e.g., T-shirts with character illustrations) or theme-driven (e.g., mugs or posters featuring famous lines from your book).

- **Partner with Merchandising Companies**: Platforms like Redbubble, Teespring, and Etsy make it easy to create and sell branded merchandise. Alternatively, you can partner with a professional merchandising company to handle production, fulfillment, and distribution for a wider reach and more polished products.

- **Offer Limited Editions or Bundles**: Creating exclusive or limited-edition merchandise can drive demand. Consider offering a bundle that includes signed copies of your book along with a piece of merchandise (like a T-shirt or tote bag) for fans who want to feel like they're part of something special.

Example: After regaining your rights, you partner with an online merchandising platform to create a line of T-shirts and mugs featuring popular quotes from your book. You promote the merchandise through your website and social media, and it becomes a hit with your fan base, generating additional income.

Tip: Keep your merchandising strategy aligned with your brand and audience. Quality and relevance are key to ensuring that your merchandise resonates with fans and generates sales.

4. Licensing Your Work for Games, Apps, or Other Media

Beyond books and merchandise, your intellectual property may have potential in other forms of media, such as mobile games, apps, or interactive experiences. Licensing your book's world, characters, or storylines for these formats can unlock new revenue and help you reach an even broader audience.

- **Pitch Your Work to Game or App Developers**: If your book features rich world-building or strong visual elements, consider approaching game developers or app creators to pitch your story as the basis for a mobile game or interactive app. These developers are always looking for unique content, and adapting a pre-existing book can be appealing.

- **Negotiate Licensing and Creative Control**: When licensing your work for games, apps, or other media, ensure you maintain some degree of creative control to protect the integrity of your story. Negotiate terms that provide you with ongoing royalties or profit participation, as these formats can generate significant long-term revenue.

- **Expand into Interactive Storytelling**: Platforms like Episode or Choices allow authors to create interactive, choose-your-own-adventure-style stories. If your book lends itself to this format, consider adapting it for one of these platforms to engage readers in a new way.

Example: A mobile game developer approaches you to license your fantasy novel for a game adaptation. You negotiate a licensing agreement that includes a share of the profits and some creative oversight to ensure that the game remains faithful to the original story. The game becomes a hit, boosting both your book's sales and your income from the game.

Tip: When exploring multimedia adaptations, work with an agent or attorney who specializes in intellectual property to ensure your rights are protected, and that you receive fair compensation for licensing your work.

Exploring new revenue streams through audiobooks, foreign markets, and merchandising is a smart way to extend the life and profitability of your book. By branching out into different formats, licensing deals, and creative products, you can reach new audiences and maximize the financial potential of your work. Whether you're creating an audiobook, expanding internationally, or turning your book into a brand, these strategies will help you build a lasting legacy for your writing.

Protecting Your Intellectual Property: Monitoring for Infringement and Misuse

As an author, your intellectual property (IP) is your most valuable asset. Once your publishing contract has ended, it's critical to take proactive steps to protect your rights and ensure that your work isn't being used or distributed without your permission. In this section, we'll cover how to monitor for infringement, what to do if you discover unauthorized use of your work, and the steps you can take to enforce your rights and protect your creative property.

1. Regularly Monitor Online Platforms and Marketplaces

The internet is a vast and accessible space, which makes it both an opportunity and a challenge for authors. Your work can reach global audiences, but it can also be more vulnerable to piracy and unauthorized distribution. Keeping a close eye on where your work appears is essential for protecting your intellectual property.

Here's how to monitor online platforms:

- **Search for Your Work**: Conduct regular searches for your book's title, key phrases, and your author name on popular platforms like Amazon, eBay, Google, and piracy websites. Pay attention to listings for unauthorized eBook downloads, counterfeit physical copies, or unlicensed adaptations.

- **Use Google Alerts**: Set up Google Alerts for your book title and author name to receive notifications when your work is mentioned online. This is an easy way to keep tabs on any unauthorized use without having to manually search for it constantly.

- **Monitor Social Media**: Keep an eye on social media platforms where users may be sharing pirated or unauthorized versions of your book. If you come across any illegal uploads or links to pirated copies, take action to have them removed.

Example: You notice that your book is being offered as a free PDF download on an unauthorized website. By setting up a Google Alert for your book title, you quickly receive a notification and can take action before the file spreads widely.

Tip: While monitoring for piracy is important, remember that some uses of your work (like brief quotations in reviews) fall under "fair use" and may be permissible. Focus on stopping truly harmful infringements like full-text copies being distributed without your permission.

2. Take Immediate Action Against Piracy and Unauthorized Use

If you discover that your work is being distributed without your consent, it's crucial to act quickly to minimize the damage and prevent further infringement. There are several legal and practical steps you can take to address unauthorized use of your intellectual property.

Here's what to do if you find your work being misused:

- **Send a DMCA Takedown Notice**: The **Digital Millennium Copyright Act (DMCA)** allows you to request that websites hosting unauthorized content remove your work. Send a DMCA takedown notice to the site's administrator or platform (such as Amazon or Google) outlining the infringement and requesting immediate removal of the content. Most platforms have clear instructions for submitting these requests.

- **Reach Out to the Infringer Directly**: In some cases, the person distributing your work may not realize they are infringing on your rights. A polite but firm email requesting that they take down the unauthorized content can often resolve the issue without needing to escalate to legal action.

- **Consult a Lawyer**: If you're dealing with a serious case of infringement—such as a large-scale piracy operation or someone profiting from unauthorized sales of your work—consult an intellectual property attorney. They can help you take legal action, including sending cease-and-desist letters or pursuing compensation.

Example: You discover a website selling counterfeit physical copies of your book. After confirming the unauthorized sale, you send a DMCA takedown notice to the website's hosting provider, which results in the removal of the illegal listing.

Tip: Keep copies of all correspondence and evidence of the infringement, including screenshots, URLs, and communication records. This documentation will be useful if you need to escalate the issue legally.

3. Register Trademarks for Key Elements of Your Work

In addition to copyrights, consider protecting key elements of your book (such as titles, character names, or logos) by registering them as trademarks. Trademarks offer an additional layer of protection, especially if you plan to expand your book's brand through sequels, spin-offs, merchandise, or adaptations.

Here's how to use trademarks effectively:

- **Identify Protectable Elements**: Consider what aspects of your book's branding are unique and could be valuable as trademarks. For example, if your book has a distinctive title, series name, or logo that you plan to use in future projects or merchandise, trademarking these elements can prevent others from using them.

- **File a Trademark Application**: In the United States, you can file for trademark protection through the United States Patent and Trademark Office (USPTO). The process involves submitting an application, paying a fee, and providing examples of how the mark is being used in commerce (e.g., book covers, websites, or merchandise).

- **Monitor for Infringement**: Once your trademark is registered, you'll need to monitor its use to ensure no one else is profiting from your brand. If someone uses your trademarked elements without permission, you can take legal action to stop them.

Example: You trademark the title of your book series and its distinctive logo, which you plan to use on merchandise. A few years later, you discover another author using a similar title for their series, and you're able to send a cease-and-desist letter to stop them from infringing on your trademark.

Tip: Trademarks are especially useful if you plan to build a brand around your book, such as creating a series or launching related merchandise. Consult with a trademark attorney to ensure you're filing your application correctly and protecting your brand effectively.

4. Use Licensing Agreements to Control the Use of Your Work

One way to prevent unauthorized use of your work is by creating clear licensing agreements with any party that wants to use your intellectual property. Licensing your work can open new revenue streams, but it's essential to have a well-defined agreement that outlines how, when, and where your work can be used.

Here's what to include in a licensing agreement:

- **Scope of Use**: Clearly define the scope of the license, including what rights the licensee has (e.g., the right to distribute, reproduce, or adapt the work). Specify whether the license is exclusive or non-exclusive, and outline the duration of the agreement.

- **Royalties and Payments**: Include details about how you will be compensated for the use of your work. This could involve royalties, flat fees, or profit-sharing arrangements. Make sure the terms are clearly defined to avoid disputes.

- **Creative Control**: Retain control over how your work is adapted or used, especially if the license involves creating derivative works (like a film adaptation). Include clauses that allow you to approve significant changes or adaptations to protect the integrity of your original work.

Example: A publisher in a foreign market wants to license the rights to translate and distribute your book. You create a licensing agreement that specifies the scope of their rights, the royalties they will pay you, and your approval over significant changes to the content.

Tip: Always consult an intellectual property attorney when drafting licensing agreements to ensure that your rights are protected and that the agreement is enforceable.

Protecting your intellectual property requires ongoing vigilance and proactive action, especially after your publishing contract has ended. By regularly monitoring for unauthorized use, taking swift action against infringement, registering trademarks, and using clear licensing agreements, you can safeguard your creative work and continue to profit from your intellectual property. Maintaining control over your rights will ensure that your book's success and legacy are preserved for years to come.

Quick Tips and Recap

- **Set Up Monitoring Systems**: Use tools like Google Alerts to regularly monitor online platforms and marketplaces for unauthorized use of your work.

- **Take Action Quickly**: If you discover infringement, send a DMCA takedown notice or contact the infringer directly to resolve the issue before it spreads.

- **Document Everything**: Keep detailed records of any infringement, correspondence, and actions taken to protect your work in case legal action is needed.

- **Register Trademarks**: Consider trademarking key elements like book titles, series names, or logos to protect your brand and prevent unauthorized use.

- **Use Licensing Agreements**: When licensing your work, create clear agreements that define the scope of use, royalties, and your level of creative control.

- **Consult Professionals**: Work with intellectual property attorneys to help you draft strong contracts, register trademarks, and pursue legal action if necessary.

By actively monitoring and protecting your intellectual property, you can ensure that your creative work remains safe and profitable in the long term.

Renegotiating Contracts: Revisiting Terms for Future Success

"Renegotiating contracts is a strategic opportunity to ensure that the terms continue to serve your business interests and adapt to new challenges and opportunities." — JACK WELCH, FORMER CEO OF GENERAL ELECTRIC

Welcome to Chapter Twenty-Four, "Renegotiating Contracts: Revisiting Terms for Future Success," where we brush off the old contracts and give them a sprightly new spin. Think of it as giving your aging car a fine tune-up—because even the most solid agreements can benefit from a little tweaking to keep them purring along the highway of your career.

This chapter is all about the art of the deal—the sequel. We'll guide you through the when, why, and how of contract renegotiations, ensuring you approach the negotiation table armed with a clear vision, a sharp pencil, and a firmer handshake. Whether it's because the market has shifted, your career trajectory has skyrocketed, or simply because it's Tuesday, you'll learn how to advocate for terms that better suit the current you, not the you from five years ago.

So, roll up your sleeves and ready those negotiation muscles, because we're about to dive into the nitty-gritty of ensuring your contracts are keeping pace with your ambitions. It's time to align your agreements with your ascending star—let's make sure your contracts are as dynamic and evolving as your career!

Identifying When to Renegotiate: Key Triggers and Timing

Contract renegotiations are a natural part of an author's career, especially as circumstances change, markets shift, and your work gains traction. Knowing the right time to revisit and renegotiate your contract is crucial to maximizing your potential and ensuring your agreement reflects your current value. In this section, we'll explore the key triggers that signal it's time for renegotiation and how to approach the timing strategically.

1. Career Milestones and Success Indicators

One of the clearest indicators that it's time to renegotiate your contract is when you hit significant career milestones or achieve notable success. This is the point where your leverage is at its highest, and you can advocate for better terms that reflect your growing stature in the literary world.

Here's what to look for:

- **Bestseller Status**: If your book hits a major bestseller list (such as the New York Times or Amazon's top-selling titles), this is a prime opportunity to renegotiate for better royalties, advances, and marketing commitments. Bestseller status demonstrates to your publisher that your book is in high demand, giving you leverage to ask for more favorable terms.

- **Sales Growth**: Consistent growth in book sales over time is another key trigger. If your book is performing well in the marketplace, your original royalty rate may no longer reflect the demand for your work. In this case, it's time to renegotiate for a higher percentage of profits.

- **Award Recognition**: Winning literary awards or receiving significant acclaim can also provide the perfect moment to renegotiate your contract. This recognition increases your marketability, and your publisher may be willing to offer better terms to retain your next project.

Example: After your debut novel becomes a bestseller, you approach your publisher to renegotiate for a higher royalty rate and a larger marketing budget for future works. Your newfound success gives you leverage to secure these improved terms.

Tip: Keep track of your book's performance, awards, and reader feedback. Having this data at your fingertips will help you build a strong case when you begin renegotiation talks.

2. Shifts in the Market or Industry Trends

The publishing landscape is constantly evolving, and market shifts can impact your contract's relevance. Whether it's the rise of new distribution platforms, changes in reader behavior, or technological advancements (like the growing popularity of audiobooks), these external factors can signal the need for contract updates.

Here's how to spot market-based triggers:

- **New Distribution Models**: If your contract doesn't account for newer formats like audiobooks or digital subscriptions, it's time to renegotiate. These formats are booming, and your contract should reflect your ability to capitalize on these trends.

- **Genre Popularity**: If your genre experiences a sudden surge in popularity (such as the growing demand for dystopian fiction or true crime), this can be a reason to revisit your terms. Publishers may be more willing to invest in marketing and promotion when they see a demand for your genre.

- **Changes in Publishing Platforms**: The rise of self-publishing and platforms like Amazon Kindle Direct Publishing (KDP) has shifted the power dynamics between authors and traditional publishers. If you're finding success with self-publishing or are considering hybrid publishing models, you can leverage this to renegotiate more favorable terms.

Example: Your book, a sci-fi thriller, becomes part of a wave of interest in the genre due to the success of a popular TV show. You use this momentum to renegotiate your contract, asking for higher royalties on digital and audiobook sales, which are now key revenue streams.

Tip: Stay informed about market trends and the performance of your genre. If you see a shift that impacts your book's potential, use it as a reason to start renegotiation talks.

3. End of Contract Term or Rights Reversion Opportunities

Another natural point for renegotiation is when your contract's term is approaching its end, or when specific clauses—such as rights reversion—are about to take effect. This is your chance to reassess the entire agreement and decide whether you want to extend the relationship or seek new opportunities.

Here's what to consider:

- **Contract Expiration**: Most publishing contracts have a set term, after which you and your publisher can renegotiate or part ways. When your contract is nearing its expiration, evaluate whether the terms still serve your career goals. If not, this is the ideal time to push for better terms or explore other publishers.

- **Rights Reversion**: If the rights to your book are about to revert to you, such as when a book goes out of print or a certain number of years has passed, you can renegotiate the contract to regain control. From there, you can explore new deals for reprints, sequels, or other adaptations.

- **Upcoming Projects**: If you're planning to pitch a sequel, spin-off, or new project to your publisher, consider using this moment to renegotiate your overall agreement. This way, you can secure more favorable terms for the new project while revisiting terms for your existing work.

Example: Your publishing contract is about to expire, and you have a new project in the works. You approach your publisher to renegotiate the terms of your next book, asking for a higher advance and more creative control over the marketing strategy.

Tip: Review your contract for clauses related to term length, renewal options, and rights reversion. Use these clauses to time your renegotiation efforts effectively.

4. Career Growth and Increased Market Value

As your career evolves, your market value increases. Whether you've developed a loyal readership, grown your platform through social media, or expanded into other creative endeavors (like podcasts or speaking engagements), these achievements strengthen your case for renegotiating.

Here's how to leverage career growth:

- **Platform Expansion**: If you've built a substantial following on social media, grown an email list, or developed a strong personal brand, you're in a stronger position to negotiate higher advances or royalties. Publishers recognize the value of an author who can engage their audience and drive book sales.

- **Multiple Projects**: If you've published multiple successful books or diversified your creative portfolio (such as writing across genres or publishing a non-fiction work), your value as an author increases. Use this expanded portfolio to renegotiate for better terms across all future projects.

- **Industry Relationships**: Building relationships with other authors, editors, and industry professionals can provide you with the knowledge and leverage you need to negotiate better deals. If you've established yourself as a thought leader or gained credibility in the industry, publishers may be more willing to accommodate your requests.

Example: After building a large following on social media, you approach your publisher to renegotiate your contract. You emphasize the value of your platform in promoting future books and ask for higher royalties and a more significant marketing investment.

Tip: Document your career growth and platform expansion to provide evidence of your increased market value. Showing concrete numbers (e.g., social media followers, newsletter subscribers, or podcast listeners) strengthens your case during negotiations.

Identifying the right time to renegotiate is essential for securing terms that reflect your current value and future potential. Whether it's due to career milestones, market shifts, contract expiration, or personal growth, recognizing the right triggers and timing your approach strategically will help you enter the negotiation table with confidence. By staying proactive, you ensure your contracts evolve along with your career.

Assessing Your Current Contract: What Needs Updating

Before heading into contract renegotiations, it's important to take a close look at your existing agreement to identify which terms may need updating. Whether your career has evolved, market trends have shifted, or your book's performance has exceeded expectations, ensuring your contract reflects your current situation is key to securing better terms. In this section, we'll explore how to assess your contract effectively, with a focus on key clauses that may need adjustment.

1. Reviewing Royalty Rates and Payment Structures

One of the most critical aspects of any publishing contract is the royalty rate—the percentage of sales you earn from each book sold. Over time, your initial royalty rates may become outdated, especially if your book has performed well or if you've developed a stronger author platform. Here's how to assess this part of your contract:

- **Evaluate Current Royalty Rates**: Compare your royalty rate to industry standards. Are you receiving the typical percentage for print books, eBooks, or audiobooks? If your royalty rates fall below the average, especially after significant sales or success, this is an area to push for an increase.

- **Consider Different Formats**: Make sure your contract covers royalties for all formats, including digital (eBooks) and audiobooks. These markets continue to grow, and if your contract lacks strong terms in these areas, now is the time to negotiate for higher royalties or expanded coverage.

- **Check for Escalator Clauses**: Some contracts include escalator clauses, where your royalty rate increases after hitting certain sales milestones. Review whether your contract has these clauses and whether you've surpassed any thresholds that should trigger a higher payout.

Example: After two years of consistent sales, you realize your royalty rate for eBooks is lower than industry standards. During renegotiations, you ask your publisher to raise your eBook royalties to match current market rates, reflecting your book's digital success.

Tip: Research typical royalty rates in your genre and for different formats before renegotiating. This will help you make a more compelling case for an increase.

2. Evaluating the Advance Structure

Advances are the upfront payments you receive when signing a publishing contract. While these payments are recouped against royalties, a higher advance shows the publisher's commitment to your work and provides financial stability. If your book has performed better than anticipated or your platform has grown, consider renegotiating your advance terms.

Here's what to consider:

- **Reassess the Advance Amount**: If your original advance was modest and your book has exceeded expectations, you may be able to negotiate a higher advance for future projects. Publishers are often willing to increase advances for authors who've proven their marketability.

- **Evaluate Payment Schedules**: Advances are often paid in installments (e.g., upon signing, manuscript delivery, and publication). Review your payment schedule and negotiate for more favorable terms, such as receiving a larger percentage upfront or spreading out payments in a way that better aligns with your needs.

- **Unrecouped Advances**: If your previous advance hasn't been fully earned out (i.e., your royalties haven't covered the advance), it may affect your ability to negotiate a higher advance for future works. Be prepared to address this with your publisher and provide a plan for how you'll drive stronger sales in the future.

Example: Your book has sold far better than expected, and you realize that your original advance was relatively small compared to its success. In your renegotiation, you ask for a larger advance for your next book, citing your strong sales and growing reader base as justification.

Tip: Use sales data, awards, and positive reviews to back up your request for a higher advance. Demonstrating the publisher's return on investment can make them more willing to invest more upfront.

3. Revisiting Rights Clauses: What You've Granted vs. What You Retain

Your contract's rights clauses dictate who controls various aspects of your book's distribution, licensing, and adaptation. It's important to revisit these clauses, especially if your book has gained traction and there's potential for foreign translations, film or TV adaptations, or other media.

Here's what to look for:

- **Subsidiary Rights**: Subsidiary rights cover additional ways your book can be exploited, such as foreign translations, audiobooks, film rights, and merchandise. If your publisher holds these rights but hasn't actively pursued opportunities, consider renegotiating to retain more control or share in the decision-making process.

- **Territorial Rights**: Make sure you understand the geographic scope of your rights. If your contract only covers certain regions (such as North America), there may be untapped markets elsewhere. During renegotiation, you can request to expand the geographic rights or regain control of unused territories.

- **Reversion of Rights**: If your book is no longer actively being promoted or selling well, review the reversion clauses. These allow you to regain rights to your book and republish or explore new opportunities. Make sure your contract includes clear conditions for rights reversion and renegotiate if the terms seem restrictive.

Example: Your book has seen strong international interest, but your publisher hasn't pursued foreign translation rights. In your renegotiation, you request that these rights revert to you so you can pursue foreign deals independently or through an agent.

Tip: If your publisher hasn't actively pursued subsidiary rights (like foreign translations or film adaptations), use this as leverage to regain control or negotiate for a more active role in decision-making.

4. Reassessing Marketing and Promotion Commitments

Another area to evaluate is your publisher's marketing and promotion commitments. As an author, you want to ensure that your publisher is investing in the promotion of your book to maximize its reach. If your book has proven its potential, renegotiating for a stronger marketing push can increase your visibility and long-term success.

Here's how to assess this part of your contract:

- **Review Marketing Obligations**: Look at what your publisher is contractually obligated to do in terms of marketing and promotion. Does the contract specify a certain amount of marketing spend, or is it vague? If marketing support has been lacking, push for more concrete commitments during renegotiations.

- **Ask for More Involvement**: If you have a strong personal platform or know your audience well, you may want to negotiate more involvement in the marketing strategy. This can include collaborating on marketing campaigns, approving promotional materials, or even receiving a larger portion of the marketing budget.

- **Negotiate for New Formats**: With the rise of digital marketing, social media, and book influencer campaigns, your original contract may not cover these areas adequately. During renegotiation, push for modern marketing strategies that take advantage of digital and social platforms to boost visibility.

Example: After successfully building a large social media following, you realize that your publisher hasn't capitalized on this audience for marketing purposes. In your renegotiation, you request a larger marketing budget and more collaboration on social media campaigns to drive sales.

Tip: Present your publisher with a clear marketing vision, showing how an increased investment in promotion (especially digital marketing) could drive higher sales and expand your audience.

5. Assessing Creative Control and Approval Rights

Creative control refers to how much input you have on decisions related to cover design, marketing materials, and adaptations. If you feel that your current contract limits your ability to influence these aspects, now is the time to renegotiate for more say in the creative process.

Here's what to review:

- **Cover Design and Layout**: If you were dissatisfied with the cover design or layout of your previous book, request more approval rights over these elements. A contract that allows for input on design choices can help ensure that the final product aligns with your vision.

- **Adaptations and Licensing**: If your book has the potential for film, TV, or merchandise adaptations, ensure you have some creative oversight over these projects. While you may not have full control, retaining approval rights over major changes can help preserve the integrity of your work.

- **Title and Editorial Input**: Some contracts grant publishers the right to change titles or make significant editorial changes. If this was a point of contention in your last project, renegotiate to ensure you have the final say in these areas.

Example: You were unhappy with the original cover design of your book, feeling that it didn't represent the tone or genre effectively. In your renegotiation, you request greater involvement in the cover design process and the ability to approve final designs.

Tip: If your contract offers limited creative control, consider bringing examples of how your involvement could improve the final product. Demonstrating your expertise in your audience or genre will help justify your request.

Assessing your current contract thoroughly is the foundation of successful renegotiation. By identifying areas that need updating—whether it's royalty rates, advances, rights, marketing, or creative control—you can enter the negotiation process with a clear understanding of what to ask for. A well-prepared author is more likely to secure favorable terms that reflect their growing career and market potential.

Building a Strong Case for Better Terms: Leveraging Your Success

When renegotiating your contract, one of the most powerful tools you have is the success you've already achieved. By demonstrating your book's performance and your own personal growth as an author, you can make a compelling case for better terms, whether that's higher royalties, a larger advance, or more creative control. This section will guide you through how to leverage your success effectively and use it to your advantage during renegotiations.

1. Showcase Sales Figures and Market Performance

One of the strongest indicators of success is how well your book has performed in the marketplace. If your book has sold well or exceeded expectations, this can give you substantial leverage when negotiating for better terms. Here's how to present your book's sales figures effectively:

- **Gather Sales Data**: Collect sales reports from your publisher, retail platforms (like Amazon, Barnes & Noble, or independent bookstores), and any other relevant sources. Focus on key metrics such as total units sold, performance over time, and sales spikes during promotions or media coverage.

- **Compare to Industry Standards**: If your book has outperformed similar titles in your genre, use this as a comparison to show how well it's done. Publishers are more likely to offer better terms if your book has performed above expectations for your market niche.

- **Highlight Consistency**: If your book has demonstrated consistent sales over time, rather than a brief spike at launch, emphasize this. Steady, long-term sales are valuable to publishers, as they indicate continued interest and demand for your work.

Example: You present data showing that your debut novel sold 50,000 copies in its first year—double the average sales for similar books in your genre. You use this as evidence to justify a higher advance and royalty rate for your next book.

Tip: Be specific and detail-oriented when presenting sales figures. Break down your book's performance by region, format (print, digital, audiobook), and time period to give a comprehensive picture of its success.

2. Leverage Awards, Critical Acclaim, and Media Recognition

Beyond sales, accolades such as awards, critical acclaim, and media recognition can significantly strengthen your case for better contract terms. Publishers are eager to work with authors who have garnered attention and credibility in the industry, as it makes your work more marketable.

Here's how to leverage your achievements:

- **Highlight Major Awards or Nominations**: If your book has been nominated for or won literary awards, make sure this is a centerpiece of your renegotiation case. Awards enhance your reputation as an author and can boost the perceived value of your work in the marketplace.

- **Showcase Reviews and Media Coverage**: Gather reviews from notable publications, respected critics, and influential bloggers. If your book has been covered in mainstream media (such as TV interviews, magazine features, or podcast appearances), include this as well.

- **Cite Positive Reader Feedback**: Reader reviews on platforms like Amazon, Goodreads, or social media can also be valuable. Positive reader feedback shows that your book resonates with its target audience, which can help convince the publisher to invest more in future works.

Example: Your book was nominated for a prestigious genre award, and several major publications gave it glowing reviews. You include these accolades in your renegotiation proposal, demonstrating that the book's success goes beyond sales figures.

Tip: Present a balanced mix of critical reviews, award recognition, and reader testimonials. This combination shows both industry and audience validation, which can be highly persuasive.

3. Demonstrate Audience Engagement and Platform Growth

A growing author platform—whether through social media, email marketing, or public speaking—can be a powerful asset when renegotiating your contract. Publishers value authors who actively engage with their readers and can help drive book sales through their own promotional efforts.

Here's how to leverage your platform growth:

- **Provide Social Media Metrics**: Share data on your social media following, engagement rates, and the reach of your posts. Publishers look favorably on authors who can promote their work directly to a large, engaged audience.

- **Highlight Newsletter and Email List Growth**: If you have an email list, show its growth over time and the open rates of your newsletters. Email marketing is a valuable tool for driving book sales, and a strong list demonstrates your ability to reach readers effectively.

- **Public Speaking or Event Participation**: If you've built a reputation through public speaking, workshops, book tours, or other events, include this as part of your platform. A proven ability to connect with readers in person can add significant value to your renegotiation efforts.

Example: Your social media following has grown by 50,000 followers over the past year, and you've consistently engaged with readers through posts, live Q&A sessions, and book giveaways. You use these metrics to show your publisher that you've expanded your reach and can help promote future projects more effectively.

Tip: Don't just focus on the size of your platform—emphasize engagement. Publishers want to see that your audience is active and responsive, not just large.

4. Use Comparative Data from Similar Authors

When making your case for better terms, it can be helpful to compare your performance to that of similar authors in your genre or niche. This shows the publisher where you stand relative to your peers and highlights your unique strengths.

Here's how to use comparative data:

- **Research Comparable Authors**: Find authors in your genre with similar careers or books, and look at their contracts, advances, or sales (if publicly available). Use this data to show that you deserve terms on par with or better than what similar authors are receiving.

- **Highlight Competitive Advantages**: If you have a larger platform, better sales, or more critical acclaim than other authors in your genre, make this clear in your negotiations. Show the publisher why your success justifies improved terms.

- **Cite Industry Trends**: Use trends in your genre or the broader publishing industry to support your request. For example, if authors in your genre are seeing increased demand for audiobooks or international rights, use this as a reason to negotiate for higher royalties or a bigger advance.

Example: After researching similar authors, you discover that many of them are receiving higher royalty rates for digital sales. Armed with this knowledge, you negotiate for a royalty increase, pointing out that your sales performance and platform growth are comparable to or better than these other authors.

Tip: Be tactful when using comparisons. Focus on demonstrating your value rather than framing it as a competition with other authors. Publishers appreciate collaborative approaches over adversarial ones.

5. Present Your Vision for Future Projects

Your renegotiation is not just about past success; it's also about what you plan to achieve in the future. A clear vision for your upcoming projects can convince the publisher that investing in you will yield long-term returns.

Here's how to pitch your future:

- **Outline Upcoming Books or Series**: If you have plans for a sequel, series, or entirely new book, present an outline to your publisher during renegotiations. Show how these projects build on your existing success and have strong market potential.

- **Pitch Multi-Format Opportunities**: If you envision your work expanding into other formats, such as audiobooks, foreign translations, or film/TV adaptations, include this in your proposal. Demonstrating the cross-media potential of your work can justify higher royalties or advances.

- **Set Long-Term Career Goals**: Frame your request for better terms as part of your broader career growth. Explain where you see your career going and how the publisher can play a key role in helping you achieve those goals.

Example: You present your publisher with a proposal for a three-book series, including a detailed plan for marketing and promotion. You explain that this series has strong potential for foreign rights sales and merchandising, making the case for a larger advance and a more comprehensive marketing commitment.

Tip: Focus on how your vision aligns with the publisher's goals. Show that investing in your future work will be mutually beneficial and lead to continued success for both parties.

Leveraging your success is the foundation of a strong renegotiation strategy. By presenting data on your sales, audience engagement, critical acclaim, and future projects, you can make a compelling case for better contract terms. Your success not only validates your past work but also signals your future potential, giving publishers every reason to offer more favorable terms that align with your growth as an author.

Negotiation Strategies: How to Secure a Favorable Outcome

Now that you've built a strong case for better terms, the final step in your contract renegotiation process is securing a favorable outcome at the negotiation table. Whether you're pushing for higher royalties, a larger advance, or more creative control, having effective negotiation strategies is key to ensuring your publisher meets your expectations. In this section, we'll explore proven techniques that will help you navigate the negotiation process with confidence and increase your chances of success.

1. Start with a Clear Understanding of Your Goals

Before you enter any negotiation, it's essential to have a clear understanding of what you want to achieve. This means defining your goals and knowing which terms are non-negotiable versus areas where you're willing to compromise. When you have a clear sense of your priorities, you'll be in a stronger position to advocate for yourself.

Here's how to prepare:

- **Identify Key Priorities**: Are higher royalties your top priority, or is securing a larger advance more important? Are you focused on gaining more control over marketing, or do you want a more favorable contract for future projects? Knowing your key goals will guide your negotiation strategy.

- **Prepare Backup Options**: It's unlikely that you'll get everything you want, so it's important to have backup options in mind. For example, if the publisher can't meet your request for a higher advance, you might instead push for more favorable royalty rates or a stronger marketing commitment.

- **Rank Your Asks**: Prioritize the issues you want to address, ranking them from most important to least important. This will help you stay focused on what matters most and make concessions on less crucial points if needed.

Example: Your top goal is to secure higher royalties for eBook sales, but you're also interested in renegotiating your marketing commitments. You prepare by ranking these goals, knowing you might compromise on marketing if you get the eBook royalty rate you want.

Tip: Be clear about your bottom line—what you're willing to accept and what would make you walk away from the deal. This will give you confidence and prevent you from settling for less than you deserve.

2. Use Data to Back Up Your Requests

Successful negotiations are often grounded in facts and data. By using solid evidence to support your requests, you can make a more compelling case for why your publisher should agree to better terms. Data not only strengthens your argument but also helps you stay objective during the negotiation process.

Here's how to use data effectively:

- **Present Sales Figures**: Provide specific data on your book's sales, including units sold, growth trends, and comparisons to industry standards. Publishers respond well to hard numbers, so show how your book has outperformed expectations or similar titles in your genre.

- **Cite Industry Benchmarks**: Research standard royalty rates, advances, and marketing commitments for authors in your genre or at your career stage. Use this information to show how your current contract compares and why you're asking for improvements.

- **Demonstrate Audience Engagement**: Share metrics on your social media following, email list growth, and audience engagement. Publishers value authors who can actively promote their work, and strong audience data can justify better terms.

Example: You provide your publisher with sales data showing that your book consistently sold above average for your genre over the past year. You also highlight your growing email list and social media following, which positions you as an author with strong promotional capabilities.

Tip: Present your data in a clear and organized way. Whether it's a visual chart showing sales growth or a bullet-point list of key metrics, make it easy for your publisher to understand the evidence supporting your requests.

3. Be Open to Compromise and Creative Solutions

While it's important to advocate for what you want, flexibility is key in any negotiation. Sometimes, the publisher may not be able to meet your exact terms, but they might offer alternative solutions that still work in your favor. Being open to creative compromises can help both parties reach a mutually beneficial outcome.

Here's how to stay flexible:

- **Find Middle Ground**: If your publisher can't offer a higher advance, perhaps they can provide more robust marketing support or a higher royalty rate on future projects. Explore different ways to balance the contract in a way that satisfies both parties.

- **Consider Non-Monetary Concessions**: If financial terms are a sticking point, look at other areas where the publisher might be willing to negotiate. For example, you might request more creative control over your book's cover design or approval rights for foreign translations.

- **Negotiate Contract Length**: If you're hesitant about committing to long-term terms, negotiate for a shorter contract length or a more flexible renewal clause. This gives you the option to renegotiate again in the near future if circumstances change.

Example: Your publisher isn't able to offer the advance you were hoping for, but they're willing to increase their investment in marketing your book and offer a higher royalty rate on future sales. You accept this compromise, recognizing the long-term benefits of better promotional support.

Tip: Approach negotiations with a mindset of collaboration, not confrontation. A cooperative tone can help foster goodwill and lead to creative solutions that benefit both you and the publisher.

4. Know When to Push and When to Pause

Effective negotiators know when to push for more and when to step back and give the other side time to consider their options. Negotiations can take time, and publishers may need to consult with various departments before making a final offer. Understanding the right moments to press forward and when to be patient can help you secure a more favorable outcome.

Here's how to balance assertiveness and patience:

- **Push When You Have Leverage**: If you've built a strong case based on sales performance, audience growth, or critical acclaim, use this leverage to push for better terms. This is especially true if the publisher is eager to retain you for future projects.

- **Pause to Let Them Consider**: If the publisher needs time to evaluate your requests, give them space to do so. Pressuring them too quickly may lead to a hasty decision that's less favorable for you. Allow time for thoughtful consideration, especially for complex requests like higher advances or subsidiary rights.

- **Follow Up Thoughtfully**: If the negotiation process drags on, follow up with your publisher in a polite but firm manner. Remind them of your key points and reiterate your enthusiasm for reaching a mutually beneficial agreement.

Example: During your negotiation, you press for a higher royalty rate based on your strong sales data. The publisher is hesitant, so you give them time to consider the request and come back with a counteroffer. After a few weeks of back-and-forth, you agree on a slightly higher royalty rate and more marketing support.

Tip: Negotiations often involve multiple rounds of offers and counteroffers. Be patient, but stay firm on your core requests, and don't be afraid to ask for clarification or more information if needed.

5. Consider Using a Literary Agent or Attorney

If negotiations become complex or you feel uncertain about certain legal aspects of your contract, it might be time to involve a professional. Literary agents and attorneys specialize in contract negotiations and can help you navigate tricky clauses, avoid potential pitfalls, and secure more favorable terms. While they will take a percentage of your earnings, their expertise can lead to better deals in the long run.

Here's how to involve a professional:

- **Hire a Literary Agent**: A literary agent can handle contract negotiations on your behalf, using their industry knowledge and connections to secure the best possible terms. They can also help you find new opportunities for foreign rights, film adaptations, and other licensing deals.

- **Consult an Intellectual Property Attorney**: If you're concerned about the legal intricacies of your contract, an attorney can review it and advise you on specific clauses related to rights, royalties, or creative control. They can also negotiate directly with your publisher if necessary.

- **Collaborate for the Best Outcome**: If you already have a literary agent or attorney, work closely with them to identify your key goals and ensure they're advocating for your interests. Regular communication throughout the negotiation process will help you stay aligned.

Example: You've built a strong case for renegotiation but are unsure about certain legal clauses related to subsidiary rights and royalties. You consult an intellectual property attorney, who advises you on the best approach and helps you renegotiate these specific terms.

Tip: If you're working with an agent or attorney, make sure to be clear about your priorities and maintain regular communication. Their expertise can help you achieve better results, but they need to fully understand your goals.

Negotiating for better terms requires a combination of preparation, flexibility, and strategy. By setting clear goals, backing your requests with data, staying open to creative solutions, and knowing when to push or pause, you can navigate the negotiation process with confidence. Whether you're seeking higher royalties, a larger advance, or more control over your creative work, these strategies will help you secure a favorable outcome and ensure your contract aligns with your evolving career.

Quick Tips and Recap

- **Define Your Goals**: Identify your top priorities (royalties, advance, marketing, etc.) and be clear on what you're willing to compromise.

- **Use Data to Strengthen Your Case**: Back up your requests with sales figures, audience engagement metrics, and industry benchmarks to demonstrate your success.

- **Be Flexible**: Stay open to creative solutions, such as non-monetary concessions or alternative payment structures, if your publisher can't meet your exact demands.

- **Know When to Push and When to Pause**: Apply pressure when you have leverage, but give the publisher time to evaluate complex requests.

- **Consider Professional Help**: If negotiations are complicated, consult a literary agent or intellectual property attorney to help you secure better terms.

- **Stay Focused on Long-Term Goals**: Ensure that the contract aligns with your career trajectory and prepares you for future success.

With these strategies, you'll be better equipped to negotiate a contract that reflects your value and supports your long-term goals as an author.

Legal Recourse: Protecting Your Interests

"Protecting your interests isn't just a defensive measure; it's an essential aspect of nurturing and preserving the integrity of your work."
— BOB IGER, FORMER CEO OF THE WALT DISNEY COMPANY

Welcome to Chapter Twenty-Five, "Legal Recourse: Protecting Your Interests," where we don our judicial robes and polish the gavel. It's time to ensure that when the literary world throws curveballs, you're not just ready to catch them—you're ready to throw them right back with legal finesse.

Think of this chapter as your legal shield and sword. Here, we delve into the thrilling (and sometimes chilling) world of copyright disputes, breach of contract, and all the legal armory you need to safeguard your creative empire. We'll explore every tool at your disposal, from sternly worded letters to courtroom showdowns, ensuring you know how to defend your work without turning into a courtroom drama protagonist.

So, tighten your tie, straighten your arguments, and prepare to stand firm. After all, your creations are more than just words on a page—they're a part of your legacy. Let's ensure they're protected with the same passion with which they were penned!

Understanding Breach of Contract: Recognizing and Addressing Violations

A breach of contract occurs when one party fails to uphold their end of a legally binding agreement. In the publishing world, this can happen in various ways, from a publisher not paying royalties on time to failing to promote your book as outlined in your contract. Understanding what constitutes a breach and knowing how to address it are critical to protecting your rights as an author.

In this section, we'll explore how to identify a breach of contract, the steps you should take if a violation occurs, and the best practices for resolving these issues before they escalate.

1. Types of Breach in Publishing Contracts

Not all breaches of contract are the same, and understanding the different types can help you assess the severity of the situation and decide on your course of action. Here are the most common types of breaches in publishing contracts:

- **Material Breach**: A material breach is a serious violation that undermines the entire purpose of the contract. For example, if your publisher fails to pay you royalties or doesn't release your book according to the agreed-upon schedule, this would likely be considered a material breach. These types of breaches typically allow the injured party (you) to terminate the contract and seek damages.

- **Minor Breach**: A minor breach (or partial breach) occurs when one party doesn't fulfill a specific part of the contract, but the breach doesn't completely negate the agreement. For example, if a publisher delays payment by a few weeks but eventually fulfills their obligation, this might be a minor breach. While not grounds for contract termination, it could warrant compensation or other corrective actions.

- **Anticipatory Breach**: This type of breach occurs when one party indicates, either through words or actions, that they won't fulfill their contractual obligations in the future. For instance, if your publisher informs you they won't be able to publish your book within the agreed timeframe, this may be an anticipatory breach. In such cases, you can often take legal action before the breach actually happens.

Example: If your publisher is contractually obligated to release your book by a certain date but fails to do so, and this delay causes you financial harm (e.g., missing out on a marketing window), this would likely be considered a material breach.

Tip: Always keep detailed records of contract timelines, communications with your publisher, and any issues that arise. Having this documentation will be essential if you need to take legal action.

2. Identifying a Breach: Red Flags to Watch For

Recognizing when a breach has occurred is not always straightforward, especially if it's a minor or anticipatory breach. Being proactive about tracking your contract terms and publisher performance can help you spot potential violations before they cause significant harm. Here are a few red flags to watch for:

- **Delayed or Missing Royalty Payments**: If you notice that your royalty statements or payments are consistently late, missing, or incorrect, this is a common red flag of a potential breach. Publishers are legally obligated to pay you the agreed-upon royalties in a timely manner.

- **Failure to Meet Deadlines**: If your contract includes specific deadlines for publication, editing, or marketing, and the publisher consistently misses these deadlines without explanation, it may be a breach of contract.

- **Inadequate Promotion or Marketing**: If your publisher has committed to promoting your book (such as arranging book tours, social media marketing, or press releases) and they fail to meet these obligations, this can also be a breach of contract, particularly if it affects your book's success.

- **Changes in Contract Terms Without Consent**: If your publisher attempts to change key terms of the contract (such as royalty rates or rights ownership) without your written consent, this could be a serious breach.

Example: You notice that your royalty payments have been inconsistent for several months, and your publisher has stopped responding to your inquiries. After reviewing your contract, you realize they are in violation of the payment schedule, and you decide to take action.

Tip: Keep copies of all communications with your publisher, including emails, contracts, and payment records. If you notice any discrepancies or delays, bring them to your publisher's attention immediately to resolve the issue before it escalates.

3. Steps to Address a Breach of Contract

If you believe your publisher has breached the contract, there are several steps you should take to address the issue and protect your interests. Handling the situation professionally and systematically can often lead to a resolution without needing to escalate to legal action.

- **Review the Contract**: Before taking any action, review your contract carefully to understand the specific terms related to the breach. Make sure you understand your publisher's obligations and the remedies available to you if they fail to meet them.

- **Document the Breach**: Collect evidence of the breach, including emails, royalty statements, contract clauses, and any other relevant documentation. Make detailed notes of the dates and nature of the breach, and how it has impacted you financially or professionally.

- **Communicate with Your Publisher**: Reach out to your publisher in writing (email is typically sufficient) to notify them of the breach. Be clear, professional, and direct, outlining the specific issues and referencing the relevant sections of your contract. Request a resolution or corrective action within a reasonable timeframe.

- **Send a Formal Notice of Breach**: If the initial communication doesn't resolve the issue, you may need to send a formal notice of breach. This is a legal document that outlines the breach and your intent to take further action if it is not remedied. In many cases, this can prompt the publisher to take corrective steps.

Example: After noticing several missed royalty payments, you send your publisher an email outlining the breaches and asking for an explanation. When they don't respond, you follow up with a formal notice of breach, giving them a two-week deadline to rectify the situation.

Tip: Remain calm and professional in all your communications. The goal is to resolve the issue amicably if possible, and escalating too quickly can strain the relationship unnecessarily.

4. When to Escalate: Seeking Legal Recourse

If the publisher fails to address the breach after your formal notice, you may need to escalate the situation. Legal action is often a last resort, but it may be necessary if the breach is significant and the publisher is unresponsive. Here are your options for legal recourse:

- **Mediation**: Mediation involves working with a neutral third party to resolve the dispute outside of court. This can be a quicker and less costly option than litigation, and it allows both parties to negotiate a solution.

- **Arbitration**: Arbitration is a more formal process where a third party (an arbitrator) reviews the evidence and makes a binding decision. Many publishing contracts include arbitration clauses as a way to resolve disputes without going to court.

- **Litigation**: If mediation and arbitration fail, or if the breach is serious enough, you may need to file a lawsuit. In this case, you'll work with an intellectual property attorney to pursue damages and/or termination of the contract through the legal system.

Example: After several failed attempts to resolve a serious breach of contract, you decide to seek legal representation and pursue arbitration, as outlined in your contract. The arbitrator rules in your favor, and your contract is terminated, allowing you to seek a new publisher.

Tip: Before pursuing legal action, consult an attorney who specializes in publishing or intellectual property law. They can help you understand the best course of action and what to expect during the process.

Understanding a breach of contract and taking appropriate action is vital for protecting your rights as an author. Whether it's a minor breach or a serious violation, staying informed, documenting the issue, and communicating professionally with your publisher are key steps to resolving the situation. In cases where the breach cannot be resolved amicably, knowing your options for legal recourse ensures that you can protect your creative work and your career.

Copyright Infringement: Defending Your Intellectual Property

As an author, your work is your most valuable asset, and protecting it from unauthorized use is essential. Copyright infringement occurs when someone uses your work without your permission, violating the exclusive rights you hold as the creator. Whether it's unauthorized reproduction, distribution, or adaptation, defending your intellectual property is crucial to maintaining control over your creative output and ensuring you're fairly compensated.

In this section, we'll cover what constitutes copyright infringement, how to identify when your work has been used unlawfully, and the steps you can take to protect your rights and seek legal recourse.

1. What Constitutes Copyright Infringement?

Copyright law gives authors the exclusive rights to their creative works, including the right to reproduce, distribute, perform, display, and create derivative works. Infringement occurs when someone uses your work in one of these ways without your permission, violating the protections afforded to you under copyright law.

Here's what counts as infringement:

- **Reproduction Without Permission**: Copying or reproducing your work without authorization is a direct violation of your copyright. This includes making unauthorized copies of your book (digital or physical) and distributing them.

- **Unauthorized Distribution**: If someone distributes your work—such as uploading it to a website, offering free downloads, or selling pirated copies—they are infringing on your rights. This can happen in both online and physical marketplaces.

- **Derivative Works**: Creating a derivative work (such as a film, TV series, or merchandise) based on your book without your consent is a form of copyright infringement. This also includes unauthorized translations of your work.

- **Public Performance or Display**: If your work is performed, read aloud, or publicly displayed without your authorization (e.g., public readings or dramatizations of your book), this could also be a form of infringement.

Example: You discover that someone has uploaded a PDF of your entire book to a website offering free downloads, without your permission. This is a clear case of copyright infringement, as it violates your exclusive right to distribute your work.

Tip: Copyright protection is automatic when you create an original work, but registering your copyright with the appropriate legal body (such as the U.S. Copyright Office) strengthens your ability to enforce your rights in court.

2. Identifying Copyright Infringement: Red Flags and Common Scenarios

Spotting copyright infringement isn't always straightforward, especially in the digital age where content can be easily shared and reproduced across multiple platforms. Being vigilant about how your work is being used and distributed is key to catching infringements early and taking swift action.

Here are common red flags to watch for:

- **Unauthorized Copies Online**: One of the most common forms of infringement occurs when your book is illegally uploaded to websites that offer it for free download. Keep an eye on piracy websites, file-sharing platforms, and even social media pages that may be distributing your work without consent.

- **Pirated Physical Copies**: In some cases, infringers may produce counterfeit physical copies of your book and sell them through online marketplaces or at unauthorized retailers. This is particularly common with popular titles.

- **Unapproved Translations**: If your book has been translated into another language without your approval, and it's being sold or distributed, this is a clear violation of your copyright.

- **Unauthorized Adaptations**: If your characters, plot, or setting are being used in a way that creates derivative works (like fan fiction, films, or merchandise) without your permission, this could be an infringement of your intellectual property.

Example: You stumble upon a website offering an unauthorized Spanish translation of your book, which is being sold for profit. This is copyright infringement because you have not granted anyone the rights to create or sell a translation.

Tip: Set up **Google Alerts** for your book's title and your name to help you monitor any unauthorized mentions or uploads of your work. Regularly search for your book on piracy websites or unauthorized marketplaces.

3. Steps to Defend Your Copyright

Once you've identified a case of copyright infringement, it's important to take swift action to stop the unauthorized use of your work and protect your rights. Here's a step-by-step guide on how to defend your copyright:

- **Document the Infringement**: Before taking any action, gather evidence of the infringement. This could include screenshots of the offending website, URLs where your book is being illegally sold or distributed, and any correspondence you've had with the infringer (if applicable). Make sure to keep detailed records, as this will be important if the situation escalates to legal action.

- **Send a Cease-and-Desist Letter**: A cease-and-desist letter is a formal request for the infringer to stop using your work immediately. This letter should outline the specific infringement, reference your copyright ownership, and demand that the infringing content be removed. Cease-and-desist letters are often effective, especially when sent by an attorney.

- **Submit a DMCA Takedown Notice**: The **Digital Millennium Copyright Act (DMCA)** allows you to request that online platforms remove infringing content. Most websites, including major platforms like Amazon, YouTube, and Google, have specific processes for filing DMCA takedown notices. If your book is being illegally distributed online, submitting a DMCA notice can quickly get the content removed.

- **Contact the Infringer Directly**: In some cases, the person infringing on your copyright may not be aware that they're violating the law. A polite but firm email or message informing them of the infringement and requesting that they remove your work can often resolve the issue without escalating the situation.

Example: You find a website offering an unauthorized download of your eBook. You send a DMCA takedown notice to the site's hosting platform, which results in the immediate removal of the infringing content.

Tip: When sending cease-and-desist letters or DMCA notices, remain professional and clear in your language. Include specific details about the infringement and reference the law that supports your claim to strengthen your case.

4. Pursuing Legal Action for Copyright Infringement

If cease-and-desist letters or takedown notices don't resolve the issue, or if the infringement is severe, you may need to consider pursuing legal action. Filing a lawsuit for copyright infringement can result in the infringer being ordered to stop using your work and potentially paying damages for any financial harm they caused.

Here's what you need to know about taking legal action:

- **Consult an Intellectual Property Attorney**: If you're dealing with a serious case of copyright infringement, it's best to consult an attorney who specializes in intellectual property law. They can advise you on the best course of action, help you assess the strength of your case, and represent you in court if necessary.

- **Determine Damages**: In a copyright infringement lawsuit, you may be entitled to monetary damages. This can include compensation for any lost sales or profits, as well as statutory damages (set amounts of money awarded by law) if your copyright is registered.

- **File a Copyright Infringement Lawsuit**: If the infringer refuses to comply with your demands, filing a lawsuit may be your best option. A successful lawsuit can result in the infringer being ordered to pay damages and legal fees, and it can also stop them from continuing to use your work.

Example: After discovering a company producing merchandise based on characters from your book without your permission, you consult an intellectual property attorney and file a copyright infringement lawsuit. The court rules in your favor, ordering the company to stop selling the merchandise and pay damages.

Tip: If your work is registered with the U.S. Copyright Office, you have a stronger legal case and can pursue statutory damages. Make sure to register your copyright as soon as possible to strengthen your ability to take legal action if needed.

Defending your copyright is essential to protecting your creative work and ensuring you maintain control over how it's used and distributed. By staying vigilant, addressing infringements swiftly, and using the legal tools at your disposal, you can safeguard your intellectual property and prevent unauthorized use of your work. Whether through cease-and-desist letters, DMCA notices, or legal action, you have the power to defend your rights and protect your legacy as an author.

Dispute Resolution: Mediation, Arbitration, and Litigation

When conflicts arise in the world of publishing—whether it's a contract dispute, copyright infringement, or a breach of agreement—resolving the issue effectively and efficiently is crucial. Fortunately, there are several pathways to resolving legal disputes, ranging from informal negotiations to formal legal proceedings. Understanding your options can help you navigate conflicts and protect your interests without unnecessary stress or financial burden.

In this section, we'll explore three primary methods of resolving disputes: mediation, arbitration, and litigation. Each method has its advantages and disadvantages, and knowing which one is right for your situation can save you time, money, and frustration.

1. Mediation: Finding a Collaborative Solution

Mediation is one of the least formal methods of dispute resolution, often used when both parties want to resolve the conflict outside of court in a collaborative and amicable way. In mediation, a neutral third party (the mediator) helps both parties come to a mutual agreement.

Mediation is often a good first step in resolving publishing disputes, especially when you want to preserve a working relationship with your publisher or another party. It's designed to be a non-adversarial process, where the goal is for both sides to reach a fair settlement without the need for a lengthy legal battle.

Here's how mediation works:

- **The Role of the Mediator**: The mediator is a neutral party who facilitates discussion and negotiation between you and the other party (such as your publisher or an infringer). Their job is to guide the conversation, help clarify the issues, and propose possible solutions. However, the mediator does not make any binding decisions—both parties must agree on the resolution.

- **The Mediation Process**: During mediation, each party presents their side of the issue, and the mediator helps identify common ground.

Through discussion and compromise, the goal is to reach a settlement that both parties find acceptable. The process is typically confidential, and any agreement reached is legally binding once signed by both parties.

- **When to Use Mediation**: Mediation is most effective when both parties are open to negotiation and willing to compromise. It's often used for contract disputes, royalty disagreements, or minor copyright issues where the goal is to avoid escalating to more formal legal action.

Example: You and your publisher disagree over the royalty payments owed to you, but you both want to maintain a good working relationship. You decide to use mediation to reach a fair agreement without going to court.

Tip: Mediation is generally faster and less expensive than arbitration or litigation. It's a great option for resolving disputes quickly and collaboratively, especially when you want to avoid the time and cost of a lawsuit.

2. Arbitration: A Binding Decision Without Going to Court

Arbitration is a more formal process than mediation, but it's still an alternative to going to court. In arbitration, a neutral third party (the arbitrator) listens to both sides of the dispute and makes a binding decision. Arbitration is often used when parties want a final resolution without the time and expense of a full trial.

Many publishing contracts include an arbitration clause, meaning that if a dispute arises, you're required to go through arbitration instead of litigation. Arbitration can be faster than litigation and typically involves less public exposure, but the decision made by the arbitrator is legally binding and can't be easily appealed.

Here's how arbitration works:

- **The Role of the Arbitrator**: The arbitrator acts like a private judge. After hearing both parties' arguments and reviewing the evidence, the arbitrator makes a decision on how the dispute should be resolved. Unlike mediation, the arbitrator's decision is binding, meaning both parties must adhere to the ruling.

- **The Arbitration Process**: Arbitration is more structured than mediation but less formal than court litigation. Both sides present their case, including evidence and witnesses if necessary. The arbitrator then makes a decision based on the facts and the law. The decision is final and legally enforceable.

- **When to Use Arbitration**: Arbitration is often required if it's outlined in your contract, but it can also be a good choice when you need a binding decision but want to avoid the cost and complexity of litigation. It's commonly used for larger contractual disputes or when a publisher fails to meet significant obligations.

Example: Your contract includes an arbitration clause, and after a serious breach of contract, you pursue arbitration to seek damages from your publisher. The arbitrator rules in your favor, and the decision is binding.

Tip: Review your publishing contracts carefully to see if they include an arbitration clause. If so, you'll need to pursue arbitration instead of litigation when a dispute arises.

3. Litigation: Taking Your Case to Court

Litigation is the most formal method of dispute resolution and involves taking your case to court. In litigation, both parties present their case before a judge (and sometimes a jury), and the court makes a legally binding decision. Litigation is often used for more serious disputes, such as large financial claims, significant copyright infringement, or when other methods of resolution have failed.

While litigation can be costly and time-consuming, it may be necessary if the dispute cannot be resolved through mediation or arbitration. Litigation also allows for a more comprehensive presentation of evidence, expert testimony, and a final ruling that can have wider implications (such as setting a legal precedent).

Here's how litigation works:

- **The Role of the Court**: In litigation, a judge (and possibly a jury) hears both sides of the case, reviews the evidence, and makes a legally binding ruling. The court's decision can include financial compensation, injunctive relief (such as ordering the other party to stop certain actions), or other remedies.

- **The Litigation Process**: Litigation involves several stages, including filing a lawsuit, discovery (where both parties exchange evidence), pre-trial motions, and the trial itself. After the trial, the court will issue a ruling, which can be appealed in some cases. Litigation is a public process, and court records are generally available to the public.

- **When to Use Litigation**: Litigation is often a last resort when other methods of dispute resolution have failed, or when the stakes are too high to settle through mediation or arbitration. It's used for serious breaches of contract, significant financial disputes, or when the parties cannot agree on a resolution through other means.

Example: After discovering widespread copyright infringement of your book, you file a lawsuit against the infringer, seeking damages and an injunction to stop further distribution of your work. The court rules in your favor, and the infringer is ordered to pay damages and cease all unauthorized distribution.

Tip: Litigation is often expensive and time-consuming, so it's important to consult with an intellectual property attorney before pursuing this option. However, if the stakes are high and other methods of resolution have failed, litigation may be the best course of action to protect your rights.

4. Choosing the Right Method of Dispute Resolution

Choosing the right method of dispute resolution depends on the nature of your conflict, the terms of your contract, and your long-term goals. Here's a quick comparison to help you decide which method might be best for your situation:

- **Mediation**: Best for collaborative resolutions, where both parties are willing to negotiate and preserve the relationship. It's non-binding but effective for smaller or more straightforward disputes.

- **Arbitration**: Ideal for disputes where a binding decision is needed without the full complexity of a court trial. It's often required by contract and faster than litigation.

- **Litigation**: Necessary for serious disputes or when other methods have failed. Litigation offers a thorough legal process but is time-consuming and costly.

Example: If your publisher has missed several royalty payments and discussions have failed, you may first try mediation. If that doesn't resolve the issue, you could pursue arbitration (if required by your contract) or litigation, depending on the severity of the breach.

Tip: Always consult with a legal professional before deciding on a method of dispute resolution. They can help you understand the potential outcomes, costs, and benefits of each option based on your specific case.

Dispute resolution is an important part of protecting your rights and interests as an author. Whether through mediation, arbitration, or litigation, understanding your options and knowing when to escalate a dispute can help you resolve conflicts effectively and maintain control over your work. Each method has its place, and by choosing the right one, you can minimize stress and maximize the likelihood of a favorable outcome.

Hiring Legal Representation: When and How to Seek Professional Help

While some publishing disputes can be resolved through direct negotiation or informal processes, there are times when the complexity or severity of the issue requires professional legal help. Hiring legal representation can be crucial in protecting your rights, ensuring that your contracts are fair, and navigating disputes that are beyond your expertise. Knowing when and how to seek the right legal professional can make all the difference in securing a favorable outcome.

In this section, we'll discuss when it's time to bring in a lawyer, how to find the right one for your needs, and what to expect when working with legal representation.

1. When to Hire a Lawyer: Recognizing the Need for Professional Help

Not every contract disagreement or legal issue requires the immediate involvement of an attorney. However, certain situations call for professional expertise, particularly when the financial stakes are high or the legal matters are complex. Here are some scenarios where it's wise to seek legal help:

- **Serious Contract Disputes**: If you're facing a major contract dispute—such as a significant breach of contract, unclear contractual obligations, or disputes over royalties—hiring a lawyer ensures that your rights are protected and that you receive what you're owed.

- **Copyright Infringement**: When your intellectual property is being infringed upon (such as unauthorized use of your book, characters, or ideas), and cease-and-desist letters or DMCA notices haven't resolved the issue, you'll need an attorney to help you pursue legal action.

- **Complex Contract Negotiations**: If you're negotiating a high-stakes book deal, multiple contracts with various publishers, or foreign rights agreements, an experienced attorney can help you navigate complex terms and secure the best deal.

- **Litigation**: If mediation or arbitration has failed and you're considering litigation, you'll need a lawyer who specializes in intellectual property or publishing law to represent you in court.

- **Unclear Legal Obligations**: If you're uncertain about the terms of your contract, your rights, or potential liabilities, consulting with an attorney can clarify your obligations and help you avoid future legal problems.

Example: You discover that a company is producing merchandise featuring characters from your book without your consent, and the infringement is widespread. After sending cease-and-desist letters with no response, you decide to hire an attorney to file a lawsuit for copyright infringement.

Tip: Don't wait until the issue has escalated beyond control. If you're unsure about your legal standing, seek professional advice early to avoid costly mistakes or long-term consequences.

2. Finding the Right Lawyer: Key Qualities to Look For

Not all lawyers are the same, and when it comes to publishing disputes, it's important to hire someone with specific expertise in intellectual property law, contract law, and the publishing industry. Here's how to find the right lawyer for your needs:

- **Look for Industry-Specific Expertise**: Publishing law is a specialized field, so seek out an attorney who has experience working with authors, publishers, or intellectual property disputes. A lawyer with knowledge of the book industry will be familiar with the unique challenges authors face, such as subsidiary rights, royalties, and contract terms.

- **Check Credentials and Experience**: Look for an attorney who has a proven track record in handling cases similar to yours. Whether it's contract negotiation, copyright infringement, or litigation, ask about their experience and success rates in these areas.

- **Evaluate Communication Skills**: Good communication is key when working with a lawyer. They should be able to explain complex legal terms in a way you can understand and keep you updated on the status of your case. Choose someone who is responsive and willing to answer your questions.

- **Consider Fees and Payment Structure**: Legal representation can be expensive, so it's important to understand the lawyer's fee structure before hiring them. Some attorneys charge an hourly rate, while others work on a contingency basis (where they only get paid if you win the case). Be clear about fees upfront to avoid surprises later.

Example: You're negotiating a major book deal that includes foreign rights, film adaptations, and merchandise. You hire a lawyer who specializes in publishing contracts to review the terms, ensuring that you retain control over key rights and maximize your earnings.

Tip: Ask other authors or professionals in the publishing industry for recommendations. A referral from someone who's been in a similar situation can lead you to a trustworthy and experienced attorney.

3. What to Expect When Working with a Lawyer

Once you've hired a lawyer, understanding how the process works will help you get the most out of the professional relationship. Here's what to expect when working with legal representation:

- **Initial Consultation**: Most lawyers offer an initial consultation, during which they'll review your case, assess the legal issues, and provide advice on the best course of action. This is your opportunity to explain the situation and ask questions about how they plan to handle your case.

- **Strategic Planning**: After reviewing your case, your lawyer will develop a strategy to achieve the best outcome. Whether it's negotiating with the other party, preparing a lawsuit, or sending a formal notice, your attorney will guide you through the legal steps.

- **Regular Updates**: Throughout the process, your lawyer should keep you informed about the status of your case, including any negotiations, filings, or developments. Clear communication is key, so don't hesitate to ask for updates if needed.

- **Collaborative Efforts**: While your lawyer will handle the legal heavy lifting, you'll need to provide information, documents, and input throughout the process. Be prepared to collaborate with your attorney by providing relevant materials, such as contracts, royalty statements, or evidence of copyright infringement.

- **Negotiations and Legal Filings**: Depending on the nature of your case, your lawyer may engage in negotiations with the other party or file formal legal documents on your behalf. If the case goes to court, they'll represent you in hearings or trials.

Example: Your publisher is withholding royalties, and you've decided to take legal action. Your lawyer reviews your contract, gathers evidence of the breach, and begins negotiations with the publisher to resolve the dispute. If negotiations fail, your lawyer files a lawsuit to recover the unpaid royalties.

Tip: Stay organized and keep detailed records of all communications, payments, and legal documents. This will help your lawyer build a stronger case and ensure a smoother legal process.

4. Maximizing the Value of Legal Representation

Hiring legal representation can be a significant investment, so it's important to make the most of your lawyer's expertise. Here's how to maximize the value of legal representation:

- **Be Prepared**: Before meeting with your lawyer, gather all relevant documents, contracts, and evidence. The more organized and prepared you are, the easier it will be for your attorney to assess the situation and build a case.

- **Ask Questions**: Don't be afraid to ask questions if you're unsure about legal terms, procedures, or strategies. A good lawyer will explain things clearly and ensure that you're fully informed about the process.

- **Follow Your Lawyer's Advice**: While it's important to advocate for your interests, remember that your lawyer is an expert in the field. Trust their advice and follow their recommendations, especially when it comes to negotiations, settlements, or legal filings.

- **Communicate Regularly**: Keep in touch with your lawyer and provide updates if new developments arise. Regular communication ensures that both you and your lawyer are on the same page throughout the legal process.

Example: During a copyright infringement case, you provide your lawyer with detailed evidence of unauthorized use, including screenshots, royalty statements, and correspondence. Your preparation helps the lawyer build a strong case, leading to a successful resolution in your favor.

Tip: Legal disputes can take time to resolve, so be patient and trust the process. By staying engaged and working closely with your attorney, you can help ensure the best possible outcome.

Quick Tips and Recap

- **Know When to Hire a Lawyer**: Seek legal representation for serious contract disputes, copyright infringement, complex negotiations, or litigation.

- **Find the Right Lawyer**: Look for industry-specific expertise in publishing or intellectual property law, with a proven track record in handling similar cases.

- **Be Prepared and Organized**: Gather all relevant documents, contracts, and evidence before meeting with your lawyer to ensure a smoother legal process.

- **Communicate Effectively**: Maintain regular communication with your lawyer and ask questions to stay informed about your case and legal options.

- **Understand Legal Fees**: Clarify your lawyer's fee structure upfront, whether hourly, contingency-based, or flat rate, to avoid surprises later.

- **Follow Professional Advice**: Trust your lawyer's recommendations during negotiations, settlements, or legal proceedings to achieve the best possible outcome.

These strategies will help you make the most of legal representation and ensure that your rights are protected throughout any publishing-related legal matters.

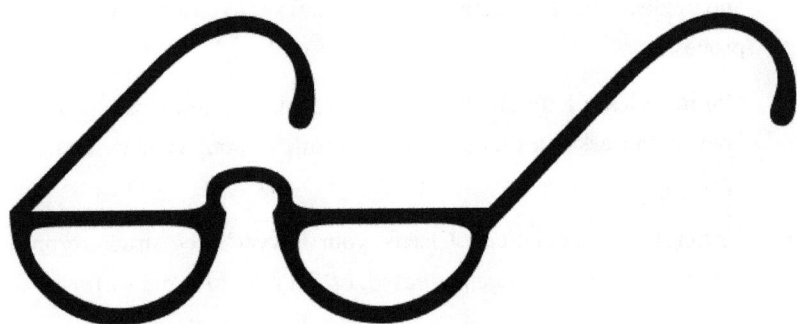

Conclusion

Empowering Your Publishing Journey

A s you close the final chapter of this book, it's clear that navigating the legal and business complexities of publishing is not just an essential part of your journey as an author—it's a critical tool for long-term success. From understanding publishing rights and negotiating favorable contracts to protecting your intellectual property and managing financial disputes, this book has equipped you with the knowledge and strategies needed to safeguard your creative work, maximize your earnings, and assert control over your publishing career.

At its heart, the publishing industry thrives on the creativity and passion of authors like you. But alongside that passion must be a deep understanding of the business and legal landscape that governs the industry. Knowing your rights, asserting your value, and protecting your work are not just legal necessities; they are acts of empowerment that allow you to fully own your success.

Here's a recap of the core lessons to carry with you as you move forward:

- **Master Your Contracts**: Every contract you sign defines your career's trajectory. Always approach negotiations with clarity, confidence, and a well-informed understanding of key clauses—like grant of rights, advances, royalties, and options for future works. By ensuring your contracts are in your favor, you're setting the foundation for a prosperous and controlled career.

- **Leverage Subsidiary Rights**: Don't let your book's potential end with publication. Subsidiary rights—such as film, TV, audiobooks, foreign translations, and merchandising—are valuable assets that can significantly boost your financial success. Understanding and negotiating these rights effectively can unlock new revenue streams and expand your book's reach beyond borders.

- **Stay Vigilant and Protect Your Work**: Your intellectual property is your most precious asset. Always be proactive in securing your copyrights, monitoring for infringement, and taking swift action if your work is used without permission. Whether through legal notices, DMCA takedowns, or lawsuits, defending your creative output ensures that you remain in control of your legacy.

- **Know When to Seek Help**: While you've learned a great deal about the legal landscape, don't hesitate to seek professional help when needed. Lawyers, literary agents, and financial experts can provide valuable guidance, helping you navigate complex contracts, handle disputes, and maximize your earnings. Having the right support system can make all the difference in your publishing journey.

- **Adapt and Evolve**: The publishing industry is dynamic, and so are your rights as an author. As your career progresses, continually revisit your contracts, renegotiate terms, and stay aware of new opportunities to expand your reach. The more proactive you are in adapting to industry changes, the more control you will have over your creative and financial future.

As you step into the next phase of your career, remember that the knowledge you've gained from this book isn't just about understanding legal jargon or signing contracts. It's about empowering you to take charge of your path, assert your worth, and ensure that your hard work and creativity are rewarded.

The world of publishing can be full of twists and turns, but with the right tools and a strategic mindset, you're more than prepared to thrive. Whether you're negotiating your first book deal or managing a growing body of work, you now have the legal and business acumen to navigate the challenges ahead with confidence.

Your words hold power, and so does your understanding of the business behind them. Continue writing, creating, and building your legacy with the peace of mind that you are fully in control of your rights, your earnings, and your future. This is just the beginning of a long and rewarding journey, and you are now better equipped than ever to embrace it.

Here's to your success—may you continue to write stories that not only inspire but also bring the recognition and rewards you rightfully deserve.

Where Do We Go from Here?

As you reach the conclusion of "Legal Ink: Navigating the Legalese of Publishing," it's clear that mastering the legal and business aspects of the publishing world is about more than contracts and copyright—it's about empowering you to fully own and shape your career as an author. Beyond the skills and knowledge you've gained here, your journey is one of continuous growth, where staying informed, building meaningful connections, and protecting your creative legacy are all part of a long-term vision for success. In this closing section, we'll explore some essential final takeaways that will equip you not only to navigate today's publishing challenges but to thrive and lead with confidence, balance, and impact in an ever-evolving industry.

Lifelong Learning and Adaptability

The publishing world is an ever-evolving landscape, and as an author, maintaining a mindset of lifelong learning and adaptability is one of your greatest assets. Just as you continue to develop your craft, staying informed about industry trends, digital advancements, and changing legal standards is essential for ongoing success. Think of this book as a solid foundation—but one that's meant to be built upon. Engage with new resources, attend workshops, join online forums, or participate in author communities. By keeping yourself up-to-date, you're ready not only to seize opportunities but also to avoid pitfalls and make empowered choices in a rapidly changing market.

Building a Network of Resources and Allies

As you move forward, remember that you're not on this journey alone. Building a network of trusted advisors—legal professionals, literary agents, publishing experts, and even fellow authors—can provide invaluable support and insights at every stage of your career. When you're faced with a contract decision or a rights question, having people who understand your goals and can guide you is a huge advantage. Beyond professional relationships, consider mentoring other authors as well. Sharing what you know and learning from the experiences of others strengthens the author community, creates lasting bonds, and empowers each member of this network to make informed, confident choices.

Looking Beyond Individual Success: Impacting the Publishing Industry

Each time an author negotiates fair terms or asserts control over their intellectual property, they help set a positive precedent that benefits the entire industry. By making informed decisions and standing up for your rights, you contribute to a shift toward greater transparency and fairness in publishing. When authors like you bring knowledge and confidence to the negotiation table, publishers notice— and this can gradually shift industry standards. Your empowered stance has the potential not only to shape your own career but also to inspire others, creating a ripple effect of change. The more authors who understand and exercise their rights, the stronger and more respected the creative community becomes as a whole.

Maintaining Balance and Well-Being

While it's crucial to handle the business side of your career, it's equally important to nurture your creativity and well-being. Striking a balance between your creative work and the business tasks of managing contracts, rights, and royalties helps prevent burnout and keeps your passion alive. Consider setting boundaries with your business matters, allowing yourself time to enjoy the creative process without distraction. Celebrate your successes, even the small ones, and find ways to rejuvenate creatively. Remember that your well-being is a vital part of a sustainable career, and keeping a healthy balance will help you stay inspired and productive in the long run.

A Vision for the Future of Creative Work

As you close this book and embark on your next chapter, recognize that you're not just crafting stories—you're helping to shape the future of the publishing industry. The way you approach your career, protect your rights, and manage your business sets a standard for a new generation of authors who will view their creative work through both artistic and entrepreneurial lenses. By merging creativity with empowered ownership, you're leaving a legacy that transcends words on a page. You are part of a new wave of authors who own their stories and control their careers, and as you continue to grow, you're paving the way for others to follow.

READ ON for a bonus chapter!

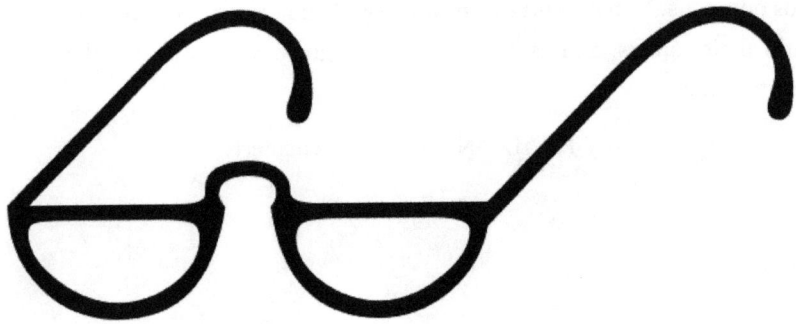

The Role of Agents and Lawyers: Enhancing Your Legal and Commercial Outcomes

"Having a good agent and lawyer is like having a GPS and a good set of brakes: one helps you to find where you're going, and the other makes sure you can stop before anything crashes."
— JAMES PATTERSON, AUTHOR

Welcome to the Bonus Chapter, "The Role of Agents and Lawyers: Enhancing Your Legal and Commercial Outcomes," where we lift the curtain to reveal the unsung heroes behind literary success stories. Think of agents and lawyers not just as your advisors, but as your career's backstage crew, ensuring the show goes on without a hitch.

Here, we dive into the dynamic duo of the publishing world. Agents, with their keen market insights and fierce negotiation skills, are like your personal booking agents for the best gigs in town—securing deals, managing rights, and sometimes playing the bad cop so you can remain the beloved artist. Lawyers, on the other hand, are the guardians at the gate, armed with legal jargon that's as protective as a dragon's scales, ensuring every contract you sign is as tight as a drum.

So, whether you're looking to land a lucrative deal or navigate the treacherous waters of intellectual property law, this chapter will show you how these professionals help turn your literary dreams into well-protected, financially sound realities. Let's toast to the agents and lawyers—because with them on your side, you're not just writing stories; you're building an empire.

Literary Agents: Navigating the Marketplace and Securing Deals

A literary agent is often the first line of defense for authors entering the publishing world. These professionals act as gatekeepers, career strategists, and advocates, helping authors secure deals with publishers, negotiate contracts, and manage their creative careers. For many authors, a literary agent is an indispensable ally, bringing industry insight, negotiation expertise, and long-standing relationships with publishers to the table.

In this section, we'll explore the crucial role of a literary agent in navigating the often-complex publishing marketplace and securing the best possible deals for your work.

1. The Role of a Literary Agent in Your Career

A literary agent is more than just someone who finds you a publisher. Their job is multifaceted, ranging from career development to negotiating terms that protect your financial and creative interests. Here's what a literary agent does:

- **Manages Submissions**: One of the most important roles of a literary agent is submitting your manuscript to the right publishers. Agents have established relationships with editors and know which publishers are the best fit for your book. They save you from the dreaded "slush pile" and help ensure your manuscript gets in front of decision-makers.

- **Negotiates Contracts**: Once a publisher shows interest in your book, your agent steps in to negotiate the terms of the deal. This can include everything from advances and royalties to subsidiary rights and reversion clauses. The goal of the agent is to ensure that you receive fair compensation and retain as much control over your work as possible.

- **Provides Career Guidance**: Beyond book deals, agents also help you strategize your long-term career. Whether it's choosing the right project to pursue next, expanding into new genres, or navigating the world of film or TV adaptations, your agent can offer invaluable guidance.

- **Handles Business Affairs**: Agents take on much of the business side of being an author, allowing you to focus on your writing. This includes negotiating marketing and promotion efforts, foreign rights, and even audiobook deals. In some cases, agents also assist in building your brand as an author.

Example: An author signs with a literary agent who has strong connections in the fantasy fiction market. The agent submits the manuscript to top publishers, secures an offer from a well-known house, and negotiates favorable terms, including a large advance and retention of film rights.

Tip: While literary agents typically take a percentage of your earnings (usually 15%), their ability to secure better deals often results in higher overall income and stronger protections for your work.

2. How Agents Navigate the Publishing Marketplace

The publishing industry is vast and constantly evolving, with different trends, imprints, and preferences across various publishers. Literary agents are well-versed in this landscape, acting as your guides to ensure your book finds the right home.

- **Industry Connections**: Agents have long-established relationships with editors, publishers, and even media professionals. They understand what each publisher is looking for and have a finger on the pulse of what's trending in the marketplace. This knowledge allows them to target the right publishers for your work, maximizing the chances of getting a deal.

- **Market Positioning**: One of the key advantages of having an agent is their ability to position your book within the market. They know how to frame your manuscript in a way that appeals to publishers, whether it's highlighting the book's commercial potential or aligning it with current trends. Agents also know how to time submissions, making sure your book stands out when publishers are actively seeking new content.

- **Multiple Submissions**: Agents often submit your work to multiple publishers simultaneously, increasing the likelihood of receiving multiple offers. This gives you more leverage in negotiations, as agents can create a competitive bidding situation between publishers. This can result in better financial deals, more favorable contract terms, and greater marketing support for your book.

Example: Your literary agent submits your thriller manuscript to several imprints that specialize in suspense novels. Two publishers express interest, leading to a bidding war. As a result, you receive a larger advance and better contract terms.

Tip: Trust your agent's expertise in positioning your book. They know how to tailor submissions to the specific preferences of publishers, making it more likely that your manuscript will get picked up.

3. The Agent's Role in Negotiating Deals

Once a publisher expresses interest in your work, the negotiation phase begins. Literary agents are expert negotiators, and their goal is to secure the best deal possible while protecting your rights. Here's what you can expect during the negotiation process:

- **Advance and Royalties**: Your agent will negotiate the size of your advance (the upfront payment you receive before the book is published) and the royalty rate (the percentage of each sale you earn). A skilled agent knows how to push for higher advances and royalties while ensuring that the terms are reasonable and achievable.

- **Rights and Ownership**: Agents help protect your ownership of the book's rights, including subsidiary rights (such as film, TV, and foreign translations). They negotiate to ensure that you retain control over as many rights as possible, allowing you to earn additional income from these sources in the future.

- **Contract Terms**: Beyond the financial aspects, agents negotiate the fine print of the contract, ensuring that clauses related to publication timelines, marketing commitments, and reversion rights are in your favor. This ensures that you're not locked into a bad deal or left with limited control over your work.

Example: Your agent negotiates a higher royalty rate for eBook sales and retains the right to sell foreign translation rights independently, allowing you to earn additional revenue from international markets.

Tip: Agents work for you, so it's important to communicate your priorities during the negotiation process. If retaining certain rights (such as film or merchandising) is important to you, make sure your agent knows.

4. The Benefits of Working with a Literary Agent

Working with a literary agent offers several key benefits that can elevate your career and ensure your long-term success as an author:

- **Access to Top Publishers**: Agents have access to large publishing houses and influential editors that are often closed off to unagented submissions. This gives you a competitive advantage in the marketplace.

- **Expert Negotiation**: Agents are skilled negotiators who understand the nuances of publishing contracts. They can secure better financial terms and protect your rights in ways you might not be able to on your own.

- **Career Strategy**: Beyond securing deals, agents help you develop a long-term career strategy. Whether it's advising you on which projects to pursue or helping you expand into other formats, they play a critical role in shaping your career.

- **Time and Energy Savings**: Agents take on much of the administrative and business-related work, allowing you to focus on your writing. From managing submissions to handling royalty payments, they keep the business side of your career running smoothly.

Example: After landing a successful book deal, your agent helps you strategize your next steps, advising on follow-up projects and expanding your reach into audiobooks and foreign markets.

Tip: Choose an agent who aligns with your career goals and values. A strong working relationship with an agent who understands your vision can lead to long-term success.

Literary agents are powerful allies in the publishing world, guiding you through the complexities of the market and ensuring your work is positioned for success. From navigating submissions to negotiating contracts, their expertise can significantly enhance your commercial outcomes and protect your creative rights. By working with a skilled agent, you can focus on what you do best—writing—while they handle the business of turning your literary dreams into reality.

Rights Management: Leveraging Agents for Subsidiary and Foreign Rights

When it comes to maximizing the financial and commercial value of your book, subsidiary and foreign rights are essential. Subsidiary rights go beyond the initial book deal, offering opportunities for film adaptations, TV series, audiobooks, merchandising, and more. Meanwhile, foreign rights open the door for your book to be translated and sold in international markets, significantly expanding your reach.

This is where your literary agent becomes invaluable. Agents are not just skilled at securing the initial publishing deal—they are experts at leveraging subsidiary and foreign rights to ensure that your book continues to generate income long after the initial release. In this section, we'll explore how agents manage these rights, the opportunities they unlock, and how they negotiate on your behalf to secure lucrative deals.

1. What Are Subsidiary Rights?

Subsidiary rights refer to the rights to exploit your book in different formats and mediums beyond the printed or digital version. These rights are a goldmine for authors, offering multiple streams of income from various formats and adaptations. Here are the most common subsidiary rights your agent will manage:

- **Film and TV Rights**: One of the most valuable subsidiary rights is the right to adapt your book into a film, TV series, or streaming content. An experienced agent will help you retain as much control as possible over these rights, ensuring that you're compensated fairly if your book is picked up by Hollywood or a production studio.

- **Audiobook Rights**: The audiobook market has exploded in recent years, and selling the rights to create an audiobook version of your book can be highly profitable. Your agent will help you navigate audiobook deals, securing the best terms with audiobook publishers or production companies.

- **Merchandising Rights**: If your book lends itself to merchandise, such as action figures, clothing, or other branded products, your agent can negotiate deals with companies that want to license your characters or intellectual property for products.

- **Dramatic Rights**: If your book is suited for live performances, such as stage plays or musicals, dramatic rights allow for adaptations in theaters. These rights are especially important for books with strong characters and compelling narratives that translate well to the stage.

- **Serial Rights**: Your agent can also negotiate for first serial rights (the right to publish excerpts of your book in magazines, newspapers, or online publications before the book is released) and second serial rights (excerpts published after the book's release). These deals can help build early buzz and generate additional revenue.

Example: Your literary agent negotiates a deal for your novel to be adapted into a Netflix series, ensuring that you retain creative control over key aspects of the adaptation while securing a generous upfront payment for the film rights.

Tip: Retaining as many subsidiary rights as possible during your initial book deal negotiation allows your agent to sell those rights separately, often leading to more lucrative deals than if they were bundled with the main contract.

2. How Agents Negotiate Foreign Rights

Foreign rights allow your book to reach a global audience by being translated and sold in international markets. These rights can be a significant source of income, especially if your book appeals to readers in non-English-speaking countries.

Here's how your agent will manage and negotiate foreign rights:

- **International Book Fairs**: Agents often attend major international book fairs (such as the Frankfurt Book Fair or the London Book Fair), where they meet with foreign publishers and rights buyers to pitch your book for translation deals. These events are prime opportunities for agents to secure deals with foreign publishers interested in translating and distributing your work in their country.

- **Multiple Territories**: Foreign rights can be sold on a territory-by-territory basis, meaning your book could be sold in multiple countries, each deal generating separate revenue. Agents will negotiate these deals with foreign publishers, ensuring that you retain control over the quality of the translation and the marketing of your book in each country.

- **Royalty Terms and Advances**: Just like with your initial book deal, your agent will negotiate advances and royalty rates for foreign rights deals. They will also ensure that the contract terms protect your interests, including securing payment schedules, translation approvals, and marketing commitments.

- **Long-Term Strategy**: Some agents specialize in international markets and can help you develop a long-term strategy for expanding your global reach. This includes timing your foreign rights sales to coincide with major events (like film adaptations) or the release of sequels, ensuring that your book maintains momentum internationally.

Example: After securing a successful book deal in the U.S., your agent pitches your novel to foreign publishers at the Frankfurt Book Fair. Several publishers express interest, and your agent negotiates translation deals for Germany, France, and Japan, securing significant advances in each market.

Tip: Foreign rights deals can sometimes be more lucrative than domestic deals, especially in markets where your genre or subject matter has strong appeal. Make sure your agent is well-versed in the international market to take full advantage of these opportunities.

3. Why Retaining Rights Matters

One of the most important strategies in negotiating your initial book deal is retaining as many subsidiary and foreign rights as possible. Many publishers will try to acquire these rights as part of the overall deal, but allowing your agent to sell them separately often results in higher earnings for you.

Here's why retaining rights is important:

- **Higher Earnings Potential**: By retaining film, TV, audiobook, and foreign rights, your agent can sell them to the highest bidder, rather than including them as part of a bundled deal with your publisher. This often leads to more competitive deals and higher advances.

- **Creative Control**: When you retain certain rights, such as film or merchandising rights, you have more control over how your work is adapted. This ensures that your vision remains intact and that any adaptations reflect your original intent.

- **Multiple Revenue Streams**: Retaining subsidiary rights opens the door to multiple revenue streams, allowing you to earn money from different markets and formats beyond the initial book sale. This diversification can be especially valuable if your book has broad appeal across different mediums.

Example: By retaining film rights during the negotiation of your book deal, your agent later sells the rights to a major studio for a large sum, allowing you to retain creative input on the screenplay and character development.

Tip: Always consult with your agent before agreeing to sell any subsidiary or foreign rights as part of your main publishing contract. They can advise you on the best strategy for retaining rights and maximizing future revenue.

4. Maximizing the Value of Subsidiary and Foreign Rights

With the help of your agent, subsidiary and foreign rights can significantly extend the life and reach of your book. Here's how agents ensure you get the most value from these rights:

- **Timing**: Agents know when to sell subsidiary and foreign rights to maximize their value. For example, selling film rights after your book has gained significant popularity can lead to more competitive offers from studios, while waiting to sell foreign rights until after a major award win or high-profile media coverage can increase interest from international publishers.

- **Bundling Rights**: Sometimes, bundling certain rights together—such as selling audiobook and foreign rights to the same company—can lead to a better deal. Your agent will evaluate when it makes sense to bundle rights and when it's more advantageous to sell them separately.

- **Maintaining Flexibility**: A good agent will negotiate contracts that allow for flexibility, ensuring that you can continue to exploit rights in the future. For example, if you retain merchandising rights, you may be able to license your characters for new products or media years after the book's release.

Example: After your book gains popularity, your agent successfully negotiates a package deal that includes foreign rights for multiple countries and an audiobook adaptation, securing a larger advance than if the rights had been sold separately.

Tip: Stay involved in the process and work closely with your agent to understand the timing and strategy behind subsidiary and foreign rights sales. Your input can help shape the direction of future deals and adaptations.

Rights management is a key component of your long-term success as an author. By leveraging the expertise of your agent, you can unlock valuable opportunities in film, TV, audiobooks, merchandising, and international markets. Retaining control over your subsidiary and foreign rights allows you to maximize earnings, maintain creative control, and expand your book's reach far beyond its initial publication. With the right strategy, these rights can turn a successful book into a global phenomenon.

Lawyers: Ensuring Legal Protection and Contractual Security

While agents focus on securing deals and managing your career, lawyers play an equally critical role in protecting your legal rights and ensuring that every contract you sign is airtight. Lawyers, particularly those with expertise in publishing and intellectual property law, are your legal safety net—guarding against unfavorable contract terms, navigating complex legal issues, and ensuring that your intellectual property is fully protected.

In this section, we'll explore the vital role that lawyers play in ensuring legal protection and contractual security, why it's essential to have one on your team, and how they collaborate with your agent to safeguard your long-term interests.

1. Why You Need a Lawyer in Publishing

The publishing world is filled with intricate legal documents, intellectual property rights, and financial arrangements that can be difficult to navigate without legal expertise. Having a lawyer on your team provides you with the legal knowledge needed to protect your rights, your income, and your creative work. Here are the key reasons you need a lawyer:

- **Complex Contracts**: Publishing contracts can be lengthy and filled with legal jargon that's easy to overlook or misinterpret. A lawyer ensures that every clause is fully understood and in your best interest, from royalty rates to reversion rights and non-compete clauses.

- **Intellectual Property Protection**: As an author, your work is your intellectual property, and you must ensure that it's legally protected. A lawyer will help you secure copyright, trademark important assets like book titles or character names, and ensure that your rights are upheld in case of infringement.

- **Dispute Resolution**: Whether it's a breach of contract, royalty disputes, or copyright infringement, a lawyer will represent your interests and guide you through the legal processes involved in resolving disputes, ensuring the best possible outcome.

- **Maximizing Legal and Financial Benefits**: Lawyers can also identify opportunities to negotiate better financial terms or secure additional protections in your contract, ensuring you get the maximum legal and financial benefits from your publishing deal.

Example: You receive a contract from a major publisher offering a lucrative deal, but it includes a non-compete clause that restricts you from publishing other works in the same genre for several years. Your lawyer helps you renegotiate this clause to protect your creative freedom while maintaining the value of the deal.

Tip: Always have a lawyer review any contract before you sign it, even if you have an agent. Lawyers are trained to spot potential legal pitfalls and can ensure that your rights are fully protected.

2. How Lawyers Safeguard Your Contractual Security

When you sign a publishing contract, you're entering into a legal agreement that will govern your relationship with the publisher for the duration of the deal—and sometimes beyond. This is where a lawyer's expertise is critical. They ensure that the contract terms are clear, enforceable, and fair, protecting your rights as an author. Here are some specific ways lawyers safeguard your contractual security:

- **Reviewing Contract Terms**: Lawyers meticulously review every clause in your contract to ensure it aligns with your best interests. This includes advance payments, royalties, subsidiary rights, marketing commitments, and more. They ensure that the terms are clearly defined, without ambiguous language that could be used against you later.

- **Negotiating Favorable Clauses**: Lawyers work with your agent to negotiate clauses that benefit you. This might include ensuring you retain ownership of subsidiary rights, securing a fair royalty structure, or including reversion clauses that allow you to reclaim your rights after a certain period.

- **Protecting Against Exploitation**: In some contracts, publishers may include terms that favor them at your expense, such as excessive control over your future works, restrictive options for sequels, or hidden fees that reduce your earnings. A lawyer will identify and push back against these exploitative terms to protect your long-term interests.

- **Handling Disputes**: If issues arise with your publisher—such as non-payment of royalties, failure to meet publication deadlines, or disputes over the use of your work—your lawyer can step in to handle these disputes. They may negotiate a resolution or, if necessary, pursue legal action to enforce your rights.

Example: Your publisher includes a clause in your contract that grants them the right to publish all future works in the same genre, limiting your ability to work with other publishers. Your lawyer renegotiates this clause, ensuring you retain creative control and flexibility for future projects.

Tip: Even if you're confident in your agent's ability to negotiate deals, lawyers bring an additional layer of legal expertise that ensures your contracts are not only favorable but also legally sound.

3. Protecting Your Intellectual Property

One of the most critical roles a lawyer plays in your publishing journey is protecting your intellectual property (IP). As an author, your book is your creation, and it's essential to secure your ownership of it to prevent others from exploiting or infringing on your rights. Lawyers help you navigate the complex legal landscape of IP protection, ensuring your work is fully safeguarded. Here's how:

- **Copyright Registration**: While copyright protection is automatic when you create an original work, formal copyright registration strengthens your legal claim if someone infringes on your work. Your lawyer will handle the process of registering your copyright, ensuring that your rights are recognized and enforceable in court.

- **Trademark Protection**: If your book title, characters, or series name have significant commercial value, a lawyer can help you file for trademarks to protect these assets. This is especially important for authors who expand into other markets, such as merchandising or adaptations.

- **Enforcing Your Rights**: If your work is used without your permission—whether it's being distributed illegally, adapted into unauthorized formats, or otherwise infringed upon—your lawyer will help enforce your rights. This could involve sending cease-and-desist letters, filing DMCA takedown notices, or pursuing legal action against the infringer.

- **Negotiating Licensing Agreements**: If you plan to license your work for adaptations (such as film, TV, or merchandising), your lawyer ensures that the licensing agreements are clear, protect your IP, and fairly compensate you for the use of your work.

Example: Your book gains widespread popularity, and a third-party company begins selling merchandise featuring your characters without your permission. Your lawyer files a trademark to protect your characters and sends cease-and-desist letters to stop the unauthorized use of your intellectual property.

Tip: Protecting your IP early in your career can prevent costly legal battles down the line. A lawyer can help you understand what aspects of your work are eligible for IP protection and guide you through the legal process.

4. Working with Agents and Lawyers as a Team

Agents and lawyers often work hand-in-hand to ensure that your career is both creatively fulfilling and legally secure. While agents focus on securing deals, expanding your reach, and managing your career, lawyers provide the legal expertise needed to protect your rights and maximize your long-term success.

Here's how agents and lawyers collaborate to benefit you:

- **Contract Negotiation**: Your agent handles the initial negotiation with publishers, securing favorable terms. However, your lawyer steps in to review the legal language, identify potential pitfalls, and negotiate legal clauses that ensure your contract is fair and enforceable.

- **Subsidiary and Foreign Rights**: Your agent may secure subsidiary or foreign rights deals, but your lawyer will review the legal contracts associated with these deals to ensure that you retain as much control and financial benefit as possible.

- **Dispute Resolution**: If a dispute arises with your publisher or another party, your agent may attempt to resolve it through informal channels. If the issue escalates, your lawyer steps in to enforce your rights and pursue legal remedies, such as litigation or arbitration.

Example: Your agent secures a lucrative film adaptation deal for your book, but the production company includes several legal terms in the contract that could limit your creative control. Your lawyer reviews the contract and negotiates changes, ensuring that you retain veto power over key creative decisions.

Tip: Communicate openly with both your agent and lawyer about your goals, concerns, and priorities. A strong collaboration between these professionals ensures that your career is protected from both a business and legal standpoint.

Lawyers play an essential role in ensuring that your publishing contracts are legally sound, your intellectual property is protected, and your long-term interests are safeguarded. By working closely with your lawyer, you can navigate the complexities of the publishing world with confidence, knowing that your creative and financial rights are fully protected. Whether you're negotiating a book deal, licensing your work for adaptations, or protecting your intellectual property from infringement, a skilled lawyer ensures that every aspect of your career is legally secure.

When to Hire an Agent or Lawyer: Timing and Choosing the Right Professional

Knowing when to bring an agent or lawyer on board is as important as understanding their roles in your publishing journey. While not every author needs an agent or lawyer right from the start, there are key moments in your career when their expertise becomes crucial. Whether you're negotiating a major book deal, expanding into new formats like film or audiobooks, or protecting your intellectual property, having the right professionals in your corner can significantly impact your success.

This section will guide you through the key indicators of when to hire an agent or lawyer, how to choose the right one, and what to look for in a long-term professional relationship.

1. When to Hire a Literary Agent

A literary agent is a valuable asset at various stages of your writing career, but it's important to understand when their services are most beneficial. Here are some situations where hiring a literary agent can make a major difference:

- **Ready to Submit to Publishers**: If you've completed a manuscript and are ready to submit it to traditional publishers, having an agent is essential. Many large publishing houses do not accept unsolicited manuscripts, meaning your work won't even be considered without representation. Agents know the right people in the industry and can pitch your book directly to editors, giving it a better chance of being picked up.

- **Negotiating Multiple Offers**: If your book has garnered attention from multiple publishers, a literary agent is crucial in navigating the competitive landscape. Agents have the experience and industry knowledge to create bidding wars between publishers, driving up advances and improving contract terms.

- **Exploring Subsidiary and Foreign Rights**: If you're interested in selling film rights, foreign translation rights, or other subsidiary rights, an agent can handle the complexities of these negotiations. They will connect with professionals in these specialized fields to help you maximize your book's earning potential.

- **Seeking Long-Term Career Development**: Agents do more than just secure a single book deal—they help authors develop long-term careers. If you're looking to build a body of work, expand into new genres, or explore media opportunities (such as film adaptations or speaking engagements), an agent is the perfect partner to help you strategize for the future.

Example: You've finished your debut novel and have received positive feedback from beta readers. You're ready to submit to traditional publishers, but you want to ensure your book lands with the right publisher and on favorable terms. Hiring an agent helps you get your manuscript into the right hands and negotiate a strong deal.

Tip: Don't rush into hiring an agent. Make sure your manuscript is polished, and research agents who have experience in your genre. A good agent will be selective about the clients they take on, and they should believe in the long-term potential of your career.

2. When to Hire a Lawyer

While agents handle the business side of your career, **lawyers** ensure that your legal rights are protected. You may not need a lawyer for every contract, but there are specific situations where hiring one is essential:

- **Reviewing or Negotiating Complex Contracts**: If you're signing a publishing contract with significant financial terms or complex legal language, a lawyer is essential. Lawyers ensure that every term is clear, enforceable, and in your favor. This is particularly important for contracts involving intellectual property, subsidiary rights, or long-term commitments.

- **Handling Copyright and Trademark Protection**: If you need to formally register a copyright or trademark your book title, series name, or character names, a lawyer will guide you through the legal processes and ensure that your intellectual property is fully protected.

- **Dealing with Disputes or Legal Issues**: Whether it's a royalty dispute with your publisher or unauthorized use of your intellectual property, a lawyer can help resolve the issue. They'll manage negotiations, send cease-and-desist letters, or represent you in court if necessary.

- **Entering New Markets or Media**: If you're expanding into film, TV, audiobooks, or merchandising, the contracts associated with these deals can be complex. A lawyer will ensure that your rights are protected, you receive fair compensation, and that you maintain creative control over your work where possible.

Example: You've been offered a six-figure deal for the film rights to your book, but the contract includes complicated legal terms related to creative control, royalties, and distribution. You hire a lawyer with experience in entertainment law to review the contract, negotiate better terms, and ensure your rights are protected in the adaptation process.

Tip: Even if you feel confident in your agent's ability to handle business negotiations, always have a lawyer review any contract before signing. Lawyers have specialized legal expertise that can catch potential issues your agent may miss.

3. Choosing the Right Agent or Lawyer

Once you've decided it's time to hire an agent or lawyer, the next step is choosing the right one for your specific needs. Here's how to find the perfect professional to join your team:

- **For Agents**:
  - **Specialization in Your Genre**: Make sure the agent you choose has experience working with authors in your genre. If you write science fiction, for example, an agent with connections in that market will know the editors, trends, and readers that matter most.

  - **Track Record of Success**: Look for an agent with a proven track record of securing deals for authors like you. Don't be afraid to ask about past deals, client success stories, and how they plan to position your book in the marketplace.

  - **Long-Term Fit**: You'll be working closely with your agent, so ensure that they understand your long-term career goals. A great agent is one who can guide your career over time, not just secure a single deal.

- **For Lawyers**:
  - **Expertise in Publishing Law**: Choose a lawyer who specializes in publishing or intellectual property law.

Publishing contracts have specific terms and nuances that a general lawyer may not fully understand.

- **Experience with Authors**: A lawyer who has worked with authors before will be familiar with the common challenges you face, from royalty disputes to protecting your IP in international markets.

- **Clear Communication**: Your lawyer should be able to explain complex legal terms and clauses in plain language. Make sure they're accessible and willing to answer your questions throughout the legal process.

Example: You're considering two agents to represent you—one with experience in multiple genres and another who specializes in your specific niche. You choose the latter because they have strong relationships with editors in your genre and understand the market better.

Tip: Ask for referrals from other authors in your network. A personal recommendation from a trusted source can help you find an agent or lawyer with a strong reputation and the skills you need.

4. Building Long-Term Professional Relationships

Working with an agent or lawyer isn't a one-time transaction—it's an ongoing relationship that can last throughout your career. Here's how to build strong, long-term relationships with these professionals:

- **Communicate Regularly**: Keep your agent or lawyer informed about your goals, concerns, and new opportunities. Regular communication ensures that they're always working in your best interests and are aware of your evolving career path.

- **Trust Their Expertise**: Both agents and lawyers bring a wealth of industry knowledge to the table. While it's important to be involved in decisions, trust their guidance, especially when it comes to legal terms or industry trends you may not be familiar with.

- **Foster Mutual Respect**: A successful relationship with an agent or lawyer is built on mutual respect. Be clear about your expectations, but also be open to their advice and insights. By working together as a team, you'll be able to make informed decisions that benefit your career.

Example: You've been working with the same agent for years, and they've helped you expand into new genres and markets. By maintaining open communication and trusting their expertise, you've built a successful, long-term partnership that has led to multiple book deals and media opportunities.

Tip: Reevaluate your relationships with your agent or lawyer periodically. As your career evolves, you may need different services or a new approach. Don't be afraid to make changes if necessary.

Knowing when to hire an agent or lawyer is essential to navigating the complex world of publishing with confidence. Whether you're ready to secure your first book deal, negotiate a subsidiary rights agreement, or protect your intellectual property, having the right professionals on your team can make all the difference. By choosing agents and lawyers who understand your vision and offer the expertise you need, you'll be well-positioned to achieve long-term success while protecting your creative and financial interests.

Quick Tips and Recap

- **Hire an Agent When Submitting to Publishers**: If you're ready to approach traditional publishers, an agent can get your manuscript into the right hands and negotiate better deals.

- **Leverage Agents for Career Development**: Agents are not just deal-makers—they help shape your long-term career by securing subsidiary rights, foreign deals, and advising on project choices.

- **Consult a Lawyer for Complex Contracts**: Always have a lawyer review any publishing, film, or subsidiary rights contract to ensure your legal and financial interests are protected.

- **Protect Your Intellectual Property**: Hire a lawyer to register copyrights, trademarks, and defend your rights against infringement or unauthorized use.

- **Choose the Right Professional**: Look for agents who specialize in your genre and lawyers with experience in publishing law. Always prioritize clear communication and proven success.

- **Build Long-Term Relationships**: Stay in regular communication with your agent and lawyer, trust their expertise, and work together as a team to advance your career.

By knowing when to hire an agent or lawyer and selecting the right professionals, you'll safeguard your creative work, negotiate stronger deals, and set yourself up for lasting success in the publishing world.

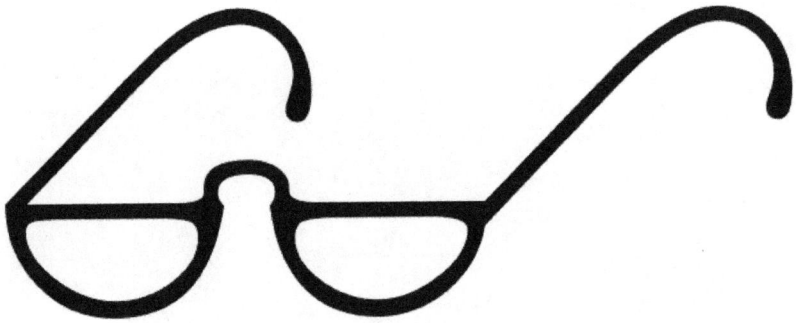

Resources

The Empire Builders and Blueprint Series

Welcome to the Resource section of the Empire Builders Series: Masterclasses in Business and Law. Here, we provide a carefully curated collection of practical tools and materials designed to complement the strategies and insights discussed throughout the series. This section is your gateway to deeper understanding and application, offering everything from sample agreements and checklists to detailed case studies and guidelines. Whether you're forging a new business, protecting intellectual property, or planning for expansion, these resources are intended to empower you with the necessary tools to effectively implement and navigate the complex landscape of business and law. Embrace these resources as your companion in building and sustaining a robust empire.

Empire Builders Series:
Masterclasses in Business and Law

In the dynamic world of business, where innovation intersects with opportunity, success often hinges not only on creativity but also on a deep understanding of the legal and operational landscapes. The Empire Builders Series is meticulously designed to arm aspiring entrepreneurs, seasoned business owners, creative professionals, and legal experts with the comprehensive knowledge and strategies needed to navigate these complexities and build lasting empires.

Each book in the series serves as a foundational pillar, offering expert guidance and actionable insights in specific areas of business and law; tailored to foster growth, innovation, and success in today's competitive marketplace:

1. **Brick by Brick**: This guide acts as your blueprint for building a business from the ground up. It offers essential strategies, legal insights, and operational tactics crucial for establishing a solid foundation for any business venture.

2. **Mark Your Territory**: Dive deep into the world of trademarks with this essential guide, designed to help you protect and effectively leverage your brand in today's competitive market.

3. **From Idea to Empire**: Transform your entrepreneurial dreams into reality with this exhaustive guide to business planning. Learn how to craft a compelling business plan that not only attracts investors but also sets the stage for a successful enterprise.

4. **Beyond the Pen**: Safeguard your creative works and master the intricacies of copyright law with this expert guide, tailored specifically for writers, artists, musicians, and digital content creators.

5. **Legal Ink**: Demystify the complex legal landscape of publishing with practical advice on negotiating contracts and protecting intellectual property, essential for authors and publishers.

The Empire Builders Series stands as a testament to the power of knowledge and the importance of mastering the strategic and legal aspects of business management. Each book is designed not merely to inform but to inspire action and lead to success. Embark on this journey to build your empire, one masterclass at a time.

Brick by Brick:
The Entrepreneur's Guide to Constructing a Company

The first book in the Empire Builders Series: Masterclass in Business and Law is "Brick by Brick: The Entrepreneur's Guide to Constructing a Company."

Summary: "Brick by Brick" is an indispensable resource for entrepreneurs who are poised to transform their innovative business ideas into successful enterprises. This comprehensive guide meticulously outlines the complexities of business formation, providing detailed, step-by-step instructions and vital insights into the legal, operational, and strategic aspects of starting and running a thriving company.

Part 1: Laying the Foundation – Focuses on selecting the appropriate business entity, delving into the legal implications of each option and the economic considerations vital for establishing a solid foundation for your business.

Part 2: Operational Mechanics – Discusses the operational aspects of setting up partnerships and LLCs, navigating corporate governance, maintaining corporate records, and managing capital and shareholder relationships effectively.

Part 3: Advanced Strategic Planning – Offers insights into managing structural changes, handling stock and ownership issues, expanding operations across state lines, and deploying tax strategies to ensure compliance and optimize financial performance.

Part 4: Implementation Tools and Resources – Provides practical tools such as sample agreements, startup task checklists, and comprehensive guidelines for drafting business plans and the incorporation process, enabling entrepreneurs to effectively implement their business strategies.

"Brick by Brick" not only serves as a guide but acts as a complete blueprint for building a robust business capable of thriving in today's competitive market. It arms aspiring entrepreneurs with the necessary knowledge and tools to navigate the complexities of business formation. From drafting your first business plan to preparing for incorporation, this book delivers invaluable insights and practical advice to establish a strong foundation and sustain growth.

Mark Your Territory:
Navigating Trademarks in the Modern Marketplace

The second book in the Empire Builders Series: Masterclass in Business and Law is "Mark Your Territory: Navigating Trademarks in the Modern Marketplace."

Summary: "Mark Your Territory" provides an indispensable resource for anyone involved in the branding and legal aspects of their business, offering a comprehensive guide to understanding, acquiring, and effectively managing trademarks. This book is crucial for ensuring that trademarks, which are vital assets to any business, are properly protected and leveraged.

Part 1: Fundamentals of Trademarks – Introduces the basics of trademarks, including their legal framework, the process of trademark selection and registration, and their importance in identifying business sources and ensuring product quality.

Part 2: Strategic Trademark Management – Focuses on the ongoing management of trademarks, detailing strategies for maintaining rights, monitoring for infringements, addressing challenges in digital marketing, and managing global trademark portfolios.

Part 3: Advanced Topics in Trademarks – Delves into more complex issues such as preventing trademark dilution, managing renewals, understanding the specific needs of service marks in advertising, and navigating the intricacies of trademark licensing and emerging legal trends.

Part 4: Practical Tools and Resources – Provides practical aids like sample trademark filings, management checklists, and insightful case studies, equipping readers with tangible tools and real-world examples to apply the concepts discussed effectively.

Designed for entrepreneurs, business owners, and legal professionals, "Mark Your Territory" equips readers with actionable strategies and essential tools for effective trademark management. It ensures that readers can maintain their brand's uniqueness and legal protections, thus securing a competitive edge in the marketplace.

From Idea to Empire:
Mastering the Art of Business Planning

The third book in the Empire Builders Series: Masterclass in Business and Law is "From Idea to Empire: Mastering the Art of Business Planning."

Summary: "From Idea to Empire" offers an indispensable roadmap for entrepreneurs eager to transform their innovative ideas into successful businesses. This comprehensive guide equips readers with a strategic blueprint for drafting robust business plans that attract investors and serve as a roadmap for navigating the transition from startup to thriving enterprise.

Part 1: Conceptualizing Your Business – This section lays the groundwork by assisting readers in defining their business vision, understanding market needs, analyzing competitors, and setting clear business objectives. It also guides readers in selecting an effective business model that aligns with their long-term goals.

Part 2: Strategic Planning – Delve into creating detailed marketing strategies, operational plans, and financial projections. This part covers risk management and technological integration, ensuring the business plan is both innovative and executable.

Part 3: Articulating Your Plan – Focuses on the actual drafting of the business plan, including how to write an engaging executive summary, develop compelling proposals, and master communication and negotiation tactics with potential investors and partners.

Part 4: Execution and Review – Outlines the necessary steps to launch the business successfully, monitor its performance, and make adjustments based on real-world feedback and market dynamics. This section also explores strategies for sustainable growth and long-term viability.

"From Idea to Empire" is more than a mere planning manual; it's a strategic guide that provides budding entrepreneurs with the necessary knowledge, tools, and confidence to build a business capable of facing today's market complexities. With practical advice, real-world examples, and essential resources, this book is a vital tool for anyone ready to evolve their business concept from idea to a profitable empire.

From Idea to Empire: Abridged Edition

The third book in the Empire Builders Series: Masterclass in Business and Law is "From Idea to Empire: Abridged Edition."

Summary: "From Idea to Empire: Abridged Edition" delivers the essential roadmap for turning business ideas into successful enterprises—streamlined for readers seeking concise and actionable insights. While the original edition provides an expansive resource with success stories and detailed case studies, this abridged version focuses solely on the strategic elements of business planning, offering the tools needed to conceptualize, design, and execute a winning business strategy.

By eliminating supplementary stories and focusing on the practical frameworks, this edition is perfect for readers eager to dive straight into the mechanics of business planning without distraction. It provides the knowledge required to develop robust business models, articulate compelling proposals, and successfully launch and grow a business in today's dynamic marketplace.

Part 1: Conceptualizing Your Business – Laying the Foundation – In this section, readers learn how to define their business idea, identify market needs, analyze competitors, and set clear objectives. It introduces essential business models and helps entrepreneurs align their vision with long-term goals.

Part 2: Strategic Planning – Mapping the Path to Success – Here, readers will discover how to design effective marketing strategies, operational plans, and financial projections. Topics like risk management and technological integration are covered to ensure every business plan is both realistic and innovative.

Part 3: Articulating Your Plan – Communicating with Precision and Impact – This section emphasizes the importance of clarity in communication. Readers will learn how to craft compelling executive summaries, develop strong proposals, and master negotiation strategies for working with investors and partners.

Part 4: Execution and Review – Launching and Scaling with Purpose – The final section covers essential steps for launching a business successfully, monitoring performance, and making real-time adjustments. It also addresses strategies for sustainable growth, long-term resilience, and market adaptation.

About This Edition:

The Abridged Edition is crafted for readers who prefer a focused, no-frills approach to business planning. By presenting the core methodologies from the original book in a concise format, this version allows entrepreneurs to absorb key concepts quickly and efficiently. Whether you're a first-time entrepreneur or a seasoned business owner, this streamlined guide provides the essential tools needed to transform an idea into a thriving business.

Why This Edition Matters:

"From Idea to Empire: Abridged Edition" underscores that great business planning doesn't require lengthy explanations—it requires clear strategies and actionable frameworks. This edition emphasizes the importance of focus, discipline, and adaptability in building a successful business.

Designed to complement busy entrepreneurs, it delivers the same powerful strategies as the original book but in a more accessible format. Readers can quickly refer to specific sections, apply the knowledge, and move forward with confidence in their business endeavors.

"From Idea to Empire: Abridged Edition" is the perfect companion for entrepreneurs who need to move swiftly from concept to execution. With straightforward advice and practical insights, this edition equips readers to create robust business plans and take decisive action toward building their own empire.

Beyond the Pen:
Copyright Strategies for Modern Creators

The fourth book in the Empire Builders Series: Masterclass in Business and Law is "Beyond the Pen: Copyright Strategies for Modern Creators."

Summary: "Beyond the Pen" serves as a crucial guide for artists, writers, musicians, and digital creators who seek to effectively navigate the complexities of copyright law and protect their creative assets. This comprehensive resource provides a deep dive into the mechanisms, legal frameworks, and strategic practices necessary to safeguard intellectual property in today's rapidly evolving digital landscape.

Part 1: Understanding Copyright Law – This section lays the groundwork by covering the essentials of copyright, including how to register works, the extent of legal protection available, and the nuances of international copyright laws. It equips creators with the crucial knowledge needed to assert and defend their rights.

Part 2: Navigating Use and Fair Use – Focuses on the vital concept of fair use, offering real-world scenarios and detailed guidance on how to handle copyright infringements and resolve disputes effectively without compromising creative freedom.

Part 3: Licensing and Monetization – Explores strategic approaches to structuring and managing licensing agreements, understanding diverse revenue models, and handling collaborations, ensuring creators can monetize their works effectively while maintaining control over their usage.

Part 4: Copyright in the Digital Age – Addresses the challenges and opportunities presented by new technologies, digital rights management, and online content sharing platforms. This part also examines the impact of social media on copyright and anticipates future trends that could influence creators' rights.

"Beyond the Pen" is more than just a legal manual; it is a strategic resource that empowers creators to protect, manage, and prosper with their intellectual property in today's interconnected market. Packed with practical examples, expert advice, and actionable strategies, this book is an indispensable tool for anyone looking to navigate the legal challenges and seize the opportunities in the modern creative landscape.

Legal Ink:

Navigating the Legalese of Publishing

The fifth book in the Empire Builders Series: Masterclass in Business and Law is "Legal Ink: Navigating the Legalese of Publishing."

Summary: "Legal Ink" offers an indispensable guide for authors seeking to navigate the complex world of publishing contracts. This comprehensive book demystifies legal jargon and provides a clear roadmap to understanding and managing the intricacies of publishing agreements effectively.

Part 1: The Grant of Rights – This section explains the various types of publishing rights, offering guidance on how to negotiate and manage these rights effectively to safeguard the author's interests.

Part 2: Your Obligations – Details the commitments authors must uphold under publishing contracts. It emphasizes the implications of these obligations for an author's literary career and advises on managing multiple contractual commitments.

Part 3: Getting Your Book to Market – Covers the practical aspects of the publishing process from the final manuscript preparation to marketing and distribution. This part ensures authors understand the steps involved and their roles in bringing their book to market.

Part 4: Follow the Money – Breaks down the financial components of publishing contracts, including advances, royalties, and accounting clauses. It offers crucial advice on how to negotiate for fair compensation.

Part 5: Parting Ways – Discusses strategies for effectively managing the conclusion of a publishing agreement, including rights reversion and contract termination, providing tactics for authors to regain control of their work.

"Legal Ink" acts as more than just a guide—it's a strategic tool for any author looking to deeply understand and master the legal framework of publishing contracts. With this book, writers are equipped to make informed decisions, negotiate better terms, and ensure their rights are protected throughout their publishing journey. It is an essential resource for anyone looking to confidently handle the legalities of publishing and secure the success of their work in the competitive marketplace.

The Empire Blueprint Series:
Case Studies for Business Success

Welcome to the Case Studies section of The Empire Blueprint Series: Case Studies for Business Success. This collection serves as an essential companion to the theoretical knowledge presented in the earlier volumes. Here, we delve into real-world applications and successful business practices through detailed case studies, showcasing how various entrepreneurs and businesses have navigated challenges, seized opportunities, and achieved success in their respective fields.

In this series, you will encounter a variety of scenarios that illustrate the practical implementation of business strategies and legal frameworks. Each case study not only highlights successes but also discusses the obstacles faced and lessons learned along the way. Whether you're a budding entrepreneur, a seasoned executive, or a legal professional, these insights will provide you with invaluable perspectives and tools to enhance your own business endeavors.

Each book in the series includes:

1. **70 Case Studies in Vision, Strategy, and Personal Branding**: This volume explores the journeys of entrepreneurs who have effectively crafted their visions and built strong personal brands. It highlights strategies for aligning personal values with business goals and creating a lasting impact in the marketplace.

2. **70 Case Studies in Leadership, Innovation, and Resilience**: This volume examines leaders who have driven innovation and fostered resilience within their organizations. The case studies showcase their approaches to overcoming challenges and inspire others to cultivate a culture of adaptability and forward-thinking.

3. **74 Case Studies in Growth, Digital Presence, and Legacy Building**: This volume delves into the strategies employed by businesses that have successfully navigated digital transformation and growth. It emphasizes the importance of establishing a strong online presence and building a legacy that resonates with future generations.

Each case study in The Empire Blueprint Series: Case Studies for Business Success is crafted to offer actionable insights and inspiration for readers. By examining these real-world examples, you will gain a deeper understanding of the strategies that drive business success and how to apply these lessons to your own ventures.

70 Case Studies in Vision, Strategy, and Personal Branding: The Foundations of Success, Volume 1

The first book in The Empire Blueprint Series: Case Studies for Business Success is "70 Case Studies in Vision, Strategy, and Personal Branding: The Foundations of Success," Volume 1

Dive deeper into the essential elements of business success with Volume 1: 70 Case Studies in Vision, Strategy, and Personal Branding. This volume not only presents a wealth of real-world examples but also serves as a practical toolkit for aspiring entrepreneurs and seasoned professionals alike. Here, you will find a curated collection of resources designed to complement the case studies and enhance your understanding of effective business practices.

From strategic planning templates and personal branding frameworks to time management guides and storytelling techniques, these resources empower you to implement the insights gleaned from the case studies. Explore practical tools for optimizing your online presence, launching impactful marketing campaigns, and engaging audiences across various platforms.

With a focus on innovation and adaptability, this resource section is your go-to companion for navigating the complexities of today's business landscape. Whether you're looking to craft an inspiring vision, develop effective strategies, or build a standout personal brand, the materials provided will equip you with the actionable insights needed to achieve meaningful success. Embrace the tools and inspiration within these pages, and take your entrepreneurial journey to new heights.

70 Case Studies in Leadership, Innovation, and Resilience: building a Thriving Enterprise, Volume 2

The second book in The Empire Blueprint Series: Case Studies for Business Success is "70 Case Studies in Leadership, Innovation, and Resilience: Building a Thriving Enterprise," Volume 2

Enhance your understanding of effective leadership with Volume 2: 70 Case Studies in Leadership, Innovation, and Resilience: Building a Thriving Enterprise. This resource section is designed to complement the rich insights presented throughout the volume, providing you with practical tools and frameworks to elevate your leadership journey.

Within this section, you'll find a variety of resources that address the core themes of this book—leadership, innovation, and resilience. From templates for developing effective communication strategies to guides on fostering a collaborative corporate culture, these materials are crafted to support your growth as a leader. Explore negotiation techniques, emotional intelligence assessments, and frameworks for ethical leadership that will help you build trust and loyalty within your teams.

The resources also include practical tips for embracing digital transformation and integrating innovative technologies into your business practices. Learn how to leverage these tools to drive growth, enhance customer engagement, and maintain a competitive edge in today's dynamic market.

With a focus on creating lasting value and building a legacy, this section equips you with actionable insights and strategies to navigate challenges with confidence. Whether you are an entrepreneur launching a new venture or an executive steering an established enterprise, these resources will empower you to lead with purpose and resilience.

Dive into these valuable tools and insights, and discover how to turn challenges into opportunities, fostering an environment where innovation and sustainable growth thrive.

74 Case Studies in Growth, Digital Presence, and Legacy Building: Strategies for Long-Term Success, Volume 3

The third book in The Empire Blueprint Series: Case Studies for Business Success is "74 Case Studies in Growth, Digital Presence, and Legacy Building: Strategies for Long-Term Success," Volume 3

Unlock the secrets to sustainable success with Volume 3: 74 Case Studies in Growth, Digital Presence, and Legacy Building: Strategies for Long-Term Success. This resource section is designed to enhance your understanding and application of the powerful insights shared throughout the volume, providing you with practical tools and strategies for thriving in today's competitive landscape.

Resources

In this section, you'll find a wealth of resources that align with the key themes of this book—growth, digital engagement, and legacy building. From templates for strategic goal-setting and growth frameworks to guides on optimizing digital marketing efforts, these materials will help you implement the actionable insights gained from the case studies.

Explore best practices for storytelling and community engagement in the digital realm, along with practical tips for leveraging social media to amplify your brand's presence. Discover frameworks for navigating the complexities of innovation and operational efficiency, ensuring your business not only grows but flourishes sustainably.

The resource section also emphasizes the importance of legacy building, offering tools for effective succession planning and community involvement. Learn how to align your everyday decisions with your long-term vision, ensuring that your enterprise leaves a lasting impact for future generations.

Whether you are an entrepreneur embarking on a new venture, an executive scaling operations, or a professional seeking to elevate your digital presence, these resources will empower you to lead with purpose and confidence. Dive into the practical tools and insights provided here, and equip yourself to navigate challenges, innovate boldly, and create a meaningful legacy.

In conclusion, the Resource section of the Empire Builders Series and Empire Blueprint Series serves as valuable extensions of the learning journey you've embarked upon. By utilizing these carefully chosen tools and materials, you are better equipped to apply the principles and strategies discussed in the series to real-world scenarios. Each resource has been tailored to enhance your understanding and effectiveness in the realms of business and law, ensuring you have the practical support necessary to navigate challenges and seize opportunities. We hope these resources prove instrumental in helping you build and sustain your business empire, transforming knowledge into actionable success.

L. A. Moeszinger also known as simply "L" is the face behind the AuthorsDoor Leadership Program: AuthorsDoor Series: *Publisher & Her World*, AuthorsDoor Advanced Series: *Publisher & Her World*, and AuthorsDoor Masterclass Series: *Publisher & Her World*. The program comprises, books, courses, and workbooks. The courses expand upon the books. The workbooks go into further detail, outlining step-by-step instructions. Courses are *free*; books and workbooks are available for purchase on Amazon and other retailer sites. She has been launching the careers of self-publishers since 2009, and she also writes the AuthorsRedDoor.com blog on writing, publishing, and marketing. L is also the co-founder of The Ridge Publishing Group and its imprints.

She is an American author, publisher, and creator who resides in Coeur d'Alene, Idaho, with her husband and two dogs. She writes under the pseudonyms: Ann Patterson and Ann Carrington for her business law pieces; L. A. Moeszinger for her writing, publishing, and marketing pieces; Lori Ann Moeszinger for her biblical books and personal pieces; and a handful of others for her Manhattan Diaries series. She believes strongly in faith, blessings, and working her butt off . . . and she thinks one of the best things about being an author-publisher—unlike the lawyer she used to be—is that she can let her passion out.

Original Package Design
© 2024 AuthorsDoor Leadership Program
Cover Design: Eric Moeszinger
Author Photo © 2023 Edwin Wolfe

Parent Website: https://www.RidgePublishingGroup.com and

blog site https://www.PublisherAndHerWorld.com

Publisher Website: https://www.GuardiansofBiblicalTruth.com and

blog site https://www.Jesus-Says.com

Author website: https://www.LAMoeszinger.com and New Youniversity sites:

https://www.NewYouniversity.com, https://www.ManhattanChronicles.com

Bridge Website: https://www.AuthorsDoor.com and

blog site https://www.AuthorsRedDoor.com

Entertainment website: https://www.EthanFoxBooks.com and

blog site https://www.KidsStagram.com

Want More?

The ideas in this book are expanded upon throughout the AuthorsDoor Leadership Program of books, courses, and workbooks. Follow our Facebook page. Join our Facebook private group. Watch our YouTube channels (AuthorsDoor Group, Authors Red Door #Shorts, and Publisher and Her World at Ridge Publishing Group). Listen to our Podcast channel (Publisher's Circle); or email me: *Hello@AuthorsDoor.com*

AuthorsDoor Hubs

Get insights from the articles we write on our *website* (AuthorsDoor.com). You'll find more publications to help authors sell better, pitch better, recruit better, build better, create better, and connect better. You are also invited to visit our *blog* and find out what we're talking about now. Sign up for our *AuthorsDoor Leadership Program Newsletter* and join the conversations going on there with our private community (Publisher's Circle); visit: *www.AuthorsRedDoor.com*

Publisher & Her World Blogs

Enter a world where the sometimes shocking and often hilarious climb to the top as an author-publisher is exposed by a true insider. Faced with on-going trials and tribulations of the world of self-publishing, L. A. Moeszinger is witty and sometimes brutally candid in her postings. If you enjoy getting the inside scoop on the makings and thoughts behind self-publishing, this is the blog for you! *www.PublisherAndHerWorld.com*

This

book was art

directed by John Jared.

The art for both the cover and the

interior was created using pastels on toned

print making paper. The text was set in 10 point Times

New Roman, a typeface based on the sixteenth-century type designs

of Claude Garamond, redrawn by Robert Slimback in 1989.

The book was printed at Amazon and IngramSpark.

The Managing Editor was Jack Clark. The

Production was supervised by

Jason Reed and Ed

Warren.